ACRL Publications in Librarianship no. 54

Literature in English:
A Guide for Librarians in the Digital Age

edited by

Betty H. Day
William A. Wortman

Association of College and Research Libraries
A division of the American Library Association
Chicago, 2000

The paper used in this publication meets the minimum requirements
of American National Standard for Information Sciences–Permanence
of Paper for Printed Library Materials, ANSI Z39.48—1992.∞

Library of Congress Cataloging-in-Publication Data

Literature in English : a guide for librarians in the digital age / edited by Betty H. Day
[and] William A. Wortman.
    p. cm. -- (ACRL publications in librarianship ; no. 54)
    Includes bibliographical references and index.
    ISBN 0-8389-8081-3 (alk. paper)
    1. English literature--Bibliography--Methodology. 2. English
literature--Bibliography--Data processing. 3. Libraries--Special collections--English
literature. 4. English literature--Study and teaching. I. Day, Betty H. (Betty Harris) II.
Wortman, William A., 1940- III. Series.

Z2001.A2 L57 2000
[PR21]
016.82--dc21

                                  00-024213

Printed in the United States of America.

03 04 02 01 00   5 4 3 2 1

Acknowledgments

The editors wish to thank all the chapter authors for their hard work and for their patience and forbearance with our editorial meddling; we also thank the reviewers of the ACRL Publications in Librarianship Committee, and their chair, John Budd, for expeditious and thorough reading of the manuscript. Bonnie Fannin, of the Miami University Libraries, provided considerable computer help to Bill Wortman, and Alice Wortman provided editorial assistance at a crucial point: sincere thanks to both of them.

We dedicate this collection to
Susan H. Wortman and John L. Day.

Table of Contents

Part Two. Readers and Services

Introduction:
Collaborative Partnerships

Betty H. Day
University of Maryland

William A. Wortman
Miami University

Whether you are new to the field of librarianship or are simply taking on a new assignment in reference and/or collection development in the field of literature in English, you have already made a good first step by selecting this volume for guidance. It and an earlier publication, *English and American Literature: Sources and Strategies for Collection Development* (1987, now out of print),[1] are companion works written by librarians who are members of the English and American Literature Section (EALS) of the Association of College and Research Libraries (ACRL), a division of the American Library Association (ALA). This book is an example of one of two kinds of resources that can help you develop the understanding and skills needed to provide effective collections and services—publications and professional organizations.

EALS is just such a professional organization. Membership in it brings one into a network of subject specialists who are working actively in the field of literature librarianship and who share common concerns related to the acquisition, organization, and use of information sources related to the study and teaching of literature written in

English. In addition to the pleasures of active involvement with other librarians doing virtually the same work as you and sharing your subject and professional interests, EALS provides some very practical assistance. The organization began as the English and American Literature Discussion Group in 1982, became a full-fledged section in 1992. Every summer at the annual meeting of the ALA, EALS presents a program on relevant topics, such as electronic texts (1998) and Southern literature (1999). General membership meetings at both annual and midwinter ALA meetings provide an opportunity to discuss issues and share professional concerns related to the field. Working on one of the EALS committees or participating in one of the discussion groups (Literary Reference or Nineteenth-Century Materials) provides an opportunity to both learn and help shape the future of the profession. The EALS Web site (http://www.library.yale.edu/eals/) provides further information about the organization and includes links to its newsletter, *Biblio-Notes*, and information about the electronic discussion list, EALS-L, an interactive forum for discussion of issues, assistance with reference questions, and reviews of new electronic or print resources. *Biblio-Notes* is published twice a year (print and online) and contains EALS news and brief articles on literature librarianship. Scott Stebelman, past-editor of *Biblio-Notes*, maintains a Web site listing "Studies of Interest to English and American Literature Librarians" that includes books and articles on librarianship, reference sources, and relevant developments in the field of English studies.[2] Two additional ACRL discussion groups are of interest—the *MLA International Bibliography* in Academic Libraries Discussion Group and the Electronic Text Centers Discussion Group. Both run business sessions and programs at the annual and midwinter ALA meetings and maintain listservs.[3]

Membership in the Modern Language Association of America (MLA) is another valuable professional investment.[4] In addition to the specialized literature divisions and discussion groups, the Methods of Literary Research Division and the Bibliography and Textual Studies Discussion Group both run programs at annual meetings and provide contacts helpful in bridging the professions of literary studies and librarianship. A subscription to *PMLA* comes with membership and provides a means of keeping current on conferences, new publications, and announcements of new serials or changes in publication. The MLA also produces the *MLA International Bibliography*, our field's essential source of research in literature, linguistics, and related areas such as film, folklore, and culture studies (see Judy Reynolds's chapter here on teaching use of the MLAIB), and publishes useful books and studies (discussed below). Membership in MLA also brings what might be seen as a mixed blessing—inclusion on the mailing lists for major scholarly and literary publishers, a major resource for collection development.

As for publications, there is a small library of basic guides to literary reference books and resources and of up-to-date essays on professional and scholarly issues. James L. Harner's *Literary Research Guide: An Annotated Listing of Reference Sources in English Literary Studies* is core among these books.[5] Harner's work organizes the reference literature by general resources, national literatures, and related topics, and follows a general pattern from guides to research and methodology, to guides to primary and secondary literature, periodicals, background reading, and genre studies. The organization is helpful in guiding the novice librarian to the right reference resource, and Harner's evaluations also provide invaluable assistance in learning appropriate sources for literary scholarship.

Michael J. Marcuse's *A Reference Guide for English Studies*, although current only through the mid-1980s, is seen by Harner as "thorough in its annotation, usually judicious in selection and evaluation [and] a valuable complement to the present *Literary Research Guide*" (11).[6] Although Harner's three editions supersede Margaret C. Patterson's *Literary Research Guide*, her volume is still helpful to the novice literature librarian because her introduction outlines strategies for analyzing literary research problems and suggests methodologies for identifying appropriate resources for the needed information.[7]

Harner and Marcuse guide the researcher to dictionaries, handbooks, and historical studies, but several nonreference works also are useful to the new literature librarian. Three in particular—*Critical Terms for Literary Study, Redrawing the Boundaries: The Transformation of English and American Literary Studies*, and *Introduction to Scholarship in the Modern Languages and Literatures*—provide basic statements of the major critical and theoretical approaches, a theoretical context for the recent changes in literary scholarship and criticism, and a survey of the major active areas of current literary scholarship.[8] *Redrawing the Boundaries* and *Introduction to Scholarship* are cited frequently throughout these pages.

✳ ✳ ✳ ✳ ✳ ✳

The chapters in this book fall naturally into two broad sections, one dealing with resources and collections and the other with readers and services. They are anchored by three essays that were originally given as papers at the EALS 1995 ALA program titled "The Humanities and the Librarian: A Collaborative Partnership," and all deal explicitly or implicitly with the fact of and need for collaboration as we respond to changes that have occurred in the past fifteen or more years and step into the new century.[9] Following that program, as the editors and the EALS Publication Committee thought about how to proceed and what topics to take up, we found that the authors themselves were each offering their own selection of topics of interest and importance; thus, this book has grown organically from our collective experience and individual enthusiasms. The changes we have all experienced run as motifs through the chapters here, even though each writer has a different view of them, and the reader can see this collection as a continuing conversation.

Readers and Services

Readers in our libraries are primarily undergraduate students, graduate students, and faculty. We know them as individuals who come to the reference desk, e-mail us requests for new books and journals, ask us to talk to their classes, complain about our storage policy or the freeze on new subscriptions, invite us to their colloquia, and so forth. We know them, too, as groups, specifically the Department of English with its particular curriculum, degree programs, reading lists for honors or MA students, lecture or reading series, and so forth, but also the institution itself with its distribution requirements, demographic character, and climate of intellectual inquiry. We may also be familiar with the local nonacademic community of independent scholars, retirees, high school students, and avid readers of the kind of literature we collect. Incidentally, we have tried to use the term *readers* throughout in place of *users* or *patrons* in hopes of more accurately reflecting the reality of literature librarianship and to assert the essential value of literature: one does not use it, one reads it.

Students and teaching seem in the ascendancy as institutions recommit themselves to undergraduate education. Perhaps, as recently suggested, a new "learning paradigm" is developing to replace the long-existing "teaching paradigm."[10] This new paradigm may be seen in a widespread emphasis on critical thinking, on teaching and student portfolios, on the deliberate use of a diverse range of instructional methods and student activities. Concern for undergraduates must inform collection development and reference service, and librarians must be alert to their real needs; they are usually not able to speak for themselves, in the sense that they know what they need and ask for it. The professor doing research and the graduate student writing a thesis know definitely (and tell us) that they need a new journal or a specific edition, but undergraduates make rather inchoate demands for late hours, constant service, or food courts; and often when they ask for specifics in the collection, it turns out we already have them, they just cannot find them. They do not need a better collection so much as they need help using the collection we have.

Librarians, therefore, must understand the learning process and use this understanding to design our services. Judy Reynolds, in her chapter on the *MLA International Bibliography*, discusses how best to teach effective use of this key tool and other literary reference resources at three distinct levels—early undergraduates in composition and general literature courses, junior and senior majors, and graduate students. She grounds her specific recommendations about what is appropriate and needed at each level in a review of relevant research into learning, the profession's guidelines for library and information literacy, specific suggestions from working librarians, and her own considerable experience. She gives valuable insight into the actual instructional situations in which most of us find ourselves.

Candace R. Benefiel and Michael Adams place their discussion of literary reference work, "Literary Reference into the New Century," within the context of a changed literary canon, expanded range of research and course interests, and the uneasy, if exhilarating, cohabitation of traditional print and new electronic resources (see the next section for more on the canon issue). In their view librarians must push undergraduates to use the full range of resources—they should "not become so enamored of electronic sources that they are unwilling to use print materials" (p. 250)—and must push themselves to expand and develop their own knowledge and reference abilities:

> As literary research becomes increasingly interdisciplinary, the demands on literary reference librarians also grow so that a librarian must not only have specialized knowledge of the field as a whole but must also be a generalist at ease with sources in a number of more-or-less related fields. . . . such fields as history, cultural and gender studies, psychology, philosophy, and religion (p. 253).

Although faculty tell us what they need, we must look beyond their immediate requests and try to understand the nature of their work as it is carried out today. Faculty are under intense pressure to teach well, to reach a high level of scholarly productivity, and to be systematic and rigorous in their use of theory. The requirements for tenure and promotion, even for entry-level positions, have ratcheted up, so that teaching, however good, is seldom enough. The new "learning paradigm" requires that faculty not merely lecture about what they know but that they also involve their students, elicit their responses, and create a classroom and syllabus through which students discover and learn for themselves. Interestingly, studies of the nature of scholarly work in the humanities indicate that a high percentage of faculty research is triggered by teaching.[11] The reverse also may be true—that research and publication eventually lead to new courses. Most departmental curriculums allow for both one-time courses and considerable flexibility within multisection courses so that the classroom can be a

laboratory in which experiments can be made in interpreting, juxta-
posing texts, tracing "traditions," and reexamining literary and cultural contexts.

Along with expectations of increased research productivity has
come a demand for methodological sophistication and self-reflection.
This is the age of theory, and literary theory is a:

> . . . self-consciousness . . . about the implications of
> [practical criticism] by examining its philosophical, meta-
> physical, linguistic, social, and political assumptions and
> effects. Literary theory, in short, is literary criticism that
> puts its own discourse into question.[12]

If today's faculty sometimes seem more concerned with their own
statements than with the literature they are talking about, this leaves
librarians more than ever responsible for the library's literature collection and services, including the instruction of undergraduates and
graduate students in the most effective use of our increasingly complex resources. We also may be less clear than in the past about the
nature of faculty research and teaching; we need, therefore, an explanation of the current faculty mentality.

J. Paul Hunter describes—from his vantage point as a member of
the University of Chicago's English department—a "new kind of historicist climate" within which there have been three kinds of change in
literary study:

> First is the return to historical questions and a deep
> interest in where texts come from, what their loyalties,
> contexts, and cultural implications may be, and what
> kinds of impact they have had initially and subsequently.
> Second is the movement in English and in language de-
> partments more generally toward cultural studies and
> the widespread attention to issues of multiculturalism
> in rethinking basic courses. Third is the way the popu-
> lation and distribution of faculty skills in English de-
> partments are beginning to change as our territory en-

larges and faculty areas of expertise overlap less frequently . . . (p. 291).

His chapter develops the nature of these changes and their implications for librarians: "The move to historicism in literary studies has
a number of important ramifications in how faculty and students use
their time and what kinds of materials they study in what ways . . ." (p.
294).

Hunter's observation provides a smooth transition to Stephen E.
Wiberley's chapter in which he reports the results of an ongoing, extensive analysis of how literary scholars use library collections and of
the ways different scholarly concerns draw on library collections. His
chapter culminates his and his collaborators' earlier publications and
proposes a "typology of literary scholarship." Literary scholars and critics, he shows, who work in the different areas of descriptive bibliography, editing, historical studies, criticism, and theory each make different uses of different library resources. The resources we need to provide to those who are working and teaching in our institutions depend,
then, on the kind of work they are doing. The question is not, of course,
whether literary scholars need the library but, rather, what kinds of
resources and services they need:

> Consequently, librarians who develop collections in lit-
> erature must keep their eyes on fields their predeces-
> sors did not have to follow. Also, they must stay abreast
> of new trends, particularly those that their local faculty
> find most important (p. 314).

Staying abreast is partly a matter of reading, but it also means
being aware of our own faculty and students and their interests, courses,
research, publications. "If we regard librarianship . . . as a process of
communication," explains Marcia Pankake, then, "faculty liaison plays
a pivotal role" (p. 319). The collections we build and maintain, the
services we provide, the tools we have acquired and mastered must be
made known to our users, but, conversely, we need to know our users
and their particular interests, needs, and ways of doing their own jobs.

Pankake describes some steps we can take to discover our faculty's and students' interests and to determine which materials and services best meet their needs. She also describes some of the activities and programs she has established at Minnesota that have served as a model for at least a generation of librarians:

> Librarians who anticipate patrons' needs, who respond to local interests . . . , who provide access to and deliver materials in innovative ways, who create new online reference, teaching, and research tools, who do research and publish—these librarians contribute directly to the credit, if not the glory, of their institutions (p. 335).

Literary Canons

Faculty self-consciousness and the "new historicist climate" inevitably entail a reexamination of the nature of literature and literary study. The so-called canon wars or culture wars of the past two decades might be seen as an inevitable reformulation of both the content of the canon and the process of its formation, whether one views the results as beneficial or deleterious. Librarians too have been affected by these reexaminations, and several of the chapters in this book refer to them. Adams and Benefiel provide the most extensive overview and also discuss the implications of the changes in canon on reference services.

Richard Heinzkill has argued in a much-cited article that there are "canons," not a single canon: literary, popular, women, gay, ethnic, African-American, regional, postcolonial, genres, etc.[13] The canon having been expanded—or the canons multiplied—we must be sure to build collections that incorporate them. In his chapter, Heinzkill offers a remarkably rich annotated guide to bibliographies for selectors overwhelmed by the abundance of new writers, literatures, critical approaches, and theoretical statements. He reminds us that there are real pleasures and comforts in retrospective collection development where we select titles that have been tested and proved, work from lists compiled by knowledgeable bibliographers, our silent partners, and build purposefully.

Several canons are all in play at one time, but we need to be especially aware of two kinds of canons: the teaching canon and the research canon. The teaching canon is perhaps best seen in textbook anthologies and English department curriculums. As for the figures taught, the MLA has commissioned periodic surveys of curriculums. In 1992, Bettina J. Huber reported that as far as texts go, "The major works and authors remain preeminent in the courses surveyed, though nontraditional texts were cited among the works respondents had recently added to their required readings." The methods of literary study also remained traditional:

> Similarly, the great majority of respondents subscribe
> to traditional educational goals for their courses. These
> aims revolve around providing students with the his-
> torical and intellectual background needed to understand
> the primary texts they are assigned and helping them
> appreciate the merits of these texts. A good many re-
> spondents think it important to introduce considerations
> of race, class, and gender . . . . Such new orientations
> have not replaced traditional goals, however.[14]

Three years later, Huber reported again that four out of five English departments offer survey courses and that the writers covered are "largely traditional."[15] Huber's generally ameliorative view has not gone unchallenged,[16] and we should remember that complex elements are at play in what is taught and what is learned. Teaching at the lower levels may rely on anthologies that present a de facto canon, but teachers augment them with other books or do not ask students to read cover to cover, whereas students themselves resist textbooks for all kinds of reasons, from rebellion to indifference. Any anthology's influence and authority are undoubtedly limited.

The research canon, meanwhile, may be quite different. Faculty do not necessarily teach what they study. *Gravity's Rainbow* probably makes it to few syllabi despite its nearly irresistible attraction to critics. With 324 citations in the *MLA International Bibliography*, as of mid-1999, it is the most-written-about, post-1960 work in English, nearly half again that of its closest competitor, Toni Morrison's *Beloved*, which is closing in fast (Joseph Heller's *Catch 22* comes in third). That the research has changed over the past forty years will surprise no one. A simple analysis of *MLA International Bibliography* citations on three pairs of authors (one man and one woman; one long canonical, the other only recently so) over the past thirty-five years gives one view of this shift. In 1963–1975, there were over twenty times more articles on Dryden than on Behn, but in 1996–1998, there were nearly twice as many on Behn as on Dryden; in 1963–1975, there were twice as many articles on Lawrence as on Woolf, but in 1996–1998, there were nearly three times as many on Woolf; in 1963–1975, there was one article on Morrison and 241 on Bellow, but in 1996–1998, there were over four times as many on Morrison. So, on the one hand, the traditional canon of English and American literature has been reformed, reshaped, resized, and redefined to include a wider range of writers and writings, new ways of categorizing and combining the literature, and new deliberate tentativeness about canonizing; and, on the other hand, several distinct canons are being set up in parallel, each developing its own set of canon-making features, such as anthologies and reference books.

Resources and Collections

Not only the syllabus, but also the formats of literature have changed—what might be called literary technology. Although texts—poems, novels, stories, plays—remain central, we now find them on the Web, CD-ROM, and floppy disks, as well as in print or microform. Although scholarly and critical output flourishes, it now occurs through e-mail, as strings on listservs and newsgroups, in electronic journals, and, perhaps soon, in electronic monographs. On the one hand, we have electronic editions of well-known literary works, reference sources, and scholarly journals. On the other hand, we also have an increasing range of literary resources available only on disk or through the Internet; of CD-ROM and Internet products that combine text, images, and commentary; of individual Web sites devoted to an author or a work; and of metasites that collect links to many related sites. Aside from the difficult issues of cost, intellectual property rights, and usability entailed in these electronic resources that affect all areas of our libraries, not just literature, there are issues of access and quality that seem to have uniquely literary facets.

Shelley Arlen's chapter on textual and literary Web sites describes this constantly changing array and provides a "webliography" of some 150 items and an extensive bibliography. As important as the individual sites and services mentioned, however, are the seventeen categories she identifies, including electronic text repositories, literature sites (for genres, periods, regions), discussion lists, newsgroups, newsletters and journals, associations, metasites, etc. Librarians can simply copy her listings, but they also can maintain updated listings within the categories appropriate to their own situations and needs.

Timothy Shipe's *cri de coeur* for catalogers and cataloging argues that if we want effective access, we must provide accurate, consistent, and professionally meaningful description, classification, and cataloging for electronic texts, Web sites, and other digital resources. These resources should be included as equal partners with traditional resources, and catalogers' professional expertise is needed to describe this new category of library resource, to improve standardization of these resources, and to help define and identify quality in them. Shipe adds that the question of whether (or how) to catalog individual sites within metasites and gateways was earlier asked about microform sets (such as *Early English Books*), and he suggests that after the catalog provides hot links to full-text resources, the distinction between catalog and collection has been obliterated.

Access is also a key issue in Perry Willett's discussion of electronic text collections, whether they are managed as a distinct electronic text center or, less formally, as just another part of the general collection. Librarians must meet student and faculty needs, provide a suitable level of service, and maintain equipment, software, and links. To create and maintain a full-fledged electronic text center is a daunting prospect that requires "equipment and resources, ongoing funding for reference staff, equipment replacement, operating system and application software upgrades, and technical support" (p. 271–72), not to mention the need for librarians who have both technological skill and subject knowledge. Providing this level of access also ensures a quality of both resource and service comparable to that which we have traditionally offered for print resources.

Literature remains essentially a print field, however. The MLA echoes this sentiment in its "Statement on the Significance of Primary Records," and Susan L. Peters discusses the statement, some of the supporting evidence accompanying its release, and librarians' responses, which have been sympathetic, yet realistic. The principles we have followed in developing and maintaining our print collections undoubtedly should be followed with electronic resources as well. Willliam A. Wortman's chapter on the nature of literature collections expands on this point and on the related question of "literary information," that is, the secondary literature of scholarship, criticism, reference, and pedagogy that we draw from for our collections. Collections must serve readers' immediate curricular and research needs, of course, but we also hope to collect so as to demonstrate how literature has been produced. At its simplest, this means we should collect an accurate representation of a work's transmission through a typical sequence of published texts, from first editions through various subsequent editions and formats to, in the case of significant examples, scholarly editions.

A key quality issue is selection of the most suitable literary texts, but John L. Tofanelli asks (p. 119), "How—in this welter of activity, theoretical dialogue, and new products—are librarians to recognize what is of importance?" New electronic editions, expensive scholarly editions, and a plethora of inexpensive paperbacks and gifts beckon the librarian on one hand; while on the other, intense and arcane discussions of editorial principles and procedures intimidate librarians acutely aware of their obligation to select the "best" texts, print or electronic, for their students and faculty. After an overview of textual studies in general, Tofanelli explains the recently dominant "eclectic" theory of copy-text developed by Thomas Greg and Fredson Bowers; the new, alternative concept of "versions"; and the likely roles of, and determinants of quality in, electronic editions. His chapter clarifies a complex issue in both its historical development and its current debate and practice.

For Scott Stebelman, the quality issue is not so much a matter of individual texts as it is of the collection as a whole: "collection assessment is a systematic attempt to evaluate the adequacy of the library to support local research and teaching" (p. 187). He discusses both client-centered and collection assessment techniques, and covers a range of special considerations, including the as-yet-untested area of assessing the adequacy of a collection's electronic resources. Traditional assessment is still focused on print collections, but with the addition of electronic texts, extensive use of electronic journals, and consortial arrangements that build resources somewhere outside the library, this will change. Sheer number of volumes is decreasingly a meaningful measure, but quality of resources and access to them remain central concerns.

Institutional Context

Actually, we may have been mistaken about the canon wars; the real war was about costs and accountability and took place not inside but, rather, outside the English departments, as a recent president of the MLA has pointed out:

> . . . the site of the battle has shifted from the curricular and methodological clashes of the 1970s and 1980s to economic and institutional pressures that, however much these conflicts may have exacerbated them, have now taken on a life of their own [so that we are called to] 'systematically address issues of cost, productivity, efficiency, and effectiveness as a prerequisite for increases in public sector investments.'[17]

Whether or not higher education has become a "mature industry" fated to transform or die, as some have suggested, it is definitely constrained. Further, institutions' use of part-time and temporary faculty, their misunderstanding of the nature and limitations of digital resources (print is not dead, digital not free), and their continuing inability to provide adequate funding for library resources and facilities certainly affect the print collection and its primary readers, members of English departments.

Libraries have been especially constrained. Statistics compiled by ARL (and no doubt repeated in other academic libraries) show that although expenditures for serials and monographs went *up* 142 per-

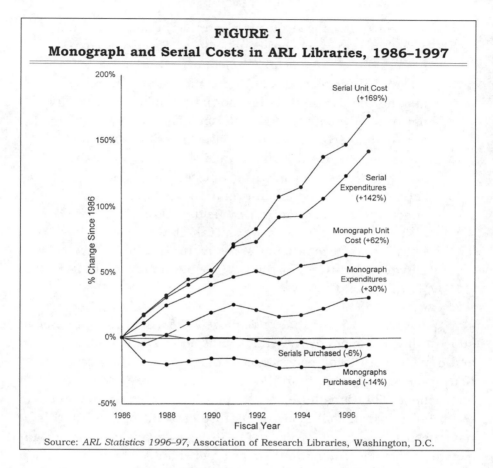

FIGURE 1
Monograph and Serial Costs in ARL Libraries, 1986–1997

Source: *ARL Statistics 1996–97,* Association of Research Libraries, Washington, D.C.

cent and 30 percent respectively from 1986 to 1997, the actual number of serials and monographs added to collections *decreased* 6 percent and 14 percent respectively, because of even greater increases in per unit costs of serials and monographs and static or declining budgets.[18] (See figure 1.) However, this is not a simple contrast between what went up and what went down:

> The academic and research library environment is complex. To some extent, these trends are tied to the transformational nature of new technologies and networking capabilities. Although most monograph and serial titles are still produced in paper format, traditional formats

are being challenged by the electronic production and dissemination of scholarly publications. Electronic communication and the establishment of networks, consortia, and inter-institutional agreements are similarly making the distribution of information more effective, not only for digitized materials, but for printed books and/or photocopies, as well. Other possible explanations for the trends mentioned above include the strong emphasis on scientific and technical research, expectations for timely information, and the twigging effect of specialization in new fields of knowledge. No matter what the underlying causal relations, research libraries are exchanging some of the traditional archival imperatives for the user demands of "information here and now."[19]

What the ARL report does not show is the extent to which we are substituting document delivery and online access for actual ownership and providing our local readers access to consortial resources in addition to (or as a substitute for) locally held resources. Reference and instructional librarians have seized upon the new electronic products to revitalize instruction about the nature of academic resources and have used the willingness of faculty to let us explain an important electronic tool not familiar to them as an opening to slip in instruction about related traditional resources. Forced to rethink our collecting choices in the face of budget cuts and publishers' contining output of print and electronic resources, and with the benefit of consortial options and support, we now can take a new look at what faculty are publishing, the curriculum and course syllabi, and student capabilities, and use increasingly precise circulation and connect statistics to rethink the nature of resource needs and the collection in our own library. More from ARL:

> Library roles are being redefined as the academic community undergoes changes. . . . This data compilation does not assess, for example, the quality of an organiza-

tion in meeting user needs. Such answers can only be found by library staff who systematically explore with users their real needs and then design better service delivery systems at the local level.[20]

Conclusion

Where once we helped gather and preserve the tradition, now we collaborate in the continuing renewal, remaking, and reassembling of the literary canon. There is a new sense in which we build a core collection. Working in the consortial context and with a range of document delivery procedures and electronic access technologies, we now must think more clearly and seriously about what exactly is needed in our own local library and about ways to collaborate with faculty to be sure that we are right and that we help students. We have become, in a sense, more the librarian-professional and less the librarian-bibliographer or librarian-scholar, and are valued more for our ability to design Web pages, create links to electronic texts, and initiate undergraduates into the *MLA International Bibliography* and less for our knowledge of literature.

Not only, then, are we re-creating library resources and library services, we are rethinking what a library is and, particularly, what a library is that serves students and faculty studying and researching—that is, reading—in the field of English-language literature. Today we must retain our print and paper based knowledge while outflanking digitally adept but quite naive undergraduates and resurrecting computer-challenged senior professors whose scholarship and teaching could be enhanced by knowledgeable work with new resources. In this environment of expansion and change, the librarian for English-language literature must move comfortably through both traditional sources for literary scholarship and new areas of inquiry and their associated resources. To borrow Perry Willett's summary of working with electronic text collections, "Management of these collections [print as well as electronic] will require technical and subject understanding, creativity, and a willingness to experiment" (p. 278).

Notes

1. *English and American Literature: Sources and Strategies for Collection Development*, ed. William McPheron, Stephen Lehmann, Craig Likness, and Marcia Pankake (Chicago: ALA, 1987).

2. Scott Stebelman, "Studies of Interest to English and American Literature Librarians," Mar. 1999, http://gwis2.circ.gwu.edu/~scottlib/english.html (18 Aug. 1999).

3. "*MLA International Bibliography* in Academic Libraries Discussion Group." Subscribe at listserv@gwuvm.edu (send the message <subscribe mlaib yourfirstname yourlastname>) and see the Web page at http://gwis2.circ.gwu.edu/~scottlib/mla.html; "Electronic Text Centers Discussion Group." Subscribe at listserv@rutvm1.rutgers.edu (send the message <subscribe etextctr yourfirstname yourlastname>).

4. See the MLA's Web site at http://www.mla.org.

5. James L. Harner, *Literary Research Guide: An Annotated Listing of Reference Sources in English Literary Studies*, 3d ed. (New York: MLA, 1998). See also Harner's Web site for revisions and additions: "Literary Research Guide," 16 Aug. 1999, http://www-english.tamu.edu/pubs/lrg (18 Aug. 1999).

6. Michael J. Marcuse, *A Reference Guide for English Studies* (Berkeley: Univ. of California Pr., 1990).

7. Margaret C. Patterson, *Literary Research Guide*, 2d ed. (New York: MLA, 1983).

8. *Critical Terms for Literary Study*, ed. Frank Lentricchia and Thomas McLaughlin (New York: MLA, 1990); *Redrawing the Boundaries: The Transformation of English and American Literary Studies*, ed. Stephen Greenblatt and Giles Gunn (New York: MLA, 1992); *Introduction to Scholarship in the Modern Languages and Literatures*, 2d ed., ed. Joseph Gibaldi (New York: MLA, 1992).

9. The chapters by Paul Hunter, Marcia Pankake, and Stephen Wiberley were originally given as papers in the program "The Humanist and the Librarian: Creating a Collaborative Partnership," at the annual meeting of the ALA, Chicago, June 1995.

10. Robert B. Barr and John Tagg, "From Teaching to Learning: A New Paradigm for Undergraduate Education," *Change* 27 (Nov./Dec. 1995): 12–25.

11. On research triggered by teaching, see John M. Budd, "User-Centered Thinking: Lessons from Reader-Centered Theory," *RQ* 34 (1995): 487–96; Clara M. Chu, "The Scholarly Process and the Nature of Information Needs of the Literary Critic: A Descriptive Model" (Ph.D. diss., Univ. of Western Ontario, 1992).

12. Robert Young, "Literary Theory," *Year's Work in English Studies* 62 (1981): 17–18.

13. Richard Heinzkill, "The Literary Canon and Collection Building," *Collection Management* 13 (1990): 51–64.

14. Bettina J. Huber, "Today's Literature Classroom: Findings from the MLA's 1990 Survey of Upper-Division Literature Courses," *ADE Bulletin*, no. 101 (1992): 52.

15. ———, "What's Being Read in Survey Courses? Findings from a 1990–91 MLA Survey of English Departments," *ADE Bulletin*, no. 110 (1995): 45.

16. For a skeptical view of this survey, see Will Morrisey, Norman Fruman, and Thomas Short, "Ideology and Literary Studies, Part II: The MLA's Deceptive Survey," *Academic Questions* 6, no. 2 (1993): 46–58.

17. Herbert Lindenberger, "Must We Demonize One Another?" *MLA Newsletter* 29, no. 3 (1997): 3–4.

18. "Monograph and Serial Costs in ARL Libraries, 1986–1997," *ARL Statistics 1996–97: A Compilation of Statistics from One Hundred and Twenty-one Members of the Association of Research Libraries*, comp. Martha Kyrillidou, Michael O'Connor, and Julia C. Blixrud (Washington, D.C.: ARL, 1998), 8.

19. Ibid., 9.

20. Ibid., 17.

Chapter 1
The Nature of Library Collections

William A. Wortman
Miami University

Library collections of English and American literature consist of texts and information resources added or linked for our readers. Use of the word *text* avoids the materiality of *book* or *periodical* but recognizes that people read and that literature cannot be adequately represented by the word *information*. Literary texts—poems, novels, and plays—are not information, but there is a wide range of information about all aspects of literary history, authors, publishing, and study and teaching that belongs with the texts in collections. Literature is uniquely (wonderfully) physical, of course; we have spent our reading lives with books, newspapers, and magazines in our hands and our professional lives unpacking, shelving, and repairing the books and magazines, the videotaped movies and plays, and the archives of manuscripts and letters that have traditionally made up collections. New electronic resources have expanded and altered the formats of literature and, to some extent, the appropriate services. There is a physicality about them, too—an almost sensuous power in "calling up" a Web site with a poem, a picture, or even a recording that appears instantly at the click of the mouse, day or night, at home or in the office. These have not, however, supplanted the traditional print and media resources. We will continue to add books, periodicals, and other materials while at the same time finding ways to link new electronic texts and information resources through our libraries. To build and maintain effective, appropriate collections and to make fullest and best use of the new resources, we must understand the nature of literary texts, the literary information needs of students and faculty, and the kinds of collection management issues inherent in literature, all of which are the concerns of this chapter.

We ought to talk about all English-language literature, not just English and American, and, further, distinguish between literature and literature**s**. The latter indicates a variety of discrete literatures; the former assumes an essential commonality. I prefer the singular: there is one, worldwide English-language literature today, its writers speaking from a myriad of specific places and in a myriad of distinct dialects, and its readers diverse and eclectic. The geography of literature has changed, and in the presence of a Rushdie, a Walcott, a Gordimer, even American literature is insular and provincial. Not only is there incredible variety within this literature, but also there is a varied and extensive literature of scholarship and criticism about it.

These collections of English-language literature in academic libraries exist chiefly to serve students and faculty, and most academic libraries have a clearly stated, quite focused mission to support instruction and research. Both instruction and research, however, have been unusually fraught during the past two or three decades. It is easy enough to point to problems, to those developments that, in the words of Stephen Greenblatt and Giles Gunn, are "significant departures rather than important continuities."[1] Greenblatt and Gunn's introduction to *Redrawing the Boundaries: The Transformation of English and American Literary Studies*, an MLA collection of the early 1990s that attempted to synthesize and legitimize many of the changes that occurred in the 1970s and 1980s and that continue to concern many of us, provides a succinct overview of these "departures." Our students come from more diverse backgrounds than ever before. Literature itself has undergone a "reconception," so that we talk of "texts" rather than "works," question the image of "an individual author toiling in isolation from history and society to bring into being a work of personal artistic authenticity," and acknowledge the power of readers to make texts their own. Practitioners of literary studies are "self-conscious about the shifting conditions of their own making and remaking." Above all, we have lost the confidence that literature and literary study make up a single domain and have, instead, come to recognize a multitude of domains with many boundaries:

> Foregrounding the issue of boundaries has reminded us that literature is not something given once and for all but something constructed and reconstructed, the product of shifting conceptual entitlements and limits. Not only is the canon of literary works in any genre fashioned by a simultaneous perambulation and transgression of boundaries but the very concept of the literary is itself continually renegotiated (p. 2).

Departures, disconnections, change, redrawn boundaries are indeed all features of the field of English-language literature, yet the ground, the earth of the field, remains the texts that people read, teach, think, and write about and that readers of all kinds enjoy and treasure, however much they also debate and disagree about them. Our collections remain our essential continuity: literature lives in libraries.

Texts

Librarians' responsibility is twofold: we provide our users what they want and make use of, and we develop and maintain a collection that reveals the nature of literary resources, primarily texts. Some of the confusion in the changes that have swept our field is the result of the expansion of what counts as text and thus is taught and studied. For librarians, the issue is practical, not theoretical: for us, texts are the things literary people read, teach, and study. The literature librarian ultimately deals with texts and understands that texts are varied and multiple. If, then, we want to provide collections that accurately reveal the real nature of literary culture, we must be sure to recognize and be able to demonstrate the real complexity of textual production, dissemination, and reception.

The Nature of Texts

Text is the central fact of literature. Current critical and scholarly thinking agrees (on the whole) that we need to distinguish the literary work from the (often many) texts that can embody it. Further, it describes the conditions of textual creation, production, dissemination, reception, and preservation, as well as textual variation and indeterminacy, the importance of historical context and conditions, the historical sequence of the multiple texts of a single work, and conditions affecting reception.[2] *Text* also has come to be preferred by theorists who resist the idea that a literary work exists in some unique and ideal state and prefer to think of "literature" as discourse or performance.[3]

Every text has a history. A text is a process as well as a finished product. Each text is a version of a larger or different text intended by its author and also a fragment of the total body of literary texts. A text is seldom satisfactorily explicit; it needs mediation and interpretation. There are all sorts of texts—poems, plays, short stories, novels, the texts of theory and criticism, cultural texts such as the Declaration of Independence, even cultural objects such as Barbie dolls. A text can be an image as well as a word, a dance as well as a poem, aural and kinetic as well as static and typographic; and any given work often (if not always) exists in multiple textual versions and forms. Every text is created, published, distributed to readers, transmitted from one form to another, received, and read. *Hamlet* exists in three contemporary versions apparently written by Shakespeare, in a host of scholarly, popular, and professional (acting) versions, in countless productions for stage, screen, radio, television, and classroom, and as a kind of cultural artifact whose broad presence allows it to be used intertextually by, for example, Mark Twain and Tom Stoppard.

What do our readers make of the multiplicity? Some focus on the texts themselves, others on the author or the literary and social culture that might account for this variety. The former, the textual scholars, are further divided into those who want to edit one single text out of the multiplicity and those who want to display the multiplicity itself. The traditional scholarly edition analyzes multiple texts and tries to discover the author's final intentions about the text and distinguish these from false starts, publisher's intrusions, and printer's errors (discussed more fully below and, especially, in John Tofanelli's chapter). At the other extreme, however, is something like the *Rossetti Archive* under development by Jerome McGann in which all of Rossetti's multiple texts (both manuscript and printed) are being collected, digitized, and made available precisely for the purpose of indicating the richness of textual multiplicity.[4]

Scholars in the latter group are perhaps influenced by the newly developed field of the history of books and publishing. Since the 1970s, when several new books (or new editions of older ones) were published, a history-of-the-book movement has developed that seems, more than earlier manifestations of scholarly attention to publishing history, to be interested in the dynamics of literary publishing. It concerns itself with the agents and process of the production of texts, which today continue to show much the same pattern as in earlier times: progression from manuscript to serial or book; collaboration of author and editor; distribution and dissemination over time and place; influence of bookseller, librarian, and teacher; reception by readers who themselves are influenced in their reading by their own personal histories.[5] The reality of what people have read, attended, or heard, especially when viewed with an awareness of the effects of race, class, and gender, has opened a new window on literature. This current history-of-the-book approach is neatly summed up by Michael Winship in his discussion of the nineteenth-century American publishers Ticknor and Fields:

> Common to the work of these scholars, and to that of recent book historians and bibliographers, is the basic understanding that literature is a human institution— part of a matrix of social and cultural forces from which it emerges—and not a pure or abstract ideal separated or independent from history. No published text, literary or otherwise, exists in isolation: rather, it is the collaborative effort of many people—authors and editors, papermakers and printers, publishers and readers, among others—and it acts as a political force in the social and cultural worlds of these historical collaborators.[6]

There may be a danger, however, of too much attention to books, as if they were the single or the essential embodiment of our texts. Publication in parts started at the end of the seventeenth century, continued on into the nineteenth, and by the 1870s was pretty well supplanted by serialization in periodicals.[7] We know that a large share of literary texts first saw publication in a periodical, yet there is a tendency to think of the book publication as somehow more important and primary in value, if not in time. Periodical serialization, starting in the nineteenth century, not only provided a steady flow of new fiction but also placed this fiction in the varied literary contexts embodied in each particular magazine. Novelists were often first encountered in a magazine setting controlled by a journalistic editor. In the nineteenth century, periodicals reached tens of thousands, but books only thousands. Today the numbers might be reversed, but still most poetry and short fiction and many novels (or excerpts) see first publication in periodicals, now "little" rather than commercial magazines. Virtually every new book of poetry and short stories published in the United States includes an acknowledgments section in which the writer thanks editors of the little magazines where the poems or stories first appeared. This from Mary Oliver's *West Wind* is typical: "My thanks to the editors of the following magazines in which some of these poems, sometimes in slightly different form, have previously been printed," followed by a list of the magazines.[8] The poet's first reader is a magazine editor.

Kinds of Texts

The discussion so far has emphasized the nature of texts, mainly their multiplicity and the process of their production and transmission. Now I want to describe the *kinds* of texts that we should consider collecting. Nearly forty years ago, F. W. Bateson published a short article describing what a library collection supporting doctoral-level study ought to consist of, and his points, appropriately modified, make sense in all kinds of libraries.[9]

Manuscripts. Manuscripts are the handwritten (typed or word-processed) texts preceding printed, published texts. Frequently these reveal something of the author's process of writing through drafts and revisions, or they reveal changes in the author's text suggested or imposed by a publisher. Bateson called for actual manuscripts when available, but also for published facsimiles. The need for manuscripts of printed literature is probably less widely felt today (except for scholarly editing) than the need for manuscripts of essentially manuscript literature, that is, literature created before the invention of printing. The interest in the "material book" mentioned above is shared by medievalists who have developed a "materialist philology" that studies the ways the physical details and condition of each manuscript yield information "about the text's audience, its purpose and even the intention an individual scribe may have had in producing a particular copy."[10]

Original editions. These are the first and other editions in an author's lifetime whose form of publication (including corrections, revisions, and nonverbal elements such as illustrations) was presumably authorized by the author. Libraries are collecting original editions in our own day, of course, and through rare book dealers, microform, reprint, and now electronic texts, we acquire original editions or facsimiles of earlier material. Our interest is both the verbal authority and the material reality of the publications. Books are not the only original editions: as just mentioned, for the past 150 years periodicals have been the original place of publication for many, if not most, literary texts. In addition, then, to first editions and other original book editions, we should try to develop our holdings of literary periodicals. Current literary magazines exist in superabundance, but purposeful selection from among them is the challenge; older titles, though expensive, are relatively available and accessible through a number of major microform projects.[11]

Subsequent editions. Much of our literature exists as a sequence of editions. In the nineteenth century, Victorian novels and other literature typically appeared in print as a three-decker, a one-volume reissue, and various cheap reprints ("railway libraries," yellowbacks, etc.), sets of collected works, and American editions (often pirated).[12] Conditions in the United States were somewhat different, but even here publishers had many ways to introduce and reintroduce their wares. Today there is a fairly uniform sequence of publication going from little magazine to clothbound book to paperback (trade or mass market), with some opportunity along the way for book club or foreign editions and for participation by a range of trade, university press, and small press publishers. A full understanding of literary publishing, not to mention of the presence of literary works in the larger culture, has to acknowledge publishers' entrepreneurial zeal.

Scholarly editions. A scholarly or critical edition generally has the following features. Its editor has:

• identified the texts of a work that have some degree of authority (including manuscript, original, and most subsequent editions in the author's lifetime);

• selected a copy-text from among these that will serve as the base text for resetting and as primary authority for words, spelling, and punctuation;

• compared (collated) the various texts to discover variants and distinguished those variants that seem to be errors or a publisher's intrusions from those that are the author's revisions;

• emended (or not) the copy-text with revisions felt to be intended by the author;

• provided a thorough record of the textual history, variants, and emendations to the copy-text.

Although a full, scholarly edition is a sizable and costly volume, the edited text itself can be used in less expensive, more serviceable editions.[13]

The MLA's Committee on Scholarly Editions has issued a "Statement of Aims and Services" that summarizes current guidelines for print-format editorial projects. These are the product of nearly four decades of thinking about editorial principles and methods, largely initiated and formed by Fredson Bowers.[14] More recently, however, Bowers's influence has been modified by new editors dealing with new texts in a new scholarly and institutional context. Large-scale editions such as those encouraged by the MLA starting in the 1960s seem to be winding down (see, for example, the Newberry–Northwestern Melville and the Iowa–California Clemens), but other projects continue that will provide sound, important scholarly editions, such as the Nebraska Cather or the Oxford George Eliot. Graduate students still do carefully supervised scholarly editions for dissertations. (See chapter 4 for further discussion of this central scholarly activity.)

Student editions. Designed specifically for students in high school and college, these editions usually have a sound text, an introduction to the historical and literary contexts, and content annotations. Sometimes they also include a selection of critical articles or ancillary documentation such as the author's letters or selections from the manuscript. Norton Critical Editions are the most familiar example, and the Bedford Books series mentioned by Paul Hunter in chapter 11 is a recent entry. Paperback series from Penguin and Oxford University Press also qualify.

Anthologies. Although anthologies today infrequently print original, previously unpublished material, they do provide an important context for literary texts and often bring hitherto little-known writers to our attention. Modern anthologies can be of the best-of-the year variety (such as the annual *Best American Poetry*, New York: Scribner, 1988–); can define a genre, movement, regional, or other gathering (such as *Seventh Generation: An Anthology of Native American Plays*, edited by Mimi Gisolfi D'Aponte, New York: Theatre Communications Group, 1999); or can be, as textbooks, a kind of canon-making collection.

Material Texts and Primary Records

Our printed texts continue to be produced in massive quantities by increasingly multinational, conglomerate-controlled publishers. Each year English-language literature librarians have a worldwide set of some 20,000 book titles to select from. Fortunately, most of us work with a far smaller number from a smaller section of the whole, but we do struggle with the dispersal of publishing, the constant shifting of publishers' interests, the rise and decline of small press houses, and the similar diversity and instability of little magazines and journals. Table 1 provides detailed publishing figures for poetry, fiction, drama, and general literature and language from 1880 through 1997, relative to the entire United States output. (Similar figures for nineteenth- and early twentieth-century British publishing have been compiled and graphed by Simon Eliot.[15])

TABLE 1
Literary Publishing in the U.S., 1880–1997

Year	Total	Fiction	Literature	Language	Poetry & Drama
1880	2,076	292	106		111
1890	4,559	1,118	183		168
1900	6,356	1,278	543		400
1910	13,420	1,539	2,042	200	752
1920	6,187	1,123	301	195	453
1930	10,027	2,103	539	215	696
1940	11,328	1,736	536	319	738
1950	11,022	1,907	591	148	531
1960	15,012	2,440	726	228	492
1970	36,071	4,862	3085	472	1,474
1980	46,743	2,835	1,686	529	1,179
1990	62,039	5,764	2,049	649	874
1997	65,796	7,963	2,729	1,056	1,545

Periodicals add even more. The *Index of American Periodical Verse 1996* lists 20,214 poems by 6,914 poets in 298 little magazines, and the 1996 *American Humanities Index* lists some 40 plays, 8,120 poems, and 1,750 short stories from about 400 American magazines. At the same time, Dramatists Play Service and Samuel French added some 150 new plays to their catalogs, although very few plays are published by nonspecialist publishers and, indeed, relatively few plays see publication at all, not even in acting editions. A glance at the credits sections of the most recent volumes in the *Best Plays* or *Best Women's Stage Monologues* series shows at least 50 percent of the selections are from unpublished plays. The dramatic text may exist essentially on the stage, not on the page, but the other genres depend on the page, almost uncountable numbers of them.[16]

Overwhelmed as we might be by present publishing, the MLA seemingly urges us to save everything from the past as well. Its 1995 "Statement on the Significance of Primary Records" calls for preservation of virtually all evidence of printed texts, echoing history-of-the-book attitudes described above:

> [I]t is crucial for the future of humanistic study to make
> more widely understood the continuing value of the ar-
> tifacts themselves for reading and research . . . . Texts
> are inevitably affected by the physical means of their
> transmission; the physical features of the artifacts con-
> veying texts therefore play an integral role in the attempt
> to comprehend those texts. . . . [A]ll objects purporting
> to present the same texts . . . are separate records with
> their own characteristics . . . .[17]

These primary records are, of course, manuscripts, periodicals, and books, the original and subsequent editions, the trade, book club, and mass-market paperback editions, and the anthologies—all containing the text in question. For a book of even moderate popularity, the range of printed editions is usually quite extensive.

Primary records present the text and reveal much about its transmission from publisher through bookseller, library, and school to readers, both upon initial publication and over the (often long) life of the work itself. Analytical bibliographers and textual editors study the physical evidence for better understanding of the text itself, while literary historians and students of reading look at the outward appearance of the text's package and what is known about its marketing for "significant indicators of how the text . . . was regarded by its producers and how it was interpreted by its [original and later] readers."[18] (See chapter 3 for a more complete discussion of the statement and librarians' responses to it.)

This official concern for the materiality of literary texts ought to be tremendously reassuring for those of us who came to librarianship to be keepers of books and periodicals rather than literary scholars or information scientists, but it does place new responsibilities on us. No single library can advance very far in the collection, bibliographic control, and management of the full range of primary records for even one work. Each library must first collect the reading editions and the scholarly editions needed, but then each also should try to collect at least a partial representation of the full range of editions for some few works. Libraries also should collect collaboratively so that someone has, for example, all the Penguin, Modern Library, Tauchnitz, and Samuel French editions and so that someone has nearly all the editions of a given work. We must act responsibly toward the statement and realistically in our own situations.

Electronic Texts

The MLA "Statement" may have been elicited by the rather sudden arrival of electronic texts in the scholarly world. It explicitly reacted against the assumption that digital texts could replace printed texts and create a virtual library at once less costly (through savings in production, storage space, and maintenance) and more accessible ("open" day and night with a potentially infinite range of texts available to all). Theirs was not a Luddite fear for print-based jobs or nostalgia for a fading era but, rather, a reasoned and principled analysis of the nature of literary culture. Literature has been print based and its three-dimensionality cannot be replicated in a computer image, and, more practically, the technology is not yet ready. Optical character recognition scanning is not accurate enough for literary texts, so any text of scholarly quality has to be typed by hand, and any hypertext features also must be added by hand. The anticipated savings in production costs have not materialized.

Nevertheless, some electronic literature, such as hypertext fiction, is new. See the Web site "Hyperizons: Hypertext Fiction" (http://www.duke.edu/~mshumate/hyperfic.html) where the genre is defined, bibliographies maintained, and links provided to fiction itself, criticism, and theory. This site also has links to so-called hypertext poetry and to other fictions and narratives that are developments in the Web culture. Hypertext proponents such as George P. Landow see a connection with poststructuralist theory:

> [L]ike much recent work by poststructuralists, such as Roland Barthes and Jacques Derrida, hypertext reconceives conventional, long-held assumptions about au-

thors and readers and the texts they write and read. Electronic linking . . . embodies Julia Kristeva's notions of intertextuality, Mikhail Bakhtin's emphasis upon multivocality, Michel Foucault's conceptions of networks of power, and Gilles Deleuze and Félix Guattari's ideas of rhizomatic, "nomad thought." The very idea of hypertextuality seems to have taken form at approximately the same time that poststructuralism developed, but their points of convergence have a closer relation than that of mere contingency, for both grow out of dissatisfaction with the related phenomena of the printed book and hierarchical thought.[19]

Landow further asserts that a "central fact about the digital word lies in its intrinsic separation of text from the physical object by means of which it is read." In this, of course, it is in direct opposition to the material text, and this apparent antimateriality is perhaps a large part of the appeal of digital texts. Disembodied and democratized by removal from the material form of the printed book and the book's context of bookstore, library, and classroom, they become "free" and freed from any taint of canon. They are infinitely variable and manipulable in the reader's (or "accessor's") hands, yet they can return to their essential form. One can call up the same text on different computers in different places at different times, print out the text on any of a range of printers, download to one's own disks or hard drives, and then cut and paste the text at will; and one can do this today or tomorrow or fifty years form now and yet the essential text remains in memory (barring digital deterioration, discussed further below). Similarly, Richard A. Lanham praises the "metamorphic power" through which words, images, sound, and motion are converted into one digital file that enables new links, new forms, new teaching, new learning, new aesthetic, and intellectual culture.[20]

At the moment, however, most electronic texts reinforce the power of traditional printed texts and the scholarship surrounding them. Thousands of electronic literary texts are currently available on the Internet, ranging from single poems to complete novels, and are designed to appeal to a variety of readers and serve a variety of purposes. Most are there simply to be read and include only the most rudimentary information beyond the text itself, nothing more than author and title. They are, in effect, cheap paperback books missing both cover and title page but with the title and author's name penciled onto the first page. If, however, an editor describes the printed source in adequate detail, uses HTML markup language that allows a degree of hypertextuality, and provides links to, say, informative and educational images and annotations, an electronic text of this sort may be read in any literature course—or could even be produced as a project in a literature course. A third level of electronic text—the scholarly electronic edition—demands adherence to two sets of guidelines. It depends on careful, principled selection of the base printed text that is copied, and this text must be produced using a sophisticated and standard markup language. The MLA's Committee for Scholarly Editions recently issued a draft version of "Guidelines for Scholarly Electronic Editions," the essence of which is:

> The content of an electronic [scholarly] edition differs little from that of a print edition. It should be appropriate, complete, and coherently conceived. The criteria for what is to be included in an electronic critical edition will generally be more expansive than those for a comparable printed edition, because of the computer's inherent ability to organize and manipulate large amounts of data. In addition to materials that form part of the edition itself, an electronic edition can also make use of existing electronic materials by linking to them. . . .

> For an electronic scholarly edition, perhaps the single most crucial decision is the choice of encoding standard. . . .

> It is preferable to use the implementation of Standard Generalized Markup Language (SGML) specifically de-

vised for coding electronic texts, the Text Encoding Initiative (TEI).[21]

Strictly speaking, a digital text reproduces the text only, not any of the material publication that originally carried it. In many cases, however, there is extra-textual matter linked, and several projects are now under way devoted to creating digital versions of printed and manuscript materials that try to capture much of the three-dimensionality of the original material. Electronic books can represent the physical or material publication that originally contained the text so that readers can see illustrations, book size, format, and binding, bound-in advertisements, and whatever else was part of the published book or magazine. The electronic manuscript tries to reproduce the physical manuscript, which is particularly useful for medieval literature where manuscripts were the literary medium and texts would exist in several different manuscripts, each having unique scribal features in addition to the text. Three examples of these more complex and ambitious electronic projects are *The Electronic Beowulf* (Kevin Kiernan, director), *The Rossetti Archive* (Jerome McGann, director), and the *Dickinson Electronic Archives* (Martha Nell Smith, Ellen Louise Hart, and Marta Werner, general editors).[22]

As of this writing, no true scholarly electronic editions have been produced, but a wide range of digitized texts is available on floppy disk, CD-ROM, magnetic tape, and the Internet. Some are produced anonymously, some by volunteers for Project Gutenberg, some by individual scholars working alone or as part of larger group efforts, and some by university and commercial publishers. Although the markup usually does not approach the standards of TEI and the choice of editions preferred by the CSE, these texts certainly indicate some of the important possibilities of digital texts in libraries. As literary texts issue from the computer rather than the press, literary scholars will continue to search for answers to their questions about how these texts were produced and disseminated (and need the evidence in their libraries). As summarized by G. Thomas Tanselle:

Computerization is simply the latest chapter in the long story of facilitating the reproduction and alteration of texts; what remains constant is the inescapability of re-corded language from the technology that produced it and makes it accessible.[23]

Just as we have been able to gain an understanding of print pro-duction and build library collections that represent its nature, so should we now develop an understanding of electronic texts and our collec-tions of them.

Literary Information

Literature is not "information," literary study not "science," yet we rec-ognize that there is information about literature. A poem is not infor-mation, but there is information about poems, poets, their publishers, teachers, and readers of poems. Standard reference books, scholarly studies, author pages on the Web, vertical files with, for example, bro-chures for poetry reading series, and even collection management sta-tistics from our online systems provide a range of information about literature and its creators, producers, teachers, and readers. To build strong collections of texts requires us to think about the nature of texts and their production, but to build a collection of literary informa-tion requires us to think about those who use our collections. As aca-demic librarians, each of us in our own institution has unique pro-grams, student bodies, institutional missions, department emphases, and faculty research and teaching interests. In addition, we must un-derstand the nature of scholarship, criticism, theory, study, and teach-ing, and we must understand how they are characterized in each of our own situations. The latter requires some sense, then, of what is being taught, what the goals of our departments are, and why the cur-riculum is what it is, although we must not ignore nonmajors and non–English department interests in English-language literature.

Our readers are engaged in scholarship, criticism, study, and teaching. They also are specific individuals, and before we go very far with our own work, we must establish good working relations with them through a liaison system much like that described by Marcia Pankake (chapter 13). In addition, our readers are doing what other faculty are, so Stephen Wiberley's discussion of the collection needs of different kinds of literary study (chapter 12) and Paul Hunter's description of new historicist scholarship (chapter 11) are important reading. Finally, essays in *Introduction to Scholarship in Modern Languages and Literatures* (an MLA publication) outline several currently active areas of scholarship.[24] I will expand on two of these, biography and publishing history, and then discuss reference books and scholarly communication as two further kinds of literary information.

Scholarship

Scholarship deals with the process by which literature is composed, produced, disseminated, and received. That is, it mainly studies authorship, publishing, the book trade, and ways that new works are reviewed and recommended (or not) to the reading public and, of course, the nature of literary texts, as discussed above. There are some variations on this central purpose, such as new interests in collaborative authorship, the role of libraries, and the complex phenomenon of reading, not to mention a broadening of interest from traditional book publishing to the periodical press, secondary publishers (such as reprint and paperback publishers), and now digital publishers. Moreover, there is recognition that in many cases production means the creation of live or recorded performance. This scholarly interest has in part been simply historical: to identify what happened, by whom, when, and where. Increasingly though, in its pursuit of explanation and understanding, it has become allied with theory and broad questions about the nature of literature and the object of literary study.

Biography. Biography has long been a central element in literary study, and although, ultimately, our questions probe the process of authorship, we are also interested in basic life facts, the nature of formative influences, general participation in the events of the time, and so forth. Biographical studies that reveal an author's activities during periods of writing, specifically relationships with other writers, editors, and publishers, as well as with friends and others who may have influenced the writing, are of most interest and importance in our collections. Literary biography comes in a variety of forms, is based on a fairly standard range of biographical resources, and tries to answer a range of biographical questions. The critical biography does try to account for the writing (in contrast to the narrative biography, the psychological biography, or the biography specializing in, say, the early life), although it often deals with the content and style of the end result more than with the actual process of writing and getting published.

In addition to biographies, scholars also publish biographical resources such as chronologies, specialized studies of a writer's nonliterary interest in theater or film (for example), and editions of diaries and journals. A range of biographical resources can be collected in their original form or in printed editions produced by scholars, such as editions of letters, diaries, journals, commonplace books, authors' autobiographies and memoirs, the memoirs of acquaintances and contemporaries, as well as the nonwritten materials such as catalogs of authors' libraries or collections of saved playbills or photographs. Where these resources exist in print (or eventually in electronic editions), of course, libraries need the most scholarly and authoritative editions. Printed editions of these resources almost all deal with the same editorial and scholarly problems and issues—such as accurate transcription; indications of the writer's manuscript markings (cross-outs, deletions, revisions, underlinings, etc.); accurate dating of each item; thorough annotation that identifies individuals, locations, and events and detailed indexing.

Published letters provide a good example of these criteria. Letters are common; mention people, places, and events; are perhaps more unbuttoned than more formal writing; and often allow for a variety of specialized treatments. (Diaries and journals are similarly interesting and need scholarly treatment but are less common.) For example, Leon Edel's edition of Henry James's letters, in four volumes, actually includes not quite 10 percent of the total letters extant and available, leaving room for both specialized collections—such as between James and his brother, contemporary writers, and his English publisher—and alternative selections. Edel himself also edited two one-volume editions that each included letters not in the larger or the other single-volume collections.[25] Editorial standards of the past forty years generally mean that older editions of letters should be replaced as newer ones become available, on the expectation that these will be more complete and accurate, better annotated, and indexed in greater detail. For many authors, a popular, selective edition also is appropriate. Not only scholars and students, but also general readers want to read Keats's and Mark Twain's letters, for example, and do not need the full scholarly editions in hand if they are accessible in the library.

Although biographical study assumes *an* author, authors have always worked within a system and through a process. It is common today to talk about collaborative authorship. At its most literal, this is the recognition that nearly every writer may share preliminary work with friends, often sends it to other writers or trusted readers for critique, and, of course, has to deal with publishers' editors and readers. Jack Stillinger, in *Multiple Authorship and the Myth of Solitary Genius*, starts with the major Romantic writers but works his way to Anne Beattie with several examples of a range of degrees of collaboration between authors and others.[26] Scott Fitzgerald's advice to Ernest Hemingway about *The Sun Also Rises* and Ezra Pound's to T. S. Eliot about *The Waste Land* are well known, as is Maxwell Perkins's work as editor to a number of writers.[27] All this is, of course, to say nothing about the theoretical discussion of the concept and actuality of authorship stimulated by Roland Barthes in "The Death of the Author" and Michel Foucault in "What Is an Author?" and echoed by reader-response criticism.[28] These do not deny the fact of a person putting words on a page that are read but, rather, remind us that in the process of writing—and of turning writing into literature—additional factors affect (if not determine) how that which is read is received, defined, understood. The point is not to belittle the author but, instead, to understand the process of production and reception. Discovery of authorship must go beyond identifying the name on the title page.

Publishing, the Book Trade, and Reader. Libraries traditionally collected in publishing history but perhaps did so for quite specialized bibliographer and historian readers who were not entirely in step with their critic colleagues. Now scholars look into the dynamic relationship among printing, publishing, selling, libraries and book clubs, education, and the act of reading. The publisher's role in literary production is essentially entrepreneurial. It selects a literary manuscript to publish, oversees final editing for publication (which has always entailed some degree of alteration of the author's manuscript, from regularizing punctuation to censoring diction and narrative), distributing it to the book trade, and then maintaining the book's commercial viability through translations and subsidiary rights for paperbacks, film, TV, and audiotape. The physical work of printing actual copies of books is negotiated by the publisher from a range of options that affect the book's physical appearance and readability, as well as the publisher's investment in the number and cost of copies issued. Similarly, the publisher negotiates among a variety of selling options, including the amount, nature, and cost of advertising, book club deals, and book-store packages that can determine the extent to which a book is made known and available. If the printer is now a minor player in this pro-duction, the book trade—bookstore, book club, lending library, public library, reviewing media—does control price and availability, can am-plify or depress sales and readership, and can influence the publisher's (and even author's) willingness to support (or write) certain books rather than others.

The extent to which publisher and book trade actually influence readers is uncertain. No doubt reviews can initially encourage or dis-courage readers' choices, and the study of reviews has long been a staple of graduate theses and dissertations attempting to determine a writer's initial reception. After we look beyond the evidence of reviews, however, the scene grows more confused. Textbooks, anthologies, and student editions suggest a presence in curricula; the number of critical books, articles, and dissertations indicates scholars' interest; current editions in print indicate publishers' hopes. These kinds of evidence also suggest the existence of reading or interpretive communities as defined by proponents of reception theory.

Reception is not the same as reading. Reviewers, teachers, and critics may speak well or not of certain new books, but what readers select, what they actually read, and how they respond are quite an-other matter, and very little traced as yet. The *Reading Experience Da-tabase* being developed in Great Britain is one effort to record and quantify the actual experience of readers.[29] One group of readers whose response we often do know is that of writers. Their personal libraries, library borrowing records, journal entries, commonplace books, pub-lished reviews, teaching, and comments in letters all give insight into their own intellectual and artistic development and tastes, and information about them is contained in biographies.

As for library collections, we ought to consider the following:

- directories of current and historical publishers;
- publisher archives, or directories and indexes of them;
- histories of publishing houses and individuals, such as Michael Winship on Ticknor and Fields;
- studies or documentation of publishing and author relationships, such as Peter L. Shillingsburg on Thackeray;
- textual studies in general and of specific works, such as those in the textual history chapters of Committee on Scholarly Editions–approved editions;
- histories and studies of libraries and book clubs;
- diaries, journals, logs, anything in which readers of all sorts comment on their reading and contact with the printed word.

To which we should add and retain a rich collection of journals that carry reviews and report publishing news.[30]

Reference Books—Study and Teaching

James L. Harner's *Literary Research Guide* has become the standard bibliography of literary reference resources, and in it he aims to "describe and, in most instances, evaluate important bibliographies, abstracts, surveys of research, indexes, databases, catalogs, general histories and surveys, annals, chronologies, dictionaries, encyclopedias, and handbooks."[31] His arrangement is clear and instructive: he provides not only an annotated list of sources, but also a framework on which librarians can construct their own understanding of the field and which is itself a significant conceptual statement. For example, Harner's section on nineteenth-century British literature (in the chapter "English Literature") has these sections, each of which is appropriately subdivided:

- Research Methods;
- Guides to Reference Works;
- Histories and Surveys;
- Literary Handbooks, Dictionaries, and Encyclopedias;
- Bibliographies of Bibliographies;

- Guides to Primary Works: Manuscripts, Printed Works;
- Guides to Scholarship and Criticism: Surveys of Research, Serial Bibliographies, Other Bibliographies, Dissertations and Theses, Related Topics;
- Biographical Dictionaries;
- Periodicals (note particularly the subdivisions here);
- Background Reading;
- Genres: Fiction, Drama and Theater, Poetry, Prose.

Harner is comprehensive, but his framework makes it easy for a librarian to identify reference works appropriate for libraries of all sizes and with all manner of programs. The new librarian can work with these categories to learn the collection, to develop it as new works are published, to teach the structure to students, and to provide reference service. Harner's guide, then, is an important collection development tool.

While Harner covers English-language literature in general, James K. Bracken focuses on individual authors. His *Reference Works in British and American Literature* deals with some 1,400 specific authors and for each of them lists the available primary and secondary bibliographies, dictionaries, encyclopedias and handbooks, indexes and concordances, and specialized journals.[32] As with Harner, Bracken's comprehensiveness allows the librarian to be selective, easily identify resources for writers dealt with in courses and programs in one's own institution, and keep up-to-date with new publications. Neither Harner nor Bracken really helps us (or readers) select the "best" edition, biography, or critical study, so research guides such as Frank Jordan's *English Romantic Poets* are important. Unfortunately, they are few in number and few are very recent. Annuals such as *The Year's Work in English Studies* and *American Literary Scholarship* keep us fairly current in these areas and also with new scholarship and reference books.[33]

A key element in any reference collection are bibliographies and indexes to literary criticism and new writing. See chapter 7 for Judy Reynold's discussion of the *MLA International Bibliography*. I will only add that, as of 1999, the MLAIB's online coverage extends back to 1963, and the *Annual Bibliography of English Language and Literature*— its British counterpart—has its entire file since 1920 online. As indexing in both the MLAIB and ABELL is at least one to two years behind current publishing, readers must use the standard indexes to current periodicals to find the latest criticism. My own *Guide to Serial Bibliographies for the Modern Literatures* is an attempt to record regularly published serial bibliographies that complement or supplement the MLAIB and ABELL.[34] For the selector, a judicious selection of these complementary, supplementary bibliographies would seem appropriate, such as the checklists in the *Walt Whitman Quarterly Review*, the annual bibliography in *Victorian Studies*, the extensive book reviews in *Renaissance Quarterly*. Not to multiply examples here, but the advertisements in major journals such as *PMLA* are a bibliographic and critical education in themselves and display something of the array of contemporary scholarly and critical discussion.

Both Harner and Bracken emphasize research resources but give less guidance in selecting useful resources for lower-level students and nonmajors. The oft-scorned, but more often consulted, *Cliff's Notes* and *Masterplots* can be helpful aids to students struggling through a first reading of almost any literary work. Too often when students ask for assistance, librarians and/or instructors send the students to criticism that is even more daunting and impenetrable than the work itself. Simple plot summary can clarify novels and plays, but the more extensive help in something like *Shakespeare for Students* is probably more appropriate in most of our libraries.[35] When plot summaries are too short or *Cliff's Notes* too old (many volumes were originally written in the 1960s), we should look at more current and extensive alternatives, such as:

• Critical introductions, such as the *Dictionary of Literary Biography* and the Scribner Author Series or *Contemporary Dramatists/Novelists/Poets*, the *Oxford Companions,* and *Cambridge Guides*. More than potted recitals of biographical facts, these resources introduce writers and their themes, style, and key works in the terms of current critical discussion.

• Annotated editions, such as much-taught texts from Norton, Bedford, and Broadview. These texts offer content notes, background and context readings, and in the case of the Norton Critical Editions, a selection of critical articles.

• Collections of articles, such as in the old *Twentieth-Century Interpretations* from Prentice-Hall and now volumes from G. K. Hall and Cambridge University Press.

• Introductory monographs, such as in the various Twayne series.

• Standard classroom anthologies from Norton, Heath, Longman, etc. These include useful introductions and content notes.

• The MLA's Approaches to Teaching series. Although not directly useful for students, its volumes do help classroom faculty (and librarians) think about literary works as teachers rather than as critics.

Much is available that we can acquire to help our student readers deal effectively with literature. The trick is to set aside sufficient budget to keep it current with teaching emphases in the profession and in one's local institution, and to keep it available and usable in the face of heavy (and sometimes abusive) use.

Scholarly Communication: Monograph and Journal

Scholarly communication is a process within a system. The system consists of institutions (universities, libraries, academic departments), foundations, professional associations, publishers, and, of course, individual scholars. The process through which the scholar's reading, understanding, and writing typically develop includes study, teaching, informal discussion with colleagues, presentations at local faculty gatherings or seminars, papers read at conferences, articles published in journals, and finally publication of a book.[36] Almost any recent book's acknowledgments page lays out the process and system for us. For example, in her recent book on Henry James, Beverly Haviland thanks her undergraduate and graduate teachers, friends who supported her, colleagues with whom she discussed her project, the publisher's editor and readers. In addition, she thanks James's current literary executor and the research library where his papers are housed; she thanks national endowments for grants and her institution for research assistance (which we can imagine as reduced teaching load, office space, secretarial assistance and research assistants, travel funds); and she reveals the process through which her ideas about James developed—from courses taken and taught through conversations with colleagues, papers delivered at conferences and faculty seminars, and preliminary articles in journals to the book in hand.[37]

In this example, the scholarly monograph was the ultimate desired outcome, but the health and even utility of the scholarly monograph seem in doubt. On the one hand, although the number of monograph titles published has doubled in the past fifteen years, sales of individual titles have fallen by at least half, so that a print run of 250 to 500 copies seems standard; and of these, only 200 or so might be bought by academic libraries (thus further narrowing a book's visibility and availability). University press publishers seem under increasing pressure to show profit rather than foster high-quality, but money-losing, scholarship; library budgets have plateaued while the cost of journals, space, computer services, and books has advanced steadily. Some observers accuse both publishers and scholars of trendiness and criticize the university for pressuring tenure-hungry young faculty to publish prematurely (a tenure-tract) while solid work from seasoned faculty goes unpublished.[38]

On the other hand, however, there is evidence from citation studies that the role of the monograph remains what it has always been— an important contribution to new scholarship and the ongoing critical conversation. Although "monograph" implies simply a one-author or one-topic book, the scholarly monograph is better defined as "a book that presents new scholarship on a fairly narrow topic, rather than synthesizing the work of others, and whose primary audience is other researchers in the field, rather than students or general readers." It is different from a collection of essays, a textbook, a narrative history or biography, or a sweeping work of synthesis. The monograph may be in danger, but not because it is not still the premiere vehicle of communication in literature and the humanities; and some experiments are under way using electronic publication to make it affordable and more widely available.[39]

The effectiveness of the monograph depends not only on its content but also on its presentation, and for most writers effectiveness has to be honed through the process of conference presentation and journal publication. Journal publication in the humanities serves a different function than that in the sciences. In the latter, the journal article is a report of research that has been validated, authorized, and established; in the process of their work and their initial submission to the journal, the researchers had already communicated with other scientists, drawn on previous research for data or to carve out a niche of their own, and established the validity and significance of their research. Publication culminates the research, documents it, and places it in an archive where it can be consulted and cited in turn. Literary journal articles, on the other hand, can be better understood as part of an ongoing critical conversation. Although the literary article is indeed the culmination of reading, thinking, and writing, rigor of method and display of evidence have to be matched by the suggestiveness of ideas—and especially by the ability to engage the reader in these ideas. The text read and discussed—whether a traditional literary text or a cultural phenomenon—is of course crucial; and the critical reading does not alter this text but, rather, affects other readers and their own ongoing reading of the same or other texts.

With the arrival of the electronic journal, readers now have two formats in which to engage in the scholarly conversation and librarians two formats to manage in a time when journal costs are threatening to unbalance our collections. Whether electronic books will transform study, research, and general reading and lead the way toward a hypertext culture remains to be seen: for the moment they have, I believe, reinforced the recognition that literature is text based. Meanwhile, electronic journals are in fact proliferating and, for many librarians, creating a perhaps more immediate set of concerns than electronic literary texts. A considerable body of professional discussion is now available on a range of issues surrounding electronic journals, such as costs, archiving, and access.[40] Major journal publishers such as Elsevier and Johns Hopkins University Press are moving rapidly to provide their current journals in electronic as well as print format, and JSTOR is a major retrospective conversion project.[41]

The movement to electronic formats, budgeting problems created by rising serials costs, and improvements in document delivery services are altering not only how libraries handle serials access, but also how serials literature is defined and dealt with. Traditionally we have subscribed to journals in order to have access to their articles; increasingly it is possible to get individual articles without the journal "package" around them, so it is conceivable that many journals will cease as discrete publications and, instead, offer their contents on an article-by-article basis. Increasingly, online indexes and abstracting services link directly to the full text of articles they list. The editorial gatekeeping and added-value functions such as copyediting must continue, but the means of accessing, reproducing, and archiving individual articles will change significantly.[42]

At this writing, there is still some legitimate concern as to whether online journals are appropriate and necessary in literature collections. Costs of literary journals are so low, relatively, that commercial document delivery, traditional interlibrary loan, and electronic access do not offer significant savings. For many journals the whole issue is important, not only the single article, especially little magazines in which the editor's selection of poems and stories provides a significant context for individual texts. Literature itself invites, requires, and rewards "sustained" or "deep" reading,[43] and scholarly articles about literature need, as explained above, a similar commitment: it remains to be seen whether the online journal format really allows for and supports the kind of careful, engaged reading that is the essence of scholarly communication in literature and the humanities.

Certainly, however, a number of benefits argue for the online journal: space saved in our periodical stacks, improved service to off-campus and nontraditional students, and convenience to faculty in their offices. The activities of teaching, study, and research call upon a wide range of increasingly digitized information about literature, so that the computer has become as essential as the library in the process of reading. Study and research can only be improved if readers can consult the OED online at the moment they need it, tap into the critical conversation late at night working at home, or search the online version of literary text or a collection of online journals for a specific word or phrase. And, of course, online articles can readily be printed and read as intensively in this printed form as if they had come straight from the press.

Collection Management

Although this is not the place for an extended discussion of collection management, several issues particularly bearing on literature collections in the digital age do deserve brief mention. For more extensive discussions of the broader view, the several chapters in *Collection Management for the 21st Century* offer historical perspective and current ideas about a number of issues, and the volume as a whole is probably the most useful book on the subject at the moment.[44] In addition, regular reviews of the collection management literature in general and Scott Stebelman's ongoing bibliography "Studies of Interest to English and American Literature Librarians" and its updates in *Biblio-Notes* can keep us informed.[45]

Collection management is an ongoing process of selection to develop and maintain the collection, done within the contexts of local needs and, increasingly, of consortial arrangements, and guided by collection development policies. It starts with new resources (paper, microform, digital, and other) and continues on through repair, replacement, and preservation to removal to off-site storage or even discard. For selection of newly published materials and resources, the standard selection tools and the acquisitions procedures in our individual libraries are generally satisfactory, although they probably need to be augmented in the areas of poetry and drama, small press publications, and publications from outside the United States. Ironically, the hardest part of selection may be the literary texts themselves. Mainstream selection tools, advertisements, flyers, and publisher's catalogs abound with criticism and scholarship. Even faculty seem to request new studies more than new writing; much new writing, especially new writing that is not commercially viable, appears (and disappears) unreviewed. We cannot rely solely on what comes across our desk but, rather, must seek out resources that are truly representative. We should collaberate with colleagues in special collections, cultivate faculty who read current literature, tap the out-of-print market, and in general be alert to nonmainstream publications.

Selection of digital resources—both literary texts and literary information—involves the same criteria and policies as used for print.

Many of these resources are now being reviewed in the standard media (*Choice*, for instance), and we should work consideration of them into our regular selection routines. Although many valuable individual sites, metasites, and gateways are free and openly accessible (at the moment), we should not link sites just because they are free; they must be authoritative and useful. (See chapter 5 on electronic resources.) Costly commercial products require the same in-depth consideration that we have given in the past to large microfilm sets or encyclopedic print sets, with the significant difference that Internet databases can be purchased and managed through our consortia with costs to individual institutions apportioned as equal shares, on student FTE numbers, or on a per use basis. What we do not know yet is how to evaluate their price-to-value ratio: if no one uses them, they are too expensive; and if usage explodes, they are a treasure and a bargain. More likely is that we buy in hopes that usage will develop and that readers will find their own ways of utilizing their capabilities.

As for the ownership-access debate that has raged for well over a decade, time and commerce seem to have decided the issue, so that most of us now purchase access to digital text and information resources even though the difficult issues of archiving and long-term access have not been settled (at least not to libraries' satisfaction). Libraries have simply had to buy into digital resources as they become available and through whatever financial arrangements they could negotiate. In addition to these questions of quality and cost, there is the question of cataloging. Libraries should catalog digital resources just as carefully and thoroughly as they have cataloged print and other materials in order to provide accurate description and useful, consistent classification. Digital resources should be integrated with print and other materials in our collections, our catalogs, and our readers' minds. (See chapter 10 on cataloging.)

The procedures for selection and acquisition are probably unique to each library; we all work with a mixture, different in each institution, of vendors and dealers, direct orders and standing orders, approval plans, subscription lists, consortial arrangements, and librarian–faculty relationships. No one model works for all. As literature librarians, we probably have little influence on our overall library budgets, but we should be able to set budget allocations within our own areas where it is important to maintain a suitable balance among the various literary periods and genres, between undergraduate and faculty needs, and between established courses and new offerings, enrollment patterns, and research directions. Selection seems increasingly to involve more and more people at farther and farther removes from the individual selector. Approval plans bring in books we have never heard of, the technical requirements of digital resources require authorization or at least advice from the systems staff, and consortial agreements about online resources are made far from our library and in light of other needs than our own.

A collection development policy is useful for setting—or stating—the general direction one's collection development is going; it links literature collecting with the library's mission, builds on the existing collection, reflects the English department programs, and is appropriate to the kinds of students and faculty who use the collection. Although collection development policies are endorsed by the profession, they continue to be criticized as excessively rigid or irrelevant to our day-to-day work.[46] Policies do need to be reviewed and revised periodically as programs, faculty, and curriculums change; and they need a practical implementation. Collecting plans are an effective means of building and maintaining our collections purposefully and over the long term.[47] Just as a collection development policy is a written document, so ought our collecting plans be written down so that we can refer to them, pull them out for administrators or English departments to see, revise them as needed, and cross them off when completed.

It seems self-evident that as the universe of titles enlarges and budgets shrink, libraries must cooperate more. The history of interlibrary cooperation shows high aspirations, noble ideals, some clear successes, and a string of reality checks in which local needs and demands won out over larger-context hopes.[48] Newly formed consortia seem, however, to offer the real possibility that at last libraries can achieve meaningful cooperation at the grassroots, ordinary collection level.[49] Thus far, cooperation has been limited to shared licensing of digital resources—such as OhioLINK's agreements that provide access to *MLA International Bibliography*, Project MUSE journals, and some

Chadwyck-Healey literature databases (in a variety of budget arrangements appropriate to individual members).[50] This has been tremendously beneficial to all consortia members and has freed local funds for other purchases or provided hitherto unaffordable resources to a far wider range of library patrons. The next step—practical, coordinated collection development and management at the level of the ordinary collection that would, say, increase the range of little magazines and small presses represented, extend the authors collected, deepen collections of editions of standard writers, and let each of us build a local core within the larger consortia—can, and should, come.

Collections are dynamic: books are read, worn out, damaged, superseded; readers and programs change; new editions, new writers, new approaches flourish. The collection we built may not be the collection we have; its quality, physical condition, usefulness, and relevance may have declined. Regular review and evaluation will help us maintain the strengths we have worked to develop. We should scan our collection on the book and periodical shelves to check its physical condition, to discover overcrowding and gaps, to see it as users encounter it, and to remind ourselves of its physicality. We also should review systems data for circulation (including in-house use, ILL, reserve, and of journals as well as books), for acquisitions (including total and average per item costs in the various subjects), for cataloging (the number of volumes held, added, withdrawn, and the average number of copies in each area), and for connections to online databases and electronic texts and journals. (For more on evaluation, see chapter 6.)

A well-used collection needs constant attention to its physical condition. Review also allows us to identify items for repair, replacement, storage, and preservation treatment. A core of writers and works continues to be read regularly, and the actual physical volumes suffer higher levels of wear and tear than other areas of the collection. Sometimes this is clearly influenced by the curriculum, and it affects both primary and secondary resources: the British and American literature surveys, the masters' reading list, a popular course will send a generation or more of students to the same books again and again. On the other hand, a large proportion of books and journals have a relatively short lifetime of interest and relevance: these books should probably be removed to make way for more current and more frequently used (or likely to be used) materials. If we can develop storage facilities or cooperative storage arrangements with other libraries, we can consider relegating little-used materials to storage.

Off-site storage is a growth industry. Individual libraries, neighboring or associated libraries, and even library consortia are building off-site, warehouse-style remote storage, following the example of Harvard University's 1985 innovation.[51] Off-site storage reduces costs because it uses less expensive real estate, warehouse-style shelving and retrieval, and fewer staff; it allows libraries to retain valuable, though little-used, print resources; it is cheaper and more practical than digitization for little-used titles. Storage is one effective way to deal with brittle books that are irreplaceable or no longer available. Even if we do not (or cannot) choose to protect each individual book in a box or wrapper, simply moving at-risk items to remote storage reduces their use and unnecessary handling and puts them in facilities with appropriate environmental controls. The books are retained in the collection, and should the opportunity arise, we can give them suitable protective treatment.

The well-known preservation problems of paper resources obviously affect literature collections significantly. Nearly a century and a half of printed literature, and the scholarship and criticism appended to it, is at risk. Although popular and canonical works have been reissued in trade and scholarly editions, so much more than these exists (or existed) that a large chunk of our literary culture and our consequent understanding of it are in danger of disappearing. Various plans have been set in motion to preserve at least the intellectual content of this culture, and persistence in their execution can accomplish much. Most libraries have programs in place, and the role of literature librarians now is to select items for repair, replacement, storage, or preservation. Preservationists distinguish between the intellectual content and the physical artifact and also between preservation to retain an item and preservation to provide access to the item (or its contents). Moreover, they seem to accept that a hybrid system involving paper, microforms, and digitization is most workable.[52]

When the actual original materials are the main concern, preservation is the choice. (See chapter 3 on the MLA's "Statement on the

Significance of Primary Records" and librarians' responses to it.) If the content alone (or primarily) is of importance, a microfilm copy is easiest, least expensive, and longest lasting (permanent paper has comparable longevity but is more expensive to produce and to store). A digital copy of a microfilm or a paper original can make the content (and images of the artifact) widely available, but longevity of digital resources is an unknown. Image files are easy enough to produce by scanning, but a text file of scholarly quality needs considerable editing to correct OCR scanning errors and to add the necessary markup. In theory, an HTML or SGML file would continue to be readable with different platforms and software, provided that the file did not deteriorate or was regularly refreshed. At this time, however, digitization is more an access than a preservation technology.[53]

Conclusion

As subject specialists, we presumably have some knowledge of English-language literature that we might hope to keep alive through reading and even teaching. We must act, however, as generalists who are able to deal comfortably with all our faculty and to sympathize with students at the reference desk. Our professional specialization is in the production of print, digital, and other resources and in the development and maintenance of our own library's unique collection. The nature of literary texts is largely the history of their production (their writing, publication, distribution, and reading); scholarly, reference, and teaching resources, and the critical conversation are similarly produced. To select and build relevant and representative collections, we should know current publishing as well as historical, track publishers' lists as they merge and evolve, follow the rise and progress of little magazines, and watch the scholarly presses and learned journals adapt to new critics and theorists. With this knowledge we create core collections that both serve our readers' teaching and research needs and represent literary production.

Collection maintenance is as necessary as collection development, and probably more time-consuming. For it, a basic knowledge of issues, technologies, and procedures of preservation, repair, storage and shelving, and even basic statistical analysis is as important as our knowledge of publishing and bookselling. Just as we develop collections purposefully, so should we put similarly purposeful effort into setting up review procedures and making maintenance, preservation, and storage decisions so that the collection continues to meet the immediate study and research needs of students and faculty and to reflect the nature of literary texts and information resources. Knowing our own collection is also to acknowledge that there are weaknesses we might hope to repair and areas we will not develop in deference to (or dependence upon) other libraries' collections. Although not experts in literature, we are experts in our literature collections.

This is an exciting time. Writers continue to astound us through language, image, story, vivid characterization; scholars redraw the boundaries of the field and revitalize readers' responses to it; students discover (and think about) writing with youthful fervency; the physical heft and tactility of books and little magazines continue to please and the materiality of literature continues to be valued; electronic texts and digital resources open new ways to read, think, and teach. Our essential role remains what it has always been—to develop and maintain collections. If literature lives in libraries, it does so because we collect it, maintain its continued availability and usability, and respond to our faculty's and students' continuing needs in regard to it. Our work with library collections keeps us involved in the life of literature.

Notes

1. Stephen Greenblatt and Giles Gunn, eds., *Redrawing the Boundaries: The Transformation of English and American Literary Studies* (New York: MLA, 1990).

2. See D. C. Greetham, *Textual Scholarship: An Introduction* (New York: Garland, 1994), and ———, "Textual Scholarship," in *Introduction to Scholarship in Modern Languages and Literatures*, 2d ed., ed. Joseph Gibaldi (New York: MLA, 1993), 103–37; Jerome McGann, *A Critique of Modern Textual Criticism* (Chicago: Univ. of Chicago Pr., 1983); Peter L. Shillingsburg, *Scholarly Editing in the Computer Age: Theory and Practice*, 3d ed. (Ann Arbor: Univ. of Michigan Press, 1996); G. Thomas Tanselle, *A Rationale of Textual Criticism* (Philadelphia: Univ. of Pennsylvania Pr., 1989), esp. 11–38; William Proctor Williams and Craig S. Abbott, *An Introduction to Bibliographical and Textual Studies*, 3d ed. (New York: MLA, 1999).

3. See the table of contents in *Critical Terms for Literary Study*, 2d ed., ed. Frank Lentricchia and Thomas McLaughlin (Chicago: Univ. of Chicago Pr., 1995).

4. Jerome McGann, *The Complete Writings and Pictures of Dante Gabriel Rossetti: A Hypermedia Research Archive*, 19 Mar. 1997, http://jefferson.village. virginia.edu/rossetti/rossetti.html (22 June 1999).

5. See the Society for the History of Authorship, Reading, and Publishing (SHARP), 1999, http://www.indiana.edu/~sharp (5 Aug. 1999). See also: S. H. Steinberg, *Five Hundred Years of Printing*, 4th ed., ed. John Trevitt (New Castle, Del.: Oak Knoll, 1996); Henri-Jean Martin and Lucien Febvre, *The Coming of the Book*, trans. David Gerard (London: Verso, 1997); Philip Gaskell, *New Introduction to Bibliography* (Oxford: Clarendon, 1979); Robert Darnton, *The Business of Enlightenment: A Publishing History of the Encyclopédie, 1775–1800* (Cambridge: Harvard Univ. Pr., 1979); Elizabeth Eisenstein, *The Printing Press as an Agent of Change: Communications and Cultural Transformations in Early Modern Europe*, 2 vols. (Cambridge: Cambridge Univ. Pr., 1979).

6. Michael Winship, *American Literary Publishing in the Mid-Nineteenth Century: The Business of Ticknor and Fields* (Cambridge: Cambridge Univ. Pr., 1995), 7.

7. J. Don Vann, "Introduction," in *Victorian Novels in Serial* (New York: MLA, 1985), 1–17.

8. Mary Oliver, *West Wind: Poems and Prose Poems* (Boston: Houghton Mifflin, 1997), 65.

9. F. W. Bateson, "The Function of the Library in Graduate Study of English," *Journal of General Education* 13 (1961): 5–17; see also Eric Carpenter, "Collection Development for English and American Literature: An Overview," in *English and American Literature: Sources and Strategies for Collection Development*, ed. William McPheron, Stephen Lehmann, Craig Likness, and Marcia Pankake (Chicago: ALA, 1987), 1–19.

10. Stephen G. Nichols and Siegfried Wenzel, "Introduction," in *The Whole Book: Cultural Perspectives on the Medieval Miscellany*, ed. Stephen G. Nichols and Siegfried Wenzel (Ann Arbor: Univ. of Michigan Pr., 1996), 1–6.

11. See the *American Periodicals Series* (Ann Arbor: University Microfilms), *English Literary Periodicals* (Ann Arbor: University Microfilms), *Underground Newspaper Collection* (Wooster, Oh.: Micro Photo Division, Bell & Howell), and *Nineteenth-Century Theatre Periodicals* (Brighton, Eng.: Harvester); see also the *Index to American Periodicals of the 1700s and 1800s* and the *Index to English Literary Periodicals* (Indianapolis: Indexed Computer Systems, n.d.).

12. Richard D. Altick, "The Book Trade 1851–1900," in *The English Common Reader: A Social History of the Mass Reading Public, 1800–1900*, 2d ed. (Columbus: Ohio State Univ. Pr., 1998), 294–317; Simon Eliot, "'His Generation Read His Stories': Walter Besant, Chatto and Windus and *All Sorts and Conditions of Men*," *Publishing History* 21 (1987): 25–67.

13. See Williams and Abbott, *An Introduction to Bibliographical and Textual Studies*.

14. Greetham, *Textual Scholarship*; Fredson Bowers, *Principles of Bibliographical Description* (New York: Russell and Russell, 1962).

15. The 20,000 figure is the sum of data given in the *Bowker Annual* and the *Journal of Commonwealth Literature* about publishing output in the United States, Great Britain, Canada, and other English-speaking countries; see "American Book Title Production, 1996–1998," in *Bowker Annual: Library and Book Trade Almanac* (New Providence, N.J.: R. R. Bowker, 1999), 530, and the "Annual Bibliography of Commonwealth Literature 1997," *Journal of Commonwealth Literature* 33 (1998): 1–232. The historical data in the table are derived from Dorothy B. Hokkanen, "U.S. Book Title Output: A One Hundred-Year Overview," in *The Bowker Annual of Library and Book Trade Information*, 26th ed. (New York: R. R. Bowker, 1981), 324–29, and from the "Book Title Output and Average Prices," in *The Bowker Annual of Library and Book Trade Information* for 1982, 1992, and 1999. Note several qualifications: the per year figures are for total titles published in the United States, with no distinction made between new editions and reprints, reissues, or books originally published in Great Britain; pamphlets were included in the count and language included in the "Education" category from 1880 to 1910 (hence the large total number in 1910); the figures for fiction during the 1960s to 1980s do not adequately record mass-market publishing, which might have added 2,000 titles per year; the average yearly (not decade) increase in total output during 1880–1960 was 2.5 percent but grew to 7.8 percent starting in the 1960s. For nineteenth- and early twentieth-century British publishing, see Simon Eliot, *Some Patterns and Trends in British Publishing 1800–1919*, Occasional Papers no. 8 (London: Bibliographical Society, 1994).

16. See *Index of American Periodical Verse 1996* (Lanham, Md.: Scarecrow, 1998), *American Humanities Index* (Troy, N.Y.: Whitston, 1996), *The Best Plays of 1997–1998*, ed. Otis L. Guernsey Jr. (New York: Limelight Editions, 1998), *The Best Stage Scenes of 1997*, ed. Jocelyn A. Beard (Lyme, N.H.: Smith and Kraus, 1998).

17. Modern Language Association of America, "Statement on the Significance of Primary Records," *Profession* (1995): 27–28.

18. Ibid., 27.

19. George P. Landow, "What's a Critic to Do? Critical Theory in the Age of Hypertext," in *Hyper/Text/Theory*, ed. George P. Landow (Baltimore: Johns Hopkins Univ. Pr., 1994), 1.

20. Richard A. Lanham, *The Electronic Word: Democracy, Technology, and the Arts* (Chicago: Univ. of Chicago Pr., 1993), 11.

21. Committee on Scholarly Editions of the Modern Language Association, "Guidelines for Scholarly Electronic Editions" (section III; paragraph 3; section

I, B), 1 Dec. 1997, http://sunsite.berkeley.edu/MLA/guidelines.html (17 June 1999).

22. See these URLs: *The Electronic Beowulf*, 1999, http://www.uky.edu/ ArtsSciences/English/Beowulf/ (22 June 1999); *The Complete Writings and Pictures of Dante Gabriel Rossetti: A Hypermedia Research Archive*, 19 Mar. 1997, http://jefferson.village.virginia.edu/rossetti/rossetti.html (22 June 1999); *Dickinson Electronic Archives*, 1997, http://jefferson.village.virginia.edu/ dickinson/ (22 June 1999).

23. G. Thomas Tanselle, "Printing History and Other History," in *Literature and Artifacts* (Charlottesville: Bibliographical Society of Virginia, 1998), 326.

24. *Introduction to Scholarship in Modern Languages*, 2d ed., ed. Joseph Gibaldi (New York: MLA, 1992).

25. See Michael Anesko, "'God Knows They Are Impossible': James's Letters and Their Editors," *Henry James Review* 18 (1997): 140–48; Henry James, *Letters*, 4 vols., ed. Leon Edel (Cambridge, Mass.: Belknap Pr. of Harvard Univ. Pr., 1974–1984); *Selected Letters*, ed. Leon Edel (Garden City, N.Y.: Doubleday, 1960); *Selected Letters*, ed. Leon Edel (Cambridge: Belknap Press of Harvard University Press, 1987).

26. Jack Stillinger, *Multiple Authorship and the Myth of Solitary Genius* (New York: Oxford Univ. Pr., 1991).

27. F. Scott Fitzgerald, *Correspondence of F. Scott Fitzgerald*, ed. Matthew J. Bruccoli and Margaret M. Duggan, with Susan Walker (New York: Random House, 1980), 193–96; T. S. Eliot, *The Waste Land: A Facsimile and Transcript of the Original Drafts Including the Annotations of Ezra Pound*, ed. Valerie Eliot (New York: Harcourt, Brace, Jovanovich, 1971); A. Scott Berg, *Max Perkins: Editor of Genius* (New York: Dutton, 1978).

28. Roland Barthes, "The Death of the Author," in *Image Music Text*, trans. Stephen Heath (New York: Hill and Wang, 1977), 142–48. Michel Foucault, "What Is an Author?" in *Language, Counter-Memory, Practice: Selected Essays and Interviews*, trans. Donald F. Bouchard (Ithaca, N.Y.: Cornell Univ. Pr., 1971), 113–38. See "Reader-Response Theory and Criticism" and "Reception Theory," in *Johns Hopkins Guide to Literary Theory and Criticism*, ed. Michael Groden and Martin Kreiswirth (Baltimore: Johns Hopkins Univ. Pr., 1995), 606–11.

29. *The Reading Experience Database 1450–1914*, 1999, http:// www2.open.ac.uk/arts/RED/index.html (5 Aug. 1999); Simon Eliot, "The Reading Experience Database: Problems and Possibilities," *Publishing History* 39 (1996): 87–100.

30. See, for example, the microfilm series of publishers' archives issued by Chadwyck-Healey; Christopher Feeney, *Index to the Archives of Harper and Brothers, 1817–1914* (Teaneck, N.J.: Chadwyck-Healey, 1982); Martha Brodersen, Beth Luey, Audrey Brichetto Morris, and Rosanne Trujillo, *A Guide to Book Publishers' Archives* (New York: Book Industry Study Group, 1996);

Winship, *American Literary Publishing in the Mid-Nineteenth Century*; Peter L. Shillingsburg, *Pegasus in Harness: Victorian Publishing and W . M. Thackeray* (Charlottesville, Va.: Univ. Pr. of Virginia, 1992); Guinevere L. Griest, *Mudie's Circulating Library and the Victorian Novel* (Bloomington: Indiana Univ. Pr., 1970); Janice A. Radway, *A Feeling for Books: The Book-of-the-Month Club, Literary Taste, and Middle-Class Desire* (Chapel Hill: Univ. of North Carolina Pr., 1997); Esther Jane Carrier, *Fiction in Public Libraries, 1900–1950* (Littleton, Colo.: Libraries Unlimited, 1985); Marjorie Plant, *The English Book Trade: An Economic History of the Making and Sale of Books*, 3d ed. (London: Allen and Unwin, 1974).

31. James L. Harner, *Literary Research Guide: An Annotated Listing of Reference Sources in English Literary Studies*, 3d ed. (New York: MLA, 1998). Note also the Web site at which Harner regularly updates his book: http://www-english.tamu.edu/pubs/lrg.

32. James K. Bracken, *Reference Works in British and American Literature*, 2d ed. (Littleton, Colo.: Libraries Unlimited, 1998).

33. Frank Jordan, ed., *English Romantic Poets: A Review of Research and Criticism*, 4th ed. (New York: MLA, 1985); *The Year's Work in English Studies* (Oxford: Blackwell for the English Association, 1921–); *American Literary Scholarship: An Annual* (Durham, N.C.: Duke Univ. Pr., 1965–).

34. William A. Wortman, *A Guide to Serial Bibliographies for the Modern Literatures*, 2d ed. (New York: MLA, 1995); updated twice yearly at http://www.lib.muohio.edu/serial-bibliographies.

35. *Shakespeare for Students: Critical Interpretations*, ed. Mark W. Scott (Detroit: Gale Research, 1992).

36. See William Garvey, *Communication: The Essence of Science. Facilitating Information Exchange among Librarians, Scientists, Engineers and Students* (New York: Pergamom, 1979); *Scholarly Communication: The Report of the National Enquiry* (Baltimore: Johns Hopkins Univ. Pr., 1979); Anthony M. Cummings, ed., *University Libraries and Scholarly Communication* (Washington, D.C.: ARL, 1992), and a synopsis of this by Ann Okerson, "University Libraries and Scholarly Communication," in *Scholarly Publishing: The Electronic Frontier*, ed. Robin P. Peek and Gregory B. Newby (Cambridge, Mass.: MIT Pr., 1996), 181–99; Ylva Lindholm-Romantschuk, *Scholarly Book Reviewing in the Social Sciences and Humanities: The Flow of Ideas within and among Disciplines* (Westport, Conn.: Greenwood, 1998).

37. Beverly Haviland, *Henry James's Last Romance: Making Sense of the Past and the American Scene* (New York: Cambridge Univ. Pr., 1997).

38. A flurry of articles starting in the mid-1990s deals with this topic. See, especially, Sanford G. Thatcher, "The Crisis in Scholarly Communication," *Chronicle of Higher Education*, 3 Mar.1995, B1–2; William C. Dowling, "The Crisis in Scholarly Publishing," *Public Interest* 129 (1997): 23–37; Karen J.

Winkler, "Scholars Assess the Health and the Value of Specialized Monographs," *Chronicle of Higher Education* 26 Sept. 1997, A18; Ken Wissoker, "Scholarly Monographs Are Flourishing, Not Dying," *Chronicle of Higher Education* 12 Sept. 1997, B4–B5.

39. Bonnie Collier, "Preserving the Central Role of the Monograph," *Chronicle of Higher Education* 5 Feb. 1999, A56–57; Ylva Lindholm-Romantschuk and Julian Warner, "The Role of Monographs in Scholarly Communication: An Empirical Study of Philosophy, Sociology and Economics," *Journal of Documentation* 52 (1996): 389–404; Wissoker, "Scholarly Monographs Are Flourishing, Not Dying," B4; Dinitia Smith, "Hoping the Web Will Rescue Young Professors," *New York Times*, 12 June 1999, A17 and A19 (N).

40. There is considerable literature on electronic journals. See, for example, "Electronic Journals: A Selected Resource Guide," 23 July 1999, http://www.harrassowitz.de/ms/ejresguide.html (22 Aug. 1999); Anne Shumelda Okerson and James J. O'Donnell, *Scholarly Journals at the Crossroads: A Subversive Proposal for Electronic Publishing* (Washington, D.C.: Office of Scientific and Academic Publishing, ARL, 1995); see also Charles W. Bailey Jr., "Scholarly Electronic Publishing Bibliography," 1 June 1999, http://info.lib.uh.edu/sepb/sepb.html (16 June 1999). Also, search *Library Literature* with the subject term "electronic journals."

41. Elsevier Science, http://www.elsevier.com; Project MUSE, http://www.press.jhu.edu/muse.html; and JSTOR, http://www.jstor.org.

42. Jane P. Kleiner and Charles A. Hamaker, "Libraries 2000: Transforming Libraries Using Document Delivery, Needs Assessment, and Networked Resources," *College and Research Libraries* 53 (1997): 355–74.

43. Walt Crawford and Michael Gorman, *Future Libraries: Dreams, Madness, and Reality* (Chicago: ALA, 1995), 15, 17; Sven Birkerts, "The Owl Has Flown," in *The Gutenberg Elegies: The Fate of Reading in an Electronic Age* (Boston: Faber and Faber, 1994), 70–76.

44. *Collection Management for the 21st Century: A Handbook for Librarians*, ed. G. E. Gorman and Ruth M. Miller (Westport, Conn.: Greenwood, 1998).

45. Thomas E. Nisonger, "A Review of the 1997 Collection Development and Management Literature," *Collection Building* 18 (1999): 67–80; ———, "The Collection Development Literature of 1996: A Bibliographic Essay," *Collection Building* 17 (1998): 29–39; Ruth M. Miller, "Selected Review of the Literature on Collection Development and Collection Management, 1990–1995," in *Collection Management for the 21st Century*, 287–318; Scott Stebelman, "Studies of Interest to English and American Literature Librarians," Feb. 1999, http://gwis2.circ.gwu.edu/~scottlib/english.html (9 June 1999); *Biblio-Notes* (Chicago: ALA) and online at http://www.lib.uconn.edu/EALS/biblio/spring1999.html (3 Aug. 1999).

46. *Guide for Written Collection Policy Statements*, 2d ed., ed. Joanne S. Ander-

son (Chicago: ALA, 1996); for a skeptical view, see Richard Snow, "Wasted Words: The Written Collection Development Policy and the Academic Library," *Journal of Academic Librarianship* 22 (1996):191–94.

47. William A. Wortman, *Collection Management: Background and Principles* (Chicago: ALA, 1989), 129–31.

48. Gay Dannelly, "Cooperation Is the Future of Collection Management and Development: OhioLINK and CIC," in *Collection Management for the 21st Century*, 249–62. See also the ALA's *Guide to Cooperative Collection Development*, ed. Bart Harloe (Chicago: ALA, 1994). For history and current issues, see Richard J. Wood, "The Axioms, Barriers, and Components of Cooperative Collection Development"; and for a contrarian view, see Dan C. Hazen, "Cooperative Collection Development: Compelling Theory, Inconsequential Results?" in *Collection Management for the 21st Century*, 221–48, 263–83.

49. William Gray Potter, "Recent Trends in Statewide Academic Library Consortia," *Library Trends* 45 (1997): 416–34.

50. Gay Dannelly and David F. Kohl, "Resource Sharing in a Changing Ohio Environment," *Library Trends* 45 (1997): 435–47.

51. Ron Chepesiuk, "Reaching Critical Mass: Off-Site Storage in the Digital Age," *American Libraries* 30, no. 4 (1999): 40–43.

52. *Preservation Microfilming: A Guide*, 2d ed., ed. Lisa L. Fox (Chicago: ALA, 1996); see, especially, "Introduction," 1–22, and Appendix C, "Preservation Options," 305–9. Margaret P. Trader, "Preservation Technologies: Photocopies, Microforms, and Digital Images—Pros and Cons," *Microform Review* 22 (1993): 127–34; Abby Smith, *The Future of the Past: Preservation in American Research Libraries* (Washington, D.C.: Council on Library and Information Resources, 1999).

53. Susan Hockey, "Evaluating Electronic Texts in the Humanities," *Library Trends* 42 (1994): 676–93; Commission on Preservation and Access and Research Libraries Group, *Preserving Digital Information: Report of the Task Force on Archiving of Digital Information* (Washington, D.C.: Commission on Preservation and Access, 1996).

Chapter 2

Retrospective Collection Development and Its Bibliographies

Richard Heinzkill
University of Oregon

"Retrospective collection development involves those activities by which titles not recently published are identified and added to the collection. It contrasts with current selection, which focuses on materials that have been newly published or reviewed." So begins the chapter I wrote on retrospective collection development that appeared in the 1987 publication *English and American Literature: Sources and Strategies for Collection Development.*[1] The definition of retrospective collection development has not changed over the past decade, nor have the basic reasons for engaging in this activity or methods for doing it dramatically changed since then, although some interesting new developments have occurred on the electronic front. Because the advice given in the opening pages of the chapter in the 1987 volume still stands, for the most part, it will not be repeated in this discussion and the reader is urged to consult the 1987 volume for the complete text.

Evaluation, Canon, Electronic Texts

Almost every look at a part of the collection results in some form of evaluative statement. For instance, a cursory glance at the shelf by a visiting professor pronouncing the collection inadequate for his or her teaching purposes or users complaining the library does not have anything on their topics are judgments about the quality of the collection. Librarians also look at the collection, but in a more purposeful and systematic way and for the following reasons.

1. *To determine if a collection meets standards*: Standards here can be somewhat loosely construed. There is no accrediting body issuing either author lists or title lists of absolutely essential works for the literature collection. In fact, one of the purposes of this chapter, as of the 1987 chapter, is to identify sources that can function as a "standard" bibliography to develop a core collection. The term *core collection* is usually regarded as being synonymous with a "standard" collection. Unlike the practice of acquiring current works where the level of collecting is indicated, core collections have not adopted this approach. For instance, core collections are usually thought of as being for undergraduate work; however, a core collection for master's-level work will necessarily be more comprehensive and one for doctoral-level work still more so.

Recently, there has been more interest in comparing a library's collection to the holdings of similar or larger institutions using analysis tools such as the RLG Conspectus, OCLC/AMIGOS, and the North American Title Count. These tools certainly are helpful, but results are usually stated in poor-good-better-best terms without identifying specific titles that would indeed make a collection the best. There is a small body of professional literature on the use of these tools in collection development.[2] Most of the articles discuss overarching issues; few of them relate their use to specific disciplines and only one appears to be specifically about the area of English and American literature—the study by Jeanne Harrell, who used OCLC/AMIGOS software to evaluate the English and American literature collection.[3] This software, which is designed for all subject areas, always deals with data from the most recent ten years. Although a list of titles published in the past decade is certainly of value to an institution doing a review, the heavy use of library material older than that in literary studies argues that the results of an OCLC/AMIGOS analysis should not be the only criterion on which to judge the adequacy of the collection. Furthermore, users of this software tend to look only at the PR and PS call number ranges, but holdings in the PE and lower ranges of the PN classifications also should be examined. But more important, because of the heavy reliance in critical theory on many other disciplines, as the bibliographies cited below will testify to, evaluators of the literature collection need to look at other areas that directly support the literature program, such as fundamental works in philosophy, psychology, anthropology, etc. Many of the literary theory titles lie outside the literature, P–PZ sections in the Library of Congress classification scheme.

2. *To upgrade the support of an established academic program*: Established programs in English have broadened. Literature is no longer narrowly defined and perhaps collecting has not kept pace. Upgrading may require additional funding as either a one-time infusion or an addition to the base budget. Supporting documentation for funding requests often includes an appraisal of the affected part of the collection. The sources listed in this chapter will help with that appraisal.

3. *To support a new academic program, such as Gay and Lesbian Studies or Multicultural Studies*: The bibliographer is involved in acquiring material to support a new program or new research interests on campus. Retrospective bibliography provides guidance in giving the collection the necessary depth for supporting new programs.

4. *To restore balance to the existing collection*: For whatever reason, selection of titles in certain areas may have been neglected. Filling gaps in the collection is an important task for the literature bibliographer. Retrospective bibliographies point the way.

5. *To gather data for management decisions about preservation or storage*: Preservation procedures such as repairing, boxing, and restoring older titles are very expensive. At any or all of these decision points, the literature bibliographer may be called on for guidance, guidance determined by consulting titles that can be used as the basic bibliographies in the field. Determining what titles to send to storage in effect is asking what should stay on the library's open shelves. The

minimal answer is the core collection. Local interest will help determine which titles, in addition to the core collection, should be retained. Retrospective bibliographies can help one make informed decisions about preservation efforts and weeding for storage.

6. *To establish the strength of the collection when writing and reviewing collection development statements*: Often the collection development statement indicates what level the collection is presently at and what level is the desired collecting goal. Retrospective bibliographies have a role to play in determining these levels.

7. *To determine the extent to which there is regional support for the program that might substitute for local ownership*: The growth of regional union catalogs, such as OhioLINK and Orbis in the Pacific Northwest, and the electronic interlibrary loan (ILL) capabilities of larger bibliographic utilities, such as OCLC, are becoming an important factor in collection development. The dramatic improvement of ILL services occasions a different perspective on neighboring literature collections. Users will always want titles on the shelf when they visit their local library, but the ease of obtaining books the library does not own or that are checked out has significantly increased in the past ten years. Now, thanks to the convergence of Web versions of library catalogs, e-mail, and private express parcel shipping services, titles can be obtained from other libraries in a regional consortium more quickly than the local library can recall a book in circulation on the patron's own campus! Typically, the request to obtain the material is conveniently done from the OPAC terminal in the library, office, or home without having to visit in person any special desk or office. Furthermore, present fiscal realities mean that, in most areas, a library can no longer have a comprehensive collection. Therefore, in today's electronic environment the bibliographer should evaluate access to titles and not just consider local holdings. Use of retrospective bibliographies assists in this process.

The Canon

In 1987, I wrote that, arguably, "there is a scholarly consensus, sometimes shaky but nevertheless present, about which authors constitute the canon of English and American literature."[4] The rumbling beginning to shake the foundation of the canon then has since grown into a full-fledged earthquake in which canonical structures have fallen. For collection development purposes, I propose that instead of speaking of canonical authors, we refer to our "classical" authors, authors such as Dickens, Austen, Dickinson, and Anderson, who have been taught over the past fifty years. They are part of the record of literary scholarship. However, they have been supplemented—some would go further and say rightfully usurped—by other authors previously neglected or unknown. Persons writing from an ethnic perspective and women constitute the majority of these "new" writers. Therefore, the selector should be aware that the core collection of ten years ago is quite different from the core collection of today. I am not referring just to twentieth-century literature, but to all earlier periods as well. No matter what the century, the authors said to constitute the canon for that particular era have changed and will probably continue to change. However, this does not mean that older versions of the canon as represented in literary histories and bibliographies, such as the *New Cambridge Bibliography of English Literature* (Watson 1969–1977), can be passed by. It is just that the older, more traditional sources should not be taken as the final word on the scope of present-day literary studies.

Electronic Texts

Perhaps the most intriguing development in retrospective bibliography is the advent of electronic texts.[5] One of the earliest offerings of electronic texts is Project Gutenberg. For this endeavor, interested persons key in out-of-copyright works and submit the computerized text to the director for incorporation into the database. Project Gutenberg has been criticized for propagating older editions when newer scholarly editions exist, for allowing inaccuracies to creep in because of careless typing, for idiosyncratic selection of titles because contributors are volunteers following their own interests. Project Gutenberg pleads guilty to all counts. Inasmuch as the project exists through the efforts of unpaid volunteers, it considers itself a success, and so do many other observers, if for no other reason than that the availability of a text through one's computer is seen as better than not having the text accessible in an electronic format. Project Gutenberg is not the only effort to make literary electronic texts available over the Web. Project Bartleby, originally mounted at Columbia University, sought "to represent with 100% accuracy an original work" in an electronic format "available free to the public for educational purposes."[6] Knowing that Project Bartleby, consisting of all out-of-copyright titles from thirty-seven authors, has logged thirty-five million hits between its inception in 1994 and May 1998 prompts one to pause and wonder about the impact of electronic literary texts and what librarians should do to make texts available in several formats. Electronic texts may turn out to be more popular—and access to them expected by more library users—than we realize. Anyway, these two projects are representative of the fast-growing interest in digitized texts. A list of electronic text repositories is maintained by Library Electronic Text Resource Service, at Indiana University.[7] (Electronic texts are discussed at greater length by Arlen, Tofanelli, Willett, and Wortman in this book.)

One of the goals of retrospective collection development is to provide patrons with access to older texts. The choices for the bibliographer are increasing—older texts are arriving in the library not only in printed format, but also in micro-formats, on CD-ROMs, and over the Internet. Several options, such as cataloging Internet resources with or without a hot link in the catalog, maintaining Web pages for local users, networking resources for the library's information system, and providing humanities electronic resource centers, offer some ways of providing access to computerized texts.

Which of the many formats will be favored? It is too early to tell. Possibly different formats will emerge as most appropriate for different groups of users. One of the most interesting innovations in the electronic environment is the creation of pockets of extremely rich resources for literary study on the Web by dedicated computer-savvy academics. One can assume that more of these sites will be compiled. The interesting question is how these Web-based resources eventually will mesh with in-house resources. If retrospective collection development is involved in making older texts available and electronic formats concentrate on the older texts, there are several roles now for the literature bibliographer: compiling Web sites, recommending CD-ROM resources for the library to purchase, participating in electronic resource centers, and determining what texts should be included in digital library projects.

Criteria for Works Cited

The first few pages of my 1987 discussion of retrospective bibliography mention criteria for bibliographies appropriate for retrospective collection. Those criteria will not be repeated here except to say this chapter presents a selection of titles under each topic. The works cited are not meant to be an inclusive list but, instead, single out those books and articles that combine content and layout in a way easily utilized by selectors.

Ethnic American Literatures

Asian American

Asian American literature, to generalize about the writings from several cultural backgrounds, begins with two types of writing: writings by immigrants dealing with their trials and troubles as they encounter a different culture, and those by early immigrants, usually educated in their homeland, who interpret Asian customs, religions, and philosophies for American audiences. Most of the literature by Asian Americans produced before World War II falls into one of these two categories. But after World War II many second- and third-generation Asian Americans strove to break out of these patterns. Their work exhibited a new self-confidence and dealt with a variety of themes not treated in the immigrant literature up to that time. Writers of the post–World War II group are no longer interested in presenting themselves as an exotic people who wish to be assimilated. They insist on moving beyond the long-standing stereotypes of Asians previously presented in mainstream American literature.

The implications for the selector are several: (1) Much of the creative literature of the immigrants, aside from the autobiographical books, was published in local newspapers and magazines, not easily accessible today. (2) Before World War II, the number of titles constituting the primary bibliography of this field is not large. (3) Most bibliographies concentrate on authors who began to publish in the middle 1960s. (4) Autobiography constitutes a large portion of these literatures. (5)

Many authors are one-book authors, and there are few sustained literary careers

Nothing has surpassed *Asian American Literature: An Annotated Bibliography* (1998) by King-Kok Cheung and Stan Yogi as a selection guide. If anything, it is too comprehensive; but as the compilers say, they would rather be inclusive and suggest that people simply pass by those items they are not interested in. Although that approach may work for students, it poses some hazards for the selector. The inclusiveness is most noticeable in the prose sections where individual stories in anthologies and periodicals are each given a separate entry. In the Chinese section 57 percent of the titles are newspaper stories or anthologized pieces; the rest are books. In the Japanese section, the percentage of literary pieces appearing in newspapers or anthologies is higher, 85 percent. Obviously, for selectors using this bibliography some sorting out of formats will be necessary. The coverage is divided into Chinese American, Japanese American, Filipino American, Korean American, South Asian American, and Vietnamese American. Under each heading are the primary works of prose, poetry, and drama. Secondary sources for each literature are identified as to book, dissertation, article, or interview. Two additional sections complete the volume: creative literature by non-Asians about Asians and historical, political, sociological background works about Asian Americans.

The article "Asian American Literature," by King-Kok Cheung in *Benet's Reader's Encyclopedia of American Literature* (Perkins, Perkins, and Leininger 1991), identifies the most important authors and titles and therefore can serve as a guide to a minimal core collection. Also, a serviceable bibliography of the early poets is in *Quiet Fire: A Historical Anthology of Asian American Poetry, 1892–1970* (Chang 1996).

Three other bibliographies the selector may want to consult are *Redefining American Literary History* (Ruoff and Ward 1990), *American Ethnic Literatures* (Peck 1992), and *New Immigrant Literatures in the United States* (Knippling 1996). Their coverage of primary authors is compared below. Some lists include authors of autobiographies and key nonfiction works. Coverage of secondary literature is minimal in all three titles. All of them mention anthologies, which are an important avenue for making texts available. Their coverage is as follows: (1) Chinese American literature—*Redefining American Literary History*, sixty-five authors; *American Ethnic Literatures*, eighty-nine authors; *New Immigrant Literatures in the United States*, twenty-two authors who have published books; (2) Japanese American literature—*Redefining American Literary History*, forty-three authors; *American Ethnic Literatures*, sixty authors; *New Immigrant Literatures in the United States*, twenty-seven who have published books; 3) Korean American literature—*Redefining American Literary History*, nine authors; *American Ethnic Literatures*, eleven authors; *New Immigrant Literatures in the United States*, twenty-three who have published books; 4) Philippine (or Filipino) American literature—*Redefining American Literary History*, ten authors; *American Ethnic Literatures*, sixteen authors; *New Immigrant Literatures in the United States*, fifteen who have published books.

A recently published reference work, *Asian American Literature: Reviews and Criticism of Works by American Writers of Asian Descent* (Trudeau 1999), highlights living Asian American authors. Their backgrounds are as follows: Chinese American, twenty; Japanese American, fifteen; Filipino American, five; Vietnamese American, one; Indian American, two; and Korean American, two. This a good selection of Asian American writers today. This same volume includes a few deceased authors, but too few to be considered a good cross section of the older literature.

African American literature

Most of the African American literature before the twentieth century is found in song, folklore, tales, slave and religious autobiographies, and poetry. Anthologies and reprints have done much to give access to this body of literature. In the latter half of the twentieth-century, black literature courses in almost every college and university have contributed to the demand for the works of the key black poets, novelists, and dramatists of the twentieth century. Publishers have responded by issuing these works in a variety of editions, thus making it possible for libraries to acquire them. Although the titles recommended below tend to focus on what is usually thought of as literature, the collection that serves black literature has to go far beyond literary works. If the black studies program has not already acquired titles in history, politics, and sociology dealing with the role of blacks in American society, these titles will be needed as necessary background. Also, titles in music history, folklore, and religion are vital to the study of black literature.

One of the best overviews of a black literature collection is in the *Norton Anthology of African American Literature* (Gates and McKay 1996). The bibliographical section of this work treats the authors in the various periods of American black literature. The periods are: 1746–1865 (sixteen authors), 1865–1919 (fourteen authors), 1919–1940 (twenty-two authors), 1940–1960 (twelve authors), 1960–1970 (twenty authors), and 1970–1996 (thirty-five authors). Another outstanding anthology is *Call and Response: The Riverside Anthology of the African American Literary Tradition* (Hill 1998). It lacks a separate bibliographical section, but the credits and acknowledgments could function as guide to authors and their works.

Another useful anthology for collection-building purposes is *African American Literature* (Young 1996). The selection is not as comprehensive as that of the *Norton Anthology of African American Literature*, but the eighty-six writers are representative of most genres of black literature, except drama where the editor includes only one dramatist, Bill Harris.

A group effort produced the thirty-six-page bibliography of African American Literature for *Redefining American Literary History*. Separate sections were used for anthologies, oral literature, and autobiographies. The selection of ninety-two authors includes some who are best known for their nonfiction titles. The African American section in *American Ethnic Literatures* highlights 194 authors and has an annotated list of anthologies. The titles in the twenty-five page-listing of secondary works are annotated.

For drama, Darwin T. Turner's *Black Drama in America: An Anthology* (1994) offers an excellent bibliography with separate sections for anthologies of black drama, published plays, and the secondary literature. Most other anthologies of black drama are more focused (e.g., the Harlem Renaissance or plays produced by a single theater company).

A recent serviceable study to use when looking at the fiction portion of the black literature collection is Bernard W. Bell's *The Afro-*

American Novel and Its Tradition (1997). His bibliography is in several parts: first, the forty-one authors he regards as most important; and then, the seventy-one authors he regards as secondary, followed by a healthy bibliography of secondary sources.

Black poetry can be identified through the use of various anthologies, but before turning to them, the selector should consult the introductory essay in *Spirit and Flame: An Anthology of Contemporary African American Poetry* (Gilyard 1997) for an interesting discussion about the editorial mission which guided the various compilers of early black poetry anthologies. A comprehensive selection of black poets—from James Weldon Johnson and Paul Laurence Dunbar to Kevin Young and Reginald Shepherd—is listed in *The Garden Thrives: Twentieth-Century African-American Poetry* (Major 1996). The thirty-five poets in *Every Shut Eye Ain't Asleep* (Harper and Walton 1994) constitute a more selective group, poets born between 1913 and 1962. Coming up to the present decade are the "established and emerging" poets who can be sampled in the just-mentioned *Spirit and Flame* anthology.

Latino American

Many discussions of Chicano literature treat it as being coeval with the Chicano political and labor movement of the middle 1960s, which would make Chicano literature scarcely thirty years old.[8] This view of Chicano literature ignores a tradition of Hispanic literature produced since the seventeenth century in territory that ended up within the United States of America. A third segment of Hispanic writers comprises those immigrants from Spanish-speaking territories in the Caribbean. They have come in great numbers to the East Coast and are writing from a tradition of Spanish culture, albeit modified twice over—once in the Caribbean and a second time in the United States. The selector needs to be cognizant of which Hispanic traditions are being described in the selection tools.

The outstanding reference guide for Chicano Literature of the West/Southwest is entitled just that: *Chicano Literature: A Reference Guide* (Martinez and Lomeli 1985). It has articles on the Hispanic Southwest, 1521–1848; Mexican American literature, 1848–1942; Chicano literature from 1942 to the present; contemporary Chicano novel, 1959–

1979; Chicano theater; and Chicano poetry. The biographical entries end with a listing of primary works and secondary sources. However, the sheer number of persons included mitigates against this work being used to identify a core collection; if a comprehensive guide is needed, this is it.

A trio of books with bibliographies on the Latino American literatures are: *Redefining American Literary History*, *American Ethnic Literatures*, and *New Immigrant Literatures in the United States*. In addition to identifying important anthologies, they list the primary works of authors, as follows: (1) Chicano literature—*Redefining American Literary History*, eighty-two authors; *American Ethnic Literatures*, one hundred eighty-eight authors; *New Immigrant Literatures in the United States*, forty-nine authors. (2) Puerto Rican literature—*Redefining American Literary History*, twenty-eight authors; *American Ethnic Literatures*, thirty-nine authors; *New Immigrant Literatures in the United States*, thirty-six authors. (3) Cuban American literature—*American Ethnic Literatures*, ten authors; *New Immigrant Literatures in the United States*, fourteen authors.

If obtainable, *Twenty-Five Years of Hispanic Literature in the United States, 1965–1990* (Fernandez, Bozeman, and University of Houston Libraries 1992), done as an exhibition catalog from M. D. Anderson Library, University of Houston, would be a good place to get advice on the important works. It identifies writers by geographic locale (e.g., San Francisco and East Coast).

Thirty recently published notable authors have their work listed in the bibliography in Nicolas Kanellos's *Hispanic American Literature* (1995). *U.S. Latino Literature: An Essay and Annotated Bibliography* (Zimmerman 1992) is divided into genre sections (e.g., poetry, novel, short fiction, drama) and separates out Puerto Rican and Cuban literatures in the U.S. The introduction comments on the state of Chicano, Puerto Rican, and Cuban literatures, and the annotations are excellent.

Understanding Chicano Literature (Shirley and Shirley 1988) is a small volume intended to be an introduction to Chicano literature with a list of suggested readings; another section suggests titles for the secondary literature.

Somewhat older, but still useful, is *Literatura Chicana: Creative and Critical Writings through 1984* (Trujillo and Rodriguez 1985). There are sections on poetry, novel, short fiction, theater, and so on. The introduction takes a critical look at previously published bibliographies of Chicano literature.

Chicano Poetry: A Critical Introduction (Candelaria 1986) has a more narrow focus, poetry written between 1967 and 1985, the beginning years of the Chicano renaissance. The appendix provides the primary and secondary titles connected with forty-five poets in this historical and critical work. The first couple of chapters lay out the historical background leading up to the contemporary resurgence of Hispanic authors within the United States.

El colonialismo interno en la narrativa chicana (1994) by Manuel de Jesús Hernández-Gutiérrez is the most recent of the titles in this section. Despite the language of the title, the writers covered are almost all writing in English. The bibliographical section is extensive, including about ten important creative literature titles for each year from 1980 to 1993.

Native American

Collecting Native American literature means dealing with a body of literature that is shaped by several factors: (1) *A variety of texts*: Native American literature is perhaps the most encompassing of all the ethnic literatures. It extends beyond the traditional major literary genres of novel, poetry, and drama to speeches, songs, tales, and myths, and even further from "pure" literature to travelers' reports, explorers' accounts, ethnographers' field studies, missionary correspondence, and government documents. All these constitute the texts studied in Native American literature courses. (2) *An oral culture*: Until the beginning of the twentieth century, most of the texts of interest were those coming through oral transmission, which means there is not the great number of texts that might be expected if Native Americans had turned to print early on. The process of capturing oral texts involves translating from a non-Western language into English for readers in a far different culture. (The influence of the translator on the translation is a topic of ongoing discussion in Native American Studies, a discussion selector should be aware of even though it does not usually affect selection for the simple reason that many texts exist in only one translation. The issue here is the "authenticity" of both text and translation.) (3) *The late emergence of Native American literature*: Before the 1960s, there were a few Native American novelists, poets, and dramatists, but most were not noticed outside the local audiences they wrote for. In the 1960s, however, a rising political consciousness among Native Americans inaugurated a new stream of Native American writing and also brought about a more receptive and wider reading public. Native Americans have become much more conscious of their heritage and interested in interpreting it for others. In addition, Native American literature has been given a boost by the interest of New Agers, who, often to the dismay of Native Americans, are appropriating Native American art, religion, and literature in ways not always congenial to Native Americans. Nevertheless, their interest has done much to popularize Native American culture.

The premier tool to use for grasping the scope of this field is *American Indian Literatures* (1990), edited by A. LaVonne Brown Ruoff. The last third is about resources and is presented in two parts: a bibliographic review and a selected bibliography. This latter portion includes a basic list of 103 authors and their works, along with the secondary literature for studying the oral literature; a list of critical studies; and something about titles from history, political science, and anthropology to provide the necessary supplementary material. Anthologies, which are an important part of the collection for this literature, are evaluated (pp.118–19) and identified (pp.148–49).

A good second choice is Andrew Wiget's *Native American Literature* (1985), which has a bibliography that is still helpful. It is divided into primary sources, fiction, other writings, and secondary sources. In 1986, Wiget published a bibliographical essay that can serve as a representative collection, "Native American Literature: A Bibliographic Survey of American Indian Literary Traditions."

Somewhat older, but still of value, is the slim volume *American Indian Authors: A Representative Bibliography* (1970) compiled by Arlene B.Hirschfelder. Another older work, *Native American Renaissance* (1983) by Kenneth Lincoln, is about the generation of Native American writers that began to emerge in the 1960s. His bibliography is divided into poetry, prose, anthologies, and scholarship about the writers. It is also a good source for information about nature writing within a twenty-year period.

Two recent encyclopedic works offer invaluable guidance. *Native North American Literature* (Witalic, Chapman, and Giroux 1994) is divided into two sections, one for oral literature and one for written literature. The section on oral literature includes biographies of eight orators; the section on written literature has articles on seventy authors. The *Dictionary of Native American Literature* (Wiget 1994) has long biographical and critical essays on forty authors of the past two hundred years.[9] What is valuable are the accompanying bibliographies of primary and secondary sources for each author. The remainder of the book has essays about the oral literature, oratory, songs, epics, humor, theater, fiction, and the representations of whites and native peoples in literature. The literature of native peoples living in Alaska and Canada are included.

The list of contributors in the anthology *The Remembered Earth* (Hobson 1981) is easy to consult for identifying the group of authors who were part of the first ten years of Native American literary renaissance. At the time this anthology was published, some of the authors had yet to publish their first book; others already had a title or two to their credit. An added bonus is tribal identification for each contributor.

Joseph Bruchac, the noted writer and anthologist of Native American literature, was involved in compiling *Smoke Rising: The Native North American Literary Companion* (Bruchac, Witalec, and Malinowski 1995). The thirty-seven authors represented are "among the best known and most talented" living Native Americans publishing today; collecting their works will do much to bring the Native American literature collection up to date. The inclusion of four Canadians—Jeannette Armstrong, Tomson Highway, Lee Maracle, and Daniel David Moses—accounts for the title stating the volume is North American in scope.

Literary Theory

Although literary theory was already in the ascendancy when the first edition of this chapter appeared, it was not mentioned in the discussion of retrospective bibliography. Today, any discussion of literary scholarship must address theory. Some say theory generates more heat than light when it comes to understanding literary works. Others find it the raison d'être of literary scholarship. Wherever literary theory might be in its course through the literary firmament, it cannot be ignored. When considering titles having to do with literary theory, the selector is dealing with two kinds of works: titles considered the primary texts of the theory or the important expositions of the theory, and titles applying a theory (i.e., critical studies using theoretical positions to interpret an author, work, movement, era, etc). Of course, there is a third kind of study that becomes a combination of the two by not only putting forth theory, but also generously applying it. The reason for making what may appear to be an obvious distinction is that many bibliographies are not very enlightening about what category titles fall into and, consequently, whether the selector is dealing with the primary works or the secondary works of the theory.

Although there seems to be no end of publications wanting to introduce selectors to the spectrum of literary theories, not all of them have bibliographies suitable for easy use. However, three can be recommended. The first, *Literary Theory: An Introduction* (1996) by Terry Eagleton, is widely used in college and university courses. The bibliographical section does not list titles alphabetically but, rather, in an order in which they might best be tackled by a beginner. Many of the recommended titles can be characterized as secondary literature, rather than the primary texts of theory. The second edition is not a revision but, rather, an update by means of a new chapter that relates developments in literary theory since the first edition. Aside from the footnotes to the added chapter, the bibliography in the second edition has not been updated. The second, *A Reader's Guide to Contemporary Literary Theory* (Selden and Widdowson 1993), concludes each chapter with a most helpful sorting of titles into the basic texts, introductions, and further reading. The third, *Literary Theories in Praxis* (1987), an anthology of criticism edited by Shirley F. Staton, contains a "selected bibliography" for each of the nine literary theories it shows at work.

Also worth consulting for bibliographical guidance are the articles in *Encyclopedia of Contemporary Literary Theory: Approaches,*

Scholars, Terms (Makaryk 1993), each of which concludes with a list of primary and secondary sources. The articles in *The Johns Hopkins Guide to Literary Theory and Criticism* (Groden and Kreiswirth 1994) also identify necessary titles. A third, one-volume encyclopedic work, *Encyclopedia of Feminist Literary Theory* (Kowaleski-Wallace 1997), is more specialized. Use of this reference title ensures that feminist viewpoints on various theories are represented in the collection. The reference lists for the articles are not long.

At the beginning of this decade, the Modern Language Association (MLA) commissioned a series of essays by people in the profession on the theme *Redrawing the Boundaries: The Transformation of English and American Literary Studies* (Greenblatt and Gunn 1992). The articles are still instructive reading as an orientation to recent trends in literary theory and scholarship. The bibliographies that conclude each chapter often lack balance because of their brevity; nevertheless, they are annotated and are examples of one notable practitioner's judgment of relevant titles.

The following section on literary theories identifies some bibliographies useful to the selector. In the various bibliographies cited under each theory, one can expect a certain amount of duplication of titles because the same critic or work may be important to several different theoretical positions. Labels assigned to today's critics serve more as rough indicators, rather than placement in airtight categories. Recently, one literary handbook characterized a scholar as being simultaneously: Derridean, deconstructionist, Marxist, postcolonial, and feminist. Perhaps this is an extreme example, but on the other hand, it shows it is not unusual for a critic to be a member in good standing in several critical camps.

Each theory is introduced by a few words of description in order to put the comments to the selector into some sort of context. Bibliographies have been chosen to be those of use to the selector because of their scope, authority, and presentation. Works for the scholar do not always meet these criteria and therefore are not included here because they may be too comprehensive—some indication of good, bad, and indifferent titles is more helpful to the selector—or the bibliography is arranged awkwardly and therefore not inviting for use by busy selectors with little or no support staff. At the opposite end of the scale, bibliographies in scholarly monographs may be too narrowly focused and therefore not an appropriate guide to use in determining the titles in a balanced collection.

For all the sections that follow, the fifteen chapters in Donald G. Marshall's *Contemporary Critical Theory: A Selective Bibliography* (1993) will prove most helpful. His method for each chapter is to briefly introduce a theory, then to list anthologies and surveys, twenty to thirty relevant titles; and lastly, to list the primary works of that theory's most important personages. Most entries have a one-sentence annotation.

Cultural Studies

Cultural studies does not refer to just any piece of culture criticism but, rather, to those studies inspired by a group of British social scientists working in Birmingham, England, since the 1960s. Their work draws upon various methods. One article calls cultural studies "an amalgam of literature, social history, sociology, anthropology and communications—or media—studies."[10] Broadly construed, cultural studies takes as their subject the intersection of culture and politics, examining, for example, how certain cultural artifacts—works of literature, say—are "produced" and "consumed," or how and why some things are regarded as "high culture" and some as "popular culture." In literature departments, the subject matter of cultural studies often is in the realm of popular culture; for instance, the content, producers, and audiences of films and television are favorite topics, rather than topics of a high cultural variety. Cultural studies is characterized not only by its melting pot of methodologies, but also by its original goals of confronting the establishment in all of its manifestations—political, cultural, and economic—and of being politically involved, goals that some think have not been as important in the United States. Another difference in emphasis is that British work in cultural studies is often done collectively, whereas cultural studies in the United States tends to be the work of a single person.

Another indicator of the elusiveness of cultural studies is that the Library of Congress subject headings do not corral it within one set of boundaries but, instead, direct the reader with two see references:

"Cultural Studies" see "Culture—Study and Teaching" and "Cultural Studies" see "Popular Culture—Study and Teaching." Catalogers also have used "Culture—Methodology," "Popular Culture—Methodology," and just plain "Culture" or "Popular Culture" when describing works in this field.

Whatever culture studies may or may not be, it does exist. Its practitioners may be found in many departments on campus in addition to the English department. For a composite view of the uneasiness cultural studies causes in American English departments, see the forum in *PMLA* where thirty-two letter writers voice their opinions about "the actual or potential relations between cultural studies and the literary."[11]

How is the selector to serve the eclectic needs of a cultural studies program? There are several ways. The first is to have what are the considered the basic texts. This would include the works of the founders and early writers: John Fiske, Stuart Hall, Richard Hoggart, E. P. Thompson, and Raymond Williams, all Britons whose work has given rise to what is acknowledged now as British Cultural Studies. American cultural studies takes its cues from these initial studies but at the same time has diverged enough to cause it to be designated American Cultural Studies so as to differentiate it from its British counterpart. Also other countries are recognized as having their own version (e.g., Australian Cultural Studies). Yet, the group in Birmingham remains the common ancestor of all the present manifestations of cultural studies.

The work of the literature selector in cultural studies may not be demanding because the collection may have already acquired the necessary titles useful in cultural studies for those working in the fields of radical sociology, revisionist history, communication, or media studies. Certainly, *Cultural Studies* (Inglis 1993) should be acquired as an exposition of cultural studies; its bibliography is a very good array of the most important authors in this field, from Adorno to Wright. Another volume, also titled *Cultural Studies* (Grossberg 1992), grew out of a 1990 conference. It exhibits the wide range of topics coming under the cultural studies umbrella; however, its forty-page bibliography is too generous to be used very easily for collection development purposes. Robert H. Kieft's bibliographic essay on cultural studies in *Choice* (1994) has insightful comments. Kieft says his bibliography will "look like a core list or a hit-and-miss aggregation depending on the reader's preferences and bibliographic generosity." An announced second part to survey the fields in which cultural studies has been influential was never published.

Deconstructionism

Discussions about the nature of deconstructionism seem endless. It is fairly easy to tap into the debate at any level. However, a brief definition here will help orient the reader: "Deconstruction refers to a philosophical activity initiated by Jacques Derrida in France; the first major publications appeared in the late 1960s. It is a critique of concepts and hierarchies which, according to Derrida, are essential to traditional criteria of certainty, identity, and truth, but which, nevertheless, achieve their status only by repressing and forgetting other elements which thus become the un-thought, and sometimes the unthinkable, of western philsophy."[12] The beginning selector should recognize that nearly every discipline has been touched by the thinking of Derrida and his disciples. John Rose's bibliographical essay "Deconstruction across the Disciplines" (1990) only briefly touches on the influence of deconstructionism in other disciplines; most of his commentary is about deconstructionism in its literary context. *Literary Theories in Praxis* (Staton 1987) has a minimal list of seventeen titles as being representative of deconstructionism.

The principal outpost of deconstructionism in the United States was at Yale. At least two books" have the Yale Critics as their subject. The first of these, *The Yale Critics: Deconstruction in America* (Arac, Godzich, and Martin 1983), has a bibliography of primary and secondary works for this group; the second, *Rhetoric and Form: Deconstruction at Yale* (Davis and Schleifer 1985), has a bibliography of primary and secondary sources for Geoffrey Hartman, Paul de Man, and J. Hillis Miller.

Ecocriticism

Despite the pronouncement by the headline writer for the *New York Times Magazine* that "Deconstruction is compost. Environmental studies is the academic field of the 90s,"[13] ecocriticism is not about to dethrone any literary theory; it is, however, taking its place alongside the other philosophies and approaches current in literary scholarship. Ecocriticism uses many literary theoretical approaches in order to relate nature writing to the ecological movement's scientific and polemical works. Although ecocriticism looks at nature writing everywhere, in the United States the main interest is the treatment of the American landscape in literature and history.

Interest in nature writing certainly is not new within literary studies. However, exactly where criticism of nature writing leaves off and ecocriticism begins is hard to determine, a distinction the selector need not worry about because both are wanted in the collection. Examination of the older nature writing is one of the interests of today's ecocritics, while at the same time they assess how the work of contemporary writers elucidates any part of today's environmental agenda. In doing so, ecocriticism refers to scientific studies frequently, but not exclusively; studies in art history, folklore, anthropology, philosophy, geography, among others, are cited. In fact, any written work or artifact that in any way shows humankind's relationship to the natural world is likely to catch the attention of the ecocritic. Collect broadly! The bibliographies in the field reflect the ecocritic's broad interests.

The Ecocriticism Reader: Landmarks in Literary Ecology (Glotfelty and Fromm 1996) is an anthology with a good introduction whose bibliographic notes list the most recent anthologies of nature writings and highlight essential background works in environmental history, anthropology, psychology, philosophy, theory, and literature. An ending bibliographical section identifies the "dozen titles they [persons on the Association for the Study of Literature and the Environment listserv] deemed essential reading for someone new to this field."

Another work worth perusing is *American Nature Writers* (Elder 1996). The writers who have entries in this reference work can be taken as constituting a pantheon of American nature writers in the broadest sense, meaning some are naturalists and not belletristic writers. This encompassing interest in all forms of writing about the environment is a characteristic that makes this field appealing. The concluding essays cover such relevant topics as contemporary ecofiction, forms of American nature poetry, and literary theory in nature writing.

The best comprehensive bibliographies are found in *This Incomperable Lande* (Lyon 1989). It contains two annotated bibliographies well worth looking at: one of primary authors from Edward Abbey to Ann Zwinger, the other of secondary authors. One quibble is that some of the authors that Lyon puts in his secondary bibliography are regarded as primary authors by other compilers; therefore, it is important that both of his bibliographies be used. Lyon cast his net wide by listing "natural history essays; 'rambles'; essays of travel, adventure and solitude in nature; and accounts of farm and country living . . . philosophical essays on man and nature; critical interpretation of nature literature and histories and anthologies."[14]

Two other titles provide interesting bibliographical guidance; used together, they provide a composite view of the field. Don Scheese, in *Nature Writing: The Pastoral Impulse in America* (1996), has a long bibliographical essay describing those works in conservation history, art history, geography, psychology, religion, and philosophy that can benefit the ecocritic. This is followed by a list of "recommended titles." Some of the authors in this list are usually not thought of as being nature writers (e.g., Washington Irving, William Faulkner, Ernest Hemingway). The bibliography of "further readings" in *Natural History of Nature Writing* (1995) by Frank Stewart, is about the same size as the one in *Nature Writing: The Pastoral Impulse in America*, but only about a third of the titles show up in both bibliographies. Stewart has interspersed his list of nature writing with some of the better titles in the secondary literature.

To aid instructors, the MLA published a collection of essays, *Teaching Environmental Literature: Materials, Methods, Resources* (Waage 1985), describing models and ideas for courses in environmental literature. A list of works cited by the essayists and a second list of "additional significant works" should give the selector a good picture of what support for this topic should look like.

Feminist Theory

Studies about women in literature and woman and literature have been around for quite a while; however, the picture changed radically with the women's movement of the 1960s. Women critics developed literary theories that reflected the societal critique put forth by the American women's movement. Early on, American criticism showed the influence of the French feminists. (See the article "French Feminism" in *Encyclopedia of Feminist Literary Theory* for the essential bibliography.) Although key works are referred to by most feminist critics, feminist literary theory is not considered a single theory. And like several other literary theorists, feminist critics rely on political and social commentary surrounding the topic. If the collection is strong in women's studies, many of the necessary background works will have already been selected. (See also the section below, Lesbian/Gay/Queer Theory/Gender Studies, for related topics.)

One of the best compilations of titles for a basic collection has been put together by G. Douglas Atkins and Laura Morrow in *Contemporary Literary Theory* (1989). The bibliographies in both Staton's anthology, *Literary Theories in Praxis*, and Eagleton's *Literary Theory: An Introduction* slight the French feminists.

The Encyclopedia of Feminist Literary Theory (Kowaleski-Wallace 1997) would appear to be an obvious source for enlightenment on feminist literary theory. It is, but not necessarily for the bibliographer. It lacks articles on American feminist literary theory, literary theory, or criticism; however, it does have articles on French feminism, black feminist criticism, and Asian American feminist literary theory. In addition, there are articles on aspects of criticism from a feminist perspective (e.g., canon, deconstruction, poststructuralism, feminine aesthetics, feminist poetics). All articles have brief bibliographies.

Lesbian/Gay/Queer Theory/ Gender Studies: Introduction

An overview of this section's topics looks like a Venn diagram composed of overlapping circles named gay literature, lesbian literature, queer theory, and gender studies. At the center of the Venn diagram is a single concept—same-sex desire. Each of the topic circles also shares space with one or several of the other circles in the diagram, thus showing common concerns; yet each topic also has space that is not shared—showing it can stand alone. Book titles within this imaginary Venn diagram also inhabit several circles, which means the bibliographer selecting for one area often supports several other topics.

Applicable to Lesbian and Gay Literatures. How anthologies and bibliographies define gay/lesbian literature varies. The multiplicity of scope echoes critical thinking about just what indeed gay/lesbian literature is. Some possibilities are: (1) works by an author who defines himself or herself as gay or lesbian or, as in the case of some older authors, has since been identified as closeted gay or lesbian; (2) works by gay/lesbian authors and restricted to gay/lesbian themes; (3) works by heterosexual authors on gay/lesbian themes; (4) works by authors who seemed to be unaware of their gay/lesbian desires yet a gay/lesbian orientation can be discerned in their works; (5) works with gay/lesbian themes written primarily for heterosexual readers; (6) works with gay/lesbian themes written primarily for homosexual readers. And in criticism there is similar variation: the gay critic on gay literature, the gay critic on nongay literature, the nongay critic on gay literature, and so on. The slicing and dicing of these topics is not meant to confuse but, rather, to alert the selector that while terminology in bibliographies is sometimes carefully defined, in other instances shades of definition are not explicitly stated and the user will have to determine the criteria used by the compiler of the bibliography.

Literary studies are very much a part of the lesbian and gay movements, and therefore titles of both an academic and polemical nature will be welcome. To provide these are several sources identifying the range of interest of these movements; only one is cited here—the bibliographical essay accompanying *The Lesbian and Gay Studies Reader* (Abelove, Barate, and Martin 1993). Although bibliographical essays are not always the easiest sources to use for collection development work, this one is recommended because of its extensive coverage, with sections on, for example, AIDS, contemporary memoirs, historical sources, history (China, France, Germany, Great Britain, United States), anthropology, sociology, philosophy, politics, law, and literature.

Gay and Lesbian Literature (Malinowski 1994) interfiles entries for men and women in one alphabet. Although the emphasis is on contemporary writers, "significant deceased authors from the earlier portion of the century who have exerted a major influence on contemporary gay and lesbian literature are also included."[15] This volume is international in scope with a nationality appendix: sixteen women and twenty-nine men are in the English literature list; sixty-three women and seventy-one men are in the American literature list. In typical St. James Press fashion, each biographical entry has a list of fiction and nonfiction works. There are other useful indexes (e.g., authors interested in activism, AIDS, eroticism, homophobia, etc). The body of the work is supplemented by several appendices; one simply names "additional authors" of which 275 are women, another is a checklist of anthologies of lesbian fiction.

The reference work *The Gay and Lesbian Literary Heritage: A Reader's Companion to the Writers and Their Works from Antiquity to the Present* (Summers 1995) devotes about a page to each author it includes. Author entries include bibliographies. For the selector, overviews can be found in several sections, including American Literature: Gay, English Literature: Gay, and the entries for Novel: Gay, Poetry: Gay, Dramatic Literature: Gay. The same categories are used for lesbian literature. Additional entries are included for African Americans and Native Americans and for topical entries such as mystery, coming-out stories, and travel. Editorial practice is to put titles of works in the entries while the bibliography concentrates on the secondary literature.

Gay and Lesbian American Plays: An Annotated Bibliography (Furtado and Hellner 1993) identifies nearly seven hundred plays that fit their scope of works containing "major characters whose gay or lesbian sexuality is integral to the play's message, and plays whose primary themes are gay or lesbian." A title index is coded to identify plays with major lesbian or gay themes or characters, as well as coming-out themes, cross-dressing, or transgendered characters.

Lesbian Literature. Anthologies are an important component in the collection that serves lesbian readers, especially those pursuing critical studies. One handy guide to both anthologies of literary texts and of criticism can be found in an appendix to *Gay and Lesbian Literature*. To that list of anthologies should be added *Sexual Practice/Textual Theory: Lesbian Cultural Criticism* (Wolfe and Penelope 1993). The latter has an annotated bibliography of lesbian literary critical theory, 1970–1989, which, although valuable for scholars, is not of much value as a collection development source because it cites forty-one journal articles, but not one monograph. Again, this bibliography brings home the value of anthologies that reprint journal articles. At the end of this anthology is a rather lengthy twenty-two-page bibliography of works cited in the selections that could serve as a guide to important works up to that time.

"Suggestions for Further Reading" in *New Lesbian Criticism: Literary and Cultural Readings* (Munt 1992) is a good source for the foundation works of lesbian literary criticism. Many of the seminal articles appeared in journals and have been reprinted in anthologies; other anthologies are of original contributions. This bibliography identifies thirty-five anthologies of criticism and another 115 books. The title *Lesbian in Literature: A Bibliography* (Damon, Watson, and Jordan 1975) describes the focus of this older bibliography. It is a ninety-six-page listing with a coding system for each title: major lesbian character, minor lesbian character, repressed lesbian character, and trash(!).

Contemporary Lesbian Writers of the United States (Pollock and Knight 1993) is a biographical work about one hundred "self-identified lesbian" authors who wrote between 1970 and 1992. The editors asked for nominations; they then cut the list to one hundred, but even so, a few prominent names are "conspicuously missing" because they declined to cooperate. Nevertheless, this volume represents the most prominent lesbian authors of the period. Each entry has a list of works by the author and of studies about the author. A library's collection would be enhanced by the two hundred titles of "selected non-fiction on lesbian issues" listed in an appendix. Paulina Palmer's monograph, *Contemporary Lesbian Writing* (1993), concentrates on about seventy-five lesbian works she classifies as political, comic, or thriller, and which she lists in a separate appendix. This is followed by an eight-page bibliography of theoretical and critical works up to 1992.

Patience and Sarah, published nationally as *Place for Us* in 1983, but written in 1969 by Isabel Miller (pseudonym of Alma Routsong), was a "new beginning for lesbian literature as a whole: the establishment of a literary and symbolic 'place' for lesbian writers and readers," writes Bonnie Zimmerman in *The Safe Sea of Women: Lesbian Fiction, 1969–1989* (1990).[16] Zimmerman looked at 225 lesbian texts and included 167 in her study of the lesbian novel from the watershed year 1969 to the time she concluded her study. The 167 sources she comments on are in one listing followed by seven pages of secondary sources.

It is always refreshing to tap into the enthusiasm of knowledgeable people in the field. One such resource is "Toni and Bonnie's Fab Fifty Plus One," which addresses the background studies most likely to be consulted by the literary scholar of lesbianism. Their list, which can be found in *The New Lesbian Studies: Into the Twenty-First Century* (Zimmerman and McNaron 1996), are of works "we found personally inspiring and provocative, as well as generally influential in the development of lesbian studies as a field of inquiry. Our choices reflect our individual preferences, to be sure, but we also have attempted to reflect the diversity of theoretical and disciplinary approaches current today."[17]

Gay Literature. Gregory Woods's monumental *A History of Gay Literature* (1998) starts with the Greeks and ends with Joe Orton. Although Woods discusses English and American gay literature at some length, the arrangement of both text and bibliographical references is not handy for collection development purposes, although the volume certainly should be in the library.

The Gay Novel in America (1991), by James Levin, can act as a guide to acquiring gay novels. Levin's work is a history in chronological order from Alfred Cohen's *Marriage Below Zero* (1899) through a chapter on the "enigmatic eighties." The notes section for each chapter lists the novels cited in the chapter. His definition of a gay novel is one in which the "character is aware of his homosexual feelings."

An overview of more recent gay fiction is Reed Woodhouse's *Unlimited Embrace: A Canon of Gay Fiction, 1945–1995* (1998). He discusses seventeen novels in his personal canon, which is a canon as good as any other for this recent period. In an appendix, he annotates an additional forty-two titles he finds worthwhile. Woodhouse has enough acumen to identify the emerging themes in contemporary gay fiction. *Love between Men in English Literature* (Hammond 1996) is about the treatment of homosexuality in the canonical literature from the renaissance to the twentieth century. However, the extensive bibliography does little to identify gay works not found in the mainstream, the theme of this study.

Contemporary Gay American Novelists: A Bio-Bibliographical Critical Sourcebook (Nelson 1993) has fifty-seven entries that the compiler rightly calls representative of the contemporary scene. He does not claim to adequately cover gay science fiction or gay detective fiction, and for various reasons entries on five authors he would have liked to include are not present. The introduction cites twenty titles for a basic bibliography of criticism.

The Male Homosexual in Literature: A Bibliography (Young 1982) is a promising title, but somewhat overwhelming for use in collection development. More than 4,282 unannotated entries are listed in alphabetical order by authors, who incidentally are not identified by nationality. The titles are all English-language works including translations, which accounts for the presence of Jean Cocteau and Arnold Zweig. Entries are labeled as to novel, poetry, drama, short fiction, and whether homosexuality is a "major theme."

Queer Theory. Imagine a journal article entitled "Queer theory meets X"; substitute almost anything for X, and there is almost certain to be an article with that title. Then there is queer identity, queer politics, queer culture, queer nation, and queer planet among other pairings; also just plain queer, meaning anything from a quick way of saying lesbian and gay to an ideological term with many paragraphs of philosophical baggage. *Queer* has taken on a variety of meanings. Queer theory can loosely be said to be anything that deals with queer as a category. Queerness (i.e., otherness contrasted with heterosexual, eurocentric norms, or sometimes anything not mainstream, which takes queer beyond sexuality into race and ethnicity) comes out of the lesbian and gay movements' political activism, especially as practiced in the 1980s during their initial confrontation with AIDS.

In the academy queerness is defined and debated by linguists, sociologists, and psychologists, to name just a few. In literary criticism the basic texts began appearing in 1988. Several of them say nothing about queer theory by name, but they are nevertheless works to which queer theory constantly refers. Teresa de Lauretis is usually credited with being one of the first to add theory to queer. Even though she may not have been the very first to combine the two words, it was her 1991 article that caught the attention of others and helped launch the concept into the critical vocabulary.[18] Later, as the term was appropriated by others, often in a willy-nilly fashion without rigor, she distanced herself from it, saying she was disappointed it had not prompted the discussion she had hoped it would.

Many who use the term *queer theory* deplore it being cast into the mold of other theories (i.e., something that can be summarized and lined up with other critical theories—similar to what is happening in these pages!). They maintain it should be disruptive, disjointed, and destabilizing. Therefore, they say "theory" is a misnomer; it is more in the nature of a stance. Furthermore, it should be a call to activism, which accounts for it being sometimes regarded as a subset of cultural studies. (See also the entry above in this section for cultural studies.)

Someone has quipped that queer theory results when gay and lesbian studies meets postmodernism. In many ways, that summarizes what to expect from queer theory. Yet, the relationship of queer theory to gay and lesbian studies is a prickly one. Some denounce queer theory as confusing the issues; others regard it as illuminating in addition to being the academic's contribution in the struggle for political power by lesbians and gays. In general, the collection for the study of queer theory includes titles produced by the far left of the gay and lesbian movements.

Queer Theory: A Bibliography (Nordquist 1997) illustrates how widely the term is used: 685 entries divided into queer theory, lesbian theory, sociology, psychology, linguistics, history, anthropology, art, geography, music, film, theater, politics. The literature section, which cites twenty-two books and thirty-one articles, omits several important titles to which literary scholars will want to have access. These titles are there but scattered throughout the other sections.

The Material Queer (Morton 1996) has as its agenda to present "an anthology that is intellectually effective as an inventory of concepts [in order to] resituate discussion of the queer in a broader historical and theoretical context."[19] In the introduction, Morton is highly critical of the present state of queer theory, but in railing against it, at the same time he identifies the key works, and thus his bibliography is an effective guide to the literature on the subject. A longer, ten-page "working bibliography," the final chapter in this anthology, is an excellent overview. It lists many relevant and important works. It is a listing avowedly Marxist in orientation, but then so much is in queer theory.

Gender Studies

Sometimes used as a convenient term to put women's studies and men's studies under one roof, gender studies more frequently is used as a general category, that is, gender as it is enacted in literature. One reading of the history of gender studies is to see it as a natural extension of women's studies. Women's studies originated as a reaction to, or overthrow of, the hegemonic role of the masculine view, and therefore men are very much present within women's studies and should be identified as a separate group, a sort of know-thy-enemy approach. However, this view of gender studies is contested by many feminists.

Gender wants to distance itself from biological sexuality sufficiently to make gender regarded as a separate category. Reflecting on the meaning of gender (e.g., being feminine, being masculine) helps in understanding the distinction. For example, naming some men as effeminate and some women as butch—to consider just two variations on gender—is a judgment confidently made by most of us without a lot of conscious thought. One automatically invokes the characteristics our culture says constitute masculinity and femininity and then effortlessly places the observed person on one's internalized femininity/masculinity scale. Because gays and lesbians often engage in gender bending, it is easy to see why gender is of interest in gay and lesbian studies. They and others do not see sexuality as the final determiner of gender. Lastly, although gender studies shares this entry with same-sex approaches, it does not revolve around same sex-desire.

To provide a core collection of background material to all aspects of gender studies is most desirable. But this is easier said than done. Good collections of feminist studies, gay studies, and lesbian studies will already hold the required texts. Because gender formation is cultural, works in anthropology, history, linguistics, psychology, and sociology also will be consulted by literary researchers as they are engage in work about gender. But to relate gender studies specifically to literature, there is also little guidance, probably because gender topics are so diverse. The *MLA International Bibliography* cites studies about gender in Beowulf as well as gender in cyberpunk fiction, to say nothing of gender and race, gender and ethnicity, gender and genre. Criticism participates in gender studies by elucidating the role literature has had in defining gender throughout the ages, as well as by analyzing the literature of any period from that perspective.

Pam Lieske's article on gender in the *Encyclopedia of Feminist Literary Theory* cites only twelve items, the latest one published 1990, although the work itself was published in 1997. Her bibliography of four anthologies and four monographs is a good, but minimal, start on this topic. The four anthologies she mentions should be supplemented by the anthology of reprints edited by Elaine Showalter, *Speaking of Gender* (1989). Her introduction, "The Rise of Gender," is worth reading for an orientation to gender studies in general and its role in literary studies. Linda S. Kauffman has another view of gender studies, which she states in her introduction to her challenging anthology of original contributions, *Gender and Theory* (1989).

Combining the three sources above with the bibliography that follows, AnnLouise Keating's more recent contribution about gender in the *Gay and Lesbian Literary Heritage* (Summers 1995) would constitute a good beginning to this wide-ranging topic. She summarizes current thinking on the topic in general, at the same time incorporating how literary critics have participated in the discourse about gender.

Eve Kosofsky Sedgwick's chapter "Gender Criticism" in *Redrawing the Boundaries* (Greenblatt and Gunn 1992, pp. 271–302) talks more about the determinants of sexuality than gender in our society. Although her thoughts are always worth paying attention to, her emphasis on Foucault, AIDS, and sexuality is not typical of gender studies today.

Marxist

Marxist literary theory takes the writings of nineteenth-century Karl Marx and Friedrich Engels as the foundation on which to construct a new aesthetic and a new role for literature in twentieth-century society. From the beginning Marxism has interested critics, but it was the

Western European critics of the 1920s and 1930s who put Marxism on the critical map. And their works continue to be influential with contemporary Marxists critics. Even though the selector may not be aware of any avowed Marxists among the library's patrons, Marxist theory is one of the most important literary theories the selector deals with because so many other literary theories have a Marxist component. Eagletons's book, *Literary Theory: An Introduction*, first and second editions, can be used to identify key titles (see his second edition, p. 214, fn 5, for important recent works). *Contemporary Literary Theory* (Atkins and Morrow 1989) does a good job of providing a list of the important texts, introductions, and further reading.

New Criticism

The New Critics ask two related questions: Which texts constitute literature worth studying (their answer: the traditional canon), and how should that literature be studied (their answer: close reading of the text)? In the 1920s, T. S. Eliot, I. A. Richards, and F. R. Leavis put forth the principles taken up in the 1930s by Americans John Crowe Ransom and Cleanth Brooks. Thus the selector should recognize that no collection of New Criticism is complete if its British antecedents are ignored. John Crowe Ransom's book, *The New Criticism* (1941), became the name for this aesthetic approach. The New Criciticm was the predominant critical philosophy in academic circles from the late 1930s until the early 1960s. In the past thirty years, there has been a fierce reaction in literary studies to the principles of the New Critics. One reason for paying attention to the state of the library's holding of the New Criticism is that if students in their study of other literary theories are urged go beyond New Criticism, they should be able to discover what they are reacting against! But more important, because the New Criticism was so influential in criticism and scholarship, the library needs the works of this theory to understand the literary history of a sizable part of the twentieth century.

Although the New Criticism will never regain its preeminent position among literary theories, its influence continues today in a less visible way. A collection of essays, *The New Criticism and Contemporary Literary Theory* (Spurlin and Fischer 1995), aims to put New Criticism in perspective within the multitheoried body of today's critical writing. This volume's bibliography of the primary works of ten important figures in the New Criticism school is useful, and its bibliography of twenty-seven critical works brings the secondary literature up to date.

Eagleton, in his popular *Literary Theory: An Introduction*, does not list titles alphabetically but, rather, in the sequence that one first approaching this topic should use. Many of the titles are the secondary literature, rather than the theory's primary works.

New Historicism

Stephen Greenblatt is credited with launching the New Historicism, a term he first used in 1982, and is still regarded as its guru. From a literary standpoint, New Historicism's main theme is the cultural production of texts and their reception (i.e., whose political interests are being served, whose are being oppressed openly or covertly in the process). New Historicism is perhaps best described as an approach or orientation. And as one might suspect from the name, its practitioners are often historians, usually regarded as being revisionists. Words such as power, culture, politics, ideology, and oppression show up frequently in New Historicism writings, which makes it easy to see why it shares some of the same views as works in the bibliography of Marxist criticism and cultural studies. Because early New Historicism writings are centered on the Renaissance, the erroneous assumption is sometimes made that the Renaissance is the only historical period of interest to New Historicism critics. The New Historicism view of literature can be found in the scholarship of all literary periods.

For the New Historicism, the selector will often be working in the field of history. Hopefully, the history selector has already acquired most relevant studies. If there is some doubt that this has happened, *New Historicism and Cultural Materialism* (Ryan 1996) has a well-done bibliography of New Historicism scholarship in seven historical periods, from medieval times to the twentieth century. This same bibliography has sections on the origins, aims, and issues of New Historicism. The selector may notice that many of the titles are the same ones cited in works done from a cultural studies perspective. (See the cultural studies section in this chapter.)

An excellent bibliography of the New Historicism is appended to *The New Historicism Reader* (Veeser 1994). However, one title the editor modestly omitted was the anthology he edited, *The New Historicism* (1989), which should be acquired as an introduction to the field.

Phenomenology

Phenomenology is another of the literary theories whose basis is found in contemporary philosophy. Phenomenology was founded by Edmund Husserl, and other phenomenological philosophers are Martin Heidegger and Maurice Merleau-Ponty. The literary critic most influential in applying key phenomenological concepts is Roman Ingarden. (See also the entry below on reception theory, which is closely related.)

Once again, the selector is just as concerned about acquiring titles classified in the philosophy section of the library as in the literature section. Also, having the essential texts available in their original language will be desired by faculty members. The references following the article on phenomenology in *The Johns Hopkins Guide to Literary Theory and Criticism* are a good guide to the basic works. A shorter, bare minimum list is the one in *Literary Theories in Praxis*.

Raman Selden and Peter Widdowson in *A Reader's Guide to Contemporary Literary Theory* treat the phenomenological critics as part of their discussion of reader-oriented theories. Terry Eagleton in *Literary Theory: An Introduction* discusses phenomenology, hermeneutics, and reception theory in the same chapter. Both chapters illustrate the blurring of boundaries among these theoretical approaches; therefore, the selector should also be looking at these related approaches when evaluating the collection for its phenomenological holdings.

Postcolonialism

In 1979 Edward Said published *Orientalism*, which became the catalyst for a theoretical approach now known as postcolonialism. An oversimplification of Said's premise is that the West has defined the Orient in its own terms; the East is seen as exotic, inferior, and unable to articulate its culture to the rest of the world. Several critics have been inspired by Said's book, chief among them Homi Bhabha and Gayatri Spivak. Homi Bhabha developed the concept of "colonial discourse," while Gayatri Spivak brought a feminist perspective to the discussion. These three, Said, Bhabha, and Spivak, are considered the leading lights of postcolonial theory. The selector will want to acquire all of their works.

What was called Commonwealth literature now is also called postcolonial literature. Postcolonialism as a literary theory should not be confused by the selector with postcolonial literature as a body of literature. However, one comprehensive bibliography has combined the two: *Post-Colonial Literatures in English: General, Theoretical, and Comparative, 1970–1993* (Lawson, Dale, and others 1997) consists of more than 1,300 annotated entries in alphabetical order by author. As tempting as the title is, and as good as the annotations are, the index has a hard time opening up the contents by subject, and therefore the selector may find this volume disappointing. For a more inclusive and more manageable bibliography about postcolonialism in general, the selector should refer to the twenty-one-page listing in *Key Concepts in Post-Colonial Studies* (Ashcroft, Griffiths, and Tiffin 1998).

As its title indicates, the bibliographical essay "Riches of Empire: Postcolonialism in Literature and Criticism" (Murdoch 1995) mixes the literature coming from the postcolonial world with titles of postcolonial criticism. It is a minimal and manageable listing.

A more recent bibliography in *Contemporary Postcolonial Theory: A Reader* (Mongia 1996) is heavy with citations to journal articles because that is where much of the discussion has taken place; but the citations to monographs provide a good representative list of the important critical works.

Postmodernism

In contemporary criticism, postmodernism is one of the most frequently used, misunderstood, and elusive terms. Historically, it means "the end of modernity, in the sense of those grand narratives of truth, reason, science, progress and universal emancipation which are taken to characterize modern thought from the Enlightenment onwards . . . . Postmodernism proper can then best be seen as the form of culture which corresponds to this world view. The typical postmodernist work of art is arbitrary, eclectic, hybrid, decentred, fluid, discontinuous, pastiche-like."[20] It is a wonder that anything so varied and so encompassing can be said to have any basic texts. Yet, it does.[21]

A very thorough bibliography completes the anthology *Modernism/Postmodernism* (Brooker 1992). It directs the selector to the more general titles on postmodernism, also specifically to postmodernism and literature, and finally to postmodernism and the other arts. One of the purposes of this anthology is to show differences and similarities between modernism and postmodernism, and the introduction is a good explanation of that. The short bibliography on modernism in the "further reading" section is supplementary.

John Carlos Rowe, in "Postmodernist Studies," a chapter in *Redrawing the Boundaries*, takes on postmodern fiction, the postmodern scholarly approach, and the postmodern society. His annotated bibliography of twenty titles is a good beginning toward collecting titles on postmodernism. Steven Connor's reader, *Postmodernist Culture* (1989), goes through various aspects of our postmodern society—architecture, visual arts, literature, performance, media, popular culture, politics, feminism. The bibliographies for each of these are not long and list the basic titles for each area.

The selector, after looking at the recommended bibliographies for this topic, will notice a characteristic of the literature on postmodern: the overlap of titles, that is, titles also showing up in discussions of the other critical theories. This overlap shows the extent to which other critical theories participate in the postmodern analysis of our culture and its literature. Thus, the selector should not be surprised by the relatively few unique titles in the bibliographies and should be comforted by the fact that developing the collection in other areas of criticism also serves the postmodern critic.

Poststructuralism

Poststructuralism is a label that came into critical usage in the late 1960s. It is not a theory, a movement, or an approach, but is often applied to those who started from a structuralist position but then found it wanting. Eagleton examines Jacques Derrida and Roland Barthes in his chapter on poststructuralism. Selden and Widdowson also include Derrida and Barthes in their discussion of poststructuralism and go further by including recent psychoanalytical criticism (e.g., Jacques Lacan) and the New Historicism. All of this can be rather puzzling to the bibliographer. In general, by paying attention to other recent literary theories, one also serves poststructralism. It may be comforting to know that the highly regarded *Johns Hopkins Guide to Literary Theory and Criticism* does not see the necessity of having a separate article on poststructuralism.

Psychoanalytic/Psychological

The writings of the founder of the modern study of the unconscious, Sigmund Freud, have long influenced literary critics and continue to do so. But in contemporary criticism there are two other influential psychologists—Carl Jung and Jacques Lacan. Jung's work is the basis for archetypal theory and criticism. But perhaps more influential today than either Freud or Jung (not that they can be ignored), is the French psychiatrist Jacques Lacan. Lacan published his first book in 1932, but it was not until the 1960s that his work became influential in literary circles. It seems obvious to say that the psychological treatises of these three are fundamental to the collection for working in this approach. However, there is an additional reason for acquiring titles by the Big Three: many theorists who, although not labeled as being of the psychoanalytic or psychological school, are nevertheless closely read and refer to the school's leading thinkers.

Identifying other pertinent titles for the study of literature from a psychoanalytic/psychological perspective is not as simple a task as it ought to be. Eagleton's *Literary Theory: An Introduction*, which has been frequently recommended, is too minimal. Selden and Widdowson, in their *Reader's Guide to Contemporary Literary Theory*, have not separated out the relevant titles for this approach from other poststructualist titles. Perhaps the best short list of titles of psychoanalytic criticism is the one compiled by Staton in *Literary Theories In Praxis*, which also has a section on archetypal theory. For those wanting something a bit more inclusive, the article on Jacques Lacan and the tripart article "Psychoanalytic Theory and Criticism" in *The Johns Hopkins Guide to Literary Theory and Criticism* should be consulted.

Reader Response Criticism/Reception Theory

What is the most important element in the critical equation of author + text + reader = the aesthetic experience? The critics who answer *reader* belong here. These critics have no common theory uniting them, just that they focus on the reader. Their critical approach to the reader and the act of reading varies: rhetorical (Stanley Fish), hermeneutical (Hans Robert Jauss and E. D. Hirsch Jr.), subjective (David Bleich), psychoanalytic (Norman Holland), phenomenological (Wolfgang Iser and Georges Poulet), semiotic (Michael Riffaterre and Yury Lotman). One avenue open to the selector is to look at the bibliography of each one. Less labor-intensive is using the bibliography of twenty-two items in Staton's anthology, which is a good representation of these critics. The bibliography in *A Reader's Guide to Contemporary Literary Theory* is not as balanced but can provide a start toward having resources on this topic.

Now somewhat dated, at the time it was published the annotated bibliography in the anthology *Reader-Response Criticism* (Tompkins 1980) was the most comprehensive listing of recent work in the field of reader-response criticism. It is still worth looking at. A more selective and up-to-date bibliography can be found in *Readers and Reading* (Bennett 1995). It is divided into six sections to enable the user to focus on whatever aspect is of the most interest.

Structuralism

Structuralism has its origin in the teaching of Swiss linguist Ferdinand de Saussure, whose lecture notes were published in 1916. The main disciple who applied his principles to literature is Roman Jakobson. During a long and productive life, his writings on a wide range of subjects did much to popularize structuralist thought in academic circles. Other influential structuralists are two Frenchmen—the cultural anthropologist Claude Levi-Strauss and the critic and linguist Roland Barthes, both of whom began to flourish in the 1950s. Structuralist thinking fans out from these key figures. Another philosophical study, semiotics, is closely related to structuralism.

Selden and Widdowson list basic texts, introductions, and further reading in *A Reader's Guide to Contemporary Literary Theory*.

Eagleton, in *Literary Theory: An Introduction,* prefers to list his titles in the order that he thinks a student should approach the subject and so begins with Ferdinand de Saussure's work. The bibliography in *Literary Theories in Praxis* also can be recommended.

Conclusion

In conclusion, it would useful to add a few words about the rewards of shaping the collection by acquiring older imprints. There are advantages to not dealing with the steady flow of titles in the hope that from the mass of available titles those selected will be of more than passing interest. The titles showing up in retrospective collection-building activities have already stood the test of time—granted the period of time may only be slightly beyond the recent past! Nevertheless, these titles have in some fashion made their mark, some more so than others. There is satisfaction in knowing that these titles are more likely to enrich the collection. The presumption is that bibliographies cited in this chapter as guides have been compiled by knowledgeable people. The use of published lists contributes to a certain comfort factor for the selector in that he or she is sharing the judgment of titles with more experienced people who have put together title lists. The compiler of a bibliography becomes the selector's silent partner as the bibliography is transformed into resources for local users, many of whom the selector may know personally. Also, the selector has a sense of accomplishment in knowing that because of his or her work, the collection has a better rationale, is more cohesive than before. Within the spectrum of librarianship, retrospective collection development is just one segment, but one with its own challenges and rewards. The ultimate challenge is to provide access to a better collection, thereby giving better library service. This chapter has endeavored to provide direction in meeting that challenge.

Notes

1. Richard Heinzkill, "Retrospective Collection Development," in *English and American Literature: Sources and Strategies for Collection Development,* ed. William McPheron, Stephen Lehmann, Craig Likness, and Marcia Pankake, (Chicago: ALA, 1987), 56.

2. Interested readers are referred to the special issue of *Acquisitions Librar-*

ian, no.7 (1992), which is devoted to the RLG Conspectus and includes a selective annotated bibliography of articles on the advantages and disadvantages of using the Conspectus for retrospective collection development.

3. Jeanne Harrell, "Use of the OCLC/AMIGOS Collection Analysis CD to Determine Comparative Collection Strength in English and American Literature: A Case Study," *Technical Services Quarterly* 9, no. 3 (1992): 1–14.

4. Heinzkill, "Retrospective Collection Development," 59.

5. Discussion about editorial principles for creating archives of electronic texts, sometimes called digital libraries, is flourishing. One introduction to some of the issues is *The Literary Text in the Digital Age*, ed. Robert Finneran (Ann Arbor, Mich.: Univ. of Michigan Pr., 1996). Basic documents for those undertaking these projects are Peter Shillingsburg's "Guidelines for Electronic Scholarly Editions" and the MLA's "Guidelines for Electronic Scholarly Editions." Both are available at http://sunsite.berkeley.edu/MLA/intro.html.

6. "Bartlebian Principles of Electronic Publishing," http://www.columbia.edu/acis/bartleby/bartcriteria.html (4 Aug. 1999). In November 1996, Steven H. Van Leeuwen, the original editor, closed the Columbia University Web site and, on his own, launched a new version of this project, now *Bartleby.com*, 2000, http://www.bartleby.com (19 Feb. 2000).

7. *Library Electronic Text Resource Service: LETRS*, 2 April 1998, http://www.indiana.edu/~letrs/index.html (4 Aug. 1999).

8. This section is entitled Latino American, and not Chicano, because the term *Chicano* (which derives from Mexicano) does not adequately describe the full range of writing by people of Hispanic background. Much contemporary usage mistakenly continues to equate Chicano with Hispanic.

9. *The Dictionary of Native American Literature*, ed. Andrew Wiget (New York: Garland, 1994), is the same as *Handbook of Native American Literature* (New York: Garland, 1996).

10. Ellen K. Coughlin, "In Face of Growing Success and Conservatives' Attacks, Cultural-Studies Scholars Ponder Future Directions," *Chronicle of Higher Education*, 18 Jan. 1989, A4.

11. "Forum," *PMLA* 112 (1997): 257–86.

12. Roger Fower, *A Dictionary of Modern Critical Terms*, rev. and enl. ed. (London: Routledge & Kegan Paul, 1987).

13. Jay Parini, "The Greening of the Humanities," *New York Times Magazine*, 29 Oct. 1995, 52–53.

14. Thomas J. Lyon, ed., *This Incomperable Lande: A Book of American Nature Writing* (Boston: Houghton Mifflin, 1989), 399.

15. Sharon Malinowski, ed., *Gay and Lesbian Literature* (Detroit: St. James, 1994), vii.

16. Bonnie Zimmerman, *The Safe Sea of Women: Lesbian Fiction, 1969–1989* (Boston: Beacon, 1990), xii.

17. Bonnie Zimmerman and Toni A. H. McNaron, *The New Lesbian Studies: Into the Twenty-First Century* (New York: Feminist Pr. at The City Univ. of New York, 1996), 278.

18. Teresa de Lauretis, "Queer Theory: Lesbian and Gay Sexualities, An Introduction," *Differences: A Journal of Feminist Cultural Studies* 3, no. 2 (1991): iii–xviii.

19. Donald Morton, ed., *The Material Queer: A LesBiGay Cultural Studies Reader* (Boulder, Colo.: Westview, 1996), xiii.

20. Terry Eagleton, *Literary Theory: An Introduction*, 2d ed. (Minneapolis: Univ. of Minnesota Pr, 1996), 200–201.

21. Ibid., 215, fn 14–15.

Works Cited

Abelove, Henry, Michele Aina Barale, and David M. Halperin, eds. *The Lesbian and Gay Studies Reader.* New York: Routledge, 1993.

Arac, Jonathan, Wlad Godzich, and Wallace Martin, eds. *The Yale Critics: Deconstruction in America.* Minneapolis: Univ. of Minnesota Pr., 1983.

Ashcroft, Bill, Gareth Griffiths, and Helen Tiffin, eds. *Key Concepts in Post-Colonial Studies.* London: Routledge, 1998.

Atkins, G. Douglas, and Laura Morrow, eds. *Contemporary Literary Theory.* Amherst: Univ. of Massachusetts Pr., 1989.

Bell, Bernard W. *The Afro-American Novel and Its Tradition.* Amherst: Univ. of Massachusetts Pr., 1987.

Bennett, Andrew, ed. *Readers and Reading.* London: Longman, 1995.

Brooker, Peter, ed. *Modernism/Postmodernism.* London: Longman, 1992.

Bruchac, Joseph, Janet Witalec, and Sharon Malinowski, eds. *Smoke Rising: The Native North American Literary Companion.* Detroit: Visible Ink, 1995.

Candelaria, Cordelia. *Chicano Poetry: A Critical Introduction.* Westport, Conn.: Greenwood, 1986.

Chang, Juliana, ed. *Quiet Fire: A Historical Anthology of Asian American Poetry, 1892–1970.* New York: Asian American Writers' Workshop, 1996.

Cheung, King-Kok, and Stan Yogi. *Asian American Literature: An Annotated Bibliography.* New York: MLA, 1988.

Connor, Steven. *Postmodernist Culture: An Introduction to Theories of the Contemporary.* New York: Basil Blackwell, 1989.

Damon, Gene, Jan Watson, and Robin Jordan. *The Lesbian in Literature: A Bibliography.* 2d ed. Reno, Nev.: The Ladder, 1975.

Davis, Robert C., and Ronald Schleifer, eds. *Rhetoric and Form: Deconstruction at Yale.* Norman: Univ. of Oklahoma Pr., 1985.

Eagleton, Terry. *Literary Theory: An Introduction.* 2d ed. Minneapolis: Univ. of Minnesota Pr., 1996.

Elder, John, ed. *American Nature Writers*. New York: Charles Scribner's Sons, 1996.

Fernandez, Roberta, Pat Bozeman, and University of Houston Libraries. *Twenty-Five Years of Hispanic Literature in the United States, 1965–1990: An Exhibit, with Accompanying Text*. Houston, Tex.: M. D. Anderson Library, Univ. of Houston, 1992.

Furtado, Ken, and Nancy Hellner. *Gay and Lesbian American Plays: An Annotated Bibliography*. Metuchen, N.J.: Scarecrow, 1993.

Gates, Henry Louis Jr., and Nellie Y. McKay, eds. *The Norton Anthology of African American Literature*. New York: W. W. Norton, 1996.

Gilyard, Keith, ed. *Spirit and Flame: An Anthology of Contemporary African American Poetry*. Syracuse, N.Y.: Syracuse Univ. Pr., 1997.

Glotfelty, Cheryll, and Harold Fromm, eds. *The Ecocriticism Reader: Landmarks in Literary Ecology*. Athens: Univ. of Georgia Press, 1996.

Greenblatt, Stephen, and Giles Gunn, eds. *Redrawing the Boundaries: The Transformation of English and American Literary Studies*. New York: MLA, 1992.

Groden, Michael, and Martin Kreiswirth, eds. *The Johns Hopkins Guide to Literary Theory and Criticism*. Baltimore: Johns Hopkins Univ. Pr., 1994.

Grossberg, Lawrence, Cary Nelson, and Paula A. Treichler, eds. *Cultural Studies*. New York: Routledge, 1992.

Hammond, Paul. *Love between Men in English Literature*. New York: St. Martin's, 1996.

Harper, Michael S., and Anthony Walton, eds. *Every Shut Eye Ain't Asleep: An Anthology of Poetry by African Americans since 1945*. Boston: Little, Brown, 1994.

Hernández-Gutiérrez, Manuel de Jesús. *El colonialismo interno en la narrativa chicana: El Barrio, el Anti-Barrio, y el Exterior*. Tempe, Ariz.: Bilingual Pr./Editorial Bilingue, 1994.

Hill, Patricia L., ed. *Call and Response: The Riverside Anthology of the African American Literary Tradition*. Boston: Houghton Mifflin, 1998.

Hirschfelder, Arlene B., comp. *American Indian Authors: A Representative Bibliography*. New York: Assn. on American Indian Affairs, 1970.

Hobson, Geary, ed. *The Remembered Earth: An Anthology of Contemporary Native American Literature*. Albuquerque: Univ. of New Mexico Pr., 1981.

Inglis, Fred. *Cultural Studies*. Oxford: Blackwell, 1993.

Kanellos, Nicolas. *Hispanic American Literature: A Brief Introduction and Anthology*. New York: HarperCollins College, 1995.

Kauffman, Linda S., ed. *Gender and Theory: Dialogues on Feminist Criticism*. Oxford: Blackwell, 1989.

Kieft, Robert H. "Cultural Studies: Part 1." *Choice* 31 (1994): 1683–95.

Knippling, Alpana Sharma, ed. *New Immigrant Literatures in the United States:*

A Sourcebook to Our Multicultural Literary Heritage. Westport, Conn.: Greenwood, 1996.

Kowaleski-Wallace, Elizabeth, ed. *Encyclopedia of Feminist Literary Theory.* New York: Garland, 1997.

Lawson, Alan, Leigh Dale, Helen Tiffin, and Shane Rowlands. *Post-Colonial Literatures in English: General, Theoretical, and Comparative, 1970–1993.* New York: G. K. Hall, 1997.

Levin, James. *The Gay Novel in America.* New York: Garland, 1991.

Lincoln, Kenneth. *Native American Renaissance.* Berkeley: Univ. of California Pr., 1983.

Lyon, Thomas J., ed. *This Incomperable Lande: A Book of American Nature Writing.* Boston: Houghton Mifflin, 1989.

Major, Clarence, ed. *The Garden Thrives: Twentieth-Century African-American Poetry.* New York: HarperPerennial, 1996.

Makaryk, Irene Rima, ed. *Encyclopedia of Contemporary Literary Theory: Approaches, Scholars, Terms.* Toronto: Univ. of Toronto Pr., 1993.

Malinowski, Sharon, ed. *Gay and Lesbian Literature.* Detroit: St. James, 1994.

Marshall, Donald G. *Contemporary Critical Theory: A Selective Bibliography.* New York: MLA, 1993.

Martinez, Julio A., and Francisco A. Lomeli, eds. *Chicano Literature: A Reference Guide.* Westport, Conn.: Greenwood, 1985.

Miller, Isabel. *Place for Us.* New York: Ballantine, 1983.

Mongia, Padmini, ed. *Contemporary Postcolonial Theory: A Reader.* London: Arnold, 1996.

Morton, Donald E., ed. *The Material Queer: A LesBiGay Cultural Studies Reader.* Boulder, Colo.: Westview, 1996.

Munt, Sally, ed. *New Lesbian Criticism: Literary and Cultural Readings.* New York: Columbia Univ. Pr., 1992.

Murdoch, David. "Riches of Empire: Postcolonialism in Literature and Criticism." *Choice* 32 (1995): 1059–71.

Nelson, Emmanuel S., ed. *Contemporary Gay American Novelists: A Bio-Bibliographical Critical Sourcebook.* Westport, Conn.: Greenwood, 1993.

Nordquist, Joan, comp. *Queer Theory: A Bibliography.* Santa Cruz, Calif.: Reference and Research Services, 1997.

Palmer, Paulina. *Contemporary Lesbian Writing: Dreams, Desire, Difference.* Buckingham, Eng.: Open Univ. Pr., 1993.

Peck, David R. *American Ethnic Literatures: Native American, African American, Chicano/Latino, and Asian American Writers and Their Backgrounds: An Annotated Bibliography.* Pasadena, Calif.: Salem, 1992.

Perkins, George B., Barbara Perkins, and Phillip Leininger, eds. *Benet's Reader's Encyclopedia of American Literature.* New York: HarperCollins, 1991.

Pollack, Sandra, and Denise D. Knight, eds. *Contemporary Lesbian Writers of the United States: A Bio-Bibliographical Critical Sourcebook.* Westport, Conn.: Greenwood, 1993.

Ransom, John Crowe. *The New Criticism.* Norfolk, Conn.: New Directions, 1941.

Rose, John M. "Deconstruction across the Disciplines." *Choice* 28 (1990): 439–46.

Ruoff, A. LaVonne Brown. *American Indian Literatures: An Introduction, Bibliographic Review, and Selected Bibliography.* New York: MLA, 1990.

Ruoff, A. LaVonne Brown, and Jerry W. Ward Jr., eds. *Redefining American Literary History.* New York: MLA, 1990.

Ryan, Kiernan, ed. *New Historicism and Cultural Materialism: A Reader.* London: Arnold, 1996.

Said, Edward. *Orientalism.* New York: Pantheon, 1979.

Scheese, Don. *Nature Writing: The Pastoral Impulse in America.* New York: Twayne, 1996.

Selden, Raman, and Peter Widdowson. *A Reader's Guide to Contemporary Literary Theory.* 3d ed. Lexington: Univ. Pr. of Kentucky, 1993.

Shirley, Carl R., and Paula W. Shirley. *Understanding Chicano Literature.* Columbia: Univ. of South Carolina Pr., 1988.

Showalter, Elaine, ed. *Speaking of Gender.* New York: Routledge, 1989.

Spurlin, William J., and Michael Fischer, eds. *The New Criticism and Contemporary Literary Theory: Connections and Continuities.* New York: Garland, 1995.

Staton, Shirley F. *Literary Theories in Praxis.* Philadelphia: Univ. of Pennsylvania Pr., 1987.

Stewart, Frank. *Natural History of Nature Writing.* Washington, D.C.: island Press and Covelto, Calif.: Shearwater Books, 1995.

Summers, Claude J., ed. *The Gay and Lesbian Literary Heritage: A Reader's Companion to the Writers and Their Works, from Antiquity to the Present.* New York: Henry Holt, 1995.

Tompkins, Jane P., ed. *Reader-Response Criticism: From Formalism to Post-Structuralism.* Baltimore: Johns Hopkins Univ. Pr., 1980.

Trudeau, Lawerence J., ed. *Asian American Literature: Reviews and Criticism of Works by American Writers of Asian Descent.* Detroit: Gale, 1999.

Trujillo, Roberto G., and Andres Rodriguez, comps. *Literatura Chicana: Creative and Critical Writings through 1984.* Oakland, Calif.: Floricanto, 1985.

Turner, Darwin T., ed. *Black Drama in America: An Anthology.* 2d ed. Washington, D.C.: Howard Univ. Pr., 1994.

Veeser, H. Aram, ed. *The New Historicism.* New York: Routledge, 1989.

———, ed. *The New Historicism Reader.* New York: Routledge, 1994.

Waage, Frederick O., ed. *Teaching Environmental Literature: Materials, Methods, Resources.* New York: MLA, 1985.

Watson, George, ed. *The New Cambridge Bibliography of English Literature.* 5 vols. Cambridge: Cambridge Univ. Pr., 1969–1977.

Wiget, Andrew, ed. *Dictionary of Native American Literature*. New York: Garland, 1994.

————. *Native American Literature*. Boston: Twayne, 1985.

————. "Native American Literature: A Bibliographic Survey of American Indian Literary Traditions." *Choice* 23 (1986): 1503–12.

Witalec, Janet, Jeffery Chapman, and Christopher Giroux, eds. *Native North American Literature: Biographical and Critical Information on Native Writers and Orators from the United States and Canada from Historical Times to the Present*. New York: Gale Research, 1994.

Wolfe, Susan J., and Julia Penelope, eds. *Sexual Practice/Textual Theory: Lesbian Cultural Criticism*. Cambridge, Mass.: Blackwell, 1993.

Woodhouse, Reed. *Unlimited Embrace: A Canon of Gay Fiction, 1945–1995*. Amherst: Univ. of Massachusetts Pr., 1998.

Woods, Gregory. *A History of Gay Literature: The Male Tradition*. New Haven: Yale Univ. Pr., 1998.

Young, Al. *African American Literature: A Brief Introduction and Anthology*. New York: HarperCollins College, 1996.

Young, Ian. *The Male Homosexual in Literature: A Bibliography*. 2d ed. Metuchen, N.J.: Scarecrow, 1982.

Zimmerman, Bonnie. *The Safe Sea of Women: Lesbian Fiction, 1969–1989*. Boston: Beacon, 1990.

Zimmerman, Bonnie, and Toni A. H. McNaron, eds. *The New Lesbian Studies: Into the Twenty-First Century*. New York: Feminist Pr. at The City Univ. of New York, 1996.

Zimmerman, Marc. *U.S. Latino Literature: An Essay and Annotated Bibliography*. Chicago: MARCH/Abrazo, 1992.

Chapter 3

Primary Source Material: Responsibilities and Realities

Susan L. Peters
Emory University

This chapter has two purposes. The first is to provide collection management librarians with an update and discussion of recent developments concerning primary source material, including statements formulated by the Modern Language Association and the English and American Literature Section of the American Library Association. The second purpose is to provide an intellectual framework and vocabulary regarding primary source material, regarded here as particularly important given the recent expansion in academia of the digital environment. There is much concern among librarians that the "digital world" is making great strides in increasing funding and personnel, perhaps to the detriment or neglect of the print collections, with the possibility of bringing harm to traditional scholarly research concerns and practices. By exploring these concerns, this chapter hopes to assist, in some modest way, the many librarians, particularly those in collection management and development, who face the challenges of selecting, purchasing, preserving, storing, cataloging, and deaccessioning primary source material on an almost daily basis. Few, if any, would argue with the importance of this material, but its importance is not what is in question. What is in question is the reality of preserving and storing primary source material within one's own library institution, not because of a lack of importance but, rather, because of a lack of money (for staff support, etc.), lack of space, a lack of appreciation by university administrators and non-humanities-based researchers, and in some cases, a lack of need for a particular group of material inherited, donated, or otherwise "received." Where, if anywhere, does one draw the line regarding what is kept and cared for? Who decides, and how?

In 1995, the MLA published its annual *Profession*. One-third of the issue was a section called "Significance of Primary Records" and consisted of eight essays written by members of the MLA Ad Hoc Committee on the Future of the Print Record (which, despite its name, also encompassed manuscript). The committee itself had been formed as a response to a paper read by Phyllis Franklin, executive director of the MLA, at the 1992 MLA convention. The committee had been considering how to ensure the survival of primary materials in a time of increasing electronic communication and publication, and it was made up of well-known scholars such as G. Thomas Tanselle and J. Hillis Miller and scholar-librarians Alice Schreyer, curator of rare books for the University of Chicago Library, and Everette E. Larson, of the hispanic division of the Library of Congress. In addition to the eight essays, *Profession* included a statement calling for "representatives of library, conservation, and scholarly organizations (to) form a task group to promote continued thinking and cooperative activity leading toward (1) the maximum retention and preservation of textual artifacts, as well as a refining of the selection criteria necessarily entailed, and (2) the use of responsible procedures in the creation and identification of photographic and electronic reproductions based on those artifacts."[1]

The library community responded quickly, especially librarians responsible for preservation, collection growth, and maintenance in the humanities. On December 7, 1994, Betty Bengtson, who was then chair of the Association of Research Libraries (ARL)/Preservation of Library Materials Committee (as well as the director of university libraries at the University of Washington), wrote to Phyllis Franklin, who was still executive director of the MLA. Bengtson expressed her agreement with the importance of primary source material and the MLA's interest and growing involvement in public discourse about that concern. However, she also expressed the difficulty of acting on the "principle of universal value" as outlined in the draft of the MLA statement. Bengtson went to the heart of the matter as it affects all libraries:

> The danger of not accepting the limits of available resources is that priorities will not be set. There are many more books and manuscripts in need of preservation today than can be saved with available resources. The issue of cost is critical, given the magnitude of the preservation problem and the vast number of endangered research materials. In a context where choices will be made, it is vital to distinguish between materials that have significant artifactual value and must be preserved in the original and those for which surrogates can be created through electronic, photographic, or other means.[2]

Bengtson went on to urge the MLA to work with the ARL in establishing a joint working group that can address these issues and articulate appropriate criteria.

In January 1996, the English and American Literatures Section (EALS) of the ALA, Association of Research and College Libraries (ACRL), formed an ad hoc committee headed by Steve Enniss of Emory University. Other members of the committee were myself (also of Emory University), Pat Dominguez of the University of North Carolina, Bill Wortman of Miami University (Ohio), Candace Benefiel of Texas A&M, and Laura Fuderer University of Notre Dame. Enniss in turn notified the MLA Task Force on Primary Materials, headed by Mary Case, of this group's existence and interest. Initially, the MLA committee was thinking of two plans of action: first, to educate people about the importance of primary source materials in libraries; and second, to establish a set of criteria that could be used to evaluate primary materials. By spring 1997, the second plan was abandoned and the committee decided to focus on the first.

Also by spring 1997, the EALS ad hoc committee had formulated its own statement on primary source material and, in addition, had offered to work with the MLA committee in any way possible. Perhaps only historians have as much interest in primary source material as scholars of literature and the librarians who work with these scholarly groups. After "live" meetings at ALA conferences and "electronic" meetings via the Internet, a statement was formulated by the ad hoc committee and approved by the EALS membership. This statement was subsequently published in the winter 1997 edition of the *MLA Newsletter*, as well as in the EALS newsletter *Biblio-Notes,* and reads as follows:

> The English and American Literature Section (EALS) of the Association of College and Research Libraries supports the efforts of the Modern Language Association and, more recently, the ARL-MLA joint working group in drawing attention to the issues surrounding the preservation of print materials in their original formats in the nation's libraries.
>
> Historically the survival of the print record has been threatened from forces as varied as manufacturing processes, publishing practices, environmental conditions, space limitations and deaccessioning practices, and microfilming programs. The impressive capabilities of computer technology, combined with the widespread perception that digital images can serve as surrogates for materials in their original formats, now pose a new threat to the preservation of primary source materials within our libraries. While digitization offers enhanced capability for the manipulation of texts, it has not yet been proved an effective long-term preservation strategy. In addition, digitized and microform images of texts cannot fully convey the range of information preserved

in actual artifacts themselves, and, therefore, are not appropriate replacements for the primary record in all circumstances.

The MLA Statement on the Significance of the Primary Record is a valuable document in that it makes unequivocally clear the importance of primary materials in their original formats for a host of research purposes including, but not limited to, printing and publishing history, textual criticism, reader-response studies, and reception studies.

As librarians responsible for English and American literature collections in the nation's college and research libraries, we share the MLA's concern and we support its effort to educate the academic community and the public alike about the importance of preserving primary materials. We also understand the many costs of preserving growing library collections (including the costs of buildings and facilities, staff processing time, and preservation efforts) and the necessity for clearly defined institutional priorities in managing our libraries' collections. The preservation of the print record is beyond the scope of any single institution; therefore, we recognize the necessity for cooperative collection development with other institutions. Establishing priorities—in consultation with faculty and library colleagues in our own and other area institutions—is one of the professional librarian's primary duties and responsibilities.

We strongly support the educational efforts of the MLA and the task force and believe that only by widespread understanding of research practices can the library community and the public at large act in concert to preserve the historical legacy that falls within our care. EALS will develop educational programs and carry on continuing discussion about ways to educate users, administrators, and institutions about the need to preserve primary records.

This statement came after six months of careful study and discussion by library professionals of the major ideas expressed in the articles of *Profession 95* and how they might relate to those in the library profession who are grappling with the realities that are a by-product of what these essays designate as desirable. It is important to highlight the tension expressed in the EALS statement between the desirability of maintaining all primary source documents and the economic realities that constrain all libraries. Most librarians, especially those found in research institutions, would not argue with the theory but must argue with the reality. Because the essays in *Profession 95* form an intellectual framework and provide discussion of the issues with which librarians should be familiar, a brief summary and analysis follows.

The first essay is by the textual scholar G. Thomas Tanselle and focuses on the broader, theoretical aspects of the need for primary source material. Tanselle states that he does not disparage electronic duplication, photocopying, or microfilm, but he clearly and firmly declares that they cannot and do not replace the original document: "No reproduction of a text can ever be a fully adequate substitute for the original, since every reproduction necessarily leaves something unreproduced."[3] He notes that the fact that the original is needed to compare with the copy in order to ensure accuracy is perhaps the single most important reason for keeping primary documents in their original. Other important reasons include the study of the material as physical object, as part of a production history, techniques of manufacture, implications of their physical appearance, how visual and tactile features reflect cultural trends as well as the responses of readers over the years, editing practices, etc. Perhaps Tanselle's most thought-provoking statement is the following: "It follows . . . *that the books in existing book stacks should never be abandoned*" [emphasis mine].[4] (Note: Tanselle's excellent, fully developed article "Reproductions and Scholarship" provides much detail and theoretical support for his stand.[5]) He makes no attempt to address the issues of the space or financial limits that most, if not all, academic libraries face today, or indeed will continue to face. One could argue that this concern should not be his, as the patient does not discuss the operating room layout with the doctor. I would counter that argument by saying that the patient is certainly concerned with the *results* of a particular space if the result is a removed healthy kidney instead of an inflamed appendix! As working librarians, we must understand Tanselle's principles, but we also must make sure that he, and people of similar views, will work with us to develop practical means to solve these issues.

In his essay, J. Hillis Miller articulates three obligations that the MLA must keep in mind as it looks at the future of the print record. First, it must continue supporting preservation programs, recognizing that only 25 to 30 percent of the titles printed on acidic paper can be saved. Second, it must study the effects of the electronic revolution and guide it in ways that are beneficial to scholarly interests. And third, it must "attend closely to the uses of original materials and to save as many of those artifacts as possible."[6] To this end, he recommends a joint working group with the ARL. He closes his brief essay with the admission, unlike Tanselle, that not all primary source material can be saved and that decisions must be made as to what is preserved and what is not.

Following Tanselle's and Miller's more theoretically oriented essays are seven brief essays by scholars that focus on the actual use of primary source material in a classroom, library, or research setting. All seven are well worth reading, for they provide the librarian and library administrators with the kind of knowledgeable argument and rhetoric so necessary in dealing with those who question the need for space and monetary support for material that can be microfilmed or digitized. I will briefly summarize two of the essays here. The first is "Traces of a Lost Woman" by Susan Staves.[7] The lost woman in question is the author Elizabeth Griffith, author of six plays, three novels, and other works published between 1757 and 1782. Staves points out some of the difficulties in examining an entire oeuvre by early women writers. First, they often published anonymously or under their maiden names. Second, they often published later under their married names, but because it was not uncommon to be widowed and marry again, they sometimes published under a second married name. And third, they often published material originally not deemed "worthy" by the canon-makers; it is only in the last decade or two that they are receiving scholarly interest and study by academics. In Griffith's case, if we chose to microfilm the first edition of her book *Genuine Letters* (and it is the first edition that we almost always choose for duplication), we will lose important new material included in the first volume of her second edition. In addition, in one copy of the Dublin second edition of volumes 1 and 2 (held at the Beineke Library, Yale University), the books appear mutilated: pages are missing, words and passages are crossed out, and much marginalia has been added. Importantly, however, we discover that this appears to have been done by Griffith herself as she used this copy of the second edition as a base text for making revisions intended for a possible future edition. And, Staves illustrates, what Griffith deleted is as important as what she added. Thus, if one had discarded the second edition because we had the so-called "more important first" and, further, had discarded the obviously "damaged" and "worn-out" second edition at Yale, we would have actually lost valuable, indeed irreplaceable, material.

My second example involves a use of primary source material directed toward undergraduate students as described in the article "Rekindling the Reading Experience of the Victorian Age" by Catherine Golden.[8] Golden regularly brings her nineteenth-century undergraduate literature classes to the rare book room in the Lucy Scribner Library of Skidmore College. There, her students are not only surprised at the length of the works by Dickens, Thackeray, Eliot, and others, but they also read the material as it was originally presented: as a multivolume title (often referred to as a "three decker") or as a serial installment in one of the weekly or monthly magazines, such as *Bentley's Miscellany*. As Golden points out, unlike our readers today who can thumb to the end of the text to "find out what happened," readers in the nineteenth century often had gratification delayed for months, sometimes more than a year, until the novel's culmination. In addition, these serials contained illustrations, which are often deleted in more modern printings. Further, placement of the book's title in the table of contents often gives clues as to the importance of the text and its place in the economic life of the serial and in the status of the culture of the day.

These essays give us valuable insight into the importance of primary source material in library collections and the intellectual "battery of ammunition" needed when fighting for inclusion of material in a library or the saving of that same material from the shredder. However, few librarians, especially those responsible for collection development, growth, or maintenance, would argue differently: the shredder strikes shivers in us all. What sadly creates tension between us and scholars such as Tanselle are the issues mentioned in the opening paragraph of this chapter: where do we put it, how can we store it, are we able to preserve it, can we afford to save it? Unfortunately, there are no easy answers to any of these questions. Each library, library professional, and faculty member must work with colleagues to arrive at solutions that are "workable" and that serve best for that time and place.

Confrontation and discussion of these issues have increased. In June of 1998, the Rare Book and Manuscripts Section (RBMS) of ALA sponsored an ALA preconference called "Getting Ready for the Nineteenth Century: Strategies and Solutions for Rare Book and Special Collections Librarians," which sought to address some of the problems highlighted in this chapter. Alice Schreyer, who had been on the original MLA ad hoc committee, gave the introductory remarks as part of the Plenary Session "Common Cause: Collaborating to Preserve Printed and Primary Source Materials."[9] One of the highlights of her remarks caused much amusement in the audience, for she pointed out that the unreliability of digital material has helped the preservation environment—paper is increasingly being viewed as the more stable product. A model is emerging of preserving the paper document, then creating the digital product. This in turn helps further the preservation of the paper product because the document is needed for verification of the digital product and future wear and tear on the paper will be kept to a minimum as many researchers will be satisfied using the digital text. The Library of Congress's "American Memory" project is a good example of this process now under way.

Paul Conway of Yale University, in his remarks titled "Preserving the Nineteenth Century: Challenges and Possibilities," addressed many of the issues raised in the MLA document and underscored many of the points made in the EALS response.[10] Because he expects his comments to be published soon, I will briefly comment only on the area of collaboration. Let me also remind the reader that Conway focused solely on nineteenth-century material. The idea of "saving" all material older than that does not appear to be an issue, perhaps because pre-nineteenth-century material is scarcer and therefore already highly valued, and its paper is less acidic and therefore more stable.

Conway emphasizes that nineteenth-century materials make collaboration possible, even if it might be complicated. A combination of several large academic libraries probably has the vast majority of this material, he points out, so the questions become: is it available and accessible, and is it protected and secure? Following that, Conway says that we must assign value to what we own or wish to own: "In preservation, all decisions turn on value judgments . . . . We must choose first between no action and any action and then make the right course of treatment." And this, he argues, must be done collaboratively. We have concentrated our energies on critical mass, and now we must concentrate them on critical selection in order to be sure that as much as possible of the nineteenth century is preserved and not "just a random assemblage." Here, Conway quotes the MLA "Statement on the Significance of Primary Records," which argues that all objects that purport to present the same text (multiple editions, later printings, etc.) must be preserved. His response echoes points made in the EALS statement, which argues for selection and judgment within the contexts of necessity and economic restraints and that it is "important to recognize that individuality is not necessarily rarity—and rarity—not individuality—forms but one part of a complicated assessment of value."

Leaders in the library field will no doubt plan national initiatives as we enter the next decade. Paul Conway's talk puts forth one framework for approaching collaborative selection for preservation, and doubtless there will be others. The suggested readings at the end of this chapter give clear indication that the discussion and debate has begun, and the vast, successful microfilming projects sponsored by the NEH are outstanding examples of what can be accomplished with appropriate planning and funding. However, some actions can be taken now by individuals working within academic libraries of all sizes around the country. Those with professional duties in all areas of collection management have a responsibility for preserving our cultural heritage as well as serving the research needs of our academic community. For example, one action that costs little and can accomplish much is increasing our own professional sensitivity to the issue of primary source material. To go from "It's not my problem" to "What can I do?" involves no expense but can make a difference. To reverse a common cliché, if you are part of the solution, you are not part of the problem. That simple shift in attitude might lead to creative solutions that are inexpensive and not time-consuming. The following beginning steps are all things that we as individual librarians can do:

• Work with faculty, library administrators, and other library staff in formulating criteria upon which your decisions to preserve, retain, store, or deaccession can comfortably rest. The best time to do this is when you are not facing a crisis of space, money, or time. Communicate goals, needs, and possible actions clearly to everyone involved with the collection, including circulation, cataloging, special collection, and reference staff. Do not assume that everyone agrees with you! Explain, educate, cajole, beg.

• Come to a cooperative agreement with an academic institution, or many institutions, in your region to accept material that your institution cannot retain and is not held by other institutions in the area. Also, persuade that institution to accept duplicate copies of material already held if only one copy is available in the state; this will supply a "cushion" for when materials are lost, damaged, or stolen. If duplicates are not possible, negotiate with another institution to ensure that more than one copy of an item can be retained within the geographic area.

• Check OCLC holdings before withdrawing a monograph or serial to see if a copy is available within a reasonable geographic distance from your institution. If not, offer the items to the academic institution in your area with which you have your agreement.

• Set up a system of working with "brittle books" (i.e., books on acid paper), that your current budget can tolerate. Set priorities with faculty input as to what should be reproduced. Is in-house duplication on acid-free paper a possibility? If not, are there institutions within the region with whom you can cooperate?

• If your library's stacks have reached 80 percent capacity, explore the possibility of off-site storage of library material. Planning for such a facility takes time and money but makes feasible the retention of our important, if little-used, primary materials.

The twenty-first century presents us with a digital world unimaginable only a decade ago. Librarians are feeling increasing pressure to create and maintain "digital libraries" and to devalue traditional printed texts. Those conducting scholarly research, especially in the humanities, know this devaluation is incorrect but recognize the partnership that paper text and digital text can create with each other. Indeed, digital technology has enabled scholars and researchers to access information quickly, to formulate new theoretical approaches to knowledge, and to discover provocative links between apparently disparate materials. However, the importance of the printed text must not be lost or forgotten, and the library and all formats housed within must learn to coexist, complement, and support each other.

Notes

1. Modern Language Association of America, "Statement on the Significance of Primary Records," *Profession* (1995): 28.

2. Letter from Betty G. Bengston, chair, ARL Preservation of Library Materials Committee to Phyllis Franklin, executive director, MLA, 7 Dec. 1994.

3. G. Thomas Tanselle, "Introduction," *Profession* (1995): 30.

4. Ibid., 31.

5. Thomas Tanselle, "Reproductions and Scholarship," *Studies in Bibliography* 42 (1989): 25–54.

6. J. Hillis Miller, "What Is the Future of the Print Record?" *Profession* (1995): 34.

7. Susan Staves, "Traces of a Lost Woman," *Profession* (1995): 36–38.

8. Catherine Golden, "Rekindling the Reading Experience of the Victorian Age," *Profession* (1995): 45–47.

9. Alice Schreyer, "Common Cause: Collaborating to Preserve Printed and Primary Source Materials"(paper presented at the preconference institute, "Getting Ready for the Nineteenth Century: Strategies and Solutions for Rare Book and Special Collections Librarians," of the ALA, Washington, D.C., June 1998).

10. Paul Conway, "Preserving the Nineteenth Century: Challenges and Possibilities" (paper presented at the preconference institute, "Getting Ready for the Nineteenth Century: Strategies and Solutions for Rare Book and Special Collections Librarians," of the ALA, Washington, D.C., June 1998).

Bibliography

Atkinson, Ross. "Managing Traditional Materials in an Online Environment: Some Definitions and Distinctions for a Future Collection Management." *Library Resources and Technical Services* 42 (1998): 7–20.

Buckland, Michael K. "Information as Thing." *Journal of the American Society for Information Science* 42 (1991): 351–60.

Clapp, Verner W. "The Story of Permanent/Durable Paper, 1115–1970." *Scholarly Publishing* 2 (1971): 107–24, 229–45, 353–67.

Conway, Paul. "Preserving the Nineteenth Century: Challenges and Possibilities." Paper presented at the preconference institute, "Getting Ready for the Nineteenth Century: Strategies and Solutions for Rare Book and Special Collections Librarians," of the ALA. Washington, D.C., 13 June 1998.

De Stefano, Paula. "Use-Based Selection for Preservation Microfilming." *College and Research Libraries* 56 (1995): 409–18.

George, Gerald W. *Difficult Choices: How Can Scholars Help Save Endangered Research Resources?* Washington, D.C.: Commission on Preservation and Access, 1995.

Harris, Neil. "Special Collections and Academic Scholarship: A Tangled Relationship." In *Libraries and Scholarly Communication in the United States: The Historical Dimension*, ed. Phyllis Dain and John Y. Cole, 63–70. New York: Greenwood, 1990.

Hyde, Dorsey W., Jr. "Principles for the Selection of Materials for Preservation in Public Archives." In *Archives and Libraries: Papers Presented at the 1938 Conference of the American Library Association*. Chicago: ALA, 1938.

Modern Language Association of America. "Statement on the Significance of Primary Records." *Profession* (1995): 27–28.

Schreyer, Alice. "Common Cause: Collaborating to Preserve Printed and Primary Source Materials." Paper presented at the preconference institute, "Getting Ready for the Nineteenth Century: Strategies and Solutions for Rare Book and Special Collections Librarians," of the ALA. Washington, D.C., 13 June 1998.

Wiegand, Wayne A. "The Politics of Cultural Authority." *American Libraries* 29 (Jan. 1998): 80–82.

Williams, Gordon R. "The Preservation of Deteriorating Books: An Examination of the Problem and Recommendations for a Solution." *Library Journal* 91 (1 Jan. 1966): 51–56.

Chapter 4
Critical Editions

John L. Tofanelli
Johns Hopkins University

One of the obvious purposes of literature collections in libraries is to provide users with access to the texts of literary works. This sounds relatively straightforward. But closer examination reveals questions here that are worthy of exploration. The basic and obvious question—Which works?—is clearly deserving of extensive consideration, and it is dealt with in other chapters in this book. However, there is another question, one that perhaps does not cry out so obviously and immediately for an answer—Which texts of those works? It is within the scope of this question that the present essay falls. Most specifically, this chapter concerns itself with critical editions.

Librarians who are bibliographers for literature share with textual critics a basic awareness that the variety of items claiming to contain the text of a specific work are not interchangeable. We draw upon that awareness when we make decisions about selection (Which editions of a work should the library acquire?), about preservation (Does that brittle, older edition really need to be preserved?), and even about remote storage (Which editions of a work should be kept in the library's browsable main stacks?).

The question Which texts of those works? is thus pervasive in the life of librarians who handle collection management and development for literature. We are therefore necessarily closely implicated in the concerns of textual criticism, and the dialogues going on within that field are important to us. We are concerned, for example, with discussions about the importance of preserving the printed record—those individual copies that reflect the transmission histories of works through various editions and printings. We also must be concerned with those special types of editions that aim to provide both insight into those transmission histories and improved access to the texts of the works themselves—that is, with critical editions.

We are living in a time of particular richness and complexity for critical editions. The latter half of the twentieth century has been called the "age of editing."[1] Since the 1950s, we have seen not only a proliferation in the number of critical editions being published for English and American authors (many of whom had not previously been subjects of critical editing), but also a proliferation of dialogue regarding the aims and methods of critical editing. More recently, electronic formats have introduced new possibilities for the design and conception of critical editions and thus have helped to push the theoretical dialogue in new directions. As electronic editions continue to be created and discussed, the proliferation in the theory, practice, and products of critical editing also is intensifying.

Although fecundity in any scholarly field is welcome, it also can be confusing. How—in this welter of activity, theoretical dialogue, and new products—are librarians to recognize what is of importance? There are no simple formulas to be followed. Librarians must maintain a balanced attentiveness that extends to a variety of areas, one of which is textual criticism itself. This chapter provides an introduction to some of the key issues of textual criticism as they have been formulated during our current "age of editing" and are being revisited in a digital environment.

Critical Editing

In *An Introduction to Bibliographical and Textual Studies*, William Proctor Williams and Craig S. Abbott defined the scope and purpose of textual criticism as follows: "It seeks to identify the texts of a work and their variant states, determine the relation between the texts, discover the sources of textual variation, and establish a text on a scholarly basis." They went on to point out that although textual criticism "broadly considered, . . . is the study of the history of texts, its ultimate aim is still generally thought to be the production of scholarly editions."[2]

Building on Williams and Abbott, one might say that a scholarly edition is an edition designed to have value for a scholar engaged in the historically informed understanding of texts. Of course, not all scholarly editions are critical editions. Williams and Abbott, drawing a distinction that many textual critics would regard as a basic and crucial one, asserted that scholarly editing "takes two major forms: documentary editing and critical editing."[3] Of these two forms, critical editing is the one that requires the most expansive exercise of those activities that Williams and Abbott have identified as being part of textual criticism.

G. Thomas Tanselle offered a lucid and philosophical exploration of the basic distinction between documentary editing and critical editing in his *Rationale of Textual Criticism.* According to Tanselle, diplomatic (or documentary) editing "reproduces the texts of documents," whereas the efforts of critical editing are directed toward "reconstructing the texts of works." There are various reasons why scholars might want to see the text of a document precisely as it stands. Documentary editing aims to provide this in editions that represent historically received documents through means such as transcription or facsimile. Critical editing, on the other hand, reconstructs the texts of works. In Tanselle's conception, a work is an act of "verbal communication," and there is no reason to suppose that any document provides a completely accurate representation of that intended act. Documents typically contain elements of interference or transmissional error, such as misprints, which make them unfaithful reporters of the texts of works. The texts contained in documents, therefore, "must always be suspect," and "the attempt to move closer to an intended form of a work" necessarily "entails the questioning of surviving texts" that are found in documents.[4]

Tanselle's basic terms can be used to supply us with some sense of the complex reporting requirements that critical editions have been designed to meet. In addition to providing an editorial reconstruction of the text of a work, critical editions provide a textual essay that explains the nature of the surviving texts, the methods and assumptions used in questioning them, and the manner in which the critical text was reconstructed. They also provide a textual apparatus that contains a detailed record of the relationship between the reconstructed text and those surviving texts, including a record of emendations made and of textual variants not included in the editorially reconstructed text. The aim of the textual essay and apparatus, ideally, is to allow the reader to understand and question the process by which the text of the work was reconstructed, to reopen to some degree the process of the questioning of surviving texts. Generally speaking, the bulk of the controversy for which the field of textual criticism is well known has concerned the methods and theoretical assumptions involved in the critical reconstruction of the texts of works.

Tanselle has provided a strongly purposeful definition of critical editing, one that is essentially true to the largest ambitions that have traditionally animated the work of textual critics.[5] Nevertheless, his definition posits a constellation of relationships, values, and definitions—involving works, texts, documents, and authorial intentions—that many contemporary textual critics would regard as being, at a minimum, open to question. Although I do think it is true to the history, ambitions, and nature of critical editing to start out with a strongly purposeful definition that is open to controversy, I also regard it as helpful to readers to provide along with it a more modest and minimal definition.

A more modest and minimal definition of this kind can be gathered from Tanselle and others. Referring to what might be regarded as the core and irreducible distinction between documentary editing and critical editing, Tanselle wrote: "Every artifact that carries a verbal text can obviously be treated either way: one can accept a surviving text as it stands; or one can alter it so that it conforms more nearly with some standard." Peter Shillingsburg pointed toward a similar basic definition of critical editing when he wrote that "the result of any emendation is a critical text." No matter what beliefs a textual critic may hold about literary works and their relationships to documents, authorial intentions, or social processes, the act of emendation can usefully be seen as demarcating a critical approach to the scholarly editing of texts. Emendation is a sign that the text of a document has been "questioned" (to use Tanselle's word) and, according to some standard, found wanting. As Gary Taylor has argued, "editing can be defined as the effort to establish a proximate text. The question then becomes proximate to what? Proximate to something we value." The field of critical editing is necessarily complex because the values espoused within textual criticism, as well as the methods used to bring the texts of historically received documents into closer proximity to those values, have been diverse.[6]

The Greg–Bowers Tradition

Many discussions of the theory and potential of electronic scholarly editions make explicit or implicit reference to the copy-text model of critical editing, which was outlined by W. W. Greg and further developed by Fredson Bowers, G. Thomas Tanselle, and others. Charles Ross, for example, near the start of his essay "The Electronic Text and the Death of the Critical Edition" argued that "the birth of the reader-as-editor" (which, in his view, electronic editions will enable) "must be at the cost of the death of the critical edition." He clarified the scope of his reference as follows: "I refer to the 'critical edition' as promulgated by W. W. Greg and promoted by Fredson Bowers and G. Thomas Tanselle." In the closing footnote of his "Rationale of HyperText," Jerome McGann made a somewhat more gracious nod to a past that he nevertheless envisioned as being left behind: "this essay was written in a conscious revisionary relation to W. W. Greg's great essay 'The Rationale of Copy-Text,' which had such a profound influence on twentieth-century textual scholarship."[7]

Such references make perfect sense. Textual critics, animated by new agendas and aware of the developing capabilities of electronic formats, have for some time been engaged in mapping out new possibilities for the conceptualization and arrangement of critical editions. The most obvious point of reference and departure for any reconceptualization of critical editions would logically be the theoretical model that has been dominant in Anglo-American critical editing in the latter half of the twentieth century.

This section offers an overview of Greg–Bowers copy-text theory. I start at this point for two reasons. First, because as a point of reference and departure it provides a necessary context for understanding some recent directions in textual criticism. Second, because it continues to remain an active presence in the playing field of critical editing and literary scholarship. A substantial portion of the critical editions of English and American literature that have been created, and are still being created, in our ongoing "age of editing" are either part of the Greg–Bowers tradition or substantially influenced by it. Although it is important to understand why some textual critics feel that this tradition has exhausted itself (and I will touch on some of the reasons in the following section), it also is important to start out with the recognition that (as with most of the key issues in textual criticism) there is legitimate diversity of opinion on this matter.[8]

In his 1975 essay "Remarks on Eclectic Texts," Bowers expanded on the ideas of the editor and bibliographer R. B. McKerrow to articulate a statement of his own view of the purpose of critical editions: "The aim of a critical edition, remarks McKerrow, is to reconstruct as nearly as is possible from the preserved documents what would have been an author's careful fair copy of his work. One must comment that this ideal edition envisages a careful fair copy of the latest and most comprehensive form and in any case is a theoretical concept."[9]

It is a theoretical concept, on the one hand, because it plays a role within a specific theory of critical editing. But it also is a theoretical concept in the sense of being hypothetical because it cannot be assumed that such a document—a "careful fair copy of the latest and most comprehensive form" of a work—ever existed. Even for those cases in which an author did provide his or her publisher with a careful fair-copy manuscript to use as the basis of a printed edition and where that manuscript is still extant, there is no general reason to assume that that manuscript should represent the "latest and most comprehensive form" of the work. The author ordinarily would have had the option of making revisions at any later stage (for example, during proofs or after the printing of the first edition). In positing this basic theoretical concept—the envisaged careful fair copy of the latest and most comprehensive form of the work—Bowers acknowledged at the outset that the text the critical editor wishes to reconstruct is one that

may never before have existed in integrated form in any single historical document.

Bowers's ultimate aim was to arrive at "an established critical
text embodying the author's full intentions."[10] "Careful fair copy" is
important to the ideal of "full intentions" because it is a state in which
the text is most fully under authorial control in all of its details. Any
printed text, by contrast, will inevitably contain a variety of departures
from an author's careful fair-copy manuscript. These departures can
include both transmissional errors (such as misprints) and deliberate
restylings of textual details by compositors or publishers. "Latest and
most comprehensive form" is a theoretical ideal because, apparently, it
is assumed that the work is growing in a meaningful way toward some
ideal embodiment intended by the author, and an earlier form would
therefore stop short of the author's full intentions.

An example of how these two theoretical ideals—"careful fair copy"
and "latest and most comprehensive form"—can come into play in
Bowers's approach to critical editing can be found in his essay "Some
Principles for Scholarly Editions of Nineteenth-Century American Authors." Hawthorne is the sample case, and Bowers clearly had in mind
The Centenary Edition of the Works of Nathaniel Hawthorne for which
he served as textual editor and which was at that time (1962) just
beginning publication.[11]

Bowers observed that Hawthorne's characteristic punctuation in
the fair-copy manuscripts that are extant for some of his novels is
distinctively meaningful with regard to matters such as emphasis, pa-
renthesis, and subordination. Evaluation of the evidence reveals, further, that the widespread departures from Hawthorne's manuscript
punctuation style in the first editions of those novels and its replacement by a more conventional "printing-house style" can be attributed
to the printers, rather than to any authorial second thoughts. The issue of Hawthorne's punctuation is used by Bowers as evidence intended to demonstrate both the validity of a posited editorial principle—
that an extant authorial manuscript should ordinarily be regarded as
having "paramount authority" for the text of a work—and the relevance
of that principle to Hawthorne's case. Although the manuscripts have
paramount authority, Bowers's argument continued, they cannot be

the sole basis from which a critical edition is derived: for the first editions do contain verbal departures from the manuscripts and some of these departures can reasonably be attributed to revisions made by Hawthorne in proof.[12] To put the situation in terms of Bowers's definition of the aims of a critical edition, we might say that although Hawthorne's manuscripts meet, more or less, the theoretical ideal of authorial "careful fair copy," they do not meet the theoretical ideal of "latest and most comprehensive form" of the work.

Bowers's approach to this textual situation was to establish a critical text by means of eclectic editing. Eclectic editing, as Bowers defined it (and as it has been generally understood), involves the "selection of variants between two or more authoritative texts" in order to reconstruct editorially a "composite text" judged to reflect the authorially intended work more fully and accurately than any single preserved document. Bowers's eclectic procedures in the editing of Hawthorne's *Marble Faun*, for example, involved choosing his fair-copy manuscript as the base text for the critical edition and following it wherever there was no reason to depart from it, but also selecting, and incorporating into the text he was critically establishing those verbal variants from the first edition that could be reasonably judged to be the products of authorial revision.[13]

Although eclectic editing as a general practice is nearly as old as textual criticism itself, the specific approach to eclectic editing promoted by Bowers and exemplified in his approach to Hawthorne does represent a distinctive tradition. The distinctive tradition of eclectic editing finds its point of origin in the theory of copy-text as first articulated by W. W. Greg in his seminal essay "The Rationale of Copy-Text."[14] In this essay, Greg articulated a theory of how an editor might select, approach, and think about the document he or she takes as the basis for a critical edition and how that document might be worked with, along with other authoritative documents, in the establishment of a critical text.

Greg broke down the concept of text in general, and of copy-text in particular, into two elements: *substantives*, or the verbal matter of the text; and *accidentals*, or the formal texture of a text, including spelling, punctuation, capitalization, and word division. He pointed out that this distinction is "practical, not philosophic" and that it is based on the fact that scribes and compositors have reacted differently to these two types of textual elements—in general, aiming at faithfulness to substantives but taking liberties, as they saw fit, with accidentals.[15] Although every transmission of a text creates fresh opportunities for the introduction of corruptions of any kind, the accidentals of a text are, in Greg's view, the aspect most consistently vulnerable to deliberate alteration.

Because each printing of a text provides new opportunities for the introduction of transmissional errors and also for the nonauthorial restyling of accidentals, Greg's idea was that the editor should choose as the basis for a critical text an edition that was as close as possible to the author's manuscript. (For the period with which Greg was dealing—the sixteenth to seventeenth century—the manuscript itself, which would have been the most obvious choice, would typically be no longer extant.) If it was evident that an author had made revisions to a later edition, those revisions judged to be authorial should, Greg argued, be incorporated back into a critical text based on the earliest and least corrupt textual embodiment of the work.[16]

Greg's essay, as many have pointed out, was animated by historical concerns specific to the sixteenth- to seventeenth-century period that was his focus. Bowers's own analysis of that historical grounding and its implications is provided in his "Greg's 'Rationale of Copy-Text' Revisited." He pointed out that during the period of Greg's primary concern, 1550–1650, the English language was "in a state of flux" with regard to matters such as spelling, capitalization, and punctuation, noting that "the widest variety of accidentals prevailed within a general framework of acceptability." Whereas any printing of a text would ordinarily reflect the preferences of individual compositors in those areas, Bowers argued, subsequent printings over time would introduce additional variation as well as modernization into the accidentals of the text.[17] It is clear that, under such circumstances, the printing most immediately derived from an authorial manuscript would have the best chance of preserving something of that manuscript's accidentals.

Bowers acknowledged that Greg himself "made no specific claims for application" of his ideas beyond the historical period that was his focus, but he argued, nevertheless, that "most of his [Greg's] conclusions are as pertinent to the texts of any later period as they are to the age of Shakespeare and Jonson."[18] Although matters such as spelling have become largely standardized, the nonauthorial restyling of authorial accidentals in the publication process has continued, in Bowers's view, to be a matter requiring serious textual-critical attention. Whereas Greg was largely motivated by a philological interest in preserving an author's original spelling, Bowers argued, the editor of modern documents is largely motivated by a critical interest in preserving the author's original punctuation (the accidental that has most commonly been subjected to nonauthorial restyling in the publication of modern texts) and thereby restoring to the text the shades of meaning that that punctuation conveys.[19] In Bowers's view, Greg's key concepts—such as the distinction between accidentals and substantives, and the idea of copy-text—remain useful; and the editor of modern documents joins with Greg "in the wish to preserve as much as possible of the author's accidentals."[20]

Bowers's ideas had influence through his own theoretical writings and through the many critical editions in which he applied copy-text theory to a variety of textual situations. Most famously, perhaps, his ideas had impact on textual criticism through their institutional adaptation by the MLA's Center for Editions of American Authors (CEAA, 1963–1976), whose primary focus was the critical editing of nineteenth-century American literature. The CEAA's *Statement of Editorial Principles and Procedures: A Working Manual for Editing Nineteenth-Century American Texts* was acknowledged to be "chiefly based on the theory and practice of W. W. Greg, Fredson Bowers, and other textual scholars," and it crystallized Bowers's method into something like a step-by-step, recommended procedure.[21]

After assembling and collating "potentially relevant forms of the text," the editor's next crucial obligation, the CEAA *Statement* advises, is the choice of copy-text: "When both manuscript and printed edition are available, still the manuscript, if it is a finished or printer's copy manuscript, normally becomes the copy-text." Next, the editor must be concerned with variations from the copy-text occurring in later relevant forms of the text: "Then, since the history of printed forms of a text is almost invariably a history of increasing non-authorial error and corruption, as well as of real or potential authorial correction and revision, it becomes necessary to examine the collation of all later relevant forms, distinguishing authorial from non-authorial alteration and entering the authorial revisions into the copy-text."[22] The prescriptive tone of the *Statement*, when considered together with the fact that the work of the CEAA was supported by NEH funding, no doubt made some contribution to the flavor of the controversy that was generated by the CEAA and by Bowers's wider application of Greg's ideas.

Although the CEAA was disbanded in 1976 (due to the expiration of the NEH grant that had supported it), its essential work was continued by MLA's newly instituted Center for Scholarly Editions (currently known as the Committee on Scholarly Editions, or CSE). In an article tracing the history of the CEAA and CSE, former CSE chair Jo Ann Boydston articulated some of the continuities between the two bodies. The CSE has continued to oversee projects begun under the CEAA, and it has carried on the "tradition of establishing and publishing standards for editing along with a process of peer review that tries to ensure adherence to those standards." The "scope and purview" of the CSE are more universal than those of the CEAA had been, however, being explicitly extended to scholarly editing more generally, including nonliterary works and works from any country.[23]

The broader scope and purview of the CSE, taking into account a more widely varying range of textual situations, are in fact cited in the CSE's 1977 "Introductory Statement" as one of the reasons why it would be inappropriate for the CSE to publish a manual of editorial procedures as the CEAA had done. The tone and content of that initial "Introductory Statement" and of subsequent comparable statements of principle from the CSE have suggested a more open and philosophical attitude than the CEAA's controversial *Statement of Editorial Principles and Procedures*. It should nevertheless be observed that both the CEAA and the CSE have played an important role in facilitating the practical application of Greg–Bowers copy-text theory in the creation of critical editions.[24]

It would no doubt be possible to sort out a variety of social, economic, cultural, and institutional factors that have contributed to the creation of significant numbers of critical editions for English and American literature since midcentury. However, it is undeniable that the persuasiveness that the copy-text model has held for many textual scholars has contributed to this flourishing. As even McGann, in the midst of one of the best known critiques of copy-text theory, once acknowledged: "It is certainly true" that Bowers's theories "are the most powerful and coherent that we currently possess."[25]

As McGann would no doubt have been quick to remind us, however, every approach to critical editing is simply enabling the formulation of a certain kind of edition that is designed to facilitate the framing and answering of certain types of questions. Although many scholars have been receptive to the Greg–Bowers style of critical edition and the types of questions it allowed them to frame and answer, many have not been. Furthermore, the voices of the opposition have become more numerous, varied, and formidable, especially since the early 1980s.

Versions and Multiple Texts

As is well known, there had been controversies from the beginning regarding Bowers's wider application of Greg's ideas and about the work of the CEAA. Even the less prescriptive "Introductory Statement" of the CSE has been subjected to ideological critique. Substantial and extensive overviews of these controversies have been written, but it is not my purpose to rehearse the basics here.[26] Rather, in this section I intend to provide an account of the concept of "versions." It is a concept that has played a significant role, not simply in the critique of Greg–Bowers copy-text theory, but also in the envisioning of new types of scholarly editions that would be conceived and organized according to a different model.

Peter Shillingsburg has argued convincingly that "the ideal editorial goal for Bowers was . . . a single best text of the work." In his essay, "'Versioning': The Presentation of Multiple Texts," Donald Reiman argued for a movement away from such a goal: "there are good reasons to redirect our energies away from the effort to produce 'definitive' or 'ideal' critical editions and, instead, to encourage the production of editions of discrete versions of works." In this essay, originally delivered as a talk at the 1985 MLA convention, Reiman accurately forecast what has subsequently become one of the dominant areas of concern in textual criticism. The interest in versions might, on the whole, be described as a "textual pluralism" that has placed a new degree of emphasis on authorial revision or other intentional textual interventions that have led to the existence of multiple variant texts for a work.[27]

Hans Zeller, in his seminal 1975 essay "A New Approach to the Critical Constitution of Literary Texts," provided what is perhaps the most thorough and systematic early effort to define a concept of "versions" and to place it in opposition to the Greg–Bowers concept of the finally intended work. Essentially, Zeller asked us to consider the specific nature of the multiple authoritative documents being edited together in the copy-text model of eclectic editing.

He distinguished between "two types of multiple authority which are essentially different from one another." In the first type, "the missing original is represented by several radiating texts, from which their common original is to be reconstructed." This eclectic reconstruction is carried out through "the stemma rules of classical editing," a procedure of which Zeller approved (presumably because it is necessitated by the absence of any extant original authorial document). For the second type of multiple authority, however (the type for which Bowers's eclectic procedures were most commonly used), Zeller called into question the very use of eclectic editing: "Here *one* eclectic text is produced from authoritative documents which differ from one another in essence through the intervention of the author. This eclectic text is supposed among other things to realize the final intention of the author, as far as this is possible on the basis of the extant documents." Zeller objected to this second method of eclectic editing because, in his view, it combines elements from different authorially intended versions of the work and hence results in a "contaminated," that is, wrongfully conflated, "version unknown to the author," a version that has no historically grounded authority.[28]

A key concept here is how the term *version* is to be defined. Bowers and the CEAA (as Zeller acknowledged) did advise editors against the establishment of a single critical text combining variant elements from distinct authorial versions of a work; but they would not have agreed with Zeller's contention that copy-text editing typically involved such a practice. In his "Remarks on Eclectic Texts," Bowers, for example, explained his decision to use eclectic procedures to establish a single critical text of Fielding's *Tom Jones* (by using the first edition as copy-text and incorporating authorial substantive variants from the fourth edition) on the grounds that the first and fourth editions do not "represent quite distinctive artistic concepts." That is, Fielding in the fourth edition was simply refining the work that we know as *Tom Jones*. For Bowers, Fielding's revisions to *Tom Jones* would, then, belong in a different category than Henry James's revisions to his novels for the New York edition (a case he cited as an instance of authorial revision that does create distinct versions). [29] Although the standards of copy-text theory require that editors consider the possibility that a work may exist in more than one version, works existing in multiple versions had, on the whole, been considered to be exceptions to the norm.

Zeller, however, defined versions more sweepingly as "texts with authorial variation." His concept of what constitutes a version is based on his structuralist concept of the mode of existence of literary texts: "Since a text, as text, does not in fact consist of elements but of relationships between them, variation at one point has an effect on invariant sections of the text." Zeller denied that it is feasible to mark, as Bowers did, a borderline between authorially altered texts that do and do not constitute distinct versions. He argued that quantitative criteria regarding number of variants will not work because the introduction of a single variant (he cited change of title as an obvious case) changes the systematic relationship between all the elements of the text, resulting in a new set of relationships and hence a new version. [30]

Any work the critical editor does with authorially variant texts will therefore need, in Zeller's view, to respect the synchronic structure of the elements within each version. Eclectic editing, by contrast, creates "an arbitrary synchronization of non-synchronic elements." The attempt to reconstruct the text of the work as finally intended by its author cannot, in Zeller's view, be used to justify eclectic editing because each version "represents a semiotic system which was valid at a specific time," and all are of interest from a historical point of view. [31]

Zeller was not simply writing as a critic of Bowers. Rather, he was writing from within an alternative editorial tradition—the modern German tradition of the "historical-critical edition." In contrast to the eclectically edited clear-text editions favored by the CEAA, historical-critical editions of works existing in multiple variant authoritative documents place their emphasis on displaying in synoptic fashion the genesis and development of the literary work within and across those documents.[32] Although the idea of versions was to become increasingly important in Anglo-American textual criticism, and although Zeller is frequently cited in connection with that idea, it is interesting to note that the type of German historical-critical edition that Zeller had in mind as a counter-tradition to copy-text editing has not attained a comparable popularity.

Reiman's essay "Versioning: The Presentation of Multiple Texts" expressed a more characteristically Anglo-American attitude toward versions. He called for "the separate presentation of each major document and edition of a work," allowing for relatively light forms of editing for the removal of actual transmissional error. Reiman cited as a precursor for his concept of "versioning" not the German historical-critical edition (a model he explicitly rejected) but, rather, the long tradition of parallel-text editions, such as harmonies of the Gospels, which simply present the diverse texts side by side for comparison.[33] The present enthusiasm for hypertext editions might be regarded as continuous with Reiman's interest in parallel-text editions because hypertext editions might be considered to be a technologically agile outgrowth of the parallel-text tradition—allowing for side-by-side comparison of divergent texts, each of which retains its own integrity.

Jerome McGann has been perhaps the best known exponent of hypertext scholarly editions. Some concept of versions might be said to have played a key role throughout his theoretical writings, from *A Critique of Modern Textual Criticism* (which contains his early critique of the Greg–Bowers tradition of copy-text editing) through his more recent explorations of hypertext theory and editing and of a "materialist hermeneutics" of texts. In *A Critique of Modern Textual Criticism*, McGann cited Zeller and made use of a concept of versions that is roughly congruent with Zeller's. Like Zeller, McGann rooted his discussion of versions in a consideration of the distinctive nature of the multiple-authority situation faced by the editor of modern texts.

McGann argued that that editor typically has a "wide range of published and prepublished textual forms . . . at his disposal" and that these forms typically represent "divergent patterns of varying purposes and intentions" in which the author was involved. In McGann's view, the "first and crucial problem" facing the editor of modern works, and especially of late modern works, is "not how to discover corruptions but how to distinguish and finally choose between textual versions." He argued that copy-text editing in the Bowers tradition has obscured this problem by taking as its model the editing of classical texts (in which the aim is to reason back from variously corrupt surviving textual witnesses to an approximation of an actual historical "lost original"). Copy-text editing, however, in McGann's view, has posited for its "lost original" something that is "a pure abstraction"—"the idea of a finally intended text"—and it treats distinct authorial versions as if they were merely witnesses to that (nonhistorical) "lost original."[34]

McGann's concern with textual versions is part of his larger concern with the social nature of the processes of literary production. Whereas Bowers was ultimately concerned with the text of the work as shaped by "the author's final and uninfluenced artistic intentions," McGann is interested in the variety of texts that are generated for a work in "the process of literary production" and the ways in which those texts reflect a variety of "social interactions and purposes." Authorial intention, which is pictured by McGann as being properly responsive to such interactions rather than as purely artistic, is a key source of such textual mutations. But the intentions of other persons involved in the social institutions of literary production also are seen as having a valid role in shaping the shifting incarnations of a work. McGann argued, for example, that varied "interventions" into the text of a poem take place "as soon as it begins its passage to publication." These interventions might originate with the author or with others, such as publishers, engaged in the process of literary production. He suggested that such interventions might be seen collectively, not as "contamination" but, rather, as "a process of training the poem for its appearances in the world."[35]

Although McGann does not consistently use or foreground the term *versions* in his more recent writings, his ongoing interest in the multiple forms taken by a work is clearly continuous with the interest in versions he articulated in *A Critique of Modern Textual Criticism*. That interest, however, is now grounded in a more explicitly "materialist hermeneutics" that links him to other theorists, such as D. F. McKenzie, who explore the sociological implications of bibliographical phenomena.[36] McGann argued in *The Textual Condition* that "meaning is transmitted through bibliographical as well as linguistic codes" and that all texts involve a "laced network" of those codes. The bibliographical code includes a variety of features that have not been traditionally regarded as part of the text, such as "typefaces, bindings, book prices, page format."[37]

Focusing on bibliographical signifiers and the materiality of the text allows one to see how a new version of a work can be generated without any element of authorial revision being introduced. McGann provided an example of this in his discussion of the varying early bibliographic incarnations of Byron's poem "Fare Thee Well!" (a poem with autobiographical significance that had a bearing on Byron's personal reputation). It was first privately printed by the author for circulation among friends, then published unauthorized in a newspaper, and then published with the author's consent in a book. The scenario, as McGann described it, is one in which the author loses and then attempts to regain control of a text whose social and autobiographical significance varies according to each of these bibliographic embodiments. McGann concluded that there are "several distinct versions of . . . 'Fare Thee Well!' but each of these versions has virtually the same linguistic content."[38] What distinguishes these three texts as distinct versions of the poem, each inviting different kinds of interpretation, is not their linguistic content but their manner of being materially embodied and disseminated in various social contexts.

McGann's interest in the multiple bibliographically embodied versions of a work ultimately led him beyond a critique of any specific editorial method to one of the limitations of codex-based critical editing in general. The traditional focus of critical editing on establishing a stabilized representation of the linguistic text of the work is, in his view, a by-product of the constraints of the codex format. "The exigencies of the book form," McGann wrote, "have forced editorial scholars to develop fixed points of relation—the definitive text, 'copy text,' 'ideal text,' 'Ur text,' 'standard text,' and so forth—in order to conduct a book-bound navigation by coded forms through large bodies of documentary materials." With the advent of hypertext, however, with its more expansive navigational and representational capacities, "Such fixed points no longer have to govern the editing of documents."[39] If Greg's rationale of copy-text had been a means for moving from the multiple bibliographic embodiments of a work to a single linguistic text to represent that work, McGann's rationale of hypertext might be seen as a means of returning scholarly editions to those multiple bibliographic embodiments that now can be represented and interlinked in ways that will facilitate comparative analysis.

A general tendency of McGann, Zeller, Reiman, and many of the textual critics articulating an interest in versions has been to place an emphasis on the integrity of historically received documents and to question the validity of overarching concepts (such as the "work" and "authorial intention") that had been used to justify extensive editorial interventions into the texts of those documents. Zeller sounded a key note early on when he proposed that the concept of authorial intention as a guiding principle in critical editing should be replaced with the broader concept of the authorization of versions. In Zeller's view, Bowers's method began at the level of individual textual elements, evaluating and making choices among all variant elements of the relevant texts in the light of a posited concept of an authorially intended work. On the other hand, Zeller characterized authorial intention as "impossible to determine," and suggested that versions in whose production the author participated should be on the whole accepted as authorized except for cases of "textual faults"— clear transmissional errors that might be regarded as "intermittent suspensions of authority." Such "textual faults" would call for editorial emendation, but only after being identified and evaluated according to fairly rigorous criteria.[40]

Mary-Jo Kline has characterized the issue of versioning this way: "The current debate among literary scholars [is] over the value of eclectic clear texts versus editorial methods that retain more 'documental' elements. . . ." Certainly, an emphasis on the retention of documental elements as somehow important to the scholarly representation of versions might be regarded as a discernible line of argument running through Zeller, Reiman, and McGann. It comes to fullest flower, perhaps, in McGann's valuing of facsimiles for their ability to reproduce the bibliographical code in addition to the linguistic one. Such an emphasis moves these critics away from methods and values that have been traditionally accepted as ideally appropriate for the editing of literary works (those of eclectic critical editing) and toward methods and values that have been viewed as more appropriate for the editing of historical documents (those of documentary editing). This particular tradition of thinking about versions can be understood in Kline's terms as a part of the "continued academic debate" that has, since the 1980s, "called into question the binarism of 'historical' versus 'literary' editing."[41]

It might seem possible to say that such critics have simply moved away from an untenable idealism (the hope of reconstructing the authorially intended work) to a straightforward realism (the fact of multiple variant documents). Yet, to do so would scarcely do justice to the abiding complexities of textual criticism. There is no universal agreement about what a "version" is or as to how a "version" should be edited.[42] (This is essentially as open to controversy as the more familiar question of what a "work" is and how a "work" should be edited.) To say that many textual critics have moved away from a concern with editing works to a concern with editing versions does not mean that they have necessarily moved to more straightforward theoretical territory.

Tanselle, who probably has been the most philosophically self-aware exponent of the Greg–Bowers tradition, has acknowledged that, prior to the recent rise of interest in versions, "insufficient attention had . . . been paid to intentions other than final intention." Yet, he also has raised valid questions about the concept of versions. Suggesting that arguments emphasizing versions "do not always avoid the fallacy of confusing versions of works with texts of documents," Tanselle wrote: "There is reason to be interested in the text of any individual document, but editors of critical editions aim to go beyond documents, to works or versions of works. The works, or versions, are what they are trying to reconstruct, not what they find in documents. An eclectic process, drawing readings from different documents, can serve the goal of reconstructing an early or intermediate version just as well as a final version."[43]

Tanselle has, in fact, argued for "the necessity for eclecticism in intentionalist editing, whether or not distinct versions are involved." The editor who is oriented toward authorial intention will necessarily, in Tanselle's view, be seeking to reconstruct an intended act of "verbal communication" (whether it be a work or a version of a work). That act might span across documents and might be misrepresented by any of those documents in any number of ways. As long as the editor has taken care to distinguish the relevant documents belonging to a specific version or work, there would be no reason for refraining from an eclectic treatment of those documents because the editor's primary loyalty is not to the integrity of documents but, rather, to the integrity of the act of verbal communication that needs to be reconstructed. In contrast to Zeller's position that eclecticism produces "contaminated," or wrongly conflated, texts, Tanselle asserted that "Choosing readings from different documentary texts, far from mixing versions, may be the only way to isolate them."[44]

Peter Shillingsburg has correctly observed that "there is no objective principle for identifying the versions of the work." Much of what an editor does in seeking to identify and arrive at an editorial representation of a version depends, therefore, on how he or she defines *version*. Definitions of this term can vary widely, ranging from Shillingsburg's "a version is the ideal form of a work as it was intended at a single moment or period for the author" to Jack Stillinger's "A *version* of a work is a physically embodied text of a work." A definition that conceives of version as "ideal form" will be hospitable to a carefully circumscribed type of eclectic intentionalist editing. A definition that tends to equate *version* with *document*, on the other hand, will not be—because the "net effect" of such an equation, as Shillingsburg wrote, "is to prevent the editor of any newly edited text from extracting the work of one particular agent, say the author, from the multiplicity of variant documents." It is clear, therefore, that varying theoretical definitions of version will correspond with varying editorial approaches and will furthermore lead to varying results in terms of the text that is editorially constructed to represent any given version of a work.[45]

A careful overview of the field of discussion demonstrates that there is no single correct way to define, theorize about, or produce editions of versions. Nevertheless, it is the case that a general pattern can be identified. Versioning might be thought of, on the whole, as part of a movement away from the type of eclectic editing practice that tended typically in the Greg–Bowers tradition to establish a single critical text to represent a work. It might be thought of as a "theory of textual pluralism" (to borrow Stillinger's phrase) that places a new degree of emphasis on the integrity and significance of the multiple variant texts of a work. Unlike copy-text theory, versioning does not represent any coherent body of editorial principles (although many proponents reject eclectic editing and favor methods that are closer to those of documentary editing). Electronic formats, because of their flexible capacity to organize large and complex bodies of related texts, have been viewed as hospitable to the editorial presentation of multiple versions of a work.

Any thorough attempt to assess the status of the concept of versions in textual criticism would need to assess not simply the state of theoretical discussion, but also what is happening in the actual production of editions. After surveying the widespread theoretical interest in versions or variant texts of a work in an overview of recent textual criticism, D. C. Greetham acknowledged that "it would have to be admitted that eclectic, intentionalist editions are still being produced more often than any other form, perhaps because it will take some time for practice to catch up with theory."[46] Although the overall body of versional editions is on the increase, especially in the electronic environment, the proportion that Greetham described in 1992 has not been substantially disrupted. Whether time will close the gap between what is popular in theory and what most editors are actually doing remains to be seen.

What remains of most interest will not be the prospect of shifting patterns in the production of specific types of editions but, rather, how electronic editions might change the landscape of the discussion and the way that we think about editions. Clearly, electronic editions represent a new range of possibilities for the presentation of multiple texts and those possibilities include considerable kinds of flexibility that could be used to accommodate a variety of editorial and readerly approaches to the texts being represented.

Electronic Scholarly Editions: Theory, Practice, and Emerging Standards

One might say of electronic scholarly editions (as Shillingsburg says of electronic publication in general) that they are still in their "incunabular" stage.[47] Considering this, one cannot assume that their conventions for the representation and organization of information are worked out to the maximal potential level of sophistication. Nevertheless, it will be helpful to consider some of the ways in which scholars are currently theorizing about the potential of electronic editions and, at a more concrete level, some of the ways in which they are exploring that potential in the creation of actual electronic editions. Necessarily looming over any consideration of theory and practice is the omnipresent question of standards. For electronic scholarly editions, standards have to do not simply with scholarly accountability, but also with basic issues affecting all electronic texts, such as access and preservation. Although this section does not attempt to give a comprehensive overview of these three areas—theory, practice, and standards—it does touch on all of them in a focused consideration of some of the characteristics and potential of electronic scholarly editions.

It has been argued that printed critical editions (especially those of the clear-text variety favored by the CEAA) have contributed to a misleading impression of the stability of the texts of literary works. Critics who have made such arguments, such as McGann and Greetham, also have seen electronic editions as counteracting this misleading impression by providing for and promoting readerly engagement with the full relevant variant texts of a work. This new potential for and promotion of readerly engagement with variant texts has been seen as having various kinds of implications for the theory and practice of scholarly editing.

Greetham, for example, in his essay "Editorial Theory: From Modernism to Postmodernism," has argued that *variance* is "the innate condition of textuality" and that the proper recognition of this innate condition can be provided by a "postmodernist literary editing" that "forbids the sort of closure that the 'definitive editions' of eclecticism actively sought." The postmodern textual edition, as conceptualized by Greetham, will be distinguished by its foregrounding of its own constructed nature and by its hospitality to the "unlimited recombination of all its components." He suggested that "the posteclectic texts of current textual criticism" (among which he includes genetic texts and versioned texts) participate in this tendency, but also that this tendency will ultimately come to fulfillment only through "the facilities of electronic reader-driven editions," which will be needed to achieve the requisite "flexibility and lack of closure." "Postmodernist literary editing," as Greetham envisions it, shares values and beliefs with postmodernist literary theory because it "operates under the assumptions of poststructuralist *différence,* the continued deferral of absolute meaning" (which, in this case, would seem to mean deferral of any sense of closure as to what constitutes the text of the work).[48]

Shillingsburg's concept of editorial orientations suggests a somewhat different way of conceptualizing the potential of electronic editions and their relationship to existing traditions of scholarly editing. Shillingsburg has argued convincingly that there are multiple legitimate formal orientations in scholarly editing, each of which is grounded in distinctive beliefs about the nature and locus of authority and, consequently, about the aims and purposes of scholarly editing. One might consider as an example of an orientational perspective on electronic editions Shillingsburg's discussion of one of the emerging models for noneclectic editing in an electronic environment—the "archive" model, which he succinctly has described as "a webbed, introduced, and annotated array of existing authoritative texts."[49]

He has pointed out that such a webbed array of existing texts will be satisfactory to editors of a sociological orientation because the various forms in which a work circulated shed light on the kinds of "social, economic, and artistic exchanges" in which that work was involved. Editors of an authorial orientation, on the other hand, will not, in Shillingsburg's view, be satisfied with providing a documentary "archive" alone, because it contains only a mass of variously flawed documents and fails to provide an editorial construction, from that mass, of the authorially intended text[s] of the work. Authorially oriented editors, Shillingsburg wrote, will "in the electronic edition as in the print edition, provide an edited, critical, eclectic text." The difference in the electronic environment is that now such eclectic texts can be "webbed and cross-referenced into the archive as was never possible in the print world."[50]

Shillingsburg has written of scholarly editions in general that the textual editor has "the privilege of following the demands of his own formal orientation in preparing the text but with the corollary responsibility of providing an apparatus that will acknowledge and perhaps even suit the needs of students with other orientations as well." In an electronic edition, the area in which that corollary responsibility can be exercised has been expanded because the "apparatus" now can include an archive of interlinked relevant documents. This holds out the possibility that electronic scholarly editions might be designed so that they meet in distinctive ways the ideal goal that Shillingsburg has identified for scholarly editions in general—that they might be "genuinely rich resources for literary study, regardless of the editor's formal orientation."[51] Although some textual critics seem to imply that the advent of electronic scholarly editions heralds the triumph of one set of editorial beliefs and values over another, Shillingsburg provides a salutary reminder that the existence of multiple legitimate formal orientations will be a factor of ongoing importance in understanding the creation and use of all products of scholarly editing.

An emphasis on readerly freedom to determine how to work with textual materials in an electronic edition has been widely and variously articulated. Charles Ross, for example, in his essay "The Electronic Text and the Death of the Critical Edition," not only emphasized the freedom of users to approach the edition from a variety of perspectives, but also envisioned this freedom as displacing the idea of any critically established reading text. He wrote of "the birth of the reader-as-editor" and envisioned "*electronically layered texts* edited from data banks or archives by readers themselves." The "data banks" Ross posited are not neutrally objective transcriptions of documents but, rather, contain "textual data marked by editors." These data banks would allow readers to generate texts in accordance with varying principles: for example (in a possible scenario Ross envisioned), versions retaining all transmissive variations or versions emended to delete transmissive variations of specific types and origins. It would further be an important feature of such electronic texts, Ross argued, that they provide the "means for readers to substitute their own markup," reflecting their own textual-critical judgments, for the markup originally supplied by the editor.[52]

Ross's essay, beginning with its very title, foregrounded a disjunction between print and electronic scholarly editions. It is, nevertheless, possible to find in his essay points of continuity between them. Ross wrote, for example, that "we can't make sense of" documents "until we re-create their origins and authorities."[53] Making investigations into and judgments about the origins and authorities of documents and the textual elements within them is what textual critics have always done (and what the editor of Ross's electronic edition will be obliged to do in order to provide the requisite textual markup). Traditionally, those judgments have been conveyed to readers by means of an edition providing a critically established reading text and an accompanying apparatus. Ross asked us to reenvision radically the way in which editors convey their textual-critical judgments to readers and the way in which readers interact with editions. Nevertheless, the bottom-line concerns he saw as animating the work of both editors and readers are similar to what they have always been—understanding the origins and authorities of documents and textual variants.

To begin thinking about the character and potential of electronic scholarly editions, it is important to start out with the awareness that scholarly editing in general involves not simply a range of possible editorial approaches, but also a range of possible textual situations. Therefore, I have chosen as examples for consideration two electronic editions that cover texts from widely different historical periods: *The Wife of Bath's Prologue on CD-ROM*, edited by Peter Robinson, and *The Complete Writings and Pictures of Dante Gabriel Rossetti: A Hypermedia Research Archive*, edited by Jerome McGann. Both editions deal with works that exist in multiple authoritative documents, but the textual situation represented by those documents is in each case quite different.

The debate over the concept of versions, as detailed in the previous section of this chapter, is grounded (as Zeller made clear) in one specific type of multiple-authority situation—one in which authoritative documents differ from one another due to the presence of variations directly introduced by the author. This is a typical situation for modern texts, but not for texts (such as Chaucer's) transmitted through scribal cultures (a situation in which variation more commonly arises from practices of scribal copying and elaboration).[54] Although the type of textual situation an editor is dealing with will not determine the kind of editorial approach taken, it might be thought of as constituting a kind of playing field that does impose some boundaries on the range of meaningful possible approaches.

Chaucer's *Wife of Bath's Prologue on CD-ROM*, edited by Peter W. Robinson, is a good example of an electronic edition dealing with texts transmitted through a scribal culture. Robinson emphasized the instability of the text of the *Wife's Prologue* in his discussion of the types of variation (in wording, spelling, and letterforms) and the amount of variation to be found among the fifty-eight textual witnesses that survive from the period up to 1500. To represent this range of variation and render it susceptible to searching and analysis, Robinson includes in the CD-ROM facsimiles for all fifty-eight witnesses accompanied by searchable transcriptions that are SGML encoded to be responsive to scholarly inquiry.[55]

Although Robinson recognized the importance of making all of these materials accessible to readers, he also recognized the importance of addressing the "difficult and legitimate" questions that any reader might ask when faced with such a wide range of variant documents: "What is the relationship between the manuscripts? . . . After all, what is Chaucer most likely to have written?"[56] In *The Wife of Bath's Prologue on CD-ROM* and in the larger *Canterbury Tales* project of which it is a part, these difficult questions are addressed at different levels.

On the one hand, the CD-ROM does include one privileged text: a "very lightly edited" version of the Hengwrt manuscript text, the textual witness that Robinson judged to be most authoritative. This is offered to the user as a potential base of operation for exploring relationships among all the texts. On the other hand, in the *Canterbury*

Tales Project as a whole, the editors (making use of the advantages of electronic collation) are engaged in a larger and more ambitious effort to determine in greater detail the relationship between all of the extant fifteenth-century textual witnesses for *The Canterbury Tales* and the relative authority of the textual elements in each. As Robinson wrote of this larger effort in his introduction to the CD-ROM: "To settle, as well as one can, what Chaucer is most likely to have written for any one word in any one part of *The Canterbury Tales* we must look at every word in every one of these eighty-eight witnesses to the text."[57]

One of the strengths of electronic editions is that they allow for this kind of open-endedness and development. We do not need to wait for the final analysis of the editors in order to have access to digital representations of the materials they are working with. Furthermore, the result of current editorial analysis—the best text that has been singled out as a potential base of operations—does not place undue constraints on the user. Robinson has emphasized that scholars who disagree with the editors' opinion about which textual witness is most authoritative will be free "to ignore what we say but still make use of our edition," adding "and that is how it should be."[58]

McGann's work-in-progress, *The Complete Writings and Pictures of Dante Gabriel Rossetti: A Hypermedia Research Archive,* is proving to be an influential example of an electronic edition dealing with modern texts. McGann identifies two aspects of Rossetti's work that, in his view, encourage the editor to explore the possibilities that become available in an electronic environment. First is "the extreme 'nervousness' or 'instability' of Rossetti's texts and pictures," with each work existing in "a complex array of 'versions.'" Second is the fact that Rossetti "worked in two media" (literary and pictorial) "and he sought to integrate the work of each of these mediums into the other." These two aspects generate a variety of complex interrelationships that can, in McGann's view, best be represented through an electronic edition that makes use of "hypertextual structures" and multiple media.[59]

McGann suggests that electronic editions in general, and *The Rossetti Archive* in particular, can approximate "an ideal scholarly edition" insofar as they might "marry the respective virtues of facsimile editing and critical editing." The hypothesis of such a "marriage" is clearly part of McGann's larger effort to rethink and resolve what he calls "the long-standing tension (in editorial theory) between documentary and critical editing" (facsimile editing being one variety of documentary editing). The marriage that he envisions is one in which critical editing is no longer defined by one of the key goals that has traditionally made it recognizable and clearly distinct from documentary editing: the goal of reconstructing a maximally authoritative reading text for a work. In *The Rossetti Archive,* there is "no 'copytext' or 'basic text' or 'reading text,'" only a network of readable documents from which the user can choose. What *The Rossetti Archive* "aims to reconstruct" is "a library of all the (historically received) textually relevant states of Rossetti's writings and pictures."[60]

McGann writes of "building a database model for a full critical presentation of literary and pictorial works as they exist in their original documentary formats." The critical component, as he sees it, is incorporated into a variety of aspects of *The Rossetti Archive.* For example, the editor provides "informed commentary . . . on the historical relation and status of the various texts"; and the original materials are subjected to "rigorous formal analysis," which produces information that is then "codified in the SGML structure." The extent to which the completed *Rossetti Archive* will address such traditional concerns of critical editing as the identification and emendation of textual corruptions remains to be seen. What is clear is that McGann is asking the reader to entertain a reinvented vision of critical editing, as an activity that is primarily analytical in its aims. The virtue of "a good critical edition," in McGann's view, is its ability to expose the "structural and historical relations" of a "complete set of textually relevant documents."[61]

In thinking about electronic scholarly editions, librarians will need to be concerned not simply with the contents, goals, or theoretical groundings of specific editions, but also with the larger questions of how all electronic editions might fit together in the context of a developing viable digital library. It is for this reason that librarians need to be aware of developing standards for the encoding of textual materials designed to support humanistic research. The "Guidelines for Electronic Scholarly Editions," from the MLA's Committee on Scholarly Editions, voiced what appears to be the emerging consensus when it recommended that "It is preferable to use the implementation of Standard Generalized Markup Language (SGML) specifically devised for coding electronic texts, the Text Encoding Initiative (TEI)."[62]

At its most basic level, the *TEI Guidelines for Electronic Text Encoding and Interchange (P3)* defined "a standard form for the interchange of textual material" in humanities research. This involves a "minimal set of conventions for text encoding"—a core set of recommended or required SGML elements. In addition, the TEI provides sets of optional elements designed to encode more sophisticated kinds of textual information. The minimal set works to ensure a base level of interoperable functionality among all TEI conformant texts, and the optional sets allow for the creation of scholarly editions that address some of the complex textual-critical questions that have traditionally been addressed by critical editions.[63]

The Text Encoding Initiative began with the formation of four international scholarly working committees in 1988. The *Guidelines* were initially published in "a firstdraft version" in 1990. THe current revision (TEI P3) is numbered as the third revision. It is no longer designated as a draft, although work continues to revise and supplement it as needed (with the avowed aim of avoiding the introduction of fundamental inconsistencies). The *Guidelines* do not represent a closed system. Rather, they aim for flexibility and expandability, providing rules for how they might be adapted or modified to cover textual situations that have not been anticipated in the *Guidelines* themselves.[64]

In his essay "Textual Criticism and the Text Encoding Initiative," C. M. Sperberg-McQueen identified "three overarching goals" for electronic scholarly editions: "accessibility, longevity, and intellectual integrity." He pointed out that the TEI encoding scheme provides support for all of these goals. It "secures accessibility and longevity by providing a software- and hardware- independent notation for the creation of electronic texts." This allows those texts to be usable on any platform (accessibility), and it also allows them to survive beyond the life cycle of specific forms of software or hardware (longevity). Although the intellectual integrity of any edition must remain the responsibility of its editor, Sperberg-McQueen pointed out, the TEI encoding scheme does "provide the mechanisms needed to allow textual critics to create intellectually serious electronic editions," insofar as it provides tags designed to address "a variety of problems arising in textual criticism." Among the tags he discussed as examples are tags indicating the following features of source documents: variant readings, canceled or added material, or text that is not clearly legible.[65]

The "Guidelines for Electronic Scholarly Editions," approved by the MLA's Committee on Scholarly Editions in September 1997, outlined a number of technical and scholarly "desiderata" for electronic scholarly editions.[66] Many of these desiderata could roughly be mapped onto the three overarching goals ("accessibility, longevity, and intellectual integrity") identified by Sperberg-McQueen. Although it would be possible to value the CSE "Guidelines" as a brief and general introduction to selected key issues relating to accessibility and longevity, I believe that their most distinctive and unique contribution lies in their efforts to articulate standards of scholarly integrity for electronic scholarly editions. Such scholarly standards are not standards in the ISO sense, and may not be beyond the reach of controversy; but they can nevertheless serve as a worthy starting point for librarians who wish to consider electronic scholarly editions as part of an ongoing and evolving tradition of scholarly editing.

The "Guidelines" state that the CSE does "not prescribe a particular method of editing"; and they themselves would seem to bear witness to this. Their emphasis is on the components and functions desirable in electronic scholarly editions rather than on the application of particular editorial theories. On a question distinctly relevant to the issue of versioning (which was surveyed in the previous section of this chapter), the "Guidelines" take a catholic view: "The decision to use a single or multiple base- or copy-text, parallel texts, sequential versions or a combination of these, should be appropriate to the goal of the edition." What *is* important is that the edition contains a "textual essay" that, among other things, provides "a clear, convincing, and thorough statement of the edition's theoretical principles" and that it "sets forth the history of the text and its physical forms." It is also to be expected that the edition, taken as a whole, should be "appropriate, complete, and coherently conceived."[67]

Although the "Guidelines" do emphasize many standards of scholarly accountability that electronic editions should share in common with printed ones, they also emphasize the desirability of taking advantage of the greater expansiveness and flexibility of the electronic environment. The following may be considered as an example: "If the editor has constructed a critical text on the basis of full-text transcriptions, collation software allows the user to verify the editor's critical practice as well as to vary the editorial assumptions (e.g., by selecting another version as base text) and criteria (e.g., preservation of accidentals)."[68] Such advice allows us to identify a fourth goal for electronic scholarly editions (to be added on to the three already mentioned): flexibility. An electronic edition should be able to accommodate itself to a variety of readerly approaches to, and manipulations of, the material it includes. Adequate text encoding based on a standardized encoding system is as essential to this fourth goal as to the first three.

Although I am focusing on critical editions in this chapter as a whole, I have throughout this section on electronic editions been using the more general term *scholarly editions*. This has been deliberate. Critical editions in the print environment have tended to be characterized by a unity of purpose that makes it relatively easy to discuss their distinguishing characteristics. In the more expansive and flexible electronic environment, however, one more commonly tends to find scholarly editions that incorporate a diverse range of editorial goals. I would maintain that the traditional conceptual distinction between two forms of scholarly editing—documentary editing and critical editing—continues to make sense and that it will continue to provide a helpful context in terms of which any specific editorial goal or combination of goals might be understood. Because the electronic environment seems especially conducive to the flourishing of hybrid editions, however, it makes sense for any wide-ranging discussion to make use of the more general term—scholarly editions.

Conclusion

This essay began with the suggestion that librarians who develop and manage collections for literature have always been to some degree involved with the concerns of textual criticism. The advent of electronic scholarly editions will likely bring for many of us a closer and more self-aware involvement in those concerns. If we are to be concerned about the usability of such editions and their interoperability in the context of a digital library, we need to be able to think carefully about what usability means from a scholar's point of view. What are the purposes for which scholarly editions are used? More specifically, what are the purposes for which critical editions are used? What kinds of questions are being addressed to them? To what degree might electronic editions themselves have an influence on possible new directions for those uses and questions?

Things were simpler for us in the print environment. We knew that scholarly editions came in a variety of types designed for varying purposes, but we also knew that critical editions held a place of significant prestige among them. For those of us in research libraries, critical editions have not typically been evaluated individually. Critical editions of the works of specific authors, such as *The Clarendon Edition of the Novels of George Eliot*, are often ongoing projects that have been typically acquired on standing order. Although we might take an interest in the controversies about one or more of the volumes in such an edition, or even about the overall premises of the edition as a whole, this would largely be an intellectual interest, having little influence on acquisition decisions. Controversy is inevitable in critical editing, after all; and scholars always will want the chance to judge any edition for themselves. The stringent requirements of critical editing, as these have traditionally been understood, have meant, furthermore, that significant critical editions, even for major works, are few and far between. It is unlikely that a bibliographer for literature would want his or her user community to miss out on the specific types of insight—into the text of a work and into its transmissional history—that critical editions have aimed to provide. Even librarians at less affluent academic libraries have felt the importance of having a core collection of "standard" editions for canonical authors. It is a premise of such basic guides to collection building as *Books for College Libraries* that such editions are crucial even to collections that primarily support undergraduate study.

All of the above circumstances have created a situation in which it has not been truly necessary for us to ask ourselves detailed questions about what any given critical edition is trying to accomplish. Nor was it truly necessary for us to test the design and functionality of any such edition by addressing appropriate questions to its textual apparatus. Nor was it incumbent upon us to read the textual essay and to think about the reasons why some texts of the work were regarded by the editor as authoritative and others were not. Although many of us have taken an individual scholarly interest in such questions, there has not been any collectively perceived professional urgency requiring us as a group to take a detailed interest in them.

I would argue that the advent of electronic scholarly editions represents what should be regarded as a collectively perceived professional urgency of this kind. Electronic editions make a variety of claims, some grounded on an alleged break in continuity between print and electronic environments. We need to be able to evaluate such claims, not by simply referring them back to established conventions of printed critical editions, but by considering them in the light of the ongoing and evolving scholarly concerns of textual criticism. We need to be able to articulate what features are desirable in electronic scholarly editions and in a digital library that contains them.

Librarians are obliged to consider that there are, and always will be, a wide range of things that scholars will need and wish to do with both critically edited texts and the source materials on which those edited texts are based. With this in mind, librarians will need to have sensitivities that extend in at least three directions. What are library users doing and wanting to do with critical editions? What are some of the current and ongoing concerns of textual criticism? And, finally, what are editors and publishers currently doing? Inattentiveness to any one of these three areas could result in a loss of perspcetive. Although we need to maintain a strong focus on the current needs of our users, we also must be able to anticipate their future needs and to be on the lookout for a range of things that our users might decide (after they have been made aware of them) that they really do need, after all.

All of the products of critical editing have value of some kind. They are simply designed for different occasions or uses, or indeed for different scholarly habits. Although many scholars have recently critiqued the limitations and conventions of the textual apparatus in printed critical editions, others may feel at home with those limitations and conventions, but frustrated or lost in a hypertext environment. There are clearly valuable opportunities for user education here, but in such education we also should be attentive to what users can teach us—both about how they handle information seeking in diverse formats and also about possible desirable features in this developing genre of electronic scholarly editions.

We should not expect that all library users will wish systematically to transfer their engagements with critical editions to the format that provides the largest quantity of manipulable information. Critical editions are used by a variety of scholars and readers for a variety of purposes. Any individual may, furthermore, have different purposes in mind at different times. When the relatively continuous experience of reading a critically edited text is of paramount interest, a clear-text printed critical edition will be more efficient and helpful than the most thorough and multifaceted hypertext edition. Electronic scholarly editions cannot be regarded as superseding printed ones because, from the user's point of view, they do not provide the same balance of functions. Multiple-format scholarly editions, consisting of both print and electronic components, have already been envisioned.[69] The prospect of such editions raises the hope that scholars who currently devalue either the print or the electronic format might come to recognize that each possesses its own distinctive strengths as a vehicle for the scholarly representation of literary texts.

In his essay "Remarks on Eclectic Texts," Bowers wrote that "the main scholarly demand is for an established critical text embodying the author's full intentions (not merely one segment of them in an imperfect form) insofar as these can be ascertained by an expert who has had available all documentary sources and has devoted time and study to their transmissional history and authority."[70] Certainly, looking at such a statement now, with an awareness of the variety of alternative scholarly demands that have since been compellingly articulated, makes one aware that a great deal of water has passed under the bridge since 1975, when Bowers's essay was first published. Bowers's words can serve the useful function of reminding us of how, in a relatively short period of time, what appears to be "the main scholarly demand" can be relegated to the status of one demand among many, or even, in the eyes of some critics, removed entirely from the realm of realistic or valid scholarly demands. Because librarians build collections for future users as well as present ones, I would hope that such an example would make us cautious regarding any excessively single-minded articulations (whatever their vintage might be) of what scholars need from critical editions.

Although this quotation from Bowers provides us with a cautionary example of the potentially transitory nature of scholarly certitudes, it also provides a recognition of genuine, core, and irreducible elements in textual criticism and critical editing. Critical editions should reflect the judgments of "an expert who has had available" the relevant documentary sources "and has devoted time and study to their transmissional history and authority." Traditionally, it has been understood that those judgments will be conveyed to the reader in the form of a critically established reading text and an accompanying apparatus representing relevant textual variants. In the electronic environment, there is less universal agreement on how those judgments should be conveyed, and there is a stronger emphasis on the editorial preparation of multiple variant texts so that these will be responsive to scholarly inquiry. What I think will necessarily remain constant is that the value that we place on any product of critical editing will depend on our awareness that it contains the work of just such an expert as Bowers describes, and that it will allow us to share in that work. The value of an electronic edition is not that this expert has disappeared but, rather, that the edition more flexibly allows readers to test out their own hypotheses, to reconstruct the author's texts in different ways.

Notes

1. Fredson Bowers, "Editing a Philosopher: *The Works of William James*," *Analytical and Enumerative Bibliography* 4 (1980): 3.

2. William Proctor Williams and Craig S. Abbott, *An Introduction to Bibliographical and Textual Studies*, 2d ed. (New York: MLA, 1989), 52, 54.

3. Ibid., 55.

4. G. Thomas Tanselle, *A Rationale of Textual Criticism* (Philadelphia: Univ. of Pennsylvania Pr., 1992), is a printing of the Rosenbach Lectures delivered at the University of Pennsylvania in 1987. "Reproducing the Texts of Documents" and "Reconstructing the Texts of Works" are the titles, respectively, of the lectures dealing with diplomatic editing (39–66) and critical editing (67–93). On literary works as instances of verbal communication, see 13–15, 40. On the necessary questioning of documents, see 69.

5. For a brief history of textual criticism in the Western world, see D. C. Greetham, *Textual Scholarship: An Introduction* (New York: Garland, 1994), 295–346. On the beginnings of the scholarly editing of English literature, see Marcus Walsh, *Shakespeare, Milton & Eighteenth-Century Literary Editing: The Beginnings of Interpretive Scholarship* (Cambridge: Cambridge Univ. Pr., 1997).

6. Tanselle, *Rationale of Textual Criticism*, 63; Peter Shillingsburg, *Scholarly Editing in the Computer Age: Theory and Practice* (Ann Arbor: Univ. of Michigan Pr., 1996), 56; Gary Taylor, "The Renaissance and the End of Editing," in *Palimpsest: Editorial Theory in the Humanities*, ed. George Bornstein and Ralph G. Williams (Ann Arbor: Univ. of Michigan Pr., 1993), 129.

7. Charles L. Ross, "The Electronic Text and the Death of the Critical Edition," in *The Literary Text in the Digital Age*, ed. Richard Finneran (Ann Arbor: Univ. of Michigan Pr., 1996), 225; Jerome McGann, "The Rationale of HyperText," *Text* 9 (1996): 32 n.

8. Regarding the substantial number of critical editions that have been produced according to Greg–Bowers principles, see Greetham, *Textual Scholarship*, 335. On the ongoing production of "eclectic intentionalist editions," see ibid., 341. That the principles of Greg and Bowers continue "to be most useful and appropriate for many editions" has been asserted by Jo Ann Boydston in her "Standards for Scholarly Editing: The CEAA and the CSE," *Text* 6 (1993): 25. Those principles are, furthermore, not uncommonly called upon in the reviewing of new critical editions. See, for example, Dale Kramer, "The Compositor as Copy-Text," *Text* 9 (1996): 368–88; Joel J. Brattin, "Review Article," *Dickens Quarterly* 11 (1994): 138–47.

9. Fredson Bowers, "Remarks on Eclectic Texts," *Proof: The Yearbook of American Bibliographical and Textual Studies* 4 (1975): 34.

10. Ibid., 75.

11. Fredson Bowers, "Some Principles for Scholarly Editions of Nineteenth-Century American Authors," *Studies in Bibliography* 17 (1964): 223–28. This article had been read before the American Literature section of the South Atlantic Modern Language Association on 22 Nov. 1962.

12. Ibid., 226.

13. Bowers, "Remarks on Eclectic Texts," 55, 38. My account of Bowers's procedures with *The Marble Faun* is based on his "Textual Introduction" to that work: Nathaniel Hawthorne, *The Marble Faun: or The Romance of Monte Beni*, textual ed. Fredson Bowers, vol. 4 of *The Centenary Edition of the Works of Nathaniel Hawthorne*, ed. William Charvat, Roy Harvey Pearce, Claude M. Simpson, and Matthew Bruccoli (Columbus: Ohio State Univ. Pr., 1968), lxxiv–lxxv. For a critical assessment of *The Centenary Edition* that takes into account its historical importance, see O. M. Brack Jr., "The Centenary Hawthorne Eight Years Later: A Review Article," *Proof* 1 (1971): 358–67.

14. W. W. Greg, "The Rationale of Copy-Text," *Studies in Bibliography* 3 (1950–51): 19–36.

15. Ibid., 21–22.

16. Ibid., 24–26, 29. For exceptional cases in which authorial revision was thorough, and extended to both substantives and accidentals, Greg allowed that a revised edition could appropriately be selected as copy-text (ibid., 33–35). Bowers, in commenting on Greg's "Rationale," noted that such cases were relatively rare in the period with which Greg was concerned (1550–1650), but that they have been somewhat more common in modern times (citing as examples authors such as Walt Whitman and Henry and William James). See Bowers, "Greg's 'Rationale of Copy-Text' Revisited," *Studies in Bibliography* 31 (1978): 109.

17. Bowers, "Greg's 'Rationale of Copy-Text' Revisited," 90–91, 94–95.

18. Ibid., 91, 92. Bowers might be thought of here as making reference also to the historical focus of his own textual-critical concerns, which he has elsewhere described somewhat more clearly as: "texts that are printed, or are mixed manuscript and printed, dating roughly from the sixteenth century to the present" ("Remarks on Eclectic Texts," 44–45).

19. Bowers, "Greg's 'Rationale of Copy-Text' Revisited," 95 n. 9, 125–26, 126 n.

20. Ibid., 124–61, 127. Bowers is, however, attentive throughout to the textual-critical implications of changing historical circumstances in printing, publishing, and authorship. Those changing circumstances are capable, in his view, of qualifying in many ways the manner in which Greg's ideas might be interpreted for use in the editing of modern documents. In Tanselle's view, this essay constitutes part of Bowers's "reconsideration of his earlier, less measured response to the 'Rationale'" (Tanselle, "Editing without a Copy-Text," in *Literature and Artifacts* [Charlottesville: Bibliographical Society of the Univ. of Virginia, 1998], 247). Readers interested in the place of "Greg's 'Rationale of Copy-Text' Revisited" in the evolution of Bowers's thinking should consult Tanselle (ibid., 246–52); it has been my purpose here only to identify broad continuities.

21. Modern Language Association of America, Center for Editions of American Authors, *Statement of Editorial Principles and Procedures: A Working Manual*

for Editing Nineteenth-Century American Texts, rev. ed. (New York: MLA, 1972), ix.

22. Ibid., 4, 4–5.

23. Boydston, "Standards for Scholarly Editing," 22–23.

24. Modern Language Association of America, Center for Scholarly Editions, "The Center for Scholarly Editions: An Introductory Statement," *PMLA* 92 (1977): 583–97. On the number of editions endorsed by the CEAA and the CSE that have been "constructed along Greg–Bowers principles of eclecticism and copy-text theory," see Greetham, *Textual Scholarship*, 335.

25. Jerome McGann, *A Critique of Modern Textual Criticism* (Charlottesville: Univ. Pr. of Virginia, 1992), 35. For a good discussion of the parallel and inter-twining fortunes of documentary editing and critical editing in America, with special attention on the flourishing of both forms in the latter half of the twentieth century, see Mary-Jo Kline, *A Guide to Documentary Editing*, 2d ed. (Baltimore: Johns Hopkins Univ. Pr., 1998), 1–32.

26. The most thorough overviews of the controversies are provided in a series of essays by G. Thomas Tanselle. Three of these essays are reprinted in his *Textual Criticism Since Greg: A Chronicle 1950–1985* (Charlottesville: Univ. Pr. of Virginia, 1987). Two further essays cover the state of the discussion since 1985: "Textual Criticism and Literary Sociology," *Studies in Bibliography* 44 (1991): 83–143, and "Textual Instability and Editorial Idealism," *Studies in Bibliography* 49 (1996): 1–60. For a brief overview of these controversies, see Greetham, *Textual Scholarship*, 331–46. A critique of the CSE "Introductory Statement" can be found in McGann, *Critique of Modern Textual Criticism*, 6–8.

27. Peter Shillingsburg, "Textual Variants, Performance Variants, and the Concept of Work," *Editio* 7 (1993): 226–28. Donald Reiman, "Versioning: The Presentation of Multiple Texts," in *Romantic Texts and Contexts* (Columbia: Univ. of Missouri Pr., 1987), 179, 168. The phrase *textual pluralism* is from Jack Stillinger, *Coleridge and Textual Instability: The Multiple Versions of the Major Poems* (New York: Oxford Univ. Pr., 1994), 119. On the recent growth of interest in versions, see Greetham, *Textual Scholarship*, 340–41.

28. Hans Zeller, "A New Approach to the Critical Constitution of Literary Texts," *Studies in Bibliography* 28 (1975): 236, 256.

29. Bowers, "Remarks on Eclectic Texts," 38.

30. Zeller, "A New Approach to the Critical Constitution of Literary Texts," 236, 241. In Shillingsburg's view ("Text as Matter, Concept, and Action," *Studies in Bibliography* 44 [1991]: 69–70), Zeller offered "the most radical answer" to the question of "how much of a change or what kind of change in content is required before a *different* Version rather than an *improved* Version, results." Tanselle, in an essay roughly contemporary with Zeller's, explored that question in a manner that was more conservative, but comparably thought-provoking. See Tanselle, "The Editorial Problem of Final Authorial Intention," *Studies in Bibliography* 29 (1976): 51–67. For some subsequent noteworthy articula-

tions of a theory of versions, see Shillingsburg, "Text as Matter, Concept, and Action," 46–78, and *Scholarly Editing in the Computer Age*, 44–45; and Stillinger, *Coleridge and Textual Instability*, 118–40.

31. Zeller, "A New Approach to the Critical Constitution of Literary Texts," 256, 245.

32. On that German tradition and Zeller's relationship to it, see Hans Walter Gabler, "Introduction: Textual Criticism and Theory in Modern German Editing," in *Contemporary German Editorial Theory*, ed. Hans Walter Gabler, George Bornstein, and Gillian Borland Pierce (Ann Arbor: Univ. of Michigan Pr., 1995), 1–16. Zeller provides a brief example of historical-critical editing near the end of his "A New Approach to the Critical Constitution of Literary Texts," 250–53.

33. Reiman, "Versioning," 177, 176, 173–75.

34. McGann, *Critique of Modern Textual Criticism*, 58, 62, 57, 56–57.

35. Stephen Crane, *Bowery Tales*, ed. Fredson Bowers, vol. 1 of *The University of Virginia Edition of the Works of Stephen Crane*, ed. Fredson Bowers (Charlottesville: Univ. Pr. of Virginia, 1969), lxxvii; McGann, *Critique of Modern Textual Criticism*, 61, 62, 51–52.

36. Jerome McGann, *The Textual Condition* (Princeton, N. J.: Princeton Univ. Pr., 1991), 15. For a statement of the sociological perspective in bibliography, see D. F. McKenzie, *Bibliography and the Sociology of Texts* (London: British Library, 1986).

37. McGann, *Textual Condition*, 57, 13.

38. Ibid., 58–59. Stillinger (*Coleridge and Textual Instability*, 121–24) has explored comparable issues with regard to varying bibliographic embodiments of Coleridge's "The Rime of the Ancient Mariner."

39. McGann, "The Rationale of HyperText," 31.

40. Hans Zeller, "Structure and Genesis in Editing: On German and Anglo-American Textual Criticism," in *Contemporary German Editorial Theory*, 113, 104; Zeller, "A New Approach to the Critical Constitution of Literary Texts," 257–64.

41. Kline, *A Guide to Documentary Editing*, 192–93, 21.

42. For an analysis of issues under dispute, see Shillingsburg, *Scholarly Editing in the Computer Age*, 96–100.

43. G. Thomas Tanselle, "The Varieties of Scholarly Editing," in *Scholarly Editing: A Guide to Research*, ed. D. C. Greetham (New York: MLA, 1995), 26.

44. ———, "Textual Instability and Editorial Idealism," 35; *A Rationale of Textual Criticism*, 40; "Textual Instability and Editorial Idealism," 36. For a good example of a versional edition that is edited eclectically and according to principles of authorial intention, one might consider D. H. Lawrence, *The First 'Women in Love,'* ed. John Worthen and Lindeth Vasey, in *The Cambridge Edition of the Letters and Works of D. H. Lawrence*, ed. James T.

Boulton and Warren Roberts (Cambridge: Cambridge Univ. Pr., 1998).

45. Shillingsburg, *Scholarly Editing in the Computer Age*, 91, 44, 47 n; Stillinger, *Coleridge and Textual Instability*, 132. On the relationship between Tanselle's and Shillingsburg's concept of versions, see Stillinger, 124–29.

46. Greetham, *Textual Scholarship*, 341. For examples of ongoing "eclectic intentionalist" editions, one might consider the Cambridge editions of D. H. Lawrence and Joseph Conrad. Versional thinking has perhaps had its strongest impact in the editing of Shakespeare. See William Shakespeare, *The Complete King Lear: 1608–1623*, prepared by Michael Warren (Berkeley: Univ. of California Pr., 1989), and *The Early Quartos* volumes in *The New Cambridge Shakespeare* series (Cambridge: Cambridge Univ. Pr., 1984–). On the versional approach to Shakepearean editing, see Paul Werstine, "Shakespeare," in Greetham, *Scholarly Editing*, 268–71. For an example of a versional edition in the electronic environment, one might consider *The Complete Writings and Pictures of Dante Gabriel Rossetti: A Hypermedia Research Archive*, ed. Jerome McGann (discussed here on pp. 144–45).

47. Shillingsburg, *Scholarly Editing in the Computer Age*, 161.

48. D. C. Greetham, "Editorial and Critical Theory: From Modernism to Postmodernism," in *Palimpsest: Editorial Theory in the Humanities*, 15–17.

49. Shillingsburg, *Scholarly Editing in the Computer Age*, 165.

50. Ibid., 15–27, 165–66. For further discussion of new possibilities opened for eclectic critical editing in an electronic environment, see Tanselle, "Textual Instability and Editorial Idealism," 51–55.

51. Shillingsburg, *Scholarly Editing in the Computer Age*, 133.

52. Ross, 225, 228–29.

53. Ibid., 229.

54. For a good introduction to issues in the editing of Middle English texts, see Douglas Moffat and Vincent P. McCarren, "A Bibliographical Essay on Editing Methods and Authorial and Scribal Intention," in *A Guide to Editing Middle English*, ed. Vincent McCarren and Douglas Moffat (Ann Arbor: Univ. of Michigan Pr., 1998), 25–57. See especially pp. 39–40 on the difficulty of distinguishing between scribal and authorial variations in the editorial effort to reconstruct possible authorial versions.

55. Peter M. W. Robinson, "Is There a Text in These Variants?" in *The Literary Text in the Digital Age*, 103–12. On the use of SGML, see Geoffrey Chaucer, *The Wife of Bath's Prologue on CD-ROM*, ed. Peter Robinson (Cambridge: Cambridge Univ. Pr., 1996), accompanying manual, 60–69.

56. Peter M. W. Robinson, "Collation, Textual Criticism, Publication, and the Computer," *Text* 7 (1994): 94.

57. Chaucer, *The Wife of Bath's Prologue on CD-ROM*, manual, 10. In fact, one might say that two recognizable approaches to the scholarly editing of medieval texts are being followed here: the CD-ROM is following the "best text"

approach, while the *Canterbury Tales* project as a whole is involved in forms of analysis comparable to the stemmatics approach. On these two approaches, see A. S. G. Edwards, "Middle English Literature," in Greetham, *Scholarly Editing*, 188–92.

58. Robinson, "Text," 112.

59. Jerome McGann, "The Complete Writings and Pictures of Dante Gabriel Rossetti: A Hypermedia Research ARchive," *Text* 7 (1994) 97–98. On the influence of *The Rossetti Archive*, see McGann, "Presidential Address: The Society for Textual Scholarship, April 11, 1997: Hideous Progeny, Rough Beasts: Editing as a Theoretical Pursuit," *Text* 11 (1998): 13. For a demonstration model, see McGann, ed., *The Complete Writings and Pictures of Dante Gabriel Rossetti: A Hypermedia Research Archive Demonstration Model*, 1996, http://www.press.umich.edu/bookhome/rossetti (15 June 1998).

60. ———, "The Rossetti Archive and Image-Based Electronic Editing," in *The Literary Text in the Digital Age*, 145, 146, 155; "The Complete Writings and Pictures of Dante Gabriel Rossetti," 100. For further discussion of the traditional distinction between documentary and critical editing, see McGann, "Presidential Address," 7.

61. ———, "Rossetti Archive and Image-Based Electronic Editing," 150, 155, 152, 145. In his essay "What is Critical Editing?" McGann suggests that "the term 'critical'" used in critical editing "refers to nothing more than the comparative analysis of multiple texts." He does allow that "to define and set aside those transmissive variations that can be shown to be corruptions" is one of the functions of critical editing (*The Textual Condition*, 50), but this function does not appear to be an object of significant concern in his recent writing. It is, of course, the case that McGann locates authority in the social nexus of literary production (rather than with the author alone), and this does significantly reduce the scope and variety of transmissive variations that might be categorizable as "corruptions." On the sociological orientation in scholarly editing, see Shillingsburg, *Scholarly Editing in the Computer Age*, 21–23.

62. Committee on Scholarly Editions (CSE), Modern Language Association of America, "Guidelines for Electronic Scholarly Editions," 1 December 1997, http://sunsite.berkeley.edu/MLA/guidelines.html (25 November 1998), I.B.

63. *TEI Guidelines for Electronic Text Encoding and Interchange (P3)*, n.d., http://etext.lib.virginia.edu/TEI.html (16 March 1999), 1.3. On "Critical Apparatus," see ibid., chapter 19. The *TEI Guidelines* are also available in print: C. M. Sperberg-McQueen and Lou Burnard, eds., *Guidelines for Electronic Text Encoding and Interchange (TEI P3)*, 2 vols. (Chicago: Text Encoding Initiative, 1994).

64. On the history and planned future developments of the *TEI Guidelines*, see *TEI Guidelines*, 1.3–1.3.2. On modifying and extending the TEI encoding scheme, see ibid., Chapter 29.

65. C. M. Sperberg-McQueen, "Textual Criticism and the Text Encoding Ini-

tiative," in *The Literary Text in the Digital Age*, 51–52. For an example of the kind of functionality gained by such tagging, one might consider *The Wife of Bath's Prologue on CD-ROM*, which allows users, among other things, to limit searches to passages that have been identified by the editors as additions or deletions in the manuscript witnesses.

66. Committee on Scholarly Editions, "Guidelines," Introduction. These guidelines can usefully be read in conjunction with the CSE's statement of standards for scholarly editions in general, contained within the brochure "Aims and Services of the Committee on Scholarly Editions" (available from the MLA).

67. Ibid., V.A. 1; V.B.1; Introduction; III.

68. Ibid., II.C.1.b.

69. The editors of *The First 'Women in Love'* note that "It is planned to publish a variorum of all the states of the texts of *Women in Love*—from fragments of early versions to the first editions—in electronic form" (Lawrence, 2). That variorum is envisioned by the editors as providing a fuller representation of textual variation than the explanatory notes in the apparatus of the printed critical edition.

70. Bowers, "Remarks on Eclectic Texts," 75.

Chapter 5

Electronic Texts and Selected Web Sites for English and American Literature

Shelley Arlen
University of Florida

The current proliferation of literary texts in electronic format on the Internet has stemmed from two primary motives: first, a populist ideal of providing free access to literary works to everyone; and second, a research initiative dedicated to providing accurate documents for textual and linguistic analysis. The concerns of the first group are basically those of a publisher—to provide access to, and dissemination of, works generally in the public domain—although, increasingly, the Internet is used by writers as a vehicle for original publication. These works, distributed in a format that is legible to most software (plain or ASCII text), can be read by anyone having access to online computer networks. The movement is made up of numerous grassroots volunteers, basically "lone rangers" in the tasks of selecting, keying in or scanning literary texts, and proofreading the resulting copy.

The research-oriented group of full-text providers has a different motive. In addition to providing readable texts, this group provides authoritative texts in which the various components (words, paragraphs, chapters, etc.) may be encoded or tagged for later manipulation and study. The many encoding groups now in existence collaborate in dividing up the works and contributing to a new mission: to create a collective national digital library, following set standards and protocols with regard to scanning and digitizing texts and providing public access to them.

Thus, today, Internet users can find a multitude of texts online—fiction, poetry, drama, essays, etc.—many available at no cost and accessible to all. Some are merely "reading" copies, others are "definitive works" that can be subjected to critical textual analysis. Still others are original creations, electronic journals or works of art published on the Web that may be unavailable in any other format. Some of these full-text literary sites are proprietary, with commercial vendors offering subscriptions to them, but this chapter considers only those Web sites that are currently available without charge.

Electronic Text Revolution

One of the earliest attempts to provide access to electronic texts on the Web was by Project Gutenberg, begun in 1971 by Michael Hart at the University of Illinois and still active. Hart's original goal for the project was to collect 10,000 of the most-often-consulted books by the end of the century and to make them accessible to the consumer at no or little cost. As an all-volunteer project with little oversight, Project Gutenberg has several inherent weaknesses: the electronic text may not have been copied from the authoritative text as envisioned by the author, or it may have numerous typographical errors, unintended deletions, misspellings, and the like. And the e-text may not be complete—it might be an abridgment. Gutenberg texts tend to be available only as ASCII texts; as a result, any searching within the text is limited to the "Find" command of the Internet browser (e.g., Netscape) used. These texts are nevertheless useful to those persons wanting only a basic "reading" copy, but they should be used with caution and an understanding of their limitations. They should not be used for research purposes.

In contrast, texts provided by research-oriented groups are intended as authoritative works. One example of a provider of online texts for research needs is the Center for Electronic Texts in the Humanities (CETH), a joint collaboration of Rutgers and Princeton Universities. One of CETH's goals has been to maintain control over the texts and their format. CETH documents are authoritative and accurate, and they conform to a standardized encoding scheme, the Text Encoding Initiative (TEI), as outlined by the Association for Computers and the Humanities, the Association for Computational Linguistics, and the Association for Literary and Linguistic Computing. The text is coded so that elements or portions of it can be retrieved for analysis. The basis for the TEI standard is the Standard Generalized Markup Language, or SGML, which meets a variety of needs in terms of equipment and software compatibility, network transmission, and text analysis and manipulation. Typesetting instructions are given in brackets (<>) while, typically, the body of the text is in ASCII text. The embedded codes are not visible to, and thus offer no distractions for, the casual reader. With the onset of computer software such as Portable Document Format (PDF) that can transmit facsimiles, texts can now be duplicated in full image with any attending graphics.

The availability of e-texts has tremendous potential for use, from casual reading needs to electronic reserves in academic libraries to analysis of linguistic style. Hypertext encoding (HTML—Hypertext Markup Language) also can be added to a text. This encoding creates links to other Internet sites and can enhance the research and instructional capabilities of the Internet. A good example of the many possibilities inherent in hypertext works is the Shakespeare site at the Massachusetts Institute of Technology. The MIT site contains the full texts of all Shakespeare's works but also provides added features such as a glossary; difficult words in the text are hyperlinked to this glossary, thus enabling immediate understanding. Similarly, annotations, commentary, visual graphics, footnotes, and the like can be hyperlinked to the text, providing additional information and explanation.

A recent development that combines the features of SGML and HTML is the Extensible Markup Language (XML). Completed in 1998, XML is an easy-to-use, simplified form of SGML. HTML, the language used to publish hypertext on the Web, is an SGML language that is limited to describing predefined formats, such as headings, paragraphs, or lists. XML, on the other hand, allows for the creation of customized document types that can be published as hypertext on the Web. The next generation of HTML currently proposed, called Extensible HTML (XHTML 1.0), is a reformulation of HTML, version 4.0, in XML, for greater functionality and compatibility. A draft of XHTML 1.0 was published in May, 1999, by the World Wide Web Consortium (http://www.w3.org/TR/1999/xhtml1-19990505).

The advantages of electronic text are obvious: connection to the texts from any online location, saving of precious shelf space where square footage is at a premium, and (often) relatively low-cost and almost instantaneous access. Scholars and other individuals with interests in a particular subject or hobby have rapidly formed discussion groups on the Internet. These e-mail lists, having the power of instantaneous and simultaneous correspondence worldwide, are now considered an important mechanism for the exchange of scholarly information.

Role of the Librarian

In the midst of this electronic revolution, the role of the librarian in using this new format remains much the same: to identify resources, to create access points and finding aids to the materials, to make those sources available, and to teach a clientele how to do research using the various formats. The role remains the same, but the tools are different and increasingly require sophisticated knowledge of computer capabilities, the functionality of online resources, and computer languages. Librarians themselves are creating Web pages and providing custom-made guides to information on the Internet, all geared to local clientele needs. They must learn the specialties and limitations of Internet search engines such as AltaVista, Infoseek, Lycos, and Yahoo and must be able to teach others how to search the Web for information. In an environment in which anyone can create a Web page, the librarian's role in the evaluation process is vital. All evaluative questions that librarians have addressed to printed works now must be addressed to Internet sites: Is the work authoritative? What institution, organization, or individual created the site? What is the stated mission of the site (if any)? Is the site biased toward a certain viewpoint? When was the site created, and has it been updated? The librarian's mission of providing information, compiling guides to locate and use the available information, and assisting and teaching patrons in the research process has not changed; only the arena for information has expanded.

Creation of a Web Site

In creating a Web site for a specific library clientele, there are several things to keep in mind. The first page should function as an index to the site, alerting users to the purpose of the site and giving an overview of what it contains. The page design and format should be kept simple, offering a well-organized hierarchy of links and making it easy for users to determine what is to be found on the successive links. Creating that first page and trying to give full scope without overwhelming the user is a major challenge. Design is crucial. Color, font styles, and graphics should all be used for a purpose—to enhance the process of locating information. With the numerous excellent "megasites," or guides to the Internet literature already established, no one need reinvent the wheel. Linking to the site of another institution or to a bibliographer's well-organized site is standard procedure, provided the appropriate acknowledgment or credit is given. In this respect, several of the megasites listed below were originally created as guides to the Internet for a specific local clientele. The sites have since become exemplary ones that persons beyond the local clientele have found useful. Two such "all-encompassing" Web sites for the study of English language and literature are *Voice of the Shuttle*, from the University of California, Santa Barbara, and Carnegie Mellon's *The English Server*.

The Webliography

This listing of Web sites is necessarily selective. I have given priority to those literary e-text sites that appear to be major sites frequently accessed and referred to by other Web sites; these tend to be maintained and updated fairly frequently, and are generally associated with an academic organization or institution, though a few others are included because of their unique interest. The focus here is on previously printed works now available as public domain texts on the Web. Archival materials have not been addressed, but anyone seeking information on manuscript or other nonprint materials will find a good starting point in the American Heritage Project at the Berkeley Digital Library (http://sunsite.berkeley.edu/amher). This is by no means an exhaustive list. Given the continual growth and evolution of the Internet, there can be no "definitive" list. The sites noted here, particularly the directories and the megasites such as Yahoo and *Voice of the Shuttle* that serve as subject guides to the Internet, appear to be fairly stable ones that provide a gateway to the numerous literary riches of the Web. Categories covered are:

> A. Directories of E-Text Repositories
> B. Major E-Text Repositories
> C. Update Sites
> D. Literature by Genre—Poetry, Drama
> E. Literature by Period
> F. Literature by Region
> G. Other Specialized Literatures
> H. Author Sites
> I. Bibliographies
> J. Directories of Discussion Groups, Listservs, etc.
> K. Electronic Discussion Lists
> L. Newsgroups
> M. Newsletters and Journals
> N. Associations
> O. Computing Centers and Institutes
> P. Hypertext
> Q. Megasites

A. Directories of E-Text Repositories

American Studies Web: Literature and Hypertext
> http://www.georgetown.edu/crossroads/asw/lit.html
> Extensive variety of links, from the popular to the obscure.

Directory of Electronic Text Centers
> http://scc01.rutgers.edu/ceth/infosrv/ectrdir.html
> Available from CETH (Center for Electronic Texts in the Humani-

ties), a joint project of Rutgers and Princeton Universities, and compiled by Mary Mallery. A guide to national and international text centers and digital library projects.

Electronic Texts and Publishing Resources
http://lcweb.loc.gov/global/etext/
A Library of Congress Internet Resource Page. Links to major e-text collections, some author sites, poetry and newsletter sites, and electronic publishers.

Guides to E-Text Directories
http://www.westciv.com.au (Click on "An index of e-text indexes." "Major e-text projects" is also helpful.)
Overview of selected major directories from universities, companies, and individuals. An Australian commercial site advertising Palimpsest, a Macintosh hypertext application, but access to the e-texts is available without charge.

Library Electronic Text Resource Service (LETRS), Indiana University.
http://www.indiana.edu/~letrs/
Listing of electronic text repositories by subject and language. Also links to text analysis applications, SGML and XML links, software, and home pages for LETRS-supported texts and software.

B. Major E-Text Repositories

Alex: Catalog of Electronic Texts on the Internet
http://sunsite.berkeley.edu/alex/
Originally a 1993 research project initiated by Hunter Monroe and now maintained by Eric Morgan, *Alex* is an archive of public domain electronic texts in American literature, English literature, and Western philosophy. The content of multiple documents can be searched simultaneously. You can create PDF documents for downloading, specifying font and other format features. *Alex* also provides free searching software that can be downloaded for content analysis.

Berkeley Digital Collections
http://sunsite.berkeley.edu/Collections/
The Berkeley Digital Library has an extensive collection of primarily SGML-encoded e-texts, including the following: American

Heritage Project, Literature@SunSITE (mainly U.S. authors at present), and Online Medieval and Classical Texts.

Bibliomania

http://www.bibliomania.com/

Supported by The Data Text Publishing, Ltd., a commercial electronic publisher in the United Kingdom, Bibliomania lists works by the four categories of fiction, poetry, nonfiction, and reference in HTML and some PDF formats. Most works are in the public domain, but Data Text plans to provide up-to-date reference resources and enable free-text searches across complementary reference works.

Center for Computer Analysis of Texts (CCAT)

gopher://ccat.sas.upenn.edu:70/11/Archive

The University of Pennsylvania's CCAT has one of the largest gopher archives of e-texts. The database is WAIS-indexed for easy searching. The center provides a list of texts available through various projects, many of which require permission to access.

Center for Electronic Texts in the Humanities (CETH)

http://scc01.rutgers.edu/ceth/

One of the major e-text centers, CETH serves the humanities scholar/student involved in the creation and use of e-text applications and explores the potential of these texts. A joint 1991 project of Rutgers and Princeton Universities, CETH has been supported by grants from the National Endowment for the Humanities and the Andrew W. Mellon Foundation. Its research mission is advanced by the dissemination of information, its focus on high-quality SGML-encoded electronic texts, and the development of procedures and standards. Provides TEI guidelines and has an index of e-text centers. CETH Projects include the Medieval and Early Modern Data Bank, Oral History Archives of World War II, and How(ever), a journal of experimental feminist writing.

Electronic Text Center, University of Virginia

http://etext.lib.virginia.edu/

Links to thousands of SGML-encoded e-texts; those that are publicly accessible tend to be in the Modern English Collection, Michigan Early Modern English Materials, Middle English Collection, or British Poetry Collection.

English Server, Carnegie Mellon University

http://eserver.org

Active since 1990 in providing e-texts to the public, the English Server at Carnegie Mellon University is maintained by the CMU English department and links to novels, short stories, poetry, and drama collections as well as historical, political, and religious documents.

Humanities Text Initiative, University of Michigan

http://www.hti.umich.edu/

A major project to digitize literary texts. Includes the American Verse Project, Early Modern English Materials, the Middle English Collection, and Modern English Works. SGML-encoded texts, many of which are restricted to University of Michigan users.

Internet Public Library Online Text Collection

http://ipl.sils.umich.edu/reading/

Links to more than 10,000 e-texts, including numerous short works. The collection is searchable by author, title, or Dewey subject classification.

Internet Wiretap

http://wiretap.area.com/Gopher/Library/Classic/

gopher://wiretap.Spies.COM:70/11/Books

Dedicated to the first-amendment rights of Internet citizens, Wiretap was one of the earliest (1990) repositories of e-texts. Authors are alphabetized by their first name (e.g., Emily Bronte in the E listing) in the gopher menu.

Library Electronic Text Resource Service (LETRS), Indiana University

http://www.indiana.edu/~letrs/index.html

Provides access to scholarly e-texts and application tools primarily for the Indiana University community. Texts are tagged in SGML and conform to TEI guidelines. Includes the Victorian Women Writers Project.

Master Works of Western Civilization

http://mason-west.com/MasterWorks/index.shtml

A list of classic works with links to available texts on the Web.

The New Bartleby: A National Digital Library
    http://www.bartleby.com/
    Edited by Steve van Leeuwen, creator of Columbia University's
    Project Bartleby Archive (see below). Renamed Bartleby.com in
    2000.

Online Book Initiative (OBI)
    gopher://ftp.std.com:70/11/obi/book
    The OBI at Carnegie Mellon University is primarily a repository
    for a wide variety of public domain electronic texts: monographs,
    periodicals, census materials, etc. Mirrors and provides storage
    space/archives for other e-sites. Authors are alphabetized by first
    name in the gopher index.

On-Line Books Page
    http://digital.library.upenn.edu/books/
    Index to more than 10,000 online books that can be searched or
    browsed by author, title, or subject listing. Also provides a "Books
    in Progress/Requested" listing. Founded by John M. Ockerbloom.

Online Literary Research Tools
    http://andromeda.rutgers.edu/~jlynch/Lit/
    This page points to Internet sites pertaining to English and Ameri-
    can literature, excluding single electronic texts, and is limited to
    collections of information useful primarily to academics.

The Oxford Text Archive (OTA)
    http://ota.ahds.ac.uk/
    gopher://dept.english.upenn.edu:70/11/E-Text/Elsewhere/OTA
    As a part of the Humanities Computing Unit of the Oxford Uni-
    versity Computing Services, OTA has been collecting e-texts in
    selected languages for about 20 years and is now, with more than
    2,500 titles, one of the largest collections of e-texts. The catalog
    of scholarly editions and literary works can be viewed in plain
    ASCII text, SGML, or HTML. OTA encourages the use of format-
    ting standards, but the encoding features may vary. The site also
    features full-text search of texts, and information on the creation
    and documentation of electronic texts, as well as a software re-
    pository and an FAQ.

Project Bartleby Archive

　　http://www.columbia.edu/acis/bartleby/
　　http://www.bartleby.com
　　Founded in 1993 at Columbia University, this project became a
　　leader in establishing electronic publishing methods until its of-
　　ficial cessation and transmutation into an archive. The project
　　continues as The New Bartleby: A National Digital Library (see
　　above). The texts (mostly modernist) are either in the public do-
　　main or are under Columbia University copyright or license. The
　　high quality and accuracy of the texts is emphasized, guaranteed
　　by professional editorial standards. The project set the standard
　　for accessing individual paragraphs within a prose work. In Feb-
　　ruary 1994, this site was the first to publish a book on the Web,
　　Whitman's *Leaves of Grass*.

Project Gutenberg

　　http://sailor.gutenberg.org/
　　With a goal of providing 10,000 "most-used" e-texts in the English
　　language by the year 2001, Project Gutenberg was founded in 1991
　　by Michael Hart at the University of Illinois to encourage e-text
　　creation and free distribution for the general reader. The project
　　issues around four public domain e-texts per month. The texts
　　are high quality, but not necessarily authoritative, and are pro-
　　vided in ASCII format. The three categories of included texts are:
　　Light Literature (*Peter Pan*); Heavy Literature (*Paradise Lost*); and
　　Reference Works. The Gutenberg newsletter and discussion group
　　are other features.

Schoenberg Center for Electronic Text & Image (SCETI)

　　http://www.library.upenn.edu/etext/
　　A University of Pennsylvania site designed to provide the schol-
　　arly community with important original source material. Recently
　　initiated, the collections include English Renaissance texts and
　　Women's Studies (diaries and fiction).

Virtual Library of Virginia: Books and Other Electronic Texts

　　http://exlibris.uls.vcu.edu/viva/collect/books.html
　　The mission of this group is to build and maintain an Internet-
　　accessible collection of SGML texts and images. Some of the

publicly accessible databases are: Modern English Collection, Middle English Collection, British Poetry (1780–1910), African American Documents, and Michigan Early Modern English Collection.

C. Update Sites

Books Online, New Listings

http://digital.library.upenn.edu/books/new.html

This page lists the titles of online books that have recently been added to its index or whose entries have been recently revised.

Internet-on-a-Disk

http://samizdat.com/ioad.html

Internet on a Disk, the newsletter of electronic texts and Internet trends, publishes a column of e-texts recently added to some of the major sites.

D. Literature by Genre

POETRY

American Verse Project

http://www.hti.umich.edu/english/amverse/

A University of Michigan project to compile electronic texts of volumes of American poetry written before 1920. The full text is converted into digital form and coded in SGML using the TEI Guidelines. Includes Emily Dickinson, Paul Laurence Dunbar, Edna St. Vincent Millay, and Carl Sandburg.

British Poetry 1780–1900: A Hypertext Archive of Scholarly Editions

http://etext.lib.virginia.edu/britpo.html

Romantic and Victorian poetry, some in facsimile with illustrations. Notes and annotations, if approved, can be added. From the Electronic Text Center, Alderman Library, University of Virginia.

CMU Poetry Index of Canonical Verse (Carnegie Mellon)

http://english-www.hss.cmu.edu/poetry/

Some standard works of poetry.

Contemporary American Poetry Archives

http://conncoll.edu/Academics/departments/English/CAPA/review/index.html.old

Out-of-print volumes of poetry.

Electronic Poetry Center (University of Buffalo)
> http://epc.buffalo.edu/
> (Former url: http://wings.buffalo.edu/epc/)
> Links to electronic poetry and poetics, emphasizing poetry that is "contemporary experimental and formally innovative."

Internet Poetry Archive
> http://metalab.unc.edu/ipa/
> Sponsored by the University of North Carolina Press and the North Carolina Arts Council to make the work of selected contemporary poets accessible at little or no cost. Currently includes poems by Philip Levine, Seamus Heaney, Czeslaw Milosz, Robert Pinsky, and Margaret Walker.

Museum of American Poetics
> http://www.poetspath.com/links.html
> Links to poetry sites.

Representative Poetry Online (University of Toronto)
> http://www.library.utoronto.ca/utel/rp/intro.html
> A collection of more than 2,000 English poems from the early medieval period to the beginning of the twentieth century by more than 300 poets. Most of the poems were published in the *Representative Poetry* anthology, 1912 to 1967. Indexes are by poet, title, first line, date, and keyword.

A Small Anthology of Poems
> http://www.wmich.edu/english/tchg/lit/pms/index.html
> Seamus Cooney's Web site of poems for his English class.

Yahoo *Poetry Page*
> http://www.yahoo.com/Arts/Humanities/Literature/Poetry/
> Good guide to poetry sources, including anthologies, journals, countries and cultures, and publishers.

DRAMA

The English Server: Drama
> http://english-www.hss.cmu.edu/drama/
> Contains a number of classic and modern plays (and criticism) as well as original works.

E. Literature by Period

Corpus of Middle English Prose and Verse (Humanities Text Initiative)
> http://www.hti.umich.edu/english/mideng/

Internet Medieval Sourcebook (Medieval and Early Renaissance Literature Archive)
> http://www.fordham.edu/halsall/sbook.html

The Labyrinth Guide to Medieval Studies on the Web
> http://www.georgetown.edu/labyrinth/labyrinth-home.html

Modern English Collection (Humanities Text Initiative)
> http://www.hti.umich.edu/english/pd-modeng/

Online Medieval and Classical Library (OMACL)
> http://sunsite.Berkeley.EDU/OMACL/
>
> A collection of some of the most important literary works of Classical and Medieval periods.

Eighteenth-Century Studies Page
> http://eserver.org/18th/
>
> This collection archives works of the eighteenth century from the perspectives of literary and cultural studies: novels, plays, memoirs, treatises, and poems.

Romantic Circles
> http://www.rc.umd.edu/
>
> Devoted to the study of Romantic period literature and culture, this site consists of reviews, links to e-texts, a periodical index, bibliographies, and conference information.

The Victorian Web
> http://www.stg.brown.edu/projects/hypertext/landow/victorian/victov.html
>
> Serves as a resource for Brown University courses in Victorian literature. It contains links to Victorian texts and to information on Victorian authors, art, architecture, design, religion, philosophy, politics, society, science, and technology.

The Victorian Women Writers Project
> http://www.indiana.edu/~letrs/vwwp/
>
> Highly accurate SGML transcriptions of literary works by British women writers in the late Victorian period.

F. Literature by Region

The Australian Literature Database
> http://setis.library.usyd.edu.au/oztexts/
> A collection of eighteenth, nineteenth, and early twentieth century Australian texts.

Canadian Literature Archive
> http://canlit.st-john.umanitoba.ca/Canlitx/Canlit_homepage.html
> http://canlit.st-john.umanitoba.ca/Canlitx/Framed_Version/CanlitF.html
> Aims to electronically reprint out-of-print, out-of-copyright Canadian works of fiction, poetry, and drama.

Library of Southern Literature
> http://metalab.unc.edu/docsouth/southlit/texts.html
> Part of the Documenting the American South collection of sources, University of North Carolina at Chapel Hill.

Modern Literature (American)
> http://www.english.nwu.edu/weblinks/modern2.html
> Links to numerous e-texts and home pages.

G. Other Specialized Literatures

Index of Native American Electronic Text Resources on the Internet
> http://www.hanksville.org/NAresources/indices/NAetext.html
> Organized to make the information useful to the Native American community and educators, the site links mainly to articles, news reports, and translations of myths but does include a few fiction links and links to other Native American Web sites.

Writing Black
> http://www.keele.ac.uk/depts/as/Literature/amlit.black.html
> Resources and texts related to the works of African American writers, including Frederick Douglass and W. E. B. Du Bois.

H. Author Sites

The sites listed here and the megasites listed below in section Q include scores of individual author sites.

American Authors on the Web
> http://lang.nagoya-u.ac.jp/~matsuoka/AmeLit.html

Lists general resources for authors and numerous links to individual authors, arranged chronologically, 1550–1950.

Authors & Works
> http://yarra.vicnet.net.au/~ozlit/authors.html

British and Irish Authors on the Web
> http://lang.nagoya-u.ac.jp/~matsuoka/UK-authors.html
> A chronological listing (600 a.d. to current) of links to author Web pages and e-texts.

Yahoo *Guide to Authors*
> http://www.yahoo.com/Arts/Humanities/Literature/Genres/
> Literary_Fiction/Authors/

I. Bibliographies

Bailey, Charles W. Jr. *Scholarly Electronic Publishing Bibliography*. Version 26, 1 Aug. 1999. http://info.lib.uh.edu/sepb/sepb.html (4 Aug. 1999). Also available as pdf and doc files, at http://info.lib.uh.edu/sepb/sepb.pdf and http://info.lib.uh.edu/sepb/sepb.doc, respectively.

Bernstein, Mark. *Hypertext Bibliography*. 16 Mar. 1998. http://www.uta.edu/english/V/S5356.bib.html (1 Aug. 1999).

A Brief Bibliography of Hypertext. 1999. http://www.eastgate.com/Bibliography.html (4 Aug. 1999).

Digital Library Information Resources. 2 July 1999. http://sunsite.berkeley.edu/CurrentCites/bibondemand.cgi (4 Aug. 1999). Citations from *Current Cites*, a monthly bibliography, Jan. 1994 to the present.

Electronic Labyrinth: Bibliography. 1995. http://web.uvic.ca/~ckeep/hfl0268.html (4 Aug. 1999).

Ketchpel, Steven. *Annotated Bibliography of Digital Library Related Sources*. n.d. http://robotics.stanford.edu/users/ketchpel/annbib.html (4 Aug. 1999).

Leggett, John J., Charles J. Kacmar, and John L. Schnase, Hypertext Research Lab, Texas A&M University, *Working Bibliography of Hypertext*. n.d. gopher://ftp.std.com:70/00/obi/book/Hypertext/Texas.A.M/htbib.ascii.Z (4 Aug. 1999).

McCarty, Willard. *Selective Bibliography for Humanities Computing*. May

1996. http://www.kcl.ac.uk/humanities/cch/bib/ (4 Aug. 1999).

Stebelman, Scott. *Hypertext and Hypermedia: A Select Bibliography*. Dec. 1997. http://www.gwu.edu/~gelman/train/hyperbib.htm (4 Aug. 1999).

J. Directories of Discussion Groups, Listservs, etc.

Cover, Robin. *The SGML/XML Web Page/SGML/XML Discussion Groups and Mailing Lists*

> http://www.oasis-open.org/cover/biblio.html (4 Aug. 1999).

Directory of Scholarly and Professional E-Conferences

> http://www.n2h2.com/KOVACS/

> Compiled by a team led by Diane K. Kovacs, this directory contains descriptions of electronic conferences on academic topics. E-conferences include discussion lists, Internet interest groups, Usenet newsgroups, forums, etc. Includes text-based virtual reality systems (MUDS, MOO'S, Muck's, Mushes, etc) that are primarily for scholarly, pedagogical, or professional activities.

Listservs Devoted to Literature

> gopher://gopher.english.upenn.edu/11/Lists

K. Electronic Discussion Lists

E-mail the subscription address with the following message: subscribe <listname> <your forename> <your surname>.

AMLIT-L

> American literature
> listserv@mizzou1.missouri.edu

C18-L

> Eighteenth-Century studies
> listserv@lists.psu.edu

CETH

> Center for Electronic Texts in the Humanities
> ceth@phoenix.princeton.edu

CHAUCER

> Medieval English
> listserv@vtvm1.cc.vt.edu

CHAUCER
>Chaucer, Medieval language and culture
>listserv@unlinfo.unl.edu

CTI-TEXTUAL-STUDIES
>CTI Centre for Textual Studies
>mailbase@mailbase.ac.uk

EALS-L
>English and American Literature Librarians
>listserv@hermes.circ.gwu.edu

ENGLMU-L
>Electronic communication and literature
>listserv@mizzou1.missouri.edu

ESE
>Electronic Scholarly Editions
>listproc@ra.msstate.edu

ETEXTCTR
>Electronic text centers
>listserv@rutvml.rutgers.edu

FWAKE-L
>Finnegans Wake Discussion List
>listserv@irlearn.ucd.ie

GUTNBERG
>Developments on Project Gutenberg
>listserv@vmd.cso.uiuc.edu

HUMANIST
>Humanities and computing
>listserv@brownvm.brown.edu

HY-LIT
>Hypertext and Literary Theory
>subscribe@journal.biology.carleton.ca

LITERA-L
>Literature
>listserv@tecmtyvm.mty.itesm.mx

LITERARY
>Literature
>listserv@ucf1vm.cc.ucf.edu

LITSCI-L
>Society for Literature and Science
>liststar@humnet.ucla.edu

MEDTEXTL
>Medieval texts
>listserv@vmd.cso.uiuc.edu

MLAIB
>*MLA International Bibliography* in academic libraries
>listserv@gwuvm.gwu.edu

MODBRITS
>Modern British and Irish literature (1895–1955)
>listserv@kentvm.kent.edu

REED-L
>Early English Drama
>listserv@vm.utcc.utoronto.ca

SCHOLAR
>Natural language processing
>listserv@cunyvm.cuny.edu

SGML-LIST
>mailbase@mailbase.ac.uk

SHAKSPER
>William Shakespeare
>listserv@ws.bowiestate.edu

SHARP-L
>History of the printed word
>listserv@listserv.indiana.edu

TEI-L
>Text Encoding Initiative
>listserv@uicvm.uic.edu

VICTORIA
>Victorian studies
>listserv@listserv.indiana.edu

WWP-L
>Women's writing
>listserv@brownvm.brown.edu

XML-L
> Extensible Markup Language
> listserv@listserv.hea.ie

L. Newsgroups
alt.etext
alt.hypertext
comp.text
comp.text.sgml
comp.text.xml
usfca.cyberlit

M. Newsletters and Journals
Computers & Texts
> http://info.ox.ac.uk/ctitext/publish/comtxt/
> Newsletter of the Computers in Teaching Initiative at Oxford University.

Current Cites
> http://sunsite.berkeley.edu/CurrentCites/
> An annotated monthly bibliography of selected articles, books, and electronic documents on information technology edited by Teri Andrews Rinne; published since August 1990. An index covers 1994 to the present.

D-Lib Magazine
> http://www.dlib.org/
> Monthly journal for digital library research.

Electronic Labyrinth: Guide to Publications
> http://web.uvic.ca/~ckeep/hfl0224.html
> Links to a small sample of the institutions, publications, and journals that have an interest in hypertext.

The Humanist
> http://www.princeton.edu/~mccarty/humanist/
> Published by the Centre for Computing in the Humanities; covers all aspects of humanities computing.

Internet-on-a-Disk
> http://www.samizdat.com/ioad.html

Newsletter of e-texts and trends, 1994–present.

Journal of Computer-Mediated Communication

> http://www.ascusc.org/jcmc/
>
> A scientific, refereed, quarterly journal that publishes original essays and research reports on such topics as interpersonal and group processes in communication networks, issues of privacy, economics, and access.

N. Associations

Advanced Computing in the Humanities (ACO-HUM)

> http//www.hd.uib.no/AcoHum/aco-hum.html

Association for Computational Linguistics (ACL)

> http://www.cs.columbia.edu/~radev/acl/aclinfo.html

Association for Computers and the Humanities (ACH)

> http://www.ach.org/

Association for Literary and Linguistic Computing (ALLC)

> http://www.kcl.ac.uk/humanities/cch/allc/

Society for the History of Authorship, Reading & Publishing (SHARP)

> http://www.indiana.edu/~sharp/

O. Computing Centers and Institutes

Center for Electronic Texts in the Humanities

> http://scc01.rutgers.edu/ceth/
>
> Produces the inventory of machine-readable texts at CETH.

Centre for Computing in the Humanities

> http://www.kcl.ac.uk/humanities/cch/
>
> CCH at the School of Humanities, King's College, London, promotes the application of computing in the humanities. Sponsors seminars, a newsletter, and maintains its own academic program.

Computing in the Humanities and Social Sciences (CHASS)

> http://www.chass.utoronto.ca/
>
> CHASS at the University of Toronto (founded 1985) provides information relating to humanities computing: news, bibliographies, resources, conference dates, classes offered. Also publishes CH Working Papers (http://www.chass.utoronto.ca/epc/chwp/)

Digital Library Research Group
> http://www.clis.umd.edu/dlrg/
> The Digital Library Research Group (DLRG) at the University of Maryland at College Park conducts research on digital libraries. Problems studied include models of intermediation, interface design and compatibility, user needs, and evaluation.

Institute for Advanced Technology in the Humanities
> http://jefferson.village.virginia.edu
> The Institute, based at the University of Virginia, is designed "to expand the potential of information technology as a tool for humanities research" and to investigate the partnership of computers and cultural heritage. Provides technical support, applications programming, and networked publishing facilities.

National Digital Library Federation (NDLF)
> http://www.clir.org/diglib/
> A federation of research libraries and archives in the U.S. that operate digital libraries. Founded to enable the creation, maintenance, and preservation of dispersed digitized materials and to make them publicly accessible. Specifically focused on documenting U.S. heritage and cultures.

P. Hypertext

Balasubramanian, V. "State of the Art Review on Hypermedia Issues and Applications." Mar. 1994. http://www.isg.sfu.ca/~duchier/misc/hypertext_review/index.html (18 July 1999). A review of the literature.

Barger, Jorn. "Hyperterrorist's Timeline of Hypertext History." 4 Mar. 1996. http://www.mcs.net/~jorn/html/net/timeline.html (1 Aug. 1999).

Bosak, Jon, and Tim Bray. "XML and the Second-Generation-Web." May 1999. http://www.sciam.com/1999/0599issue/0599bosak.html (1 Aug. 1999). Article in *Scientific American*.

Bush, Vannevar. "As We May Think." 1945. http://www.theatlantic.com/unbound/flashbks/computer/bushf.htm (4 Aug. 1999). Bush's 1945 essay on the possibilities of hypertext.

Connolly, Dan. "The XML Revolution." 1 Oct. 1999. http://

helix.nature.com/webmatters/xml/xml.html (1 Aug. 1999). Article in *Nature.*

"Extensible Markup Language (XML*™*)." 21 July 1999. http://www.w3.org/XML/ (4 Aug. 1999). Provides information regarding updates on XML*™*. Documents, events, software, discussion groups, and related linkes. See especially, "The XML FAQ," by Peter Flynn et al.

"Hyperizons: Hypertext Fiction." 22 July 1997. http://www.duke.edu/~mshumate/hyperfic.html (4 Aug. 1999). A listing of hypertext fiction, e-zines, and publishers, with links to theory and criticism.

"Hypertext Resources." 1999. http://www.eastgate.com/Hypertext.html (4 Aug. 1999). Web pointers to on- and off-line hypertext resources. Includes developments in theory and practice, techniques for hypertext writers, home pages of writers, and a bibliography.

"Information about Hypertext." 5 Feb. 1997. http://lucia.lib.lawrence.edu/~gilbertp/hypertext.html (4 Aug. 1999). History, glossary, the Web, HTML guides, examples, papers, bibliography.

Institute for Advanced Technology in the Humanities. "General Publications." 9 Feb. 1998. http://jefferson.village.virginia.edu/generalpubs.html (4 Aug. 1999). Links to theoretical papers and papers that discuss specific projects, including the three papers following.

McGann, Jerome. "Radiant Textuality." 10 Feb. 1996. http://jefferson.village.virginia.edu/public/jjm2f/radiant.html (4 Aug. 1999). On the computerization of literary scholarship and criticism.

———. "The Rationale of HyperText." 6 May 1995. http://jefferson.village.virginia.edu/public/jjm2f/rationale.html (4 Aug. 1999). Discusses the relation of hypertextuality to the scholarly editing of literary documents.

Rockwell, Geoffrey. "Hypertext Places." 1998. http://cheiron.humanities.mcmaster.ca/~htp (1 Aug. 1999). Links to sites on hypertext and hypertext authoring.

Unsworth, John. "Electronic Scholarship or, Scholarly Publishing and

the Public." 1 Oct. 1996. http://jefferson.village.virginia.edu/
~jmu2m/mla-94.html (4 Aug. 1999). On electronic scholarship
in its larger cultural context.

World Wide Web Consortium. "XHTML™ 1.0: The Extensible HyperText
Markup Language: A Reformulation of HTML 4.0 in XML 1.0." 26
Jan. 2000. http://www.w3.org/TR/xhtml (1 Mar. 2000).

Q. Megasites

English Server (Carnegie Mellon)
http://eserver.org

Library Electronic Text Resource Service
http://www.indiana.edu/~letrs/

Literary Resources: Miscellaneous
http://andromeda.rutgers.edu/~jlynch/Lit/misc.html

Literature Resources
http://libraries.mit.edu/humanities/Literature/

Universal Library: Collections
http://www.ul.cs.cmu.edu/

Voice of the Shuttle: Web Page for Humanities Research; English Literature
http://vos.ucsb.edu/
Compiled by Alan Liu, English Department, Univ. of California,
Santa Barbara. See especially the pages on: Cyberculture; Technology of Writing; Science, Technology, and Culture; and Media
Studies.

Yahoo-Arts: Humanities: Literature
http://www.yahoo.com/Arts/Humanities/Literature/

Selected Bibliography

Benaud, Claire-Lise, and Sever Bordeianu. "Electronic Resources in the Humanities." *RSR: Reference Services Review* 23, no. 2 (1995): 41–50.

Chesnutt, David R. "SGML and the Digital Libraries of Tomorrow." *Journal of Academic Librarianship* 24 (1998): 232–36.

Dillon, Andrew. *Designing Usable Electronic Text: Ergonomic Aspects of Human Information Usage.* Bristol, Pa.: Taylor and Francis, 1994.

Faulhaber, Charles B. "Textual Criticism in the 21st Century." *Romance Philology* 45 (1991): 123–49.

Gates, Joanne E. "Literature in Electronic Format: The Traditional English and American Canon." *Choice* 34 (1997): 1279–96.

Gaunt, Marianne I. "Center for Electronic Texts in the Humanities." *Information Technology and Libraries* 13 (1994): 7–13.

Gaynor, Edward. "Cataloging Electronic Texts: The University of Virginia Library Experience." *Library Resources and Technical Services* 38 (1994): 403–13.

Giordano, Richard. "The Documentation of Electronic Texts Using Text Encoding Initiative Headers: An Introduction." *Library Resources and Technical Services* 38 (1994): 389–401.

Guenther, Rebecca S. "The Challenges of Electronic Texts in the Library: Bibliographic Control and Access." In *Literary Texts in an Electronic Age: Scholarly Implications and Library Services*. Ed. Brett Sutton. Urbana-Champaign: Graduate School of Library and Information Science, Univ. of Illinois, 1994.

Hart, Michael. "Project Gutenberg: Access to Electronic Texts." *Database* 13 (1990): 6–9.

Hockey, Susan. "Creating and Using Electronic Editions." In *The Literary Text in the Digital Age*. Ed. Richard J. Finneran. Ann Arbor: Univ. of Michigan Pr., 1996.

———. "Electronic Texts in the Humanities: A Coming of Age." In *Literary Texts in an Electronic Age: Scholarly Implications and Library Services*. Ed. Brett Sutton. Urbana-Champaign: Graduate School of Library and Information Science, Univ. of Illinois, 1994.

———. "Evaluating Electronic Texts in the Humanities." *Library Trends* 42 (1994): 676–93.

Hoogcarspel, Annelies. *Guidelines for Cataloging Monographic Electronic Texts at the Center for Electronic Texts in the Humanities*. Technical Report No. 1. New Brunswick, N.J.: Center for Electronic Texts in the Humanities, 1994.

Ide, Nancy, and Jean Veronis, eds. *Text Encoding Initiative: Background and Context*. Dordrecht: Kluwer Academic, 1995.

Joyce, Michael. "Nonce Upon Some Times: Rereading Hypertext Fiction." *Modern Fiction Studies* 43 (1997): 579–97.

Landow, George P., ed. *Hyper/Text/Theory*. Baltimore: Johns Hopkins Univ. Pr., 1994.

Landow, George P., and Paul Delaney. *The Digital Word: Text-Based Computing in the Humanities*. Cambridge Mass.: MIT Pr., 1993.

The Literary Text in the Digital Age. Ed. Richard J. Finneran. Ann Arbor: Univ. of Michigan Pr., 1996.

Literary Texts in an Electronic Age: Scholarly Implications and Library Services. Papers presented at the 1994 Clinic on Library Applications of Data Processing, April 10–12, 1994. Ed. Brett Sutton. Urbana-Champaign: Graduate School of Library and Information Science, Univ. of Illinois, 1994.

Lowry, Anita K. "Electronic Texts and Multimedia in the Academic Library: A View from the Front Line." In *Literary Texts in an Electronic Age: Scholarly Implications and Library Services.* Ed. Brett Sutton. Urbana-Champaign: Graduate School of Library and Information Science, Univ. of Illinois, 1994.

———. "Electronic Texts in English and American Literature." *Library Trends* 40 (1992): 704–23.

———. "Electronic Texts in the Humanities: A Selected Bibliography." *Information Technology and Libraries* 13 (1994): 43–49.

Mah, Carole, Julia Flanders, and John Lavagnino. "Some Problems of TEI Markup and Early Printed Books." *Computers and the Humanities* 31 (1997): 31–46.

Marchand, James W. "The Scholar and His Library in the Computer Age." In *Literary Texts in an Electronic Age: Scholarly Implications and Library Services.* Ed. Brett Sutton. Urbana-Champaign: Graduate School of Library and Information Science, Univ. of Illinois, 1994.

Neuman, Michael, and Paul Mangiafico. "Providing and Accessing Information via the Internet: The Georgetown Catalogue of Projects in Electronic Text." *Reference Librarian* 41–42 (1994): 319–32.

Nicholls, Paul, and Jacqueline Ridley. "A Context for Evaluating Multimedia." *Computers in Libraries* 16 (1996): 34–39.

Nunberg, Geoffrey, ed. *The Future of the Book.* Berkeley: Univ. of California Pr., 1996.

Ross, Charles L. "The Electronic Text and the Death of the Critical Edition." In *The Literary Text in the Digital Age.* Ed. Richard J. Finneran. Ann Arbor: Univ. of Michigan Pr., 1996.

Seaman, David M. "The Electronic Text Center: A Humanities Computing Initiative at the University of Virginia." *Electronic Library* 11 (1993): 195–99.

———. "'A Library and Apparatus of Every Kind': The Electronic Text Center at the University of Virginia." *Information Technology and Libraries* 13 (1994): 15–19.

———. "Selection, Access, and Control in a Library of Electronic Texts." *Cataloging and Classification Quarterly* 22 (1996): 75–84.

Shillingsburg, Peter. "Principles for Electronic Archives, Scholarly Editions, and Tutorials." In *The Literary Text in the Digital Age.* Ed. Richard J. Finneran. Ann Arbor: Univ. of Michigan Pr., 1996.

Smith, Moira, and Paul Yachnes. "Scholar's Playground or Wisdom's Temple? Competing Metaphors in a Library Electronic Text Center." *Library Trends* 46 (1998): 718–31.

Sperberg-McQueen, C. M. "The Text Encoding Initiative: Electronic Text Markup for Research." In *Literary Texts in an Electronic Age: Scholarly Implications and Library Services*. Ed. Brett Sutton. Urbana-Champaign: Graduate School of Library and Information Science, Univ. of Illinois, 1994.

————. "Textual Criticism and the Text Encoding Initiative." In *The Literary Text in the Digital Age*. Ed. Richard J. Finneran. Ann Arbor: Univ. of Michigan Pr., 1996.

————. "XML and the Future of Digital Libraries." *Journal of Academic Librarianship* 24 (1998): 314–17.

Sperberg-McQueen, C. M., and Lou Burnard. "The Design of the TEI Encoding Scheme." *Computers and the Humanities* 29 (1995): 17–39.

Sutherland, Kathryn, ed. *Electronic Text: Investigations in Method and Theory*. New York: Oxford Univ. Pr., 1997.

Unsworth, John. "Electronic Scholarship; Or, Scholarly Publishing and the Public." In *The Literary Text in the Digital Age*. Ed. Richard J. Finneran. Ann Arbor: Univ. of Michigan Pr., 1996.

Warner, Beth Forrest, and David Barber. "Building the Digital Library: The University of Michigan's UMLib Text Project." *Information Technology and Libraries* 13 (1994): 20–24.

Chapter 6

Assessment of Literature Collections

Scott Stebelman
George Washington University

All selectors, by virtue of their job descriptions, engage in collection development. To spend money allocated to build collections for their academic departments, selectors must review books on the approval shelf, rank firm order slips supplied by the vendor, evaluate gifts donated to the library, and identify new serials in emerging disciplines. As ubiquitous as collection development is in libraries, its complement—collection assessment—is undertaken much less frequently, often because of the significant time commitment and staff resources that must be allocated. Unlike collection development, which usually involves the selection of current materials as they are published or is a direct response to requests by faculty for specific titles, collection assessment is a systematic attempt to evaluate the adequacy of the library to support local research and teaching. The assessment may be global and involve the library's entire collection, or it may be limited to a subset of the collection, such as English and American literature. Collection assessment is of paramount value not only to the library, to determine the historical effectiveness of its collection-building efforts, but also to the academic programs it serves: accreditation is often contingent upon the documentation of strong core collections.[1]

Whether an assessment is global or discipline specific, the individuals responsible for the project must determine its scope. They must decide the subject boundaries, the publication formats, the publication period (i.e., retrospective versus current imprints), and the degree to which ancillary staff will assist in the evaluation. In the case of English and American literature, the selector must decide whether to include linguistics, film, and comparative literature; whether to include nonprint and electronic formats as well as print; whether to restrict assessment of secondary literature to twentieth-century or to late twentieth-century imprints; and whether to involve faculty, students, and other humanities librarians in the assessment. An important blueprint that can identify what areas to target is a preexisting collection development policy statement; some writers, in fact, have argued that it is the prerequisite for assessment.[2] The logic of such a statement seems self-evident: if a library has determined first, through the statement, what it should be collecting, the assessment project can document how successful the library has been in acquiring the necessary materials. If they do not exist, or exist in insufficient numbers, reallocation of resources is indicated.

Before undertaking a collection assessment in English and American literature, it would be useful for selectors to reacquaint themselves with the information-seeking behaviors of literary scholars. In contrast to the sciences and social sciences, in which new research studies often supplant older ones, research in the humanities is cumulative. Twenty-five hundred years encompass Sophocles's *Oedipus*, Shakespeare's *Hamlet*, and Arthur Miller's *Death of a Salesman*, yet few would argue that the twentieth-century work is superior to its predecessors. The rationale that applies to primary works also operates for secondary works: studies of Chaucer and Shakespeare published over the past sixty years are still influential today.[3] According to Richard Heinzkill, Madeleine Stern, Constance C. Gould, and Clara M. Chu, literary scholars also demonstrate a greater reliance on: monographic literature; primary works; interdisciplinary research; nonprint materials; extra-literary artifacts, such as diaries, sermons, and correspondence; and foreign-language imprints.[4] For the literary selector, the implications for collection assessment are clear: a multitude of resources, formats, and publication time frames will need to be considered.

Complicating assessment even further is determining the subjects to be assessed. Before the mid-1960s, this was relatively easy because most scholars could agree on the same set of canonized writers—Chaucer, Shakespeare, Milton, Donne, Wordsworth, Hawthorne, Melville, Dickinson, etc. As Heinzkill has noted, one of the greatest influences on canon inclusion is anthologies, and the writers covered by the two most popular anthologies used in survey courses—*The Norton Anthology of English Literature* and *The Norton Anthology of American Literature*—have their popularity reinforced with each new edition.[5] Although more women and minority writers have been included in the recent editions, selectors need to be cognizant of canon bias when basic tools are identified for the assessment. Just as a canon of writers has existed for many years, so has a canon of genres: when one thinks of English and American literature, one usually thinks of poetry, novels, short stories, and plays. However, as mentioned earlier, more scholars—especially new historicists and feminists—are including a wide variety of nontraditional texts, such as diaries and sermons, in their analysis. Related to the problem of nontraditional texts is the increased use by many literary scholars of interdisciplinary research, especially in the fields of psychology, philosophy, feminism, and cultural studies.[6] Including resources that cite these formats and subjects also must be factored into the assessment.

Before undertaking an assessment, selectors should consider a strategy that is invaluable both politically and intellectually: invite members of the English department to assist in designing and implementing the assessment methodology. Too often, assessments are undertaken unilaterally by librarians who, when finished, present the results to their departments as faits accomplis. However, if faculty have not agreed to the methodology, they may not agree with the results, and therefore they may not fully cooperate with the selector in lobbying for increased materials funding should that be a final recommendation of the report. One technique to ensure faculty participation is to establish an ad hoc committee that will plan the collection assessment. The committee can be composed of the selector, faculty, and graduate students from the English department. Because faculty and students are not trained in collection development, the selector will probably need to present methodological options to the committee. English department members, in turn, can provide precise guidance about what periodicals to include in a citation study or what contemporary authors to check in a review of the library's holdings.

In establishing a methodology for the assessment, the committee may draw on two popular measures frequently used in collection assessments: collection centered and client centered.[7] Collection-centered measures compare the collection against a recognized standard. Collection-centered measures include:

• checking the library's holdings against core bibliographies;

• checking the library's holdings against citations appearing in literary journals and monographs;

• comparing local holdings in English and American literature with those of peer institutions (members of the same consortium, of a market basket group of other universities or colleges identified by the university administration, or of a group deemed to have special relevance for the assessment);

• checking the shelves where literature books are located to determine the physical status and scope of materials.

Client-centered measures provide data on how the collection is being used. Client-centered measures include:

• circulation statistics;

• interlibrary borrowing data;

• citations appearing in faculty publications and student dissertations;

• studies cited in course syllabi;

• studies cited in study lists for the M.A. and Ph.D. comprehensives;

• user survey and focus groups.

Client-centered data can corroborate inferences made from collection-centered data. For example, user surveys may identify the same gaps disclosed by citation studies.

Collection-Centered Measures

Monograph Checklists

Books for College Libraries (3rd ed.), published by the Association of College and Research Libraries, is a good place to begin.[8] *BCL3* contains references to standard author editions, bibliographies, biographies, and secondary criticism. Although intended as an assessment tool for undergraduate collections, many—if not most—of the citations would be appropriate for graduate-level research as well. When using *BCL3*, selectors should be cognizant of the kinds of degrees offered by their institutions. John M. Budd notes that only the larger research and Ph.D.-granting institutions own a majority of the titles cited in English and American literature.[9] Another criticism commonly lodged against *BCL* is its reliance on authors within the canon; women, people of color, gay and lesbian writers, postcolonial writers, and those merely perceived as unconventional are underrepresented.[10] Published in 1986, the third edition also cites many works that no longer are in print.[11] Although the proportion of out-of-print materials may seem to negate the significance of *BCL* as a collection assessment tool, the political significance of these statistics cannot be ignored; if the proportion of cited titles owned is low, the consequences of inadequately funding the monographic budget become apparent. Because the English and American Literature section of *BCL* contains more than seven thousand references, selectors will probably want to select a sample.

A major tool that many selectors might think useful in a collection assessment project is the *MLA International Bibliography*. It indexes more than four thousand journals and hundreds of monographic titles every year. As impressive as the *MLAIB* is as a bibliographic database, it has fundamental problems as a collection assessment tool: the books cited are largely those that have been sent by the publishers to the *MLAIB*. Any attempt, therefore, to make inferences on the state of a local collection based on the monographic titles contained in the *Bibliography* is questionable. One strength the database does have is its listing of Festschriften, a format not easily tracked through other tools, and its inclusion of some foreign imprints relevant to English and American literature.

The Year's Work in English Studies is an annual literature review that evaluates hundreds of scholarly monographs published during a specified year.[12] Published by the English Association in Great Britain, it tends to cover many British monographs omitted by American review organs; conversely, its coverage of American literature is sparser. The American counterpart, *American Literary Scholarship*, has American literature as its exclusive focus.[13] Chapters are organized around major writers and literary periods, and journal articles are included as well as monographs. A particular strength of *ALS* is its inclusion of foreign-language imprints. Because critical and cultural theory have been major areas of study for the past three decades, selectors will probably want to include another annual review published by the English Association—*The Year's Work in Critical and Cultural Theory*.[14]

Because *BCL3* is more than ten years old, and the annual literature reviews usually appear two to three years after date of coverage, selectors will need to include current awareness bibliographies in their assessment. *Choice*, published monthly, would be an acceptable tool for this purpose.[15] It reviews commercial press as well as university press monographs but excludes foreign-language imprints and imprints outside North America. Although primary works are reviewed, only works by minor authors are included. Each issue of *Choice* contains a literature review on a popular topic, some of which may be germane to literary criticism.[16]

If the English and American literature assessment includes the reference collection, selectors will want to check several standard tools.[17] Among these are James L. Harner's *Literary Research Guide*, Michael J. Marcuse's *Reference Guide for English Studies*, the relevant sections of *Guide to Reference Books*, *College and Research Libraries*' annual "Selected Reference Books" review, and the annual volumes of *American Reference Books Annual*.[18] Each of these tools will have to be used cautiously, with an analysis of local holdings tied to the institution's academic program; for example, an English department that offers only an undergraduate degree does not need to have the numerous archival and manuscript reference tools cited in these books.

Serial Checklists

Reviewing the literary journal collection is a primary objective of any study. *Magazines for Libraries* offers a core undergraduate list, which can be supplemented by the literary periodicals indexed in other bibliographic annuals, such as *Humanities Index, American Humanities Index,* the *Arts and Humanities Citation Index, Index of American Periodical Verse,* and *Poetry Index Annual.*[19] The two most comprehensive literary indices—the *MLA International Bibliography* (*MLAIB*) and the *Annual Bibliography of English Language and Literature* (*ABELL*)—must be used judiciously; few (if any) libraries will want to acquire the thousands of titles indexed by these services.[20] In its attempt to be comprehensive, the *MLAIB* has not exercised much selectivity in its listings; alongside *JEGP* and *Critical Inquiry* is the *James Dickey Newsletter*. Another factor precluding complete acceptance of the *MLAIB* listings is its inclusion of many humanities and social sciences journals that may only occasionally publish an article with a literary focus. *ABELL*'s listings are fewer, but the decided British emphasis may be problematical in smaller American libraries. For listings of recent journals, selectors can consult the "New Literary Periodicals" chapter that formerly appeared annually in the *Dictionary of Literary Biography Yearbook* and the lists irregularly published in *Biblio-Notes*, the newsletter of ACRL's English and American Literature section.[21]

Nonprint Materials

No well-recognized evaluative guides exist for nonprint media. In the context of an assessment, selectors might survey the film courses that are being taught and, in consultation with the instructors, determine how well the film collection supports their courses. Films that support literature classes (e.g., biographical/critical films on particular writers, ethnic groups, or literary periods) are equally important, and provide a level of understanding that cannot be provided exclusively by the text. Another format that contributes to literature appreciation is audiocassettes—hearing T. S. Eliot or Robert Frost read his poetry contributes an interpretive element that can be incorporated into classroom discussion. In some cases, such as Middle English Poetry, hearing correct pronunciation of the original text is a precondition for understanding. A useful guide for selecting nonprint media, with a list of specific tools for each medium, is Peter V. Deekle's "Literature and Nonprint Media Resources."[22]

Citation Analysis

Core bibliographies or checklists are useful because they are often compiled by experts in the area. However, they may not reflect the studies scholars actually use in their research. One procedure that does is citation analysis. By checking the monographic or journal citations in key journals, selectors can target a wide range of subjects and publication formats for the assessment. The journals selected can be general, such as *PMLA* and *JEGP*, or they can be devoted to specific literary periods or genres. As with large checklists, a sample rather than the population of citations will need to be selected. In addition, certain decisions will need to be made: what publication dates (both for the citing journal and the cited study) to use; how many issues of each journal to consult; how to establish whether a work is primary or secondary; and whether to include articles on extra-literary subjects. Perhaps most problematical will be the method chosen for subject classification: for monographs, call numbers can be ascertained and matched with Library of Congress class numbers. However, the results can be deceptive, as with Aldous Huxley's *Doors of Perception* (classed in RM) and Samuel Taylor Coleridge's *The Statesman's Manual* (classed in BL). These books will be selected not because they are important studies about drugs or religion but, rather, because they were written by important literary figures. But the computer will count them as sociological or religious works, thus leading to data misinterpretation. The problem is more severe if nonmonographic formats are cited because the selector will have to determine, quite subjectively, how to class the item, and monitor the consistency of judgments from one article to another. These problems do not negate the value of citation analysis, but they will need to be anticipated before the analysis is undertaken.

OCLC AMIGOS

Using checklists allows one to compare local holdings against a putative core collection. As helpful as this information is, the comparison is (as noted by Budd's study) more abstract than real: only the most substantial research libraries can afford to acquire the majority of these titles. A more realistic comparison is with a library's peers (i.e., other libraries with similar holdings, student enrollment, academic programs, etc.). OCLC provides software, called AMIGOS, that allows such a comparison, provided that the libraries designated for the comparison are members of OCLC. The libraries selected in an AMIGOS study often are members of the same consortium, the same market basket group, or a unique group aggregated by the library undertaking the assessment. The strength of AMIGOS is that it provides overlap cataloging data between the peer institutions, allowing an individual library to compare its holdings in key call number ranges with that of similar libraries (or libraries it aspires to emulate); it also provides a title-by-title display, enabling libraries to examine which specific titles are unique to a collection. Jeanne Harrell describes how she used AMIGOS to compare the holdings of Texas A&M's English section with that of university-defined peer institutions; she found that her library's holdings in the PRs and PSs were higher than that of the average peer institution.[23] AMIGOS does have some design flaws that complicate analysis: two copies of a book are counted as different publications if their imprint data are not identical; and libraries may catalog, at different times, books published during the same year. Hence a book with a 1997 imprint may not be counted if the library catalogs it in 1999.[24]

Although no library has yet reported using peer departments as a comparative group, this analysis can be more productive and credible than using more artificially constructed peer groups. The National Research Council periodically undertakes a ranking of American graduate programs, and the ranking of doctoral-level English programs could be used by institutions whose English departments offer this degree. A selector could identify in which quartile his or her local English department belonged, then ask AMIGOS staff to provide data for the OCLC libraries belonging to the quartile. The comparative data obtained would probably be more acceptable to the English faculty, who might demur at data from market basket or consortial English departments whose

programs and quality markedly differ from one another.[25] A final advantage to using AMIGOS is that call number ranges used are based
on the North American Title Count; these correspond roughly to literary periods and, in some cases, genres. Hence the level of analysis can
be more detailed than just comparing the PRs or PSs within peer institutions; these same data also can be used should cooperative resource
sharing be initiated among the institutions. For example, institutions
with strong holdings in a particular period might be designated as the
primary collector for future publications in that area.

RLG Conspectus

Another tool that can be used for institutional comparisons is the Research Libraries Group Conspectus.[26] Now administered by the Western Library Network (WLN), the Conspectus allows libraries to use a
variety of assessment techniques, such as shelf scanning, list checking, shelf list analysis, and expert opinion, to determine the adequacy of
a designated collection. Worksheets with appropriate Library of Congress
class ranges are provided to assessing libraries, and collection intensity
codes, from 0 (Out-of-scope level) to 5 (Comprehensive), are assigned to
each subject area. Libraries whose institutions grant doctorates in the
subject area might be expected to have a 3 or 4 collection intensity level;
departments offering only a B.A. might be expected to have a 1 collection
intensity level. After intensity codes have been assigned, verification
studies can be made to confirm the reliability of the judgments.

Although the Conspectus provides raw empirical data for the
library's assessment, it does have some drawbacks. The Conspectus
was originally designed for large research libraries, but Mary F. Casserly,
speaking of the needs of college libraries, notes that the Conspectus
"is not the most efficient or effective method of assessing the strengths
and weaknesses of predominantly usage-based collections."[27] As Richard J. Wood notes, one problem of the LC framework is that the total
collection is not always represented by the classification numbers on
the worksheets.[28] In the area of literary theory, much important work
is classed in B and H. Another criticism has been made by the English
selector at the University of New Mexico, who questioned the verification studies used for her subject; for example, her library's holdings on

Thom Gunn, a relatively minor British poet, were to be used as a bench-mark of the collection's overall quality.[29] The problem with the English and American literature verification tool—the *New Cambridge Bibliography of English Literature*—was its age and selectivity. Many of the studies cited were dated, and the primary works were often published before modern standards of textual editing were developed.

Checking Materials on the Shelves

Because monographs are especially valued by humanities scholars, the physical state of the English and American literature collection needs to be ascertained. Selectors can target specific Library of Congress class numbers (e.g., the range for Medieval literature), sample titles within that range, and report the condition of the books. Physical characteristics to examine include the binding, deterioration of the paper, print fading, and missing pages.

In addition to reviewing the physical state of the books, the selector can judge the chronological diversity of the imprints. A collection that is strong from 1950–1970, but has significantly fewer titles published during the 1990s, is in serious jeopardy of becoming antiquated. Other features of the imprint to note are location (Does the library own few British books?) and publisher (Is the collection top-heavy in university press publications at the expense of important commercial press titles?). Finally, narrow subject areas of the collection can be targeted for review, such as the contemporary American literature collection. If several courses are taught on this subject, and only a few shelves have books devoted to it, a possible gap exists.[30] Shelf checking by its very nature is impressionistic and the observations need to be verified by more empirical measures; however, if conducted early in the assessment, it can flag potential problem areas that will need further investigation.

Client-Centered Measures

Circulation Data

The monographic checklists used in an assessment can provide two kinds of information: whether a specific title is owned, and how often it has circulated. If the latter information is captured, the literary selector can ascertain the circulation frequency of:

- books restricted to a specific literary period or genre;
- primary works as opposed to secondary works;
- specified publisher categories, such as university versus commercial presses;
- books by period of publication;
- books by language of publication;
- English and American literature books as opposed to those in other disciplines.

This information can be captured by creating a worksheet for each citation checked. Using any standard statistical software package, cross-tabulations can be made between multiple variables; for example, selectors could discover whether primary editions of Renaissance texts circulated more often than those of nineteenth-century texts, or whether current imprints were more popular for American literature users than those studying English literature.[31] Circulation data can be a useful measure of which parts of the literature collection, and what kinds of materials, are being used most heavily; together with student enrollment figures, courses taught, and number of faculty specializing in a particular area, it can help selectors determine which subareas within the collection need more attention.[32]

Interlibrary-Borrowing Data

The interlibrary loan (ILL) department should be able to provide a list of titles requested by members of the English department. These titles will indicate gaps in the collection, as well as research interests of faculty and students. However, using these titles as the basis for selection decisions can be problematic: humanities scholars use a wide variety of materials in their research, materials that may be so specialized and narrow that they may never be consulted again. For example, someone interested in knowing whether a sixteenth-century physician ever attended Oxford might want to read *A Biographical Register of the University of Oxford, 1501 to 1540* and request the book through interlibrary borrowing. However, based on that request, is the library's collection really deficient because it could not supply that title? Moreover, should the library expend the money—perhaps $100 or more because it is likely to be a reprint—to acquire it? Interlibrary-borrowing information can be useful for identifying important titles missing from the collection, or patterns of materials (e.g., eighteenth-century minor fiction writers) that are consistently used and requested. But the data must be evaluated cautiously.[33]

Course Syllabi, Reserve Lists, and Graduate Student Exam Reading Lists

An obvious tool for assessing the collection is to use English department course syllabi as checklists. Every title cited on the syllabi should be in the collection, including works from the suggested reading lists. Instructors' reserve lists also should be checked for local ownership, even though logic would suggest if a title is on reserve the library must own it; unfortunately, many reserve copies are instructors' personal copies and these will be withdrawn after the course is terminated. Like reserve lists, reading lists for the M.A. and Ph.D. comprehensive exams occasionally cite materials not owned by the library, such as older Medieval or Renaissance editions that can only be obtained through reprint or microform publishers or through out-of-print jobbers.

Faculty Publications and Graduate Student Dissertations

An unobtrusive way of gauging faculty and graduate student satisfaction with the collection is to review their publications and identify how many of the studies they cite are held by the library. The inference commonly drawn is that if the library owns a high proportion of them, the collection is adequate. However, several writers have suggested this reasoning is flawed. F. W. Lancaster summarizes the criticism:

> Some investigators have evaluated the collection of a university library on the basis of references contained in faculty publications or in doctoral dissertations produced in the university (e.g., Buzzard and New, 1983). This approach is of doubtful validity. Several investigations have shown that the 'principle of least effort' has a major effect on information-seeking behavior: the more accessible an information source, the more likely it is to be used (Allen and Gerstberger, 1968; Rosenberg, 1966,

1967). More specifically, Soper (1972, 1976) has produced results to suggest that accessibility influences citation behavior—the more accessible the source, the more likely it is to be cited. If writers are more likely to cite sources readily available in their institutional library than to cite sources not so available, an evaluation of the collection on the basis of these citations introduces a definite bias in favor of the library. Rather than use internally generated dissertations, for example, it would be preferable to draw bibliographic references from those produced in comparable departments in other universities (i.e., departments with similar research interests).[34]

Doctoral dissertations also evince other kinds of document skewing. In an attempt to cover original ground, students frequently choose topics that are narrow, such as very minor writers about whom there is little or no published research. Because the topics are narrow, the only other studies that are relevant are often other dissertations. Hence graduate students tend to cite dissertations with a frequency not observed in more seasoned scholars. The pressure to be original also disposes some students to appropriate methodologies or paradigms from other disciplines, and to cite non-English-language studies. Basing collection development on the idiosyncratic titles appearing in dissertations, written by students who will soon leave the university, would divert money away from more popular areas of research.

User Survey and Focus Groups

User perceptions of the collection can often indicate weaknesses undetected by the selector. For example, English faculty and graduate students interested in psychoanalysis may note gaps in the writings of Lacan, gaps that might have been unrecognized by a psychology department whose focus is experimental rather than clinical, or behaviorist rather than Freudian.[35] Because selectors tend to be most familiar with canonical writers and genres, spotty holdings in emerging subdisciplines or areas, such as postcolonial theory, also may need special attention. As important as user surveys are in identifying existing or potential problem areas, they can be equally useful as a public relations tool: by querying the primary user group, selectors send a message that they value the group's opinion and are sensitive to the practical consequences of strong or weak collection development—the inability of faculty (and untenured faculty are especially vulnerable) to conduct research effectively.

User surveys can be conducted in several ways. If dealing with a small population, such as exists in most English departments, surveying every member rather than a sample would be advised. The survey can be conducted through the mail, e-mail, telephone calls, or personal visits to faculty offices.[36] The latter has the advantage of allowing faculty to amplify their answers and to raise other issues of concern to them.

Another method for surveying opinion is the focus group.[37] Unlike the written survey, or the single interviewer/interviewee session, focus groups permit a facilitator to meet with a group of users (usually between eight and twelve) and to solicit responses to specific questions. Among these questions might be:

• What is the state of the journal collection? Is it adequate to meet the needs of scholars? In what areas is it strongest? weakest?

• Is the general collection adequate to meet the research needs of undergraduate students? What authors or genres are well represented? underrepresented?

• Do faculty use the nonprint media collection in their teaching? What do they think of its quality?

• Is the library acquiring cutting-edge research in the faculty's fields? What research areas need strengthening?

• Are there presses important to literary research that the library should add to its approval plan? What are they?

• Do faculty use electronic materials, either on the Web or on CD ROM, in their teaching or research? What are the most important new electronic materials for the library to acquire?

To encourage participants to provide detailed information, focus group questions need to be open-ended rather than closed. The groups also need to be facilitated by an expert in group dynamics and by someone who does not have a personal relationship with the participants; by definition, this will probably exclude the English selector. Focus group observations need to be tested and confirmed by empirical data. For example, someone may criticize the weak holdings in eighteenth-century literature when, in reality, they are quite strong.

Special Considerations

Approval Plans and Collection Development Policy Statements

Although approval plans need to be checked periodically to ensure that they reflect any curricular or research changes in the English department, their review should be an essential component of any assessment project. For example, more ethnic literature classes may have been recently approved by the department, some professional association presses (e.g., the Modern Language Association of America or the National Council of Teachers of English) need to be included, and some marginal or vanity presses need to be excluded. Limiting the review to English and American literature descriptors or to Library of Congress class numbers also may be myopic. As mentioned earlier, literary criticism is becoming increasingly cross-disciplinary, and as a consequence, selectors will need to check the approval profiles for psychology, sociology, history, women's studies, theater, linguistics, and any other area believed germane to English faculty research interests. Because collection development policy statements influence the subject and format parameters specified in approval plans, selectors also should consult the policy statements written for these disciplines. The statements may explain why the collection is weak in certain areas and may identify inconsistencies among departments that need to be reconciled. Finally, many libraries have a contemporary authors subprofile in their plan, which stipulates that the works of certain authors will automatically be shipped to the library, if the publishers are treated by the vendor. The selector should review the department's commitment to contemporary literature at this time, and if the commitment is strong, perhaps add additional writers, and if weak, consider deleting writers and the concomitant approval allocation.

Electronic Publications

The proliferation of electronic texts, which can be accessible locally or remotely, is revolutionizing the way scholars conduct research. Some institutions have invested heavily in this revolution by developing electronic text centers, which can house texts published by other vendors, digitize special collections, and point users to other storage facilities.[38] In spite of the emergence of these centers, it is unclear what impact they will have on the way humanities scholars conduct future research; studies by Wiberley, Chu, Lehmann and Renfro, and Olsen indicate that humanists continue to doubt the constructive role computers can play in research.[39] This resistance, coupled with the trend in most libraries to reduce expenditures for valued printed texts, may make faculty question the wisdom of acquiring electronic ones. (See chapters by Wiberley and Willett in this volume.)

Even if libraries do not purchase electronic texts for their own collection, they will need to provide access to the multitude of electronic documents that exist on the Web. In speaking of scholarly access, Ross Atkinson has made the useful distinction between the local collection and the ante-collection: the local collection is what the library stores in-house, and the ante-collection "is the set of all publications not held in the local collection."[40] Atkinson projects, in an electronic environment, the death of collection development as commonly understood; the user, who has the potential to access an almost infinite number of documents on the Web, becomes the selector, and the librarian, as evaluator, provides "continuous ranking and reranking of the potential utility of information units as they relate to local research and instruction."[41] Susan K. Martin makes a similar pronouncement, suggesting that in order for librarians to retain the confidence of their clientele, they need to assume the same selection authority in an electronic environment as they do in the print environment.[42]

The single most important factor transforming the nature of literary research is hypermedia.[43] Instead of reading a unitary text on a flat page, scholars can now link to a variety of texts that can only be awkwardly represented in variorum print editions. By clicking on a hyperlinked word or phrase, they can be taken to the phrase in context, to the full text of the cited work, to ancillary primary texts useful for source studies, and to secondary texts that provide critical commentary. By clicking on other words or phrases, they may view the illustrations that accompanied the original text, hear the author reading the work, or see photographs of locations cited in the text. Hypermedia materials not only provide multisensory understanding of literary artifacts, but the promise—through the economies of digitization—of altering the canon to include writers heretofore excluded.[44]

Building and assessing a local electronic materials collection is difficult. As Marianne I. Gaunt has asserted, "selectors of electronic literary texts are confronted with two impediments to selecting materials: the lack of bibliographic tools to identify them . . . and the lack of reviewing media to evaluate existing products. The lack of reviewing media is complicated by the fact that there are no broadly defined standards of what constitutes a high quality electronic text."[45] Anita Lowry, acknowledging the same problem, has provided several evaluation criteria, ranging from consideration of the software and documentation to the kind of markup language used.[46]

If Atkinson is correct, however, in emphasizing the growing value of the ante-collection, and Martin in arguing that librarians must continue to function as information arbiters, how does a selector assess the adequacy of an electronic collection that exists elsewhere? The first step might be to establish guidelines that serve as the sine qua non for both access and utilization. Among these guidelines are:

• For materials locally held, the library must own the necessary hardware to view them.

• For materials held remotely, the institution must provide the telecommunications infrastructure to gain access to them.

• For materials held remotely, faculty must own the necessary hardware to access them.

• For materials available only through subscription, the institution must provide the necessary funding to access them.

• For all electronic materials, the institution (through either the library or the campus computer center) must provide training to access and interpret them.

The failure to provide any of these resources should be acknowledged and the extent to which it compromises effective research and teaching discussed.

Because the nature and content of electronic publishing is continually changing, it is difficult for selectors to establish benchmarks, or checklists, as indices of collection adequacy. One might argue, for example, that the Early English Text Society editions are essential only for graduate-level English programs, but how does one determine appropriate level for a complex webliography, such as *The Voice of the Shuttle*, which includes primary and secondary texts, instructor syllabi, conference announcements, and other nontraditional information clusters?[47] Currently no core list of literary sites exists, but those sites that are freely (wholly or in part) accessible over the Web should be available to all literary scholars. As for resources that require a fee, libraries will have to use the same criteria (e.g., student enrollment, number of faculty, level and prestige of academic program) used in traditional funding allocations, or holdings comparisons with peer institutions, to determine whether to subscribe to the journals offered through Project Muse, the full-text databases offered by Chadwyck-Healey, and to bibliographical databases such as *Periodicals Contents Index* and the *Annual Bibliography of English Language and Literature*.

Implementation of Collection Assessment Project

The time needed to undertake and complete a collection assessment project depends on the project's objectives, scope, and number of support staff (if any) assigned to it. If the project is limited to monographs and employs only one collection-centered measure (such as checking a sample of titles from *Books for College Libraries* and *Choice*), the project could be completed within a few months. If the project includes a variety of publication formats, and uses several collection-centered and client-centered measures, the project might take several years. What is important for the selector is to determine what organizational and time constraints already exist and to factor these into a timetable. For example, a selector working without staff assistance, who also works twenty hours on the reference desk and has a heavy user education load, will need to establish modest assessment goals. After the assessment has been completed, a report will need to be written. At a minimum, the report should delineate the methodology used, the scope and limitations of the project, the results (i.e., identified strengths and weaknesses within the collection), and budgetary allocations necessary for retrospective and future purchases.[48] Ideally, the report should be co-signed by members from the original ad hoc committee that planned the assessment.

Conclusion

With the growing importance of remote access, it can be argued that the rationale to expand local collections is diminishing. If libraries can subscribe to the full-text journals available from Project Muse and JSTOR, are expensive duplicate print subscriptions still necessary? If the original editions of nineteenth- and early twentieth-century works can be accessed through *The Making of America* and other digital libraries, is the acquisition of reprint or microform copies advisable, especially given the perishability of acid paper and the resistance users have to microform formats? For many libraries that are members of regional consortia, is it necessary for every member of the consortia to have approval plans that include the same university presses? If the importance of strong local collections becomes moot, why should selectors expend their valuable time, and institutions their valuable resources, to assess a collection whose physical dimensions may be reduced dramatically in the next century?

The provisional answer to all of these questions is that both collection assessment and collection development are driven by three powerful forces: accrediting agencies, institutional enrollments, and the ability of the library to support campus research and teaching. If institutional accreditation is jeopardized because of its library's marginal holdings, the institution will no longer be able to recruit students. Related to the issue of enrollment is the library's status vis-à-vis peer institutions: a university that wants to be viewed as a major research institution will want its library to have ARL status, and for a library to have ARL status, volume count is critical. The last factor—the need for the library to support institutional research and teaching—is paramount; although conversion to electronic formats is proceeding rapidly, it will probably be decades before most humanities texts are digitized and accessible remotely.

Until that transformation occurs, the acquisition of printed texts will have the highest priority, and the assessment of these collections will be necessary to maintain the scholarly and teaching reputation of the institution. For these reasons, collection assessments in English and American literature, as with any discipline, must be planned systematically. Selectors must determine what parts of the collection they want assessed, what tools and methods they will use, what comparative bodies (e.g., peer institutions) are relevant to the assessment, and what organizational resources are available to assist them. Ideally, the library will provide additional funding for the assessment, not only in the form of support staff necessary for list checking, but also in the acquisition of other aids, such as AMIGOS software, RLG Conspectus materials, and focus group facilitators. If planned collaboratively with members of the English department, the results will be accepted more easily by library and university administrators. The greatest challenge for literary selectors is to understand the dynamics of both print-based research and electronic research that is evolving on the World Wide Web. Although humanities scholars have traditionally been resistant to new technology, the twenty-first-century scholar will, if for no other reason than necessity, be using an array of hypermedia that will redefine how knowledge is constituted and experienced. Librarians need to anticipate these changes and be forceful advocates for them if their users are to remain intellectually stimulated and professionally competitive.

Notes

1. Felix T. Chu, "Librarian–Faculty Relations in Collection Development," *Journal of Academic Librarianship* 23 (1997): 15–20.

2. See Blaine H. Hall, *Collection Assessment Manual for College and University Libraries* (Phoenix: Oryx, 1985), 1.

3. A citation count of three classic works supports this observation. For the period 1980 through May 1997, the *Arts and Humanities Citation Index* indicates John Dover Wilson's *What Happens in Hamlet?* (1st ed., 1935) was cited 54 times; Caroline Spurgeon's *Shakespeare's Imagery* (1935), 83 times; and D. W. Robertson's *A Preface to Chaucer* (1962), nearly 300 times.

4. Richard Heinzkill, "Characteristics of References in Scholarly English Literary Journals," *Library Quarterly* 50 (1980): 352–65; Madeline Stern, "Characteristics of the Literature of Literary Scholarship," *College and Research Libraries* 44 (1983): 199–209; Constance C. Gould, *Information Needs in the Humanities: An Assessment* (Stanford, Calif.: Research Libraries Group, 1988); Clara M. Chu, "The Scholarly Process and the Nature of the Information

Needs of the Literary Critic: A Descriptive Model" (Ph.D. diss., Univ. of Western Ontario, 1992).

5. Richard Heinzkill, "The Literary Canon and Collection Building," *Collection Management* 13, nos. 1–2 (1990): 51. A common misperception is that the canon has been radically altered by Marxists, feminists, and other radical scholars. However, a survey of English department chairs about the writers covered in their survey courses indicates little change has occurred. See Bettina J. Huber, "What's Being Read in Survey Courses? Findings from a 1990–91 MLA Survey of English Departments," *ADE Bulletin*, no. 110 (1995): 40–48.

6. For a discussion of the importance of interdisciplinary research in literary criticism, see Eric Carpenter, "Toward Interdisciplinarity in Literary Research: Some Implications for Collection Development," *Collection Management* 13, nos. 1–2 (1990): 75–85, and Harrison T. Meserole, "The Nature(s) of Literary Research," *Collection Management* 13, nos. 1–2 (1990): 65–73.

7. Hall, *Collection Assessment Manual for College and University Libraries*, and Barbara Lockett, ed., *Guide to the Evaluation of Library Collections* (Chicago: ALA, 1989).

8. *Books for College Libraries: A Core Collection of 50,000 Titles*, 3d ed. (Chicago: ALA, 1988).

9. John M. Budd, "The Utility of a Recommended Core List: An Examination of *Books for College Libraries*, 3d ed.," *Journal of Academic Librarianship* 17 (1991): 142.

10. See Lynn Silipigni Connaway, "An Examination of the Inclusion of a Sample of Selected Women Authors in Books for College Libraries," *College and Research Libraries* 56 (1995): 71–84.

11. Based on his sample, Budd indicates that 41.7 percent of *BCL*'s "Language and Literature" titles were out-of-print. Budd, "The Utility of a Recommended Core List," 143.

12. *The Year's Work in English Studies* (Oxford: Blackwell, 1919/20–).

13. *American Literary Scholarship* (Durham, N.C.: Duke Univ. Pr., 1965–).

14. *The Year's Work in Critical and Cultural Theory* (Oxford: English Association, 1994–).

15. *Choice* (Middletown, Conn.: ACRL, 1964–).

16. See Scott Stebelman, "Using *Choice* as a Collection Assessment Tool," *Collection Building* 15, no. 2 (1996): 4–11.

17. For an overview of literary reference taxonomies, see Scott Stebelman, "Building Literary Reference Collections," in *English and American Literature: Sources and Strategies for Collection Development*, ed. William McPheron, Stephen Lehmann, Craig Likness, and Marcia Pankake (Chicago: ALA, 1987), 156–80.

18. James L. Harner, *Literary Research Guide: An Annotated Listing of Reference Sources in English Literary Studies*, 3d ed. (New York: MLA, 1998); Michael

J. Marcuse, *A Reference Guide for English Studies* (Berkeley: Univ. of California Pr., 1990); Robert Balay, ed., *Guide to Reference Books,* 11th ed. Chicago: ALA, 1996); *College and Research Libraries* (Chicago: ALA, 1939–); *American Reference Books Annual* (Littleton, Colo.: Libraries Unlimited, 1970–).

19. Bill Katz and Linda Sternberg Katz, *Magazines for Libraries,* 9th ed. (New Providence, N.J.: Bowker, 1997); *Humanities Index* (New York: Wilson, 1975–); *American Humanities Index* (Troy, N.Y.: Whitston, 1976–); *Arts and Humanities Citation Index* (Philadelphia: Institute for Scientific Information, 1978–); *Index of American Periodical Verse* (Lanham, Md.: Scarecrow, 1971–); *Poetry Index Annual* (Great Neck, N.Y.: Poetry Index, 1982–). Robert Hauptman has provided a recommended core list of literary titles (now somewhat dated) based on the degree(s) offered by an English department. See Robert Hauptman, "Serials," in *English and American Literature: Sources and Strategies for Collection Development,* ed. William McPheron, Stephen Lehmann, Craig Likness, and Marcia Pankake (Chicago: ALA, 1987), 82–101. Additional retrospective lists are cited and evaluated in Richard R. Centing, "Evaluating Literary Journals," *Collection Management* 16, no. 4 (1992): 71–77.

20. *MLA International Bibliography* (New York; MLA, 1922–); *Annual Bibliography of English Language and Literature* (London: Modern Humanities Research Association, 1921–).

21. *Dictionary of Literary Biography Yearbook* (Detroit: Gale Research, 1980–); *Biblio-Notes* (Chicago: English and American Literature Section, ACRL Division, ALA, 1982).

22. Peter V. Deekle, "Literature and Nonprint Media Resources," in *English and American Literature: Sources and Strategies for Collection Development,* ed. William McPheron, Stephen Lehmann, Craig Likness, and Marcia Pankake (Chicago: ALA, 1987), 144–55.

23. Jeanne Harrell, "Use of the OCLC/AMIGOS Collection Analysis CD to Determine Comparative Collection Strength in English and American Literature: A Case Study," *Technical Services Quarterly* 9, no. 3 (1992): 7.

24. For a discussion of the advantages and disadvantages of using AMIGOS as a collection assessment tool, see Curt Holleman, "The Study of Subject Strengths, Overlap, and National Collecting Patterns: The Uses of the OCLC/AMIGOS Collection Analysis CD and Alternatives to It," *Collection Management* 22, nos. 1–2 (1997): 57–69.

25. The latest study undertaken by the National Research Council was in 1993 and surveyed 8,000 faculty at 274 universities. A report of the study, with rankings, is published in "Rankings of Research-Doctorate Programs in 41 Disciplines at 274 Institutions," *Chronicle of Higher Education,* Sept. 22, 1995): A21–A30.

26. The complete issue of *Acquisitions Librarian,* no. 7 (1992), consists of fourteen essays addressing the merits of the RLG Conspectus. An excellent

overview of the Conspectus methodology is Richard J. Wood, "A Conspectus of the Conspectus," *Acquisitions Librarian*, no.7 (1992): 5–23.

27. Mary F. Casserly, "Collection Development in College and University Libraries: A Comparison," in *Collection Development in College Libraries*, ed. Joanne Schneider Hill, William E. Hannaford Jr., and Ronald H. Epp (Chicago: ALA, 1991), 12.

28. Wood, "A Conspectus of the Conspectus," 12–13.

29. Claire-Lise Benaud and Sever Bordeianu, "Evaluating the Humanities Collections in an Academic Library Using the RLG Conspectus," *Acquisitions Librarian*, no. 7 (1992): 132.

30. Selectors must be careful not to make holding inferences without checking circulation data. If few books on a particular subject are not present on the shelf, their absence may be due to the subject's popularity—many of the items may be checked out. A propitious time to conduct shelf checking is the end of the semester, when most circulated items have been returned. For an overview and critique of availability studies, see F. Wilfrid Lancaster, *If You Want to Evaluate Your Library* . . . (Champaign: Graduate School of Library and Information Science, Univ. of Illinois, 1988), 90–103.

31. Establishing whether a work is primary or secondary is occasionally difficult. For example, some selectors might classify T. S. Eliot's *The Varieties of Metaphysical Poetry* and R. P. Blackmur's *Studies in Henry James* as primary, others as secondary.

32. For those selectors interested in using allocation formulas to determine collection adequacy, see the classic study by Verner W. Clapp and Robert T. Jordan, "Quantitative Criteria for Adequacy of Academic Library Collections," *College and Research Libraries* 26 (1965): 371–80, and the alternative formula provided by the ACRL in "Standards for College Libraries," *College and Research Libraries News* 47 (1986): 189–200. Lancaster provides a reasoned critique of this, and other collection assessment methods, in *If You Want to Evaluate Your Library*.

33. The Erasmus Medical Library (Netherlands) provides a model of how ILL requests can be used to develop the periodicals collection. See Ans Bleeker, et al., "Analysis of External and Internal Interlibrary Loan Requests: Aid in Collection Development," *Bulletin of the Medical Library Association* 78 (1990): 345–52. Mounir A. Khalil, "Applications of An Automated ILL Statistical Analysis as a Collection Development Tool," *Journal of Interlibrary Loan, Document Delivery and Information Supply* 4 (1993): 45–54, demonstrates how individual title data can be generated from statistical software and then submitted as purchase orders. However, for the purposes of collection assessment, the same software can aggregate important group data (e.g., class numbers) to identify gaps in the collection. To determine whether ILL group data reflect the borrowing patterns of the circulation data, and hence is

an indicator of which collection areas are under- or overused, see the formula in William Aguilar, "The Application of Relative Use and Interlibrary Demand in Collection Development," *Collection Management* 8, no. 1 (1986): 15–24.

34. Lancaster, *If You Want to Evaluate Your Library,* 28.

35. Carpenter, "Toward Interdisciplinarity in Literary Research," 80.

36. An excellent English department faculty questionnaire, used at Brigham Young University, appears in Hall, *Collection Assessment Manual for College and University Libraries,* 134–38.

37. For background reading on the focus group, see David L. Morgan, *Focus Groups as Qualitative Research,* 2d ed. (Thousand Oaks, Calif.: Sage, 1997); Richard Widdows, Tia A. Hensler, and Marlaya H. Wyncott, "The Focus Group Interview: A Method for Assessing Users Evaluation of Library Service," *College and Research Libraries* 52 (1991): 352–59; Lynn Silipigni Connaway, "Focus Group Interviews: A Data Collection Methodology for Decision Making," *Library Administration and Management* 10 (1996): 231–39.

38. The premier electronic text center is the University of Virginia's Electronic Text Center. For background information, see David Seaman, "The Electronic Text Center: A Humanities Computing Initiative at the University of Virginia," *Electronic Library* 11 (1993): 195–99.

39. Stephen E. Wiberley Jr., "Habits of Humanists: Scholarly Behavior and New Information Technologies," *Library Hi Tech* 9, no. 1 (1991): 17–21; Chu, "The Scholarly Process and the Nature of the Information Needs of the Literary Critic"; Stephen Lehmann and Patricia Renfro, "Humanists and Electronic Information Services: Acceptance and Resistance," *College and Research Libraries* 52 (1991): 409–13; Jan Olsen, *Electronic Journal Literature: Implications for Scholars* (Westport, Conn.: Mecklermedia, 1994).

40. Ross Atkinson, "Access, Ownership, and the Future of Collection Development," in *Collection Management and Development: Issues in an Electronic Era,* ed. Peggy Johnson and Bonnie MacEwan (Chicago: ALA, 1994), 97.

41. Ibid., 101.

42. Susan K. Martin, "Organizing Collections within the Internet: A Vision for Access," *Journal of Academic Librarianship* 22 (1996): 291.

43. For a discussion of how hypermedia is redefining authorship, texts, and learning, see George P. Landow, *Hypertext: The Convergence of Contemporary Critical Theory and Technology* (Baltimore: Johns Hopkins Univ. Pr., 1992). Jerome McGann provides a lucid explanation of how hypermedia will transform text generation, with examples from several HyperEditing projects, in "The Rationale of Hypertext," *Text* 9 (1996): 11–32.

44. Marlene Manoff, "The Politics of Electronic Collection Development," in *Scholarly Publishing: The Electronic Frontier,* ed. Robin P. Peek and Gregory B. Newby (Cambridge Mass.: MIT Pr., 1996), 218.

45. Marianne I. Gaunt, "Literary Text in An Electronic Age: Implications for Library Services," *Advances in Librarianship* 19 (1995): 201.

46. Anita Lowry, "Electronic Texts in English and American Literature," *Library Trends* 40 (1992): 704–23.

47. *The Voice of the Shuttle: Web Page for Humanities Research*, 3 Aug. 1999, http://humanitas.ucsb.edu/ (5 Aug. 1999).

48. For examples of collection assessment reports, see "Collection Description and Assessment in ARL Libraries," SPEC Kit no. 87 (Washington, D.C.: Office of Management Studies, ARL, 1982).

Chapter 7

The MLA International Bibliography *and Library Instruction in Literature and the Humanities*

Judy Reynolds
San Jose State University

This chapter discusses how best to teach the *MLA International Bibliography of Books and Articles on the Modern Languages and Literatures* to several levels of students. My discussion is based on a review of the literature on teaching and on the library research strategies of humanists (especially students), an e-mail survey conducted in 1997, an examination of teaching materials at LOEX and the California Clearinghouse on Library Instruction and on the Web, and on my own teaching experience. The *MLAIB* is our field's most important bibliography and is used by a diverse range of students and researchers who have different needs, knowledge, and skill levels. Just as the library profession is changing, so too are the *MLAIB* and our students. The *MLAIB*'s coverage and features are continually evolving as the boundaries of literary and language studies expand. Only change is constant.

The status of the *MLAIB* in libraries varies, according to the results of my e-mail survey.[1] Although some libraries may be teaching *MLAIB* who do not have it in electronic form, this is now uncommon. A few teaching faculty and librarians still browse the general section of the print *MLAIB*, but students enthusiastically prefer the electronic versions. For students, the print version has now become "nonexistent." Several vendors offer the *MLAIB*, and search processes and capabilities differ among vendors. The variety of versions (DOS, Windows, and Web) further complicates the matter. A library also may provide more than one version of the database—one for in-house use to suit the library's hardware capabilities and another for remote use. The decision to purchase a specific version from a particular vendor may have little to do with the effectiveness of its searching because that decision also may be influenced by factors such as remote availability, compatibility with copy cards, operating systems, and discounts offered to the purchaser's system, consortium, or library.

The aim of instruction should be to teach students how to explore and evaluate as a process of discovery. Unfortunately, even though we wish to focus our instruction on effective use of the *MLAIB* options, such as subject headings, publication year, publication type, and other clues from the records, it is currently all but impossible to ignore the perfunctory mechanics of individual interfaces so that "the emphasis is on the product rather than the process of searching."[2] Librarians now lament the amount of time they spend teaching generic mechanics, such as how to display, print, and download. Their real intention is made obvious in any review of materials on the Web and in the clearinghouses: it is to teach important *MLAIB* features. In the small amount of time we spend in class with students, and considering the fact that students use a variety of interfaces, it is incumbent upon us to provide them with transferable literary research strategies to use in searching any version of the *MLAIB* (and other language and literature resources). Today's students often have careers and families, and are interested in strategies that will enable them to make efficient use of their time. Many come from "nontraditional" backgrounds and may not yet have acquired either library or computing skills. The rest of this chapter is devoted to discussing ways to teach the *MLAIB* so that students do in fact explore, evaluate, and discover.

Background

The designers did not plan to cover everything, but the *MLAIB* is now criticized for not having been even more comprehensive. Originally, it was a classified bibliography, a model that works for organizing scientific knowledge. For the first sixty years, the *MLAIB* provided little access by subject, theme, or genre. Is it little wonder, then, that humanists did not see it as central to their research? Why are we now surprised that faculty, having spent their entire research lives in this environment, are unaware of the potential of the electronic form?

The *MLAIB* covers journal articles, books, chapters and essays in books, and dissertations on literature, linguistics, language, folklore, and scholarly literary criticism. Geographic scope includes literature of the British Isles, British Commonwealth, English Caribbean, and American, European, Asian, African, and Latin American literatures. Works on literature transmitted orally, in print, or in audiovisual media are included. Human language also is covered, which includes both natural languages and invented languages that exhibit the characteristics of human language (e.g., sign language for the deaf, Esperanto, computer-programming languages).

The *MLAIB* evolved from the *American Year Book* as a current awareness tool for researchers in literature to use in keeping abreast of publishing by American scholars about American, British, Germanic, and Romance literatures and languages.[3] As such, it served for many years as a classified bibliography, updating scholars and guiding new researchers into traditional areas of research. Access was limited largely to the study of particular authors, listed by country, subdivided by century. In the 1950s and 1960s coverage was extended to include Eastern European and then African, Latin American, and Asian literature and language. Until the 1970s brought assistance from the National Endowment for the Humanities and Mellon Foundation, most of the indexing was accomplished by volunteer scholars.

The *MLAIB* first used detailed subject headings in 1981, at last making it possible for scholars to pursue interdisciplinary topics, comparative literature, theme, genre, literary movements and approaches, theory, linguistics, and folklore. This enhancement opened doors for investigating a multiplicity of research questions. However, features that were the strengths of large, older databases in the paper-copy days can slow or limit today's options. The *MLAIB* faces especially difficult challenges in adapting the database to electronic versions. Over the years, it has developed unique categories and tags that are not always easily forced into the indexing structure of the host software. Many of the electronic versions are unable to utilize much of the wealth of the indexing. The uncertainties of electronic publishing, coupled with low profits and shortage of government and private funding, limit what innovations are possible. Probably the biggest challenge to teaching the database today is its lack of controlled vocabulary. The Modern Language Association (MLA) recognizes that the *MLAIB* would benefit not only by more standardized vocabulary for the database, but also by use of terms that could be shared by other humanities indexes, strengthening interdisciplinary research efforts.

The scope of academic research on language and literature has grown and diversified, including great debate about the literary canon. For example, the MLA's *Introduction to Scholarship* volume grew from a five page statement of principles in 1938 to a 377-page work (including a bibliography) in 1992. Only three percent of the items in the 1992 bibliography were repeated from the 1981 edition. Summarizing the above changes in scholarship, Jonathan Beck stated that as recently as the 1970s, "to 'master a field' meant that one had read everything in it," but now "we have not read everything in our field, and have no intention of trying."[4]

The *MLAIB* indexes scholarship on or relating to topics beyond the study of literature. It is a good source for folklore, providing indexing to scholarly titles using the specialized terms, and for film studies, where topics include film directly compared with literary works, film criticism and theory, directors, schools of film criticism, categories of film, cultural studies of novels and films, politics, the visual arts, aesthetics, human behavior, communication, and information processing.[5] The *MLAIB*'s indexing of the field of linguistics only partially suffices for most research in linguistics, which is becoming increasingly interdisciplinary. Students and scholars also need to search for material in very diverse fields. Linguistics topics range from social and political issues such as teaching Ebonics to highly specialized calculations of speech acts, requiring study in the fields of education, psychology, sociology, anthropology, biology, computing, and political science. As it is improbable that students outside language and literature classes will receive instruction devoted, even in part, to the use of the *MLAIB*, the search options need to be obvious even to the occasional user.

Survey respondents reported that they regularly taught related indexes in conjunction with the *MLAIB* when they dealt with subjects other than English or American literature. Foreign-language courses, for example, covered limiting by language in *MLAIB* and the use of *Lexis-Nexis*. Additional resources regularly taught include: for linguistics—*Linguistics and Language Behavior Abstract: LLBA*, *Bibliography of Linguistics*, *Language Learning*; for theater—*Lexis-Nexis*, Internet, *Humanities Index*, *Art Index*, *Social Science Index*, *International Bibliography of Theatre*, *Arts & Humanities Citation Index*; for film—*Film Literature Index*, *International Index to Film Periodicals*; and for communications—*ERIC*. Other indexes mentioned were: *Alternative Press Index*, *Women's Studies Abstracts*, *Women's Studies Index*, *LION*, *ABELL*, *WorldCat*, *Books in Print*, *Cumulative Book Index*, and library online catalogs.

General Teaching Issues

Instruction in the use of the library is best done by librarians in cooperation with teaching faculty, ideally integrated into the course work rather than just as a one-hour stand. Not only can librarians provide students with the latest information on resources in a rapidly changing information environment, but their involvement in a course also visibly demonstrates that library research is an integral part of university curriculum. All students, not just those already comfortable in the library and persistent enough to ask for one-on-one attention at the reference desk, deserve this instruction. Instruction sessions should be ADA accessible and open to the discussion of diversity. Specialized, advanced research tools such as the *MLAIB* should be introduced at the point in a student's career when their use is essential for successful completion of course work.

Goals

Clear teaching goals and objectives are necessary to justify the instruction and focus the sessions, imparting useful information in one's limited class time. Universities have general education, accreditation, or information competency guidelines or requirements, an ideal place to ensure a requirement for librarians to introduce scholarly library research strategies. In addition, the ACRL's Instruction Section established goals in its "Guidelines for Instruction Programs in Academic Libraries," and more recently, an ACRL task force issued "Information Literacy Competency Standards for Higher Education."[6] The librarian must clearly articulate the students' needs in order to gain the support for instruction time and requirements from teaching faculty and administrators. The California State University System,

---

FIGURE 1

California State University Information Competencies[7]

1. State a research question, problem, or issue.
2. Determine the information requirements for the research question, problem, or issue.
3. Locate and retrieve relevant information.
4. Organize information.
5. Analyze and evaluate information.
6. Synthesize information.
7. Communicate using a variety of information technologies.
8. Use the technological tools for accessing information.
9. Understand the ethical, legal, and socio-political issues surrounding information and information technology.
10. Use, evaluate, and treat critically information received from the mass media.
11. Appreciate that the skills gained in information competence enable lifelong learning.

for example, has drawn up a list of core abilities (see figure 1). Librarians can use such competency lists as the basis for establishing comprehensive programs on their campuses. Mutually agreed upon with the teaching faculty, these skills lists can assist librarians in establishing programs that build on basic requirements and highlight the need for advanced students to master sophisticated tools such as the *MLAIB*.

Techniques

Active Learning. For instruction to be most effective, students must take an active part in their learning. Analyzing their topics and matching them with words in a database while in class are much more effective than just listening to a lecture. "Active learning," according to Cerise Oberman,

> is built on the assumption that critical thinking is, perhaps, even more important than subject content. In other words, if students can think critically about broad general principles, then they are even more likely to be able to apply those principles to new and different problems. . . . Providing students with the cognitive tools to make informed decisions must become a keystone of library instruction. Students unable to cope with the overwhelming number of choices available to them will be further disenfranchised from the information structure.[8]

Point-of-Use Guides/Web-Based Instruction. Most librarians in the survey reported that they did not make use of *MLAIB* curricular materials available from LOEX, vendors, or other libraries. Most made up materials themselves. Most of the Web pages and material from LOEX and the California Clearinghouse on Library Instruction were point-of-use guides. They addressed issues such as printing, downloading, and executing various search options. Printed point-of-use guides appear to be evolving into Web pages, making them accessible to both in-house and remote users. One librarian in the survey reported that point-of-use guides were discontinued after the library had *MLAIB* in a

Web version. Still, for use in a class session, paper handouts are reliable and many students and faculty still prefer them. Some libraries/systems have developed standardized handouts and Web forms. Quite a few of the *MLAIB* Web pages are adaptations for products such as FirstSearch and SilverPlatter. This type of instruction may be relatively ineffective in teaching search strategy and has been developed as an adjunct to live sessions. No online tutorials were found in Scott Stebelman's list of *MLAIB* Web pages.[9]

Live Demonstrations. Demonstration is still the main mode in libraries that do not have hands-on computer classrooms, though it is becoming less the norm. Using active learning techniques, most librarians use this time to discuss with students how to improve a live search. This teaches students that they are "masters of their own fate—what they enter is exactly what they will retrieve," said one librarian.

Hands-on Instruction. Libraries are responding to student and faculty requests for hands-on instruction. Harold H. Kollmeier and Kathleen Henderson Staudt stated that the most important pedagogical factor in successfully teaching students to search the *MLAIB* and other databases online is for faculty to "watch the students' progress" and confer with them "at the terminal" as the students are "refining and analyzing a topic."[10] In order to introduce instruction at points in the course where students need it, multiple sessions of varied length may be required. Before students are set loose to search in a hands-on session, librarians recommend that the stage be set with a lecture or demonstration tied to the assignment and then followed by a half-hour of hands-on activity in the lab. This enables the instructor to circulate among students and assist them as needed. Graduate students, having more complex topics, may require individualized consultations in order to cover specialized limit options and the like.

Evaluation

It is essential to have feedback on instruction, especially as the level of student varies and the information environment is rapidly changing. Feedback enables the instructor to adapt instruction for improved learning. Although assessment can be quite elaborate, Patricia K. Cross and

Thomas A. Angelo suggested two simple questions that can quickly provide ideas for refining future sessions: What did you learn today that was new? and What would you still like to learn? [11]

Grading assignments based on a joint assignment for course-integrated library instruction will provide the librarian with the best insight into student learning. Assumptions that freshmen know that they will not find novels, short stories, and other primary works or that AltaVista includes all the scholarly literature an advanced student might need will quickly become obvious when one reviews student work. Additional discussion on evaluation techniques is available for anyone wishing to explore this topic further. [12]

Why Do We Need to Teach?

Why do we need to teach the *MLAIB*? Why is the process not self-explanatory and all teaching focused simply on describing the scope of the database and related resources? Following are some of the reasons:

• Because we teach a wide range of students, from novice freshmen to doctoral students and budding scholars in research courses.

• The search options in *MLAIB*, in any of its forms, are not obvious.

• The students may not know enough about the subject to pick a topic and use the basic options.

• The goal of instruction should be to empower students with a knowledge of the basic elements in language and literature searching regardless of what version of *MLAIB* they may use.

The students we teach run the gamut from beginning-level freshmen who just need a few references about a work they read to advanced-level graduate and doctoral students who have extensive knowledge of their subject areas, though perhaps not too detailed a mental map of the available information structure. Instruction must be targeted appropriately. Novices need assistance in constructing simple searches. At more advanced levels, students need to utilize more varied search options to find and compare themes, treatments, and theoretical approaches.

Rather than teaching traditional linear methods, such as following up interesting footnotes and titles acquired from bibliographies or serendipitous discoveries, we can engage students and retain their instructors' support by demonstrating how new technologies extend the accepted methodologies in their field. Focusing on integrating the new access methods, rather than discarding and replacing the old ways, will be more effective in eliciting support from teaching faculty, whose involvement validates our instruction for students. Teaming with teaching faculty, we need to design *MLAIB* instruction sessions and assignments that are productive and interesting processes of enlightenment rather than excruciating, time-consuming ordeals. We want to focus students on the rewards of doing research.

Instruction sessions by librarians are sometimes viewed as time spent hearing about resources that have little relevance to the specific assignment for the class. Stephen Lehmann and Patricia Renfro interviewed humanist scholars and found that, "the most fundamental distinction between researchers and librarians is perhaps the emphasis on *content* by the one and on *access* by the other."[13] One needs to gauge audience enthusiasm and match the instruction. Students develop a framework for searching, an understanding that there probably is a secondary literature to peruse and that the librarians can help them search more efficiently and effectively. There is a risk in waxing eloquent about all the things one has to offer. One discouraged graduate student confessed that she dropped out of school after being overwhelmed by an introduction to the library. She was discouraged and apprehensive that she would have to master so many scholarly sources.

Instruction in the use of the *MLAIB* must be customized to address the audience level, but because the focus of humanistic research is directed by personal response to reading, the process does not lend itself to standardization. Terry Plum and Topsy N. Smalley cautioned against the temptation to adopt the "one-size-fits-all" model. "Common everyday model search strategy approaches are found wanting because there *are* no clear-cut, lock-step procedures to doing humanities research."[14] Students' information needs evolve as they progress through the university. Although three student levels are outlined in the next section of this chapter, the categories are suggestions and should be adapted to fit the particular situation. Teaming with instructional faculty to select a topic, much like the Teaching College model,[15] focuses on tailoring instruction to the particular class assignment, thus making the link to their needs obvious to students.

Faculty Attitudes Toward Library Instruction and the MLAIB

To determine the essential elements of searching the *MLAIB*, we must first look at the characteristics of humanities researchers. Understanding the research perspective of our teaching faculty colleagues will enable us to design our instruction in concert with them to suit student learning needs. In chapter 12, Stephen Wiberley analyzes faculty research characteristics and their implications for collection development. In this chapter, I examine how these characteristics influence faculty attitudes toward instruction by librarians.

Traditional Characteristics of Literature Scholarship
Studies of the information-seeking patterns of humanists reveal that they rely heavily on searches for individuals' names, geographical areas, and historical periods.[16] Monographs, possibly because they represent large investments of scholarship, are the backbone of their work.[17] Humanists are willing to look through large lists of potential information and are happy to find a few new items. Their desire to personally review citations is hardly surprising. Online indexes retrieve items based on critics' names, words in metaphoric titles, and words in subject headings that are created with only limited authority control. There are no abstracts to provide insight into the item's content or embedded topics. It is little wonder that humanists feel they must sort through massive lists of promising titles, guessing at probable relevance.

The new electronic systems have, as yet, done little to allow humanists to delegate their research. Searching the subject, or the "aboutness," of a critical or artistic work can only be hinted at with a subject heading. Library cataloging has never seriously tried to attribute subject headings to literary works. The persistence of humanists, despite the comparatively primitive nature of their indexes, highlights their inventiveness, resourcefulness, and adaptability. Instead of being thwarted by the system, they make the best use of their time by relying on citation tracking. Electronic systems have not been heavily utilized because they do not perform very well and do not merit the investment of a scholar's time. Rebecca Watson-Boone summarized the findings of sixteen studies, saying they clearly indicate that "humanists will not use what they do not need."[18]

Attitude toward Electronic Resources

Because it is clear that, for now at least, humanists must dredge through long lists of citations, it is not surprising that they view online database searching as little more discriminating than vacuuming a floor. It is little wonder they are skeptical of librarians' urgings to use computers. Wiberley and Jones pointed out that "it is easy for librarians to lose sight of users who have limited interest in or need for technology."[19]

Reliance on computing also appears to shift the locus of control and judgment away from the researcher. This can be very uncomfortable for humanists, who have always worked alone, relying on their own judgment. Use of computers shifts the focus of research from the process of exploration and discovery to the product of the search. Teaching faculty members Kollmeier and Staudt did not welcome the librarian's role as mediator in their individual searches. They objected to the intrinsic "notion that all the important decisions about what one is looking for have been made before the search itself, and largely by someone else," and argued: "In traditional research, the researcher must possess both the ideas and the technique; when computers are used today, the researcher still has the ideas, but must appeal to a professional for the technique."[20]

The Getty study reported polarized reactions of scholars to the rush of citations from a DIALOG search. On the one hand, they felt out of control like the "sorcerer's apprentice"; on the other, they found an incredible tool, like "Las Vegas for the intellectual." They complained, however, about "the rigidity of Boolean logic, difficulty of formulating search queries, different structures and standards between databases, and difficulty in winnowing down retrieved sets."[21]

Wiberley and Jones believe that because humanists exercise little control over their primary evidence, they find information technology hardest to use. Instead of constructing tests of hypotheses, they study "products of a specific place and time and shaped by the distinctive personalities . . . The uniqueness and scatter of humanistic data invite individual, not collaborative interpretation."[22] B. J. Rahn said that humanists "lack the conceptual framework and language common to professionals in these other fields. They don't think in terms of data and its manipulation."[23] On the other hand, Smalley and Plum described the nature of publishing in the humanities and argued that the humanist transforms each piece of information: "[I]t is pointless to teach library skills in the humanities without recognition of the role of the author and recognition of the text as substratum."[24] It can also be argued that the humanist chooses to trade control over data in exchange for personal exposition: "The research process is an interpretive journey in search of meaning; the author is an active participant by bringing a unique reading."[25]

Marcia J. Bates contended that humanists cannot be assumed to be searching for specific, uniquely named topics. Although the humanist's perspective traditionally has emphasized the "ability to see broad trends, sensitivity to metaphor, ability to recognize the significance of a series of seemingly unconnected historical events," online search language, instead, involves "the mathematical precision and analytical logic required of one in using database syntax."[26] In addition, Mara R. Saule pointed out that the hierarchical nature of binary computers and databases is contrary to the humanists' world view.[27] Getty scholars felt that DIALOG "takes thinking from scholars," "eliminates my judgment and insight," and "makes you align scholarship with what it does."[28]

Bates suggested that resistance to new technology by humanists does not stem from Luddite or stubborn qualities and that the reluctance might be transformed into that technology's strongest base of support. Altering their research style "cuts deeper into the heart of their research paradigm than is the case for scientists. Change in this area automatically has more ramifications and requires more adjustments . . . Improvements in information access will reach into the daily activities of the humanities scholar the same way that a major new laboratory tool or a new experimental research technique might for the scientists."[29] As the search software begins to make the options more obvious, it should put the reins back into the hands of the scholar, who will then be more likely to utilize it.

As we work with teaching faculty to teach research with the *MLAIB*, it is important to keep in mind that reducing the number of citations for the humanists means limiting access to primary material on the basis of terms that can only hint at the world of ideas contained in the cited work. Instruction needs to emphasize options that put the researchers and their students in control of their explorations and support "fuzzy" searching for words and their connotations. If humanists are to use electronic resources, the emphasis in system development needs to be on those options that offer users some insight into and control over the search process. Options for *MLAIB* enhancements are discussed later in conjunction with levels of instruction.

What Do Teaching Faculty Think about Library Instruction?

Do faculty think students need instruction in library research? In 1990, Joy Thomas repeated her 1982 faculty study and found that little had changed. Teaching faculty were still unlikely to believe that instruction in the use of the library should be part of their classes, arguing that their curriculums were already "too full." Teaching faculty Kollmeier and Staudt felt they had sufficient skills to teach composition students to search: "We quickly dismissed the idea that we would become experts in the theory and structure of the databases: this was not our area of expertise, nor did it need to be." In contrast, Robert K. Baker's study of faculty perceptions has led him to conclude that faculty are receptive when the offer is framed in terms of the pedagogical goals of a specific course rather than on more "generic appeal." He found faculty believe that "librarians have a major role to play in creating the library as a nurturing and supportive environment."[30]

Martha Flemming found that more science and social science professors than humanities professors request more bibliographic instruction to be integrated into course work.[31] Interest in instruction may be greater in fields where online searching more closely matches traditional library research style. Only 30 percent of the four-year liberal arts colleges in Pennsylvania, Indiana, and Michigan surveyed by

Fleming in December of 1992 owned the *MLAIB*. Is it surprising that faculty who have not used indexes as a primary information source and may have done much of their formative research when the *MLAIB* was a classified index are not clamoring for instruction for their students? Because departments in the humanities disciplines tend not to be very well endowed, scholars were not strong online search advocates before the introduction of CD-ROM and Web options due to the new techonogy's high costs and uneven results.

At Earlham, a college with a history of strong support for library instruction, English professor Gordon W. Thompson found that literature students already know how to find information, but that "They needed guidance in making judgments between excellent materials and merely good ones. Above all, they need guidance in finding perspectives that challenged their own points of view . . . Until librarians teach judgment as well as information gathering," it will be difficult to make library instruction and the assignments work.[32] Students' growing interest in the Web as a resource forces us to address the issue of evaluation.[33] Librarians should stress that the *MLAIB* is restricted to scholarly publications and is comprehensive rather than evaluative, and they should suggest criteria for evaluation. We can explain the nature of the editing and refereeing process in research and the need for students to exercise individual responsibility for evaluating sources. Teaching faculty, appropriately, will continue to be responsible for teaching evaluation of critical arguments.

Offering instruction is a political issue that depends on factors such as local library resources, campus climate, and role of research in learning and course content. These factors directly impact faculty receptivity to our involvement. Integration into the required curriculum may be achieved as part of programs for general education, information literacy, or basic research skills. It is often necessary to be proactive and market instruction with individual teaching faculty, curriculum committees, and academic senates. Librarians, as the database/system selectors, have the most current information on availability and searching features, a unique perspective. Faculty will be most receptive to instruction tailored to their courses. It is imperative that librarians make teaching faculty aware of the research on student searching. The focus should be more on improving teaching and learning in courses where one has the opportunity to teach, rather than worrying about uninterested faculty. A good example is often the most winning argument for extending the instruction. Targeting specific courses will ensure that most students receive an acceptable level of instruction and help make the library's workload manageable.

Levels of Instruction

Until now, targeting student populations for appropriate instruction has largely been done on the basis of educated estimates of the student level by librarians with suggestions from instructors. Recent studies of the information-seeking habits of students and researchers in the humanities provide additional reality checks and options for measuring and tailoring instruction to the appropriate level at our local universities.

Beginning-Level Students

Kollmeier and Staudt maintain that undergraduates "tend to perceive the research paper as an information-gathering exercise, rather than a process of discovery and analysis" and that "Students' attitudes toward the usefulness of database searching were directly connected to its practical benefit for their particular assignments." According to Gloria J. Leckie, they think "in terms of a coping strategy." Lawrence L. Reed concluded that students are likely to retrieve too much and need to be taught how to search selectively. Instruction should emphasize that "research is not note-taking, it is idea tracing . . . In the online environment researching a topic involves searching, noting alternative terms and likely looking items, doing another search, noting terms, etc., and selectively recording citations."[34] Librarians in my survey commented that students are still confused about whether to expect full text, and they characterized the students' grasp of indexing, abstracting, publishing, and copyright as woefully inadequate.

Debora J. Shaw described the habits of undergraduates in her study: "The concepts of narrowing and broadening a search proved useful to some students, while others seemed to have a less sophisticated tactic of guessing the lucky word—a sort of 'pin the tail on the donkey' strategy." Students, she continued, "tended to 'escape' (using the <escape> key) from difficult situations and try different files rather than try to figure out how to overcome problems encountered."[35] Leckie felt that the expert searcher model and its assumptions just do not work for novices. These false assumptions are that students (1) have some grasp of the breadth of the field, (2) know the field well enough to focus on a specific question, and (3) will ask for help from instructor or librarian if stuck.[36] Shaw, too, found that freshmen often did not have sufficient knowledge of their subject to begin searching and needed to find the meanings of some terms first.[37] A French department instructor (a survey respondent) said that her students got stuck early in their research, and spent too much time reading about the topic before feeling "capable" of searching. She explained to them that "every day librarians are able to find detailed information on subjects they have never studied." Another librarian pointed out the need for a basic understanding of the subject prior to their search in the library: "Why track down an esoteric article on Dante when the student has yet to get even a general handle on who Dante was and what he wrote? To a certain extent this is spoon-feeding information but it gives a new student what he or she needs, namely, a foundation to build upon."

How can we adapt teaching to enhance lower-division research needs? Leckie says that we must start by working with faculty to design assignments that are not too open-ended. Freshmen (composition students and the like) may have assignments that do not really require use of a database as sophisticated as the *MLAIB*. They may never again expect to read this discipline's scholarly literature. Surveyed librarians suggested that our undergraduates are not prepared to deal with the subject matter at the point in their academic career when we introduce the *MLAIB* to them. We need to start them off with *Contemporary Literary Criticism, Humanities Index, Infotrac,* or other reference materials. "Now, with undergrads, I Unteach the *MLAIB*." Instead, they should be taught to "mine the monograph collection first." Students at campuses with limited journal holdings must use interlibrary loan even for basic sources. Nonetheless, freshmen are often strongly encouraged to use the *MLAIB* by their instructors. When this happens, the librarian should work with the teaching faculty member to make the assignment more specific, including more appropriate materials, so that the students will have a more interesting and fruitful experience.

It is important for the teaching faculty to be involved in brainstorming sessions with the students, reinforcing the concept that manipulating the topic is encouraged. Many students asking for help at a reference desk feel uncomfortable accepting the assurances of a librarian that their topic can be modified. As Leckie cautioned, overly broad topics should be pared down into workable assignments in advance. Instructors sometimes deliberately pick new authors about whom they expect little criticism has been written to prevent students from parroting someone else's material. Topics such as the American Dream are not only vague, but nearly unintelligible for English-as-a-second-language speakers, students from other countries, or young students. Clearly, this last sort of assignment is not appropriately tied to teaching how to search *MLAIB*.

Instructors who require students in introductory courses to use the *MLAIB* to locate criticism should be advised to check first that sufficient material is in the collection or available via interlibrary loan within the time frame of the assignment. They should verify that the subject has, indeed, been indexed by *MLAIB*. In the past, faculty often expected library instruction to cover how to write citations. Although this is no longer the norm, it is essential, at every student class level, to teach how to read citations and acquire the material. It is not just the entry-level student who has difficulty interpreting citations. *MLAIB* has historically been especially cryptic in its references to chapters.

The long-term goal of teaching the use of the *MLAIB* is that students learn when and how to use it in their research. What should be covered in beginning-level instruction? With an appropriately concrete assignment, instruction in the use of the library should include "(1) planning information-seeking strategies, (2) developing more effective search techniques, (3) evaluating sources and citations, and (4) navigating through the technological options."[38] The goal of instruction at this level is to provide students with knowledge of how to do straightforward, simple searches for authors or topics using the *MLAIB*. Learning objectives for beginning-level students should be to:

• understand that the *MLAIB* indexes scholarly research in language and literature;

• brainstorm the topic and terms to use in searching;

• execute a simple search, including author, title of creative work, characters;

• read a citation;

• locate items in the library;

• if items are not in the collection, know other options, such as using another index, consulting bibliographies or excerpts of criticism, or modifying the topic.

Intermediate-Level Students

Intermediate students, mainly upper-division majors and minors in language and literature, probably benefit most from library instruction. They are motivated to learn about their field but have not yet devised their own personal searching style and have little or no mental map of the structure of information in the discipline. Having done some reading in their field, they are interested in learning more. As they acquire a working knowledge of their discipline, they develop a conceptual framework that will assist them in categorizing and using the new information. Keiko Kuhara-Kojima and Giyoo Hatano found that knowledge of one's subject facilitates learning facts and provides the groundwork for judgment.[39] Students at this level want to make efficient use of their time, using whatever tools are necessary. They are more familiar than freshmen with basic search options and the vocabulary, including genres and literary techniques.

This is the prime time to assist them in identifying the basic elements to use in literature and language search systems. First, they must understand the scope of the *MLAIB*. It is an international bibliography of scholarship, not primary works, published on literature, linguistics, folklore, film, and popular culture. It is comprehensive, but not as current as less exhaustive sources. In addition to especially thorough indexing of journals, it also covers chapters in books, books, and dissertations. Searching in some versions can be limited by unique fields such as genre, language, theme, theoretical approach, and type of criticism, such as deconstructionism or feminism. It is useful for cross-disciplinary research. Survey respondents recommend it for searching film history, music history, cultural studies, academic approaches to popular culture, and printing and publishing history. However, it must be used with caution. The *MLAIB*'s subject headings are less "consistent" than is the case in many other electronic indexes, making it more difficult to teach and use.

Upper-division students have sufficient subject knowledge to put their ideas into categories and to sort citations. At this stage, Saule suggested that librarians teach students to devise a search strategy by (1) analyzing the question, (2) grouping common elements, (3) selecting the database, and then (4) outlining the mechanics.[40] Shaw found evidence that students at this level use discipline terms in the citation to evaluate citations: "The titles, subject headings, and abstracts (in the databases which had abstracts) were especially helpful in assessing relevance. . . . This is a sharp contrast with assessments by humanities graduate students, where these nontopical indicators were used in over 20% of decisions to accept or reject citations."[41] The graduate students used screening clues that required more secondary knowledge of the field, such as reputation of the author or journal.

Shaw also found that undergraduates suffer from inflexibility, and this underlines the need for these students to learn not only to brainstorm about terms, but also to spend some search time on a tentative topic, rejecting some of the items they retrieve: "Students who had done some previous searching and were looking for pieces to fit into an already-formed structure had more trouble finding the right citations than did students in the initial, exploratory search mode." Surveyed librarians reported that it is sometimes difficult to get students to consider other terminology than the exact terms used by their professors. On a campus where library instruction is integrated across the curriculum, the librarian reports that students who are already familiar with less specialized resources have difficulty understanding techniques of searching the *MLAIB*: "Students seem to understand the mechanics of searching the database, but often have conceptual problems with the MLA database search. Their level of understanding does often reflect the amount of preparation that the course instructor has given them prior to library instruction."

Students try to find a list of everything on a work or an author and then select from the long list of citations. They are still formulating their ideas while searching the *MLAIB*, looking for an idea imbedded in a title that they can use to focus their research. Because the subject headings in the *MLAIB* are inadequate to deal with metaphoric titles and imbedded themes, a keyword search is often more fruitful. "Fuzzy sets"—lists of citations that are not narrowly relevant—are to be expected in humanities searches. The *MLAIB* thesaurus, for example, lists "unspeakable" and "west" but offers no scope note or broader or related terms. A search for the subject heading "west" proves so broad as to be nearly worthless, retrieving works about West Michigan place names as well as concepts of space and society.

Upper-division students will be interested in basic strategies that put them in control of their searching. Contrasting the role of bibliographies, literature reviews, and footnotes with that of comprehensive sources such as library catalogs and the *MLAIB* would be useful for students wishing to limit the number of items they must scrutinize. Reviewing standard scholarly approaches, such as theme, genre, literary period, will provide students with a transferable model of perspectives to use each time they need to break down an assignment. This will assist them in generating terms and finding analogous material, as well as material covered as part of a broader topic. Instruction should include a review of tools that will assist students in categorizing topics and authors using the vocabulary of literary study. Handbooks and guides can provide insight about assigning terms such as Jacobean, picaresque, Romantic, or even nineteenth century.

Wiberley's research suggested that common terms are not useful and that more specific searching is the norm for humanists.[42] Although this might make sense in theory, it does not work out so well in practice in the *MLAIB*. Simple searches in the *MLAIB* for a specific author and/or title are likely to be successful. But intermediate-level search topics require more precise focus and use of subject and related terms. A search for variants of "house" misses citations using "home" or "family" that might have proved useful. Lack of control vocabulary, an inadequate thesaurus, and absence of abstracts result in inconsistent results. Inferred references cause difficulty. A citation to a work on

Shakespeare, for example, may not include subject headings for all the plays, characters, methods, and genres addressed in the cited work. Using specific language and literature terms in *MLAIB* does not always lead to satisfactory results. All too often, such a search misses relevant items. For example, a search for "novelle" retrieves few references in common with a search for "short novel." Entering the subject heading "magic realism" misses many items that include the phrase "magical realism." Although the *MLAIB* was much improved by the addition of subject access in 1981, there is no way to be sure one has used all the relevant terms on the topic. Students must understand this paradox and be advised to create multiple, key word sets. One librarian commented: "Although I do use thesauri and refer students to them, I have found that Boolean key-word searching usually yields a more valid set of hits." And another regularly advises searching for a concrete noun and then using "or" to modify the results.

Teaching students to follow up the subject headings for additional terms after an initial keyword search is probably the most effective strategy. Using as an example a topic the students have already studied with their instructor, its various segments, synonyms, and broader and narrower terms can be charted.[43] Using this template to map topics by the basic scholarly approaches enables students to visualize and manipulate research topics and peruse related terms not specified in subject headings or titles. The topic is: How is the image of travel by rail used in the works of Thomas Mann? (See figure 2.) Other categories might include title of the creative work, literary movement, or demographic groups (ethnicity, age, gender, etc.).

Use of available search options such as word list and thesaurus will introduce these students to methods for exploring variations of authors' names, synonyms, and related terms, and is a means to explore broader, narrower, and related terms. The *MLAIB* database includes about twenty subfield options that only the most dedicated students learn to use. Future Web versions could query users if they would like to search broader, narrower, and related terms as well as a list of subfields. Subjects and subfields attached to records in Web versions of *MLAIB* are not currently active links; they must be typed in manually. This severely limits efficient tracking of subject links, a powerful

---

FIGURE 2

Literature Topic Analysis

<=== Narrower Terms   Broader Terms ===>

Author name		
Mann, Thomas		

Country		
North Germany	Germany	Europe

Time Period		
1950s	Modern	20th Century

Genre		
Novel	Prose, Narrative, Stories	Works

Theme, Name of Characters, Topics, etc.		
Trains, trolleys, rail	Transportation	Journey

---

aid to discipline majors and scholars that enhances their control of their searching. The goal of instruction at this level is to teach students how to locate resources and find related materials by manipulating their searches of the *MLAIB*. Learning objectives for intermediate students should be to:

• understand the *MLAIB*'s role as a comprehensive index of scholarly research;

• learn a variety of standard approaches to use in locating language and literature scholarship (e.g., author, title, character, themes, genre, historical period, country, movement, literary technique, motif, language, linguistic topic, language system, etc.);

• follow up words in the subject headings;

• use thesaurus (if available);

• use word index (if available);

• combine terms;

• know interlibrary loan, full-text, document delivery options;

• be aware of other resources for scholarly criticism;

Learning objectives at each level assume students have mastered the previous objectives or will receive a review of essential points.

Advanced-Level Students

Graduate students have already developed searching strategies. However, they may not be aware of many of the specialized search options that the *MLAIB* offers. Now, having the ability to categorize information in their discipline, they are beginning to gain insight and added control over their searching as they learn to step back and critically evaluate system search capabilities. They begin to design alternative strategies to match the research problem. Material should be presented to them in a more consultative style, such as by presenting a problem and talking with the students about possible search processes. Stebelman, coteaching a research methods course, found lectures on categories of reference material insufficiently engaging.[44] Instead, he used active learning techniques and had students evaluate, categorize, and discuss when each reference work would be used in the research sequence.

In her 1995 study, Shaw found that "graduate students had developed the search strategies typical of humanities scholars—the tendency to cast the net as widely as possible and scan many citations quickly. A sense of individual responsibility for information retrieval is part of the searcher's self-image, highlighting the larger context of the search as one aspect of scholarly research."[45] They created large sets and weeded them using title and index terms. They selected items based on language, source of publication, and student familiarity with author's work. They preferred longer materials. The graduates used a variety of approaches including single and multiple terms, free text and control terms, "pearl growing" (citation follow-up), opting to search by subjects in retrieved citations. They revised queries, and borrowed and transferred search terms between databases. The decision to stop was often based on what could be done in one session. Printing was the biggest technological problem.

Getty scholars (not unlike graduate students) found only a few interesting items in a long list of citations but viewed this as a very good result.[46] Considering that humanists discover new references during regular reading of new books and journal articles in their specialty areas, their satisfaction with a small number of promising new items makes sense. Watson-Boone described the interactive and contemplative nature of humanists' research: "Grazing is not as much through collections, shelves, or catalogs, as through the minds of colleagues and especially within texts."[47] Shaw's graduates had difficulty incorporating serendipitous finds into their work. Students often want to use every found item regardless of relevance. She believes that as they continue their scholarship, they will likely develop techniques for storing ideas for possible incorporation into future work.[48] Surveyed librarians confirm these studies, reporting that students are happy to retrieve large sets and then "trawl" through them rather than work on a succinct search strategy. At the graduate level, footnote follow-up, the core of humanistic research, should be introduced.

For graduate students to understand the workings of the *MLAIB*, they need to know a little of the history of its structure. I use a model of information searching that contrasts the sciences and the humanities. In science, new discoveries are placed in a classified tree structure and given universal names. In the social sciences, these distinctions begin to blur, and in the humanities, they give way to an entirely different picture. Here, the vocabulary is pliable and topics are not mutually exclusive. Contrary theories are viewed as interesting rather than right or wrong. Humanists do not use one hierarchical configuration of subjects. The humanities pattern is a spiral, as shown in figure 3. Topics are viewed from many different perspectives, and the appearance changes with the angle of approach. The standard methods of study can be controlled to vary the specificity of searching. Typical critical approaches to cover at the upper-division level are individual author, country, literary period, and genre. I use this model with undergraduates, briefly discussing the utility of this approach. But it is especially useful for graduate students as a graphical demonstration of the importance of approaching a subject from different angles.

The goal of instruction at this level is to assist students to understand the *MLAIB* and manipulate it in doing an exhaustive search on their topics and to find as many related items as possible. Learning objectives for advanced students should be to:

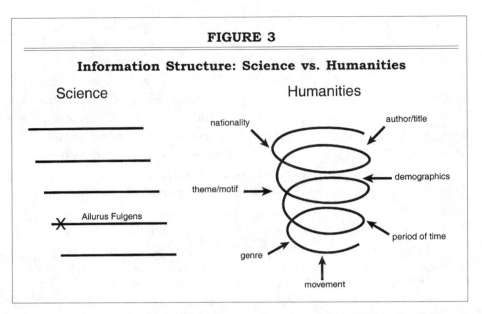

FIGURE 3

Information Structure: Science vs. Humanities

• understand humanities research using the *MLAIB* including use of metaphoric language; evaluation based on critic, source, and publisher; need to review long lists; difficulty of finding "everything" on a subject;

• understand the limits of subject headings, use of metaphoric language, variant spelling (such as Quichote, Quijote, Quixote), plurals;

• search by critic and source;

• follow up by critic and subject;

• use multiple sets in combining terms;

• use interlibrary loan, full text, document delivery options, etc.;

• become familiar with additional resources, including interdisciplinary indexes.

Our future faculty will come from the ranks of our graduate students. Building the foundation for future collegial work is essential. Instruction must provide them with transferable technology and the ability to customize a search to fit their needs. Michaelyn Burnette, Christina M. Gillis, and Myrtis Cochran initiated a proactive program of individualized collaboration with graduate students and faculty to introduce new research tools.[49] Graduates can provide valuable insights about database enhancements. Shaw's graduate students wanted greater specificity in indexing, wondering which novels were covered in an article on "The Postmodern American War Novel." They also requested finer vocabulary control to differentiate between subjects such as "second language acquisition" and "second language learning."[50] As future faculty, they need to understand and discuss the impact on their own scholarship in the humanities of decisions of access versus ownership when, in the future, they are consulted about collection development issues.

Previously, humanists may have chosen to research certain areas of scholarship because the old tools better supported such research. Getty scholars enjoyed the interdisciplinary nature of OneSearch, having the ability to explore the implications or political impact of choices and expanding research into far more interdisciplinary arenas. Doubtless, they also benefited from the efficiency of one look-up. Citing Poole's Principle of Least Effort, the Getty study stated that even scholars found electronic searching difficult and predicted that it must become easier before humanists adopt it as a standard avenue for their research.[51]

Teaching Faculty

As discussed above, teaching faculty, as seasoned scholars, have established research methods and are very familiar with the literature of their discipline. Their traditional style of research rarely involves using an index or asking a librarian for assistance. Often they only have a short break between publications to learn a new system. They are unlikely to be interested in new search strategies unless such strategies clearly offer improved results. Software for searching the *MLAIB* is becoming easier to use, offering relevant choices instead of requiring scholars to learn the software's various ways to phrase questions. It is now often available remotely for use in their quiet study places. Although systems no longer resemble early cars (requiring a crank start), they still require much manual control. The *MLAIB* has the potential to become an appealing, elegantly designed, rich resource rather than a black hole of time with questionable payoff. The goal of instruction with teaching faculty should be to keep them apprised of new options for using the *MLAIB*. Already knowledgeable about the field, many faculty absorb this new information as a dividend of being present at library instruction sessions. Newsletters, listservs, Web pages, workshops, and especially individual consultations are other modes for sharing new information with our teaching faculty colleagues. Collaboration at the curriculum design stage in the teaching of the *MLAIB* is the ideal vehicle to both update the faculty and focus the librarian on teaching and purchasing appropriate materials.

Conclusion

In our limited time with the students, we must teach the basic elements of research language and literature research strategy that can be transferred to any version of the *MLAIB*. This requires clear objectives, tailored to the particular assignment, and, for maximum success, teamwork with teaching faculty. Working with an appropriately focused topic to teach a conceptual framework, combined with a follow-up assignment using the *MLAIB*, is the key to teaching lasting research skills. Students benefit from a subsequent assignment of a draft bibliography that will provide them both the instructor's criteria and insight into the consequences of not including scholarly resources. A brief discussion of mechanics may be necessary but should be left mainly to accompanying material such as point-of-use guides, Web links or, ideally, a well-designed system that presents a searcher with options, rather than serving only those schooled in the "secrets" of the database. Continual evaluation of teaching to incorporate system innovations will keep the teaching and learning focus on issues students consistently find confusing.

Beginning students, having little knowledge of the discipline, benefit from clear and specific assignments. Their greatest difficulty with the *MLAIB* is likely to be that their library does not own the items and their assignment does not provide sufficient time to use interlibrary loan. Intermediate students, having some knowledge of their subject area, benefit from understanding how to categorize the elements of their topics and use them to broaden or narrow their searches. Advanced students need to understand how to find as much as possible on their topic in the *MLAIB*, and teaching faculty need to be updated concerning changes in searching.

Students, MLA members, and Getty scholars want to do interdisciplinary searching and doubtless benefit from the efficiency of one look-up. In their fall 1994 survey results, Shaw and Davis reported that MLA members' habits are evolving.[52] Scholars report spending less time in the library and more time writing. They often conduct the initial search online and delegate retrieval of the items to an assistant. They report problems with computer connections, learning new resources, hardware and software, and lack of sufficient instruction.

Enhancements in *MLAIB* would make it useful to a broader audience and justify its expense as a rich database that is available remotely. Although teaching will still be necessary, *MLAIB* needs to provide the searcher more obvious control in following up any title, author, or subject/subfield term. The system should ask searchers if they want to limit to fields including title and subject, as suggested by Stebelman.[53] Searching by title word only would allow *MLAIB* to develop more robust control vocabulary, while retaining the ability of scholars to search the history of the use of a term in the *MLAIB*. When a search is initiated, the user should be offered the choice of broadening or narrowing. Links could be made to the thesaurus and its tree structure of broader, narrower, or related subject headings. The subject headings should be more uniform to facilitate cross-disciplinary research, at least in the humanities. Links to a basic discipline handbook could provide more assistance for undergraduates who do not know enough about periods, national affiliation, or movement categories to break down their search. Beginning students would also benefit if it were possible for the *MLAIB* to limit a search just to items in the their library and to display local holdings and call numbers. Abstracts or annotations would increase the number of terms searched and help judge relevance. Other useful improvements include tagging local holdings, linking to cited sources, automatic "see" references for foreign-language names and terms such as Don Quixiote/Quijote/Quichote/Quichotte, an option to run the search in other databases, and coverage of new formats for scholarly information.

Our role should be to increase students' sense of control. The process of searching itself needs to be more apparent to students. Online handbooks to assist intermediate students with terms available online as links from the *MLAIB* would be especially beneficial in generating terms. The thesaurus and the word index should be imbedded in the software, actively querying students, rather than provided as an option that must be learned and invoked. The structure of the thesaurus has data that could be used to broaden, narrow, or retrieve related terms. Authority control for these headings needs to be tightened, and "see" and "see also" links should be included. Subject headings should not continue to be taken from the title words; instead, the *MLAIB* should introduce an option to limit by title words.

Librarians, as the link between students and the vendors of *MLAIB* search software and the MLA, need to be proactive in the design of systems. Live links to all subject headings and subfields is a good example of crucial areas where we need to lobby for solutions. Intermediate searchers would benefit by access to the thesaurus, absent in some Internet versions of the *MLAIB*. Studies of user behavior can provide ideas for database refinements. Shaw found that "search strategy is influenced by the searcher's ability, experience, and expectations for the search, but also by the capabilities of the search software used." Simple enhancements can be very productive. The "display of search terms in a different color was helpful in focusing the relevance assessment."[54]

This is a transitional time and a challenging and exciting time to be teaching. Students and future researchers need to learn the components of basic language and literature searching, usable with any "flavor" of the *MLAIB*. As instruction librarians, we must be advocates for better system design. Graduate students and faculty are focused on their discipline, not the information access channels. Librarians are in a unique position. Working closely with searching students and faculty, we see and select the new software versions using "real-world" criteria. We have a continuing dialog with vendors who are interested in our insights. The MLA is not just a publisher, but an integral part of the scholarly community, committed to supporting scholarship. We must work closely with it to ensure that all levels of research are well served by the *MLAIB*.

Notes

1. *MLAIB* e-mail survey, spring 1997. This paper is based on a review of the literature of studies of the information-seeking patterns of humanities scholars and university students, both undergraduate and graduate; studies of library instruction for literature or composition courses; a review of materials in the depository at LOEX and the California Clearinghouse on Library Instruction; Scott Stebelman, *World Wide Web User Aids to the MLA International Bibliography*, June 1997, http://gwis2.circ.gwu.edu/~scottlib/useraids.htm (4 Aug. 1999); use of a variety of mainly electronic renditions of the database; an e-mail survey of librarians and professors who teach the *MLAIB*. The survey was distributed via the BI-L, EALSL, Humanist, and *MLAIB* listservs in the spring of 1997. A total of twenty-seven librarians and teaching faculty responded.

2. Lawrence L. Reed, "Locally Loaded Databases and Undergraduate Bibliographic Instruction," *RQ* 33 (1993): 272.

3. Phyllis Franklin, "Pay the Piper: Creating and Maintaining the *MLA International Bibliography*," in *New Technologies and New Directions: Proceedings from the Symposium on Scholarly Communications*, ed. G. R. Boynton and Sheila D. Creth (Westport, Conn.: Meckler, 1993), 41–49; Hans Rütimann, "The MLA and the Computer," *Scholarly Publishing* 19 (1987): 18–23; Douglas Greenberg, "You Can't Always Get What You Want: Technology, Scholarship, and Democracy," in *New Technologies and New Directions*, 11–25; Eileen M. Mackesy, "A Perspective on Secondary Access Services in the Humanities," *Journal of the American Society for Information Science* 33 (1982): 146–51.

4. Jonathan Beck, "After New Literary History and Theory? Notes on the MLA Hit Parade and the Currencies of Academic Exchange," *New Literary History* 26 (1995): 704.

5. Michael Taft, "The Folklore Section of the *MLA International Bibliography*," *International Folklore Review: Folklore Studies from Overseas* 2 (1982): 61–64; L. S. Perry, "The MLA Database as a Source of Film Criticism," *Journal of Academic Librarianship* 18 (1992): 146–50. For additional resources on film, see Linda Harris Mehr and Sandra Archer, "Stand and Deliver: Providing Research and Reference Assistance at the Margaret Herrick Library of the Academy of Motion Picture Arts and Sciences," *Reference Librarian*, no. 47 (1994): 37–46.

6. See "Model Statement of Objectives for Academic Bibliographic Instruction: Draft Revision," *College and Research Libraries News* 48 (1987): 256–61; Instruction Section, ACRL, *Guidelines for Instruction Programs in Academic Libraries*, approved 9 July 1996, http://www.ala.org/acrl/guides/guiis.html (5 Aug. 1999); Task Force on Information Literacy Competency Standards, ACRL, "Information Literacy Competency Standards for Higher Education," 2000, http://www.ala.org/acrl/ilcomstan.html (1 Mar. 2000).

7. Susan C. Curzon, *Information Competence in the CSU: A Report*, Dec. 1995, http://www.calstate.edu/ITPA/Docs/html/info_comp_report.html (5 Aug. 1999).

8. Cerise Oberman, "Avoiding the Cereal Syndrome; or, Critical Thinking in the Electronic Environment," in *Information for a New Age: Redefining the Librarian*, comp. Fifteenth Anniversary Task force, Library Instruction Round Table (Englewood, Colo.: Libraries Unlimited, 1995), 116. For further reading, see Anne K. Beaubien, Sharon Hogan, and Mary W. George, *Learning the Library: Concepts and Methods for Effective Bibliographic Instruction* (New York, R. R. Bowker, 1982); *Information for a New Age*; Cerise Oberman and Katina Strauch, *Theories of Bibliographic Education: Designs for Teaching* (New York: R. R. Bowker, 1982); *Sourcebook for Bibliographic Instruction*, ed. Katherine Branch and Carolyn Dusenbury (Chicago: ACRL, 1993); *Conceptual Frameworks for Bibliographic Education: Theory into Practice*, ed. Mary Reichel and Mary Ann Ramey (Englewood, Colo.: Libraries Unlimited, 1987); *Teaching Information Retrieval and Evaluation Skills to Education Students and Practitioners: A Casebook of Applications*, ed. Patricia O'Brien Libutti and Bonnie Gratch (Chicago: ACRL, 1995).

9. Stebelman, *World Wide Web User Aids to the MLA International Bibliography.*

10. Harold H. Kollmeier and Kathleen Henderson Staudt, "Composition Students Online: Database Searching in the Undergraduate Research Paper Course," *Computers and the Humanities* 21 (1987): 155.

11. Patricia K. Cross and Thomas A. Angelo, *Classroom Assessment Techniques: A Handbook for Faculty* (Ann Arbor, Mich.: National Center for Research to Improve Postsecondary Teaching and Learning, 1988).

12. *Evaluating Library Instruction: Sample Questions, Forms, and Strategies for Practical Use*, ed. Diana D. Shonrock (Chicago: ALA, 1996).

13. Stephen Lehmann and Patricia Renfro, "Humanists and Electronic Information Services: Acceptance and Resistance," *College and Research Libraries* 52 (1991): 410.

14. Terry Plum and Topsy N. Smalley, "Research as Repatriation," *Reference Librarian*, no. 47 (1994): 163.

15. Patricia B. Knapp, *The Monteith College Library Experiment* (New York: Scarecrow, 1966).

16. Peter Stern, "Online in the Humanities: Problems and Possibilities," *Journal of Academic Librarianship* 14 (1988): 161–64; Sue Stone, "Humanities Scholars: Information Needs and Uses," *Journal of Documentation* 38 (1982): 292–313; Rebecca Watson-Boone, "The Information Needs and Habits of Humanities Scholars," *RQ* 34 (1994): 203–16; Stephen E. Wiberley Jr., "Habits of Humanists: Scholarly Behavior and New Information Technologies," *Library Hi Tech* 9, no. 1 (1991): 17–21; ———, "Names in Space and Time: The Indexing

Vocabulary of the Humanities," *Library Quarterly* 58 (1988): 1–28; ———,"Subject Access in the Humanities and the Precision of the Humanist's Vocabulary," *Library Quarterly* 53 (1983): 420–33. Stephen E. Wiberley Jr. and William G. Jones, "Humanists Revisited: A Longitudinal Look at the Adoption of Information Technology," *College and Research Libraries* 55 (1994): 499–509; ———, "Patterns of Information Seeking in the Humanities," *College and Research Libraries* 50 (1989): 638–45.

17. Scott D. Stebelman, "Vocabulary Control and the Humanities: A Case Study of the *MLA International Bibliography*," *Reference Librarian*, no. 47 (1994): 61–78.

18. Watson-Boone, "The Information Needs and Habits of Humanitites Scholars," 213.

19. Wiberley and Jones, "Humanists Revisited," 507.

20. Kollmeier and Staudt, "Composition Students Online," 149.

21. Marcia J. Bates, Deborah H. Wilde, and Susan Siegfried, "Research Practices of Humanities Scholars in an Online Environment: The Getty Online Searching Project Report No. 3," *Library and Information Science Research* 17 (1995): 34.

22. Wiberley and Jones, "Humanists Revisited," 504–5.

23. B. J. Rahn, "Humanities Faculty Members Discover New Skills in Computing Workshops," *T.H.E. Journal* 14, no. 6 (1987): 62.

24. Topsy N. Smalley and Stephen H. Plum, "Teaching Library Researching in the Humanities and the Sciences: A Contextual Approach," in *Theories of Bibliographic Education: Designs for Teaching* (New York: R.R. Bowker, 1982), 135–70.

25. Plum and Smalley, "Research as Repatriation," 162, 151.

26. Marcia J. Bates, "The Design of Databases and Other Information Resources for Humanities Scholars: The Getty Online Searching Project Report No. 4," *Online and CD-ROM Review* 18 (1994): 338.

27. Mara R. Saule, "User Instruction Issues for Databases in the Humanities," *Library Trends* 40 (1992): 598.

28. Bates, Wilde, and Siegfried, "Research Practices of Humanities Scholars in an Online Environment," 21–22.

29. Bates, "The Design of Databases and Other Information Resources for Humanities Scholars," 333.

30. Joy Thomas, "Faculty Attitudes and Habits Concerning Library Instruction: How Much Has Changed Since 1982?" *Research Strategies* 12 (1994): 209–23; Kollmeier and Staudt, "Composition Students Online," 148; Robert K. Baker, "Faculty Perceptions toward Student Library Use in a Large Urban Community College," *Journal of Academic Librarianship* 23 (1997):181.

31. Martha Flemming, "Bibliographic Instruction on Electronic Resources for the Humanities," *LIBRES: Library and Information Science Research Electronic*

Journal, 20 May 1993, ftp://ftp.lib.ncsu.edu/pub/stacks/libres/libres-3.5c. This issue is archived and can be retrieved via e-mail to Listserv@kentvm.kent.edu or via anonymous ftp to ksuvxa.kent.edu in the library directory as LIBRES LOG9305.

32. Gordon W. Thompson, "Sequenced Research Assignments for the Undergraduate Literature Student," in *Bibliographic Instruction in Practice: A Tribute to the Legacy of Evan Ira Farber*, ed. Larry Hardesty, Jamie Hastreiter, and David Henderson (Ann Arbor, Mich.: Pierian, 1993), 45.

33. Janet Martorana and Carol Doyle, "Computers On, Critical Thinking Off: Challenges of Teaching in the Electronic Environment," *Research Strategies* 14 (1996):184–91.

34. Kollmeier and Staudt, "Composition Students Online," 154, 153; Gloria J. Leckie, "Desperately Seeking Citations: Uncovering Faculty Assumptions about the Undergraduate Research Process," *Journal of Academic Librarianship* 22 (1996): 202; Reed, "Locally Loaded Databases and Undergraduate Bibliographic Instruction," 271.

35. Debora J. Shaw, "Undergraduate Use of CD-ROM Databases: Observations of Human–Computer Interaction and Relevance Judgments," *Library and Information Science Research* 18 (1996): 271, 268.

36. Leckie, "Desperately Seeking Citations," 203.

37. Shaw, "Undergraduate Use of CD-ROM Databases," 264.

38. Leckie, "Desperately Seeking Citations," 205, 207. Faculty workshops may help; see Pixey Anne Mosley, "Creating a Library Assignment Workshop for University Faculty," *Journal of Academic Librarianship* 24 (1998): 33–41.

39. Keiko Kuhara-Kojima and Giyoo Hatano, "Contributions of Content Knowledge and Learning Ability to the Learning of Facts," *Journal of Educational Psychology* 83 (1991): 253–63.

40. Saule, "User Instruction Issues for Databases in the Humanities," 606–07.

41. Shaw, "Undergraduate Use of CD-ROM Databases," 271, 264.

42. Wiberley, "Names in Space and Time," 1–28.

43. For example, see Beaubien, Hogan, and George, *Learning the Library*, 121; Martha A. Davis, "Tackle Box Strategy: Using a Matrix to Facilitate Library Research Strategy," *Research Strategies* 14 (1996): 209; Leon A. Jakobovits and Diane Nahl-Jakobovits, "Measuring Information Searching Competence," *College and Research Libraries* 51 (1990): 452.

44. Scott Stebelman, "Teaching Manuscript and Archival Resources," *Literary Research: A Journal of Scholarly Method and Technique* 12 (1987): 23–24.

45. Debora J. Shaw, "Bibliographic Database Searching by Graduate Students in Language and Literature: Search Strategies, System Interfaces, and Relevance Judgments," *Library and Information Science Research* 17 (1995): 341, 332, 335, 333, 334, 338.

46. Bates, "The Design of Databases and Other Information Resources for Humanities Scholars," 334.

47. Watson-Boone, "The Information Needs and Habits of Humanities Scholars," 212.

48. Shaw, "Bibliographic Database Searching by Undergraduate Students in Language and Literature," 333.

49. Michaelyn Burnette, Christina M. Gillis, and Myrtis Cochran, "The Humanist and the Library: Promoting New Scholarship through Collaborative Interaction between Humanists and Librarians," *Reference Librarian*, no. 47 (1994): 181–91.

50. Shaw, "Bibliographic Database Searching by Undergraduate Students in Language and Literature," 340.

51. Bates, "The Design of Databases and Other Information Resources for Humanities Scholars," 334; Bates, Wilde, and Siegfied, "Research Practice of Humanities Scholars in an Online Environment," 29.

52. Debora J. Shaw and Charles H. Davis, "The Modern Language Association: Electronic and Paper Surveys of Computer-Based Tool Use," *Journal of the American Society for Information Science* 47 (1996): 936.

53. Stebelman, "Vocabulary Control and the Humanities," 74.

54. Shaw, "Undergraduate Use of CD-ROM Databases," 264, 266.

Chapter 8

Literary Reference into the New Century

Michael Adams
City University of New York Graduate Center

Candace R. Benefiel
Texas A&M University

Reference services for English and American literature have reached a critical phase. In the past, literary scholars learned how to use library resources and relevant research methods as graduate students, and their mastery of these print indexes and bibliographies served them throughout their careers. Now, however, as literary studies have expanded with the broadening of the recognized canon of authors and have developed a more interdisciplinary bent as scholars seek historical materials and cultural artifacts to attempt to place literature in the context of its times, scholars are faced with more complex and varied sources and research methodologies. The increasing dominance of electronic resources in today's libraries also has added yet another dimension to the tasks facing the scholar. The crucial link between researchers and unfamiliar resources and technologies is the reference librarian.

The Nature of Literary Research

What exactly is literary research, and how does it affect the provision of reference services in academic libraries? Harrison T. Meserole pointed out the difficulty of adequately characterizing current practices by calling literary research "an art with many canvases" (p.72) and also pointed out that what is important is not "the nature of literary research but . . . its natures, for literary research is a multifarious undertaking, and we who practice it are an acquisitive lot who do not hesitate to range widely afield, demolishing traditional disciplinary barriers as we course in search of ways and means to add to our knowledge and competence" (p.69).[1]

The nature of literary research shapes the nature of literary reference. As reference librarians seek to assist literary researchers in obtaining information and sources, the librarians are forced, along with the scholars, to leave the safe confines of what was for so long the traditional, textual arena of literary research and move into an increasing array of multidisciplinary resources. Meserole aptly described an essential part of the literary scholarship process: "In our drive to understand all there is to understand about each . . . poem, play, or fiction, we seek out every scrap of information about the text itself, the author of the text, the facts of its publication, dissemination, printing history, reception, and the context that surround each of these inquiries."[2] Part of the broadening scope of literary research is driven by a rising sense of social and multicultural consciousness, what Eric Carpenter described as "Another factor in the trend toward new, interdisciplinary modes of inquiry [caused by] the emergence of new social movements in the 1960s and early 1970s," such as the civil rights, women's, and gay liberation movements.[3]

The relationship between new technology and the changes in scholarly information needs has been summarized by Marianne I. Gaunt:

> New technology, while facilitating new research methodologies, is making the task of those responsible for collecting the results of that research and the tools for continued research more challenging. It is not just the

> sheer volume of materials, the qualitative distinctions among them, and the ever-increasing costs with which bibliographers must contend, but the choices in format and access to be made as well: print vs. microprint (fiche/film/card), film, video, optical disc, online (interactive) communication, CD-ROM (single-station vs. LAN), machine readable datafile. Since a single work may be available in any or all formats, the choice to be made can be difficult.[4]

This multiplicity of approaches and the growing complexity of means of access to information directly influence the provision of reference services to the literary scholar, whether on professorial, graduate, or undergraduate levels. Although the well-known technophobia of older liberal arts faculty is gradually being replaced with an acceptance of the new methods of information access, many faculty are still reluctant to use electronic resources. The training they received during their student days also may not have covered some of the methods and sources used for locating primary materials and those at one time more properly considered within the realm of the historian, the sociologist, or the psychologist.

On the other hand, undergraduates, even with their increasing familiarity with the Internet and ease with electronic materials, still need extensive assistance in learning the proper use of bibliographic indexes and databases. Even more significant is the need to teach undergraduates to evaluate sources of information, to determine appropriate avenues of research, and to use resources effectively. Undergraduates must not become so enamored of electronic sources that they are unwilling to use print materials. Reference librarians, as well, must maintain their knowledge of print resources so that they will be able to identify the best sources and instruct patrons in their use. This is especially important when electronic databases cover only twenty or thirty years, but their print counterparts go back fifty to one hundred years.

In the field of literature, one deals with an ever-expanding body of works and accompanying criticism. In the sciences, for the most part, new material, even though built on the advances of the past, replaces earlier theories. In literature, texts from many centuries and cultures continue to be studied even as newer voices are added to the cumulative voice of human literary expression; and although schools of criticism shift and change, older analyses may well yet be legitimate sources for scholarly research. In this atmosphere of expansion and change, the reference librarian also must be willing to move comfortably through both traditional sources for literary scholarship and new areas of inquiry and their associated resources.

The Canon Debate

Over the past twenty years, much debate has centered on the revision or opening of the literary canon, and this war has been one of several significant changes in literary study to affect reference services. Although the academic literary world agrees that the canon is being revised and expanded, there seems to be little consensus on what the canon consists of or in what way it is being changed.

Definition of the Literary Canon

What exactly is meant by the term *literary canon*? Richard Heinzkill said it "consists of 'the' classics. They are called classics because of their literary quality, their timelessness, their universality."[5] But of what do "the" classics consist? In *The Art of Literary Research*, Richard D. Altick and John J. Fenstermaker asserted that the canon is "the list of authors and works in a nation's literary heritage—always unstable, but more so at certain times than at others—that are deemed most significant and most deserving of sustained, intensive study."[6] Our familiarity with the works in the canon, according to James Hulbert, helps us "to define other writers and relationships and to define what sort of readers and writers we are: sharers of certain cultural experiences, enjoying or aspiring to certain educational, social, literary, or critical status."[7] Henry Louis Gates Jr., more personally, called the canon "the commonplace book of our shared culture, in which we have written down the texts and titles we want to remember, that had some special meaning for us."[8] Keith C. Odom, more concretely, simply equated the British component of the canon with the table of contents in the various editions of *The Norton Anthology of English Literature*.[9]

Many commentators have posited that appearance in the standard anthologies used in survey courses constitutes admission to the canon. Similar criteria might be the tables of contents of *American Literary Scholarship* and *The Year's Work in English Studies*.

Canon Formation and the Opening of the Canon

Canon formation and revision have been increasingly important in the dialogue of literary scholars as chronicled in the journal literature. "Discussions of canons," wrote Earl Miner, "even in the necessary plural, are often conducted with a sacral hush befitting the great masterpieces being weighed and our importance in conducting the rites."[10] Revising or expanding the canon raises some significant questions about the study of literature and recording of literary history. In 1986, David S. Reynolds pointed out:

> Rewriting our literary history . . . and revising our classroom anthologies accordingly raises several key questions: what is our literary canon? Who exactly are the major writers? If we include hitherto neglected authors, what is our basis for doing so? Do we include them for literary, for historical, or for political reasons? How do we know we haven't neglected still other writers? Is there any way of accommodating the findings of both the theorists and the new literary historians? In the final analysis, we are faced with the old, alluring question: what is literature?[11]

Reynolds's actual question was, How is the canon formed? Until relatively recently, the question was not considered of great importance because the canon was, well, the canon. As Heinzkill put it: "In all innocence one might think that the canon . . . just happens, something like the formation of cream, the best comes naturally to the top. . . . We are now told that it is the keepers of society's high culture who have determined the literature worth studying from generation to generation."[12] These keepers and their criteria have changed dramatically in recent years. The current debate about the canon began as a result of the social and political movements of the 1950s and 1960s, which saw the beginnings of demands for empowerment and inclusion of racial, ethnic, and sexual minorities, as well as the rise of the feminist movement. As women and these various minorities asserted their worth in society, the issue also arose of recognizing the merits of members of these groups in a cultural context. They demanded to be viewed not as the occasional oddity of a woman who produced literature of enduring worth (as opposed to ephemeral popular fiction) or an African American whose work could not only appeal to a circumscribed segment of the population but also stand as work of value within the entire context of literature.

The culmination of the debate, although certainly not its conclusion, may have already been published. Isobel M. Findlay considered the 1992 Modern Language Association (MLA) publication *Redrawing the Boundaries: The Transformation of English and American Studies* as registering a shift in focus:

> read apocalyptically by formalists and literary historians, this reconstitution has been seen as the dangerous politicizing of literary studies and the academy, or even as the end of Western civilization; read approvingly by feminists, poststructuralists and Marxists, it is seen as a belated gesture of inclusion and liberation. What therefore becomes dramatically clear is the way that such rhetoric and polarization attest to the continuing political importance of the canon, its role in the construction of social subjects and terms we live by—nation, class, gender, ethnicity.[13]

In their introduction to *Redrawing the Boundaries*, Stephen Greenblatt and Giles Gunn described the basis of the debate on canonicity: "Where twenty-five or thirty years ago the profession was organized almost everywhere around the close reading of a stable, determinate set of masterworks, literary studies are now being reorganized in many institutions around an open series of inquiries about what constitutes literary interest in the first place."[14] Literary scholars, according to Greenblatt and Gunn, are confronted not by "a unified field at all but diverse historical projects and critical idioms that are not organized around a single center but originate from a variety of sources, some of which lie outside the realm of literary study altogether and intersect one another often at strange angles."[15]

There is, of course, some opposition to an enlarged canon, as Elizabeth Brown-Guillory observed in recounting an anecdote concerning a speaker at the 1987 MLA convention who asserted the need to retain the traditional canon and rejected all the works by women and minorities as "inferior literature."[16] Nevertheless, most who support the traditional canon have been known to admit that some change is necessary. Paisley Livingston said that among these supporters "It is also possible to recognize that some work that was previously canonical was overestimated and should now be removed from the collection."[17] One sign of this shift readily apparent to librarians can be noted in the revised 1996 edition of *Masterplots*. As the publisher's note states: "The definition of what constitutes a literary classic or masterwork shifts over time," and, accordingly, 425 new titles were added to the new edition while almost 1,000 in the 1976 set were dropped as being "today rarely addressed in schools or recognized critically."[18] Such a radical difference in what is perceived as being important to students signifies a major shift in the canon.

One group of scholars, according to Reynolds, "demand a complete revision of the American canon through the study of marginal or forgotten literature." These scholars are responding to the establishment of the canon, said Reynolds, "by critics who were blinded by various kinds of prejudice that can be eliminated only by total immersion in the unfamiliar. Popular literature, women's literature, newspaper writings, book reviews, literature by ethnic minorities" are among the untraditional writings of interest to those "calling for wholly reconceptualized literary histories."[19] Although this reasoning may seem extreme, it exemplifies the viewpoint that has made popular culture a legitimate field of study in recent decades and also has contributed to the increasingly interdisciplinary nature of literary research.

The nature of the changes in the canon can be described primarily as the growing inclusion of minority literatures, meaning works by women, racial and ethnic minorities, and gays and lesbians, reflecting a similar inclusion in society at large. Within academia as well, the face of the university alters with its changing student body. Greenblatt and Gunn pointed out that, as a result of the increasing diversity of students, "teachers of literature have found that the traditional humanistic curriculum seems less representative. This perception . . . has also forced into the open long-neglected questions about the assumptions on which that curriculum was based, the process by which it was created, the public constituencies it was perceived to address, and the intellectual and heuristic purposes it was intended to fulfill."[20] This change in what is being taught was summarized as opening up the canon by Reed Way Dasenbrock: "The established canon of English and American literature as received and taught has been seen to be a very partial representation, biased toward men from privileged classes and races. Advocates of literature by women and by marginalized social and economic groups have pressed to open up the canon, to move toward a more expansive, pluralistic view of literature with room for all sectors of society."[21]

Another aspect of the discussions of canon transformation is the establishment of multiple canons. To some extent, this has always been the norm, as canons of national literature have long been accepted. However, within the realm of literature in English (including the subset of world literature translated into English), should there be one canon or many? The view that there should be an overall canon for literature in English was summarized by Heinzkill: "On the national level we see pressure to expand what each nation regards as its canon. And as these national canons expand, new names will undoubtedly be included in the canon of literature written in English. Already some are being introduced to these other national literatures through the study of feminist literature and minority authors. From there it is only a short step to wanting to investigate these authors in their own tradition. We should, therefore, be preparing for the study of worldwide English literature."[22] Others, seeing in this establishment of a supercanon for all literature in English a continuance of the old canon, argue for a canon for each national literature or an array of canons: ones for African American literature, Hispanic literature, gay literature, etc. Nils Erik Enkvist postulated that "All bodies of text which satisfy certain definite criteria are in fact potential canons, and canons can form a hierarchy of major canons and subcanons. There can be canons of black literature or gay drama just as well as there have been canons of Elizabethan plays or of nineteenth-century novels or of the Great Writers and Great Books."[23]

Effects of Canon Transformation on the Teaching of Literature

The effects of the transformation of the canon resonate throughout literary scholarship, from the studies of distinguished professors to papers by freshmen and sophomores in survey courses. The criticism generated by the professors becomes source material for students on all levels, but although the higher-level scholars are building on an extensive basis of training in the established canonical writers and adding to their repertoire when they explore the works of newer or lesser-known writers, students usually lack a perspective in their views of literary history. Heinzkill explained how time can become an enemy of canon transformation: "There is just so much time in the school calendar and therefore what texts should be used takes on a great significance."[24] Marjorie Perloff pointed out that because "The class that reads Chopin's *Awakening* will not, in all likelihood, have time for Henry James' *Portrait of a Lady* . . . we should be under no illusion that we have replaced a 'closed' and narrow canon with an 'open' and flexible one."[25] When professors cannot "teach the new literature in addition to the old canon," wrote Dasenbrock, "something has to give, substitutions have to be made, in the classroom the canon inexorably closes down."[26]

At one time, it was thought that a well-educated person should have studied all subjects, read everything of importance that had been written. If one concedes, as one must, that great literature did not end with Homer or Shakespeare or Faulkner and is not limited to that which is written by citizens of a particular country or members of a certain race or sex, the entire field of literature has passed beyond the scope of the individual. This development can lead only to greater specialization within literary scholarship or the gradual elimination from the canon of writers once considered significant. Should current trends continue, as seems likely, there will be a sustained interest in works by minorities and women, in lesser-known writers and literatures. The canon, as Heinzkill has observed, will never again be as stable as it has been in the past, and canonical changes will occur much more rapidly.[27]

Canons and Reference Services

Given all of the above, what are the effects of this expansion and opening of the canon, at whatever rate it is taking place, on academic literary reference? Obviously, as new or different writers begin to be taught in college English classes, an upsurge of students will seek criticism of these writers, many of whom may not be covered extensively in the literature. For example, if students search the *MLA International Bibliography* for analyses of T. Coraghessan Boyle's "Greasy Lake," they will find only eleven articles on Boyle, including one in Spanish and one in German. One article is an interview with Boyle, and only one addresses the story in question directly. No explanation by a librarian that there will certainly be more Boyle criticism in the future will assuage the students' anxiety. After all, the assignment is due tomorrow. The librarian must therefore be prepared to find other (if perhaps not as scholarly) resources such as book reviews, newspaper and magazine articles, and analyses in reference works such as *Dictionary of Literary Biography* and *Masterplots*. This phenomenon is certainly not new but will become increasingly familiar as more new writers are taught. Librarians will not only need to become familiar with new reference tools dealing with the new authors and previously neglected literatures but also must actively participate in producing these tools and making sure publishers are aware of the need for reference tools that reflect the new styles of teaching and the writers covered.

The Nature of Reference Collections, Resources, and Services

The literary reference collection, whether functioning on its own or as part of a more varied reference collection, is composed of an extensive body of secondary and tertiary materials on a range of literature-related topics. The appropriate tools for the literary reference collection are discussed at length in Scott Stebelman's "Building Literary Reference Collections."[28] In addition, bibliographies that may aid the librarian in selecting or evaluating a literary reference collection also are available. For decades, librarians have relied on the various editions of *Guide to Reference Books*, which still provides a firm listing of materials useful for literary reference.[29] Walford's *Guide to Reference Material*, another massive work covering reference material in all disciplines, also should be kept in mind as a basic bibliography of literary reference materials.[30] More focused in scope, Ron Blazek's *Humanities: A Selective Guide to Information Sources* also may have value as a selection tool for literary reference collections.[31]

Two recent bibliographies of reference works for English studies will provide the most detailed coverage and undoubtedly will serve as valuable tools in developing the literary reference collection. James L. Harner's *Literary Research Guide: An Annotated Listing of Reference Sources in English Literary Study* provides annotated entries on 1,207 works (mentioning another 1,331 within the annotations), most of which are suitable for inclusion in reference collections.[32] Michael J. Marcuse's *Reference Guide for English Studies*, though older, is an excellent source for retrospective reference materials and includes helpful sections on history and the performing arts as well as other fields ancillary to the study of literature.[33] Of course, every literary reference collection should be tailored to the needs and research interests current in the institution; and in developing the literary reference collection, it may be helpful to relegate some of the less frequently used titles to the circulating stacks.

As literary research becomes increasingly interdisciplinary, the demands on literary reference librarians also grow so that a librarian not only must have specialized knowledge of the field as a whole but also must be a generalist at ease with sources in a number of more-or-less related fields. Because the profession has long expected reference librarians to be able to field questions across the entire spectrum of human knowledge, perhaps it is not too much to ask that a librarian specializing in literary reference be conversant with finding guides and other reference materials needed by literary scholars in such fields as history, cultural and gender studies, psychology, philosophy, and religion. Other fields used by literary scholars to establish contexts for their studies doubtless will suggest themselves to even the slightly experienced librarian.

Heinzkill has ably demonstrated the effects of the expansion of the canon on collection development, and many of his comments are also of interest to the librarian dealing with a literary reference collection. Anthologies, as he has noted, are an important force in determining canonicity.[34] If space in the reference collection allows, anthologies may serve as an important addition to more traditional reference tools. Other less traditional resources also might include reference tools dealing with using manuscript materials, cultural artifacts, and popular literature.

Services for undergraduates center on providing ease of access to standard reference works, indexes, and texts; and as the canon changes, reference librarians should be alert to what is being taught and add works dealing with new writers and literatures to their collections. Undergraduates have a tendency to place too much reliance on what they can find electronically and often need assistance with understanding print resources that may be either more authoritative or more appropriate to their research. Bibliographic instruction for the undergraduate student of literature becomes even more important as the variety and complexity of resources increase. Undergraduates will continue to require instruction in the basics of both library use and literary research, with continued assistance in more sophisticated resources as the level of their studies becomes more demanding.

Graduate students will need even more assistance in their research as they seek to make comprehensive searches for materials related to their thesis and dissertation topics. As more bibliographic and full-text resources become available electronically, librarians are challenged to keep graduate students (as well as faculty) up to date with these developments. Librarians can perhaps best offer assistance in a one-on-one instructional setting. This approach can be especially useful not only to beginning graduate students, but also to those with specific research problems or topics.

Literary Reference and Electronic Resources
In looking at possible changes in library services for literary researchers in the coming years, it seems clear that an important trend is the

increasing flexibility of research options. As faculty move farther afield from the traditional canon, they will need more assistance in locating materials such as manuscript collections and cultural artifacts. The literature reference librarian's skills with OCLC and RLN will allow efficient assistance with these research needs. Many research libraries have long provided their users with some form of OCLC access. With more than thirty-six million bibliographic records, the database's value as a bibliographic research resource is unparalleled. Combining this massive database with a search engine, such as WorldCat, makes it friendly even to the casual user and therefore even more important as a research tool. Because users not only are able to search by author, title, subject, ISBN/ISSN, and publisher but also can limit the results by language or year, a researcher can easily determine, for example, whether any editions of Shakespeare's *Hamlet* were published in Chinese prior to 1850. As more libraries create cataloging records for manuscript and archival materials, which might otherwise be difficult or impossible to locate, the value of WorldCat increases. It is especially useful for faculty and graduate students working on descriptive bibliographies. As the canon expands, a source such as WorldCat makes it easier to trace the various editions of primary works by the new authors and their availability.

Ironically, many faculty are left behind by their students who are usually more adept at using electronic resources. The variety of these resources available to literary researchers has increased over the past decade in degrees reference librarians of the 1970s and early 1980s would have thought unimaginable, and the number of types of these tools will clearly proliferate in the foreseeable future. Such resources as online public access catalogs, CD-ROMs, and full-text journals and books on the World Wide Web, in addition to numerous other literary Web sites, make literary research more flexible as levels of access increase and also make the duties of librarians more challenging and exciting.

The electronic versions of the *MLA International Bibliography* (*MLAIB*) as with almost any electronic database, offer obvious advantages over the print equivalent, the main one being the ability to search decades of citations at once. This is especially important for librarians whose primary patrons are undergraduates who often lack the patience to go through the traditional *MLAIB* year by year. If a patron who needs to use *MLAIB* shows some reluctance about its CD-ROM or Web versions, demonstrating the alternative may create more enthusiasm for the electronic resource.

Any librarian who frequently uses an electronic database must be thoroughly familiar with its limitations and eccentricities. If a patron researching British satire of the 1930s, for example, does not believe that searching by literary decade is impossible, retrieve an *MLAIB* citation to a work about Evelyn Waugh to show that centuries, not decades, are employed as descriptors. Because the flexibility of the electronic *MLAIB* is limited by the absence of abstracts, the librarian must learn tricks to get around this deficiency, such as learning what types of searches are best limited to the descriptor field and which ones are best performed in the entire record. Obviously, such a tool would be much more helpful to researchers if it had abstracts or at least more—and more specific—descriptors. It is up to the librarian to show users how to work around such limitations. General periodical indexes such as Gale Group's *Expanded Academic Index* and H. W. Wilson's *General Periodical Index*, which includes *Humanities Index*, offer options not available through the *MLAIB* because of the availability of abstracts. Learning to use *Humanities Index* and *MLAIB* to complement each other is a useful skill. One slight problem with such resources, especially for undergraduates, is the inclusion of book reviews. All academic librarians are familiar with the confusion created when students go to *Library Journal, Publishers Weekly, Newsweek, The New York Times Book Review*, and similar sources expecting to find articles on their subjects only to discover, instead, reviews of books on these subjects. A similar problem occurs in *MLAIB* with the inclusion of dissertations. Librarians learn to recognize the patrons for whom knowing how to exclude reviews and dissertations from search results is essential.

Graduate and faculty patrons may not have such problems, but they may have additional needs, such as learning how to use electronic resources to create a bibliography, and may need to be instructed in such skills as copying and pasting bibliographic records. Because many patrons on any level will not take the time to discover how easily the information they retrieve from electronic tools can be manipulated, this skill also must be imparted along with the usual retrieval techniques. Moreover, many patrons must be introduced to such mundane matters as being at ease with using a mouse, learning about function keys, and becoming familiar with screen displays.

Experienced librarians are very familiar with the looks of disappointment—or worse—when undergraduates learn that an electronic periodical index provides citations only, not the full text of the resources. But with the increasing number of resources such as *JSTOR, Search, InfoTrac SearchBank*, Ebsco, Ovid, *Project MUSE*, etc., providing full-text access over the Internet, this matter becomes less of a concern. Such tools make any type of research easier and allow libraries of any size to provide access to materials beyond the limitations of their budgets. As such sources grow, patrons will still experience some dissatisfaction, as with not understanding why the full text of every issue of every periodical ever published is not available or why some databases offer full text from some periodical titles, but not all. Librarians develop a sense for knowing when to explain such limitations before the disappointment develops.

Even if a library does not subscribe to one of the full-text indexing services, some individual periodicals, such as *Studies in Bibliography* (etext.lib.virginia.edu/bsuva/sb/), are available free over the Internet. A librarian specializing in English and American literature can easily determine what titles are available. Keeping up with the growth in availability requires a more determined effort. Patrons also can use such relatively inexpensive Web services as *Northern Light* (www.northernlight.com/), the *Electric Library* (www.elibrary.com/), and *UnCover* (uncweb.carl.org/) to have access to full-text periodicals.

In addition to periodical sources, a number of Web tools provide access to the full text of novels, plays, poems, short stories, and essays. As the canon grows to include more works by women and minorities that may not be available in all libraries, this access is doubly significant. These full-text sources can range from subscription services such as *LION* to free collections of public domain texts from *Project Gutenberg* (promo.net/pg/), *Bartleby* (www.bartleby.com/), the *University of Toronto English Library* (www.library.utoronto.ca/www/utel/

index.html), and many sites devoted to specific writers. The number of critical or reference works available on the Web, as with *Contemporary Authors* and *Dictionary of Literary Biography*, is bound to increase. Web concordances to the works of writers ranging from Shakespeare to Eliot, created by energetic scholars, also will grow. Reviews of Web sites in such sources as *Choice*, articles in places such as *Chronicle of Higher Education* and *The New York Times*, and sites such as the *Digital Librarian* (www.servtech.com/~mvail/new.html) and *Yahoo!* (www.yahoo.com/new/) offering weekly or daily summaries of new sites are among the ways of keeping up with new literary sites.

For the most part, such electronic tools are not replacements for traditional print sources but are highly useful as supplements to them. Librarians should therefore explain the circumstances in which they can be helpful when introducing individual researchers to them or performing instruction for classes. For example, electronic concordances allow quicker—and certainly easier—searching than their print counterparts. Web sites assembling several editions of a writer's works, as with the *Jane Austen Information Page* (www.pemberley.com/janeinfo/janeinfo.html), help create a new method of comparing texts. As with so many Internet literary sources, such sites are especially helpful to the patrons of libraries with resources limited by space or budget.

However, these sources also can present some dilemmas for literary researchers and the librarians who advise them. Did the graduate student creating a concordance to the works of a major poet cover all the poetry, and were the most reliable editions used? Should a librarian refer a patron to such a site without being able to determine its reliability? If the sources and methodology used are not explained by the creator of the site, can its reliability be easily determined? Even subscription services may not indicate which editions are the bases of the full texts they offer.

Hovering over any library are the technical glitches that can strike any online catalog, CD-ROM database (whether stand-alone or networked), or Internet access at any time. One of the more important tasks of the librarian specializing in English and American literature is that of developing a system for dealing with the inaccessibility of electronic resources, whether for minutes, hours, or days. Just as such librarians know how to approach research from several angles, they must help their patrons understand that there is rarely only one way to carry out a research project. Patrons who rely exclusively on electronic resources are placing their research at great risk. Librarians can show them the foolhardiness of searching the Web to find the birth and death dates for a writer when that information can be found more quickly in a print reference source. Likewise, librarians should recognize that for the student working at home, such a site may be the only available source.

Helping patrons understand the usefulness of both print and electronic sources will obviously continue to be considerably important for some time. For all the technological advances of recent years, it is not an exaggeration to say that libraries of the early 2000s are in the Model T era of electronic information possibilities. More and more resources now only in print form will become available in some type of electronic format and will be accessible more quickly and possibly even more cheaply. More libraries, as with the University of Virginia's *Electronic Text Center* (etext.lib.virginia.edu/), will make their special collections available on the Web. Scholars having to travel hundreds of miles to examine manuscripts, letters, and photographs could become a thing of the past. If the increasing number of these advances makes more and more demands upon librarians, they also will make the librarians who master them more and more central to the research process.

Librarians cannot be overly zealous in keeping faculty aware of new reference services and sources. Buying the *World Shakespeare Bibliography on CD-ROM* without informing the professors specializing in Shakespeare does not lead to heavy use of the product. Faculty who assume their libraries will have few research tools related to the new areas of the canon should be shown otherwise. The more faculty are kept up to date, the more aware their students are of the available resources. Librarians can schedule open houses, workshops, and other demonstrations of both new and long-established tools. Showing small groups how a CD-ROM such as *DiscLit* offers searching capabilities far beyond the Twayne author series from which it is drawn not only constitutes instruction and publicity for library resources but also is good public relations.

Librarians should be vigilant in communicating with faculty, students, and administrators about their collections and research tools, even when apathy is the common attitude. All methods of advertising library services, from user guides to Web sites, are important. Stimulating the enthusiasm of even one faculty member is bound to have positive results. As more institutions require their faculty to create Web sites for courses and ask graduate students to put their theses and dissertations on the Web, indifference to electronic information in all its formats should decline dramatically.

Conclusion

Although many libraries have a literature specialist in their corps of reference librarians, few, if any, libraries are fortunate enough to have such a specialist always available. As a result, general reference librarians from many subject backgrounds will be called upon to deal with literary questions they may have difficulty comprehending. Part of this difficulty can be alleviated through ongoing training of reference staff and the concept of baseline competencies that has been gaining momentum in academic libraries.[35]

Librarians must convey their electronic expertise to their colleagues. Not all librarians approach their use of electronic sources in the same way. Sharing their knowledge through everything from in-house training to national workshops is necessary to keep the profession strong. Librarians should be thankful that technological advances make their work, more than ever before, part of an ongoing educational process.

All librarianship is in a time of change, as has been true for the past twenty years and will doubtless be true for the next twenty, and literary reference librarianship is no exception. Tools and resources may change, the nature of the information sought may vary, but the key to access will remain the reference librarian, whether in person or via e-mail. Literary reference librarians exist because library users are not, and should not be expected to be, aware of the vast resources available to them in up-to-date research libraries. Adding another dimension with electronic resources, which may eventually put the contents of the world's libraries in the hands of every user, does not lessen the need for expert assistance in locating and using resources. If anything, the reference librarian becomes a more necessary part of the research process. In addition to helping the experienced researcher, with the expansion of library resources and services, the need for bibliographic instruction grows. An article in *Perspectives: Newsletter of the American Historical Association* recommended that graduate students in history should, if possible, take library school courses to enhance their knowledge of library research methodologies and sources.[36] If this is true for historians, and it certainly appears to be good advice, how much more so should it be for literary scholars? Literary scholarship has a closer relationship with the library and its resources than any other field in academia, and librarians must be cognizant of that fact and prepared to offer scholars the assistance they are best qualified to give. In this time of interdisciplinary research, the transformation of the canon, and the explosion of electronic resources, the versatile, well-informed reference librarian can be the literary scholar's greatest resource.

Notes

1. Harrison T. Meserole, "The Nature(s) of Literary Research," *Collection Management* 13, nos. 1–2 (1990).

2. Ibid., 71.

3. Eric Carpenter, "Toward Interdisciplinarity in Literary Research: Some Implications for Collection Development," *Collection Management* 13, nos. 1–2 (1990): 77.

4. Marianne I. Gaunt, "Machine-Readable Literary Texts: Collection Development Issues," *Collection Management* 13, nos. 1–2 (1990): 87–88.

5. Richard Heinzkill, "The Literary Canon and Collection Building," *Collection Management* 13, nos. 1–2 (1990): 52.

6. Richard D. Altick and John J. Fenstermaker, *The Art of Literary Research*, 4th ed. (New York: Norton, 1993), 6n.

7. James Hulbert, "The Problems of Canon Formation and the 'Example' of Sade: Orthodox Exclusion and Orthodox Inclusion," *Modern Language Studies* 18 (1988): 120.

8. Henry Louis Gates Jr., "The Master's Pieces: On Canon Formation and the African-American Tradition," *South Atlantic Quarterly* 89 (1990): 92.

9. Keith C. Odom, "The Canon: Does Britannia Waive the Rules?" *Conference of College Teachers of English Studies*, no. 55 (1990): 91.

10. Earl Miner, "Canons and Comparatists," in *The Search for a New Alphabet: Literary Studies in a Changing World*, ed. Harold Hendrix, Joost Kloek, Sophie Levie, and Will van Peer (Amsterdam: Benjamins, 1996), 151.

11. David S. Reynolds, "Revising the American Canon: The Question of Literariness," *Canadian Review of Comparative Literature/Revue Canadienne de Littérature Comparée* 13 (1986): 230–31.

12. Heinzkill, "The Literary Canon and Collection Building," 52.

13. Isobel M. Findlay, "'Word-Perfect But Deed-Demented': Canon Formation, Deconstruction, and the Challenge of D. H. Lawrence," *Mosaic: A Journal for the Interdisciplinary Study of Literature* 28, no. 3 (1995): 57.

14. Stephen Greenblatt and Giles Gunn, "Introduction," in *Redrawing the Boundaries: The Transformation of English and American Studies*, ed. Stephen Greenblatt and Giles Gunn (New York: MLA, 1992), 7–8.

15. Ibid., 3.

16. Elizabeth Brown-Guillory, "Emerging Voices in the American Literature Canon: New Handles on Old Pictures," *Conference of College Teachers of English Studies*, no. 55 (1990): 89.

17. Paisley Livingston, "Justifying the Canon," in *The Search for a New Alphabet: Literary Studies in a Changing World*, ed. Harold Hendrix, Joost Kloek, Sophie Levie, and Will Van Peer (Amsterdam: Benjamins, 1996),145.

18. Frank N. Magill, "Introduction," in *Masterplots*, ed. Frank N. Magill (Pasadena, Calif.: Salem, 1996).

19. Reynolds, "Revising the American Canon," 230.

20. Greenblatt and Gunn, "Introduction," 3.

21. Reed Way Dasenbrock, "What to Teach When the Canon Closes Down: Toward a New Essentialism," in *Reorientations: Critical Theories and Pedagogies*, ed. Bruce Henricksen and Thais E. Morgan (Urbana: Univ. of Illinois Pr., 1990), 51.

22. Heinzkill, "The Literary Canon and Collection Building," 59.

23. Nils Erik Enkvist, "Canons in Linguistic, Stylistic and Literary Competence," in *The Search for a New Alphabet: Literary Studies in a Changing World*, ed. Harold Hendrix, Joost Kloek, Sophie Levie, and Will Van Peer (Amsterdam: Benjamins, 1996), 80.

24. Heinzkill, "The Literary Canon and Collection Building," 59.

25. Marjorie Perloff, "An Intellectual Impasse," *Salmagundi*, no. 72 (1986): 128.

26. Dasenbrock, "What to Teach When the Canon Closes Down," 57.

27. Heinzkill, "The Literary Canon and Collection Building," 62.

28. Scott Stebelman, "Building Literary Reference Collections," in *English and American Literature: Sources and Strategies for Collection Development*, ed. William McPheron, Stephen Lehmann, Craig Likness, and Marcia Pankake (Chicago: ALA, 1987), 156–80.

29. *Guide to Reference Books*, 11th ed., ed. Robert Balay, Vee Friesner Carrington, and Murray S. Martin (Chicago: ALA, 1996).

30. *Generalia, Language and Literature, the Arts*, ed. Anthony Chalcraft, R. J. Prytherch, and Stephen Willis, vol. 3 of *Walford's Guide to Reference Material*, 6th ed. (London: Library Association, 1995).

31. Ron Blazek, *The Humanities: A Selective Guide to Information Sources*, 4th ed. (Englewood, Colo.: Libraries Unlimited, 1994).

32. James L. Harner, *Literary Research Guide: An Annotated Listing of Reference Sources in English Literary Study*, 3d ed. (New York: MLA, 1998).

33. Michael J. Marcuse, *A Reference Guide for English Studies* (Berkeley: Univ. of California Pr., 1990).

34. Heinzkill, "The Literary Canon and Collection Building," 51–52.

35. Candace R. Benefiel, Jeannie P. Miller, and Diana Ramirez, "Baseline Subject Competencies for the Reference Desk," *Reference Services Review* 25 (1997): 83–93.

36. Daniel K. Blewett, "Why History Students Should Take Library Science Classes," *Perspectives: Newsletter of the American Historical Association* 33, no. 7 (1995): 25–27.

Chapter 9

Management of Electronic Text Collections

Perry Willett
Indiana University

We are all familiar with books—we can pick one up at random and understand in a moment how it is arranged, even if we cannot read the language in which it was written. We know where the book begins and ends; we can tell where chapters start and finish. Tables of contents, indices, glossaries, and other apparatus are readily recognizable. This kind of standardization is responsible in part for the tremendous, perhaps unparalleled, success of the codex book as a technology and a format.

None of these features can be taken for granted when considering digital publications. The medium has not matured to the point of standardization and instant recognition. Electronic texts allow for different uses than books, such as full-text searching, and yet provide innumerable challenges for the librarian who chooses to acquire electronic materials for the library collection. Part of this challenge lies in just what is meant by an "electronic text." There are many kinds of electronic texts: electronic journals, digital reproductions of manuscripts, character-based electronic texts, electronic reserve collections, and others. Many electronic resources use materials in other media, such as video or audio, as well. One area of interest and study is electronic texts in the humanities, meaning text-based transcriptions of primary works in literature, history, philosophy, and linguistics. This category includes both single works, such as hyperfiction novels, and collections or databases of multiple works. Also, this includes works originally conceived of and published in electronic form, as well as those works that reproduce printed texts.

The Center for Electronic Texts in the Humanities (CETH) lists more than twenty electronic text centers at universities and academic libraries in the United States.[1] Electronic text centers that focus on humanities electronic texts have developed in academic libraries over the past decade for a number of reasons. First and perhaps foremost, humanities scholars want such centers located in the library because it is where most other humanities materials are located. The library is a familiar location for humanists, unlike computer laboratories. Also, libraries were among the first service organizations to recognize the utility and importance of electronic resources for humanities research and therefore provided support for the required technology.

Still, there is no intrinsic reason why such resources and services need to be located in libraries. Centers for social science data, which administer large data sets from the U.S. Census Bureau and other government agencies, including opinion polls, election results, and other data of interest to political scientists, economists, and sociologists, were founded at many universities as part of computing services or specific departments and not as part of the library. Now, however, many social science data services are being relocated to the library because of the advantages it offers: a neutral site, longer service hours, and central resources for describing collections and making them known. Electronic text centers for the humanities are housed in libraries for many of the same reasons.

Decisions about collection development of electronic resources start primarily with the resource itself. Collection managers should ask the same questions they ask of materials in any format: Are the contents of a particular work or collection of interest? Are the editorial decisions made when creating the electronic versions acceptable? And, in many cases, because electronic collections duplicate print collections, what benefits does an electronic version of a well-known text offer? The decisions about the quality of any given electronic resource should be no less rigorous than those made about acquiring printed (or, to use the analogous example of large, reformatted collections—microform) materials.

The first electronic text centers in U.S. academic libraries began in the late 1980s, with the Electronic Text Service of Butler Library at Columbia University and the UMLibText Project at the University of Michigan among the first.[2] With such a short history as e-text centers in general possess, and the unique combinations of interest and funding that come together to form them, each new center will be set up and operate differently. There are few criteria for what constitutes an adequate e-text collection or service.

Among these few criteria, first and foremost is that e-text collections should respond to the interests of students and faculty at the particular institution where they can be accessed. There is no consensus on how or why humanists use electronic texts. Each researcher or student seems to have a different and nuanced use for electronic texts. Some use them as an ever-expanding concordance to track down remembered passages or quoted text; others see them as virtual collections with delivery systems to retrieve works not readily at hand; still others use them to test hypotheses or answer research questions. Other uses, such as attribution studies and linguistic or stylistic analysis, also are performed with e-text collections. Any e-text center or service must allow for these various possible uses.

However, there are a number of axes along which e-text centers develop their collections and services. One axis line traces the continuum between a virtual and physical e-text center. An important choice in planning an e-text center is whether to have one at all. The creation of a public service facility and the necessity for staffing and equipment means that this will not be a trivial decision. Librarians must understand that the decision to create a special center will require additional funding for it to be properly staffed. Although it may be relatively easy to find one-time funding for equipment and resources, ongoing funding for reference staff, equipment replacement, operating system and application software upgrades, and technical support is fundamentally necessary. Given the rapid rates of change, an e-text center without ongoing funding will struggle and rapidly become a museum collection.

Typically, such centers in academic libraries include computer equipment and specially trained staff to provide assistance to a collection of electronic texts on CD-ROMs and other media. The staff would be trained in the various software and interfaces that accompany these collections and would be able to help readers as requested. This task grows increasingly complicated as the number of different collections grows with different interfaces and software in a growing variety of languages. Unlike with print collections, reference assistance with e-texts does not end with simply joining the reader with the resource; although all printed books work similarly, each e-text collection from various publishers works at least a little differently from the others, and people may need assistance just getting started. The library will have to make a definite commitment to providing adequate reference assistance necessary for the resources to be useful.

The facility's staff will require training in both the humanities and computing. An understanding of humanities research, how it is conducted and communicated, is of fundamental importance for the service to be accepted by the campus community. This understanding can be reached in a number of ways: involving library staff with advanced training or degrees in the humanities, forming an advisory board of faculty members or administrators interested in electronic texts, and using graduate students from humanities departments to staff the facility. We have found that using humanities graduate students is particularly effective because they combine their subject interest with their enthusiasm for the electronic resources in their field and act as "missionaries" among their fellow students and professors.

Because there is little standardization in functionality, the technical support required to keep a growing collection of CD-ROMs may be daunting as well. Some products work only with particular operating systems, whether Microsoft, Macintosh, or something else, or even particular versions of operating systems, such as the Hebrew version of Windows 95. Some may work under multiple operating systems;

some may be networked as part of a local area network (LAN) within the center, whereas others may work only on a single workstation (and even then, may not work well with the configuration needed for other resources). As the number of collections grows, the complexity of keeping them all working together grows exponentially. Good technical support is a fundamental requirement for the operation of an electronic text center.

It will be difficult for librarians to achieve and maintain the technical skills required for these tasks because the complexity of hardware, software, and operating systems seems to grow daily. It is more realistic to expect that librarians will oversee these tasks and manage these facilities, which still require some understanding of the technical issues involved. Unfortunately, the opportunities for training focused on e-text centers are few and shrinking. CETH, a joint Rutgers University–Princeton University project funded by the National Endowment for the Humanities, used to offer summer programs designed to teach the skills required to start and run an e-text center in a library. However, these programs have not been offered recently, and the future of CETH is in some question.[3] The Rare Book School at the University of Virginia offers general classes on electronic texts, with emphasis on textual encoding.[4] Other organizations that sponsor educational programs and conferences related to electronic texts in the humanities include The Association for Computers and the Humanities, ACRL Electronic Text-Center Discussion Group, EDUCOM, and the electronic discussion groups ETEXTCTR-L, Humanist, and TEI-L, and the Usenet newsgroup comp.lang.sgml.[5]

The advantage of creating a center is its focus on electronic texts in the humanities. Staff can offer reference service and workshops in the use of specialized skills or resources, such as how to use software for a particular collection, how to create electronic texts using optical scanners and optical character recognition (OCR) software, or encoding and format issues. Expertise can be centralized and nurtured in the center. One problem facing special e-text centers in libraries is moving this expertise and the collections into the mainstream of the library's collections and services. In many cases, e-text centers have restricted hours when the materials are available, and many or even all of the resources may be restricted to use within the facility. The resources may not be cataloged, or even if cataloged, the individual texts available on any given CD-ROM may not be analyzed in the library's online catalog, making it difficult to communicate the contents of the collections. Until the contents of e-text collections are analyzed and included in the library online public catalog, the resources of an e-text center will not be entirely integrated into the library's collections.

The opposite end of this first axis is to provide decentralized access to electronic resources in the humanities over a campus wide-area network (WAN) such as over the World Wide Web and using standard access tools such as Internet browsers. A growing number of important reference sources and collections are available this way. This type of access moves important resources out of special e-text centers, perhaps with restricted hours or access, and allows researchers to use them in their offices or homes.

Even this axis point involves choices and differences. Libraries may make use of the search engines and servers of the publishers. A growing number of vendors, such as Chadwyck-Healey and Intelex, are creating Web sites for their collections and providing access through subscription. Nonprofit organizations, such as the Project for American and French Research on the Treasury of the French Language (ARTFL) at the University of Chicago, also make their resources available over the Web to subscribers. This arrangement places responsibility for system maintenance and design with the publisher, which is certainly an attractive feature. One danger with reliance on this method, however, is that the library only buys access; should the library decide for whatever reason not to pay the subscription fee, it may lose access to the resource entirely. Librarians need to be careful in signing agreements to be sure they understand whether partial access or partial ownership is possible.

One other potential problem with relying on vendors is that each vendor will create its own interface. This presents much the same problem as with CD-ROMs: as vendors' Web sites proliferate, librarians will have to struggle to teach and maintain the separate interfaces to each of the resources. Because only a few publishers are providing this kind of service, and HTML is limited in the complexity of possible interfaces, it is not yet a problem. Should this multiplicity of interfaces become a problem, one answer would be for the library to acquire the data and develop a common interface for them across vendors and publishers. This step would require a definite commitment on the part of the library, because a good deal of technical and programming expertise is required.

Library consortia have formed in growing numbers, partly in response to this problem, to acquire and provide access to e-text collections. Virginia's VIVA and OhioLink, as well as other consortia, have been particularly effective in negotiating discounts and providing service for a broad range of public and private academic libraries, and they centralize the programming, development, and maintenance necessary for these systems to operate smoothly.[6]

For these collections to be searchable over the Internet, the electronic files must be encoded in a standardized manner. This issue of encoding formats has important ramifications for the long-term viability of electronic resources. As technologies change and as hardware, software, and operating systems change, resources designed to run on particular hardware or under certain operating systems will become obsolete. Some publishers create new versions of their materials, upgrading from DOS to Windows, for instance, or from a Windows 3.1 version to Windows 95 or NT versions. Other publishers will not be able to keep their products current with technology, and the long-term prospects for such resources is not good. The market for many of these publications or products is small. In addition, the life span of CD-ROM as a medium may be only ten to twenty years, which is much shorter than librarians expect of materials in print or microformat. Thus, the format of electronic publications has extremely important implications for the longevity of any given resource.

One solution would be to create texts in a standard format that is independent of any application software or hardware. The Standard Generalized Markup Language, or SGML, is a set of rules for creating such a format or markup language. The Hyper-Text Markup Language, or HTML, is a well-known and popular implementation of the SGML standard, but it is only one such implementation. SGML has been approved by the International Organization for Standardization as an in-

ternational standard, and has been adopted by large numbers of cor-
porations for their in-house publication programs. The many departments and divisions of the U.S. federal government have chosen the
SGML standard for its electronic publications, and a growing number
of publishers are using SGML as a format for their publications.

Because it is a so-called open standard, not belonging to any
particular hardware or software manufacturer, texts encoded following the SGML standard can be used by a variety of software and on a
variety of hardware platforms without requiring conversion. This independence, in addition to its insistence on documented files, means
that files encoded following the SGML standard will have a greater
probability of longevity over those texts in other, proprietary formats.
Put another way, as David Seaman has stated, "if it's not SGML, it's
ephemeral."[7]

One drawback to SGML has been that browsers cannot display
SGML-encoded texts in their native format. Developers of browsers found
the SGML rules too complicated for implementation, and some kind of
translation from the SGML encoding to HTML was required. Recently,
however, the World Wide Web Consortium (W3C) has approved a new
standard, called the eXtensible Markup Language, or XML. XML is in
essence a simplification, or subset, of SGML rules; and the latest version of browsers such as Internet Explorer and Netscape will be able to
display documents in XML markup languages.[8]

The SGML standard defines the rules for a markup language,
and authors and publishers have choices in markup languages that
also affect the longevity of their texts. HTML, though the most popular
of SGML markup languages, is limited in its application to electronic
texts in the humanities because it is designed primarily for how text is
displayed. Although HTML follows SGML guidelines, it is not the best
SGML format for encoding a collection of literary texts. There is nothing in HTML to tell where poems begin or end, for instance, or how to
encode a special feature of any given text.

Humanists and computing professionals have collaborated to create another implementation of the SGML standard designed specifically for humanities texts called the Text Encoding Initiative Guidelines. In the TEI Guidelines, a markup language is defined that is well

suited to encoding literary texts, linguistic corpora, dictionaries, etc. Some well-known scholars and editors have disagreed with some of the basic assumptions of the TEI and have designed their own markup languages, but a very large number of electronic text projects have adopted the TEI as the format for their collections.[9]

A second axis line in electronic texts is between large electronic text collections, such as those described above, that seek to reproduce existing works in electronic form and those works that are originally designed in electronic form. One new genre that the electronic media have spawned is "hyperfiction," and is exemplified by such classics of the genre as Michael Joyce's *Afternoon* and Stuart Moulthrop's *Victory Garden*.[10] In hyperfiction, as in hypertext in general as imagined by George Landow, Jay David Bolter, and other theorists, the text lacks a narrative center or direction with no clear beginnings or ends, leaving choices to readers who thereby collaborate with the author in the creation of the story.[11] Landow and other literary critics see a "quasi-hypertextuality" in literary works such as *Tristram Shandy* and *Ulysses*, but they believe that this new medium of hypertext will give narrative fiction entirely new options to explore.[12] Others, such as Laura Miller, have not found the reality of hyperfictions to live up to their ideal.[13]

These hyperfictions, as well as general hypertexts such as the reference guide to the classical world, *Perseus*, tie together text and software in ways that are inextricable.[14] The publisher/author/programmer (and these lines become blurred) create a total environment for the reader while allowing greater freedom in using the resulting hypertext. However, the management problem remains of obsolete software becoming unworkable at a certain point, with no possibility of extricating the texts for use with different software. Some hyperfiction authors such as Michael Joyce and William Gibson have made this impermanence part of the meaning and experience of reading the hyperfiction. (Gibson's *Agrippa: A Book of the Dead* was intentionally infected with a virus that obliterated the computer files after they were read once.[15]) After they decide to acquire hypertexts for their collections, librarians will have to accept the fact that they may become unusable after a relatively short amount of time.

Electronic texts provide the potential for changing the way literary research is done. Concordances and first-line indexes, for example, have become obsolete as the full text of works becomes available in electronic formats. Also, the ability to search whole corpora for terms and concepts will lead scholars to texts they would not have considered or with which they were not familiar. This has the possibility of widening the literary canon to include disregarded and scarce works, as well as changing altogether the way literary texts are conceived.

Librarians will be faced, for some time it appears, with acquiring and providing access to electronic collections that in some way are limited in their long-term viability. These collections or databases may be formatted in a way particular to an operating system or certain software; they may be published only in a medium with a ten- to twenty-year life span; they may be limited in some other way. The collections will comprise many formats and media, and must respond to local interests, needs, and funding. Some of the materials simply will not last as long as librarians are used to thinking of when they acquire codex books, and yet they will still be of interest and research value. Librarians will have to make trade-offs between the importance of the particular resource and the longevity of the format and medium for a while to come. Management of these collections will require technical and subject understanding, creativity, and a willingness to experiment.

Notes

1. *Directory of Electronic Text Centers*, ed. Mary Mallery (New Brunswick, N.J: Center for Electronic Texts in the Humanities, 1998), available at http://scc01.rutgers.edu/ceth/infosrv/ectdir.html (29 Sept. 1998).

2. For descriptions of the early years of these centers, see Anita Lowry, "Machine-Readable Texts in the Academic Library: The Electronic Text Service at Columbia University," in *Computer Files and the Research Library*, ed. Constance C. Gould (Mountain View, Calif.: Research Libraries Group, 1990); 15–23; John Price-Wilkin, "Text Files in Libraries: Present Foundations and Future Directions," *Library Hi Tech* 9, no. 3 (1991): 7–44.

3. See the CETH Web pages at http://scc01.rutgers.edu/ceth.

4. See the Book Arts Press Web page for more information on its courses at http://www.virginia.edu/oldbooks/.

5. Electronic Discussion Groups Related to E-text Centers: ETEXTCTR-L. ACRL Electronic Text Center Discussion Group (subscription address:

listproc@cornell.edu/; submission address: ETEXTCTR-L@cornell.edu); Humanist (subscription address: http://www.princeton.edu/~mccarty/humanist; submission address: humanist@lists.princeton.edu); TEI-L (subscription address: listserv@listserv.uic.edu; submission address: TEI-L@listserv.uic.edu.

6. See the VIVA home page at http://www.viva.lib.va.us/ and the OhioLink home page at http://www.ohiolink.edu.

7. David Seaman, "Selection, Access, and Control in a Library of Electronic Texts," *Cataloging and Classification Quarterly* 22, nos. 3–4 (1996): 82.

8. See the World Wide Web Consortium Web pages at http://www.w3.org for more information on XML.

9. See Allen Renear, "Out of Praxis: Three (Meta)Theories of Textuality," in *Electronic Text: Investigations in Method and Theory*, ed. Kathryn Sutherland (New York: Oxford Univ. Pr., 1997), 107–27, for a theoretical discussion of textual encoding. For a list of projects that follow the TEI Guidelines, see the TEI Applications Page at http://www.uic.edu/orgs/tei/app/.

10. For an overview, see Robert Coover, "Hyperfiction: Novels for the Computer," *New York Times Book Review*, 29 Aug. 1993, 1–4. Two pioneering works are Michael Joyce's, *Afternoon: A Story*, 5th ed. (Cambridge, Mass.: Eastgate Systems, 1995) and Stuart Moulthrop's, *Victory Garden* (Cambridge, Mass.: Eastgate Systems, 1991).

11. J. David Bolter, *Writing Space: The Computer, Hypertext, and the History of Writing* (Hillsdale, N.J.: Erlbaum, 1991); George Landow, *Hypertext 2.0* (Baltimore: Johns Hopkins Univ. Pr., 1997).

12. Landow, *Hypertext 2.0*, 182.

13. Laura Miller, "www.claptrap.com," *New York Times Book Review*, 15 Mar. 1998, 43.

14. *Perseus Project: An Evolving Digital Library*, ed. David Crane (Medford, Mass.: Tufts Univ., 1999), available at http://www.perseus.tufts.edu (31 July 1999).

15. William Gibson, *Agrippa: A Book of the Dead* (New York: Kevin Begos, 1992).

Chapter 10
Issues in Cataloging Electronic Texts

Timothy Shipe
University of Iowa

The most important new development affecting catalogers of English and American literature during the past decade has certainly been the advent of the electronic text as a significant component of research libraries' literary collections. Although the history of the electronic text may be said to go back almost fifty years to Father Busa's early work on the *Index Thomisticus*, the advent of the electronic primary text as a library resource to be selected and cataloged has been quite recent. For all practical purposes, the effort to bring electronic texts under bibliographic control began in 1983, when the first cataloging records of the Rutgers Inventory of Machine-Readable Texts in the Humanities began appearing in the RLIN database. Started by Marianne Gaunt with support from the Council on Library Resources and the Andrew W. Mellon Foundation, the Rutgers Inventory eventually became a project of the Center for Electronic Texts in the Humanities (CETH) at Rutgers and Princeton. CETH took a leading role in developing and disseminating cataloging guidelines, and in providing a public forum for examining the issues surrounding the cata-

loging of electronic texts.[1-2] During the past decade, descriptive cataloging rules and the Machine-Readable Cataloging format (MARC)
have been modified or enhanced to accommodate electronic texts
as a format and to make provisions for remote access to digital
resources.[3]

Although the groundbreaking project at Rutgers got under way
nearly fifteen years ago, the experience of the University of Iowa may be
more typical of research libraries in general. The first electronic literary text product to be cataloged at Iowa arrived bearing the title *The
WordCruncher Disc: A Meledy [sic] of Significant Documents, Literature
and Information on CD-ROM.*[4] This item was a hodgepodge of electronic
texts on CD-ROM sold at an astonishingly low price and intended mainly
as a demonstration of the potential uses of the WordCruncher software
(the "WCView" portion of which came bundled with the product). Iowa
cataloged this title in 1990, and the cataloger (who happens to be the
author of the present essay) puzzled for hours over how to provide
access to this strange mixture of content in an unfamiliar format. Two
problems immediately came to the forefront, and although the format
has steadily evolved, both problems remain serious concerns for catalogers of electronic texts. They are the status of electronic texts as
editions of primary works in the context of the library's literary collections and the extent to which to analyze the contents of an electronic
text product or corpus.

The contents of this particular version of the *WordCruncher Disc*
(billed as "volume 1," although I am unaware of any other volumes ever
having been issued) were expressed in the formal contents note as
follows:

> Riverside Shakespeare (complete works). Religious texts
> (New International Bible, etc.). Legislative texts (Federal
> acquisition reg., etc.). Intro to American literature (se-
> lected texts). Library of America (American authors).
> Computerized manuals (WordPerfect Corporation). Con-
> stitution/freedom papers (patriotic texts). Famous
> speeches (Lincoln, Churchill, etc.). Foreign language text
> (Dutch).

Clearly this was not intended to be a coherent literary corpus. The contents as transcribed from the container did not begin to express the eclectic nature of this compilation. To take just one example, the "Foreign language text (Dutch)" was a Dutch translation of the WordPerfect manual.

One could have gone to either of two extremes in analyzing this disc. On the one hand, the compilation could have been analyzed quite thoroughly, representing every work on the disc with one analytic entry. (This would have entailed, among other things, devising a uniform title for the Dutch translation of the electronic version of the WordPerfect manual.) On the other hand, a minimalist approach could have been taken because neither the cataloging code nor the Library of Congress Rule Interpretations required any analytic entries for this work. In the end, this cataloger opted for a compromise, representing a few of the most useful aspects of the disc with analytic added entries as follows:

Shakespeare, William, 1564–1616. Works. 1990.
Bible. English. New International. 1990.
Bible. English. Authorized. 1990.
WCView (Computer program). 1990.

As it happened, these turned out to be useful entries at the time because the product included the first electronic Shakespeare and the first electronic Bible to be acquired by the University of Iowa Libraries. The inclusion of the WCView software as an analytic entry seemed appropriate because the point of the product was to demonstrate the use of this software.

In the eight years since Iowa cataloged that first disc, we have, like many research libraries, purchased or obtained access to a large array of electronic primary texts in the humanities. Those that exist as physical objects (discs) within our collections are represented in our OPAC. But many texts that are accessible by remote access do not appear in the OPAC, particularly those for which we do not pay. And many large corpora, such as the Chadwyck-Healey products (English Poetry, Database of African-American poetry, 1760–1900, etc.) and the French texts collected in the ARTFL database at the University of Chicago, appear in the bibliographic database only as single records. Like many institutions, Iowa has barely begun to tackle the problems of analytic cataloging of full-text databases and including remote resources in our OPAC.

One dilemma is that the distinction between what is and is not in our "collection" has become increasingly problematic. Another is that, with the advent of new-generation library automation systems, the distinction between our catalogs and our "collections" also may begin to blur. A user following a "hot link" from a catalog record to a full-text version of a literary work will not care whether the text is housed on a computer in the library, the campus computing center, or Michigan or Singapore, for that matter. Nor will the user necessarily register the fact that he or she has left the OPAC for, say, an SGML browser.

The relationship between the bibliographic record and the electronic text becomes particularly interesting with the development of the Text Encoding Initiative (TEI) as the preferred scheme for applying SGML to literary texts.[5] If a text conforms to TEI, it may, in a sense, contain its own cataloging record—or at least the basic information that can be used to generate a skeletal-level cataloging record. Library catalogers were heavily involved in the development of the TEI header, which was designed to incorporate the equivalents of many of the MARC fields and to provide information about both the electronic text and its source text. Although the level of detail has been left optional, it is possible to include in the header such elements as name and subject headings that are under authority control. Not only can the metadata be encoded in such a way as to meet the standards of the Library of Congress Name Authority File and the Library of Congress Subject Headings, but it also is possible to bring names within the body of the text under authority control. For example, using tags, it would be possible to associate each place name that appears in a literary text with its standardized form in the Library of Congress authority files. (Granted, the resources required to provide such dense encoding would be prohibitive in most cases.)

The fact that the TEI standards require a header that provides much of the information required by catalogers (and which, in cases such as the one at Virginia, may actually be created by catalogers) could greatly assist efforts to bring the universe of electronic texts under bibliographic control.[6] However, the notion that the TEI header can in all cases be used to automatically generate a MARC record is premature. Even if there were a one-to-one relationship between TEI tags and MARC fields, the level of detail in tagging required to effectively map to MARC is optional in the TEI standards. Although some TEI headers are created by catalogers with national and international cataloging standards in mind, others are created by scholars and editors with no knowledge of cataloging practices. TEI was deliberately designed to permit scholars as well as librarians to create headers, and some of the required elements in the header may be composed of either unstructured prose statements or highly structured, subtagged expressions and still be considered TEI-conformant.

Furthermore, the fact remains that the vast majority of electronic texts at this time do not conform to the TEI and are not likely to do so in the near future. Catalogers will continue to be faced with a bewildering variety of electronic text resources, following numerous encoding schemes, housed locally on various physical storage media or accessible remotely through the Internet or by other means. The fact that these texts will increasingly be available via the Internet from the same workstations from which users consult the online catalog, and that a new generation of integrated library systems will provide for hot links from bibliographic records to electronic resources (through the URL in the MARC 856 field), means that there will be increasing pressure to provide bibliographic access to this ever-growing universe. In many cases, access to remote texts will be free, and institutions that formerly only had to catalog whatever they could afford to buy will want to catalog what is freely available as well.

Moreover, as was mentioned previously, many of the available texts (whether remote or locally owned) will be buried in large corpora such as ARTFL and the various Chadwyck-Healey collections. The challenge of providing analytic cataloging for these works is quite similar to that of providing cataloging for the thousands of works hidden within large microform sets. In the past, some microform publishers offered analytic catalog cards for the works included in their large sets; later, these publishers (or other vendors) began offering MARC tapes for loading into the OPAC. Now, a number of publishers of electronic texts offer, or are considering offering, similar services. The availability of MARC records should be considered an essential characteristic of any "quality" electronic text corpus, and bibliographers should include this among their major selection criteria.

Whether all of the countless literary texts now available without charge through the Internet can or even should be cataloged is another question. The poor quality or ephemeral nature of many of these texts would seem to speak against encouraging their use for curricular or research purposes by representing them in the OPAC. Indeed, bibliographers are increasingly coming to see selection of free Internet resources as one of their responsibilities. In this case, "selection" consists not of a decision whether to purchase but, rather, of a decision whether to encourage access by providing links on an index site or by providing a catalog record in the OPAC. In a sense, the selection decision becomes a cataloging decision, or more precisely, a decision about what should be cataloged.

Library "gateway" sites (sometimes called "index sites" or "metasites") have, in most cases, been designed by reference librarians, bibliographers, or the staff of electronic resource centers. But a case could be made for calling on professional catalogers to take a greater role in the organization of library index sites. Such gateway sites, intended to create a browsable order from the chaos of the Internet, serve a function similar to that of classification schemes for books: they create a logical, hierarchical approach similar to the order of books on shelves. Those who have designed such sites have tended to use very broad categories and an alphabetical listing of sites within those broad categories. But as the number of resources referred to multiplies, this approach will become less and less user-friendly and the experience of catalogers in working with well-developed classification schemes will become essential. Therefore, cataloging staff should be routinely included in the work flow for building library gateway sites and catalogers should be asked to join the teams that develop those sites.

On an English and American literature index site with ten or even twenty entries, an alphabetical scheme may be adequate. For

example, at present, one library's index site for language and literature includes, among others, the following sites in the following
order:

- The Dickens Project;
- Digital Dante Project;
- Electronic Beowulf;
- Lewis Carroll's Works Illustrated;
- Marlowe, The Complete Works of Christopher;
- Shakespeare on the Web (actually two sites).

These are intermingled with a variety of more comprehensive full-
text sites and databases, some of which are purchased, others of which
are free. The designer of this Web page insisted that users are only
interested in looking for sites in alphabetical order by the name of the
site. Interestingly, a compromise was made by providing an inverted
heading for the Marlowe site, but no such accommodation was made
for the other authors represented. This schema is adequate for the site
as it now exists; but when a site points to thousands of authors and
tens of thousands of literary texts, something akin to the "author
numbers" in the Library of Congress P schedules seems to be in
order to bring works of a single author, and possibly of a given
period, together.

Of course, the capacity for multiple links to a single site over-
comes one disadvantage of any classification scheme for books: a book
can have only one shelf location and hence may occupy only one spot
in the classification scheme. Even if multiple classification numbers
are assigned in the bibliographic record (a more feasible option in an
online catalog than in the card catalog), one of these numbers must be
"privileged" as the actual physical location of the book, the place where
a patron browsing the shelves will actually encounter it. A library must
choose to either classify all of Nabokov's works in the PG or the PS
class (i.e., define him as either a Russian or an American author) or
split his Russian- from his English-language works on the shelves.
But an index site pointing to online Nabokov texts could give access
from both American and Russian literature pages. It is catalogers

who are accustomed to thinking in terms of the most useful browsing locations in a classification scheme. Just as catalogers assign multiple headings from the subject thesaurus, they should have no trouble adjusting to the opportunity to assign multiple locations in a hierarchical subject scheme for an index site.

We are finding quite a few new tasks to which catalogers may now dedicate themselves. Beyond those mentioned above, one hears occasional murmurings to the effect that catalogers possess precisely the skills required to perform actual TEI-conformant encoding of entire texts (not just creating headers as at Virginia)—in their spare time! This raises the inevitable question of the resources needed to catalog the growing universe of electronic texts.

Academic libraries have been devoting larger and larger portions of their personnel budgets to the new electronic world. Electronic text and digital resource centers are flourishing. Staff must be devoted to managing these centers, providing the technical support needed to develop and maintain them, and educating students and faculty members about their use. Meanwhile, cataloging staffs have been gutted in accordance with the perception that cataloging—and particularly a professional cataloging staff—has become a very low priority in the new environment. The cataloging profession has been under siege for a decade or more. And now, what is needed to cope with the world of electronic resources in an era of easy remote access is precisely—catalogers! Suddenly, the cataloging departments that have dwindled to a fraction of their former size are being asked to provide coherent bibliographic access not only to materials the library purchases, but also to an almost limitless range of resources the library does not own. Furthermore, catalogers are becoming involved in the creation of new resources—for example, TEI headers for electronic texts. Unless we reexamine our decisions to de-emphasize and de-professionalize cataloging in our libraries—and unless we begin including cataloging in the staffing equation for electronic text centers—our hopes for integrating the world of electronic primary texts into our literary collections will be continually frustrated by a lack of resources, resources which we failed to appreciate when we had them.

Notes

1. Annelies Hoogcarspel, *Guidelines for Cataloging Monographic Electronic Texts at the Center for Electronic Texts in the Humanities*, CETH Technical Report No. 1 (New Brunswick, N.J.: Center for Electronic Texts in the Humanities, 1994).

2. Lisa R. Horowitz, *CETH Workshop on Documenting Electronic Texts: May 16–18, 1994, Radisson Hotel, Somerset, N.J.*, CETH Technical Report No. 2 (New Brunswick, N.J: Center for Electronic Texts in the Humanities, 1994). More information on CETH is available through its home page at http://scc01.rutgers.edu/ceth/.

3. Rebecca Guenther, "The Challenges of Electronic Texts in the Library: Bibliographic Control and Access," in *Literary Texts in an Electronic Age: Scholarly Implications and Library Services*, ed. Brett Sutton (Urbana-Champaign: Graduate School of Library and Information Science, Univ. of Illinois, 1994), 149–72.

4. *The WordCruncher Disc: A Meledy [sic] of Significant Documents, Literature and Information on CD-ROM* (Orem, Utah: Electronic Text Corp., 1990).

5. *Guidelines for Electronic Text Encoding and Interchange: TEI (P3)*, 2 vols., ed. C. M. Sperberg-McQueen and Lou Burnard (Chicago: Text Encoding Initiative, 1994).

6. Edward Gaynor, "Cataloging Electronic Texts: The University of Virginia Library Experience," *Library Resources and Technical Resources* 38 (1994): 404–13.

Chapter 11
The Return to History in English Studies

J. Paul Hunter
University of Chicago

I have spent most of my life talking with librarians—from early child-hood trying to find things in books I could not lift to scholarly excursions in archives I could not negotiate on my own—but I am used to listening, not speaking: I have always had more questions than answers. So I feel a little odd as a voice in this collection: what expertise I have to offer derives from observations about research and curricular directions rather than knowledge of library functions as such. Nor am I an expert on the nuances of library–faculty interactions: I think that we see (and know) too little of each other and that in the near future we will plainly need to see and know more. For one thing, if the projections around universities these days can be believed (and I am afraid this kind of projection can), there will probably be fewer of both of us, and we will need to discover more fully how and in what specific ways we can help each other with our particular tasks. For another, global-ization has necessarily made the professoriate more modest, at least sometimes, and our knowledge of what we do not know is growing rapidly.

The only knowledge I have that might be useful in this book involves the directions of the disciplines I practice: literary criticism, literary theory, and literary history. I do believe that the directions of academic disciplines impact the way you use your time and the tasks you take on, and some quite profound changes in the directions of literary study and in what English and other language and literature departments try to do will make major differences in library use over the next few years for both faculty and students. You may already have begun to notice the effects of some of these changes, but if I am right about the directions of the disciplines connected with literary study, the changes ahead will be much greater. What you might have noticed already is that literature faculty tend to be around libraries more these days than they were in the last few academic generations, when a good deal of what they taught and wrote came out of their heads instead of out of books and manuscripts and when private meditation on set topics seemed more important than extensive and deep—and especially historical and archival—reading. You might also have noticed that some students—especially, but not exclusively, graduate students—are showing up more often, using older, scarcer, and more unusual books and asking you more questions. I am not talking primarily now about technological and pragmatic questions involving electronic innovations and possibilities (although their impact must be significant, too), but about where to find certain kinds of texts and how to ask certain kinds of bibliographical questions. I cannot tell you exactly what the effect on you will be of the ways we are changing, but if I describe those changes accurately, I think you will be able to see implications that will affect your daily tasks and that will in turn make libraries even more responsive to my own needs. I have few complaints from the past, and among all the people in universities who annoy me and make my life more difficult, librarians rank at the bottom of my list. Still, you can see that my presence in this volume has selfish motives because I am anticipating that I am going to need even more from you in future years than I have in the past. And so will my students and colleagues.

Let me talk about three kinds of changes in literary study. I will admit from the start that my profession lately has been rather fickle and that its modes and fashions have changed more often and more radically than the design of clothes, cars, and royalty. But some longer-term trends are visible. First is the return to historical questions and a deep interest in where texts come from, what their loyalties, contexts, and cultural implications may be, and what kinds of impact they have had initially and subsequently. Second is the movement in English and in language departments more generally toward cultural studies and the widespread attention to issues of multiculturalism in rethinking basic courses. Third is the way the population and distribution of faculty skills in English departments are beginning to change as our territory enlarges and faculty areas of expertise overlap less frequently (what I want to suggest is the impact that such faculty demographics are likely to have on student needs and interests and how some considerable portion of the educational function traditionally performed by faculty may in fact shift to you). On this latter point, I might ask if even now you have not begun to notice that students, both formally and informally, come to you more often with "library questions" that used to be dealt with fairly systematically (if not always very well) in basic, usually required, bibliography courses in the "home" departments such as English.

Move to Historicism

The return to historical interests in literary studies caught a lot of people by surprise. I remember a Modern Language Association (MLA) meeting in the late 1980s when a very distinguished member of my profession—a former president of MLA, a famous deconstructionist himself, an astute observer of educational trends who had led at least two major shifts in critical direction, and a basically sensible and very nice man—became overheated, almost apoplectic, in wondering what had suddenly become of the lately fashionable interest in critical theory. In trying to account for the directional shifts that had raised historicism into prominence and radically shifted attendance at convention sessions (especially among graduate students and younger faculty), he made it clear that he had no clue about where the interest in history had come from. But plainly he felt threatened not only personally, but also in terms of what he thought the profession had come to stand for methodologically and philosophically. Where had all the once-reliable theory-thirst gone, and what was this "new" historicism stuff all about anyway?

As it turns out, his alarm was a little exaggerated; critical theory still has a firm place in the minds of most people in literary study, although its directions have shifted a lot. Essentialism as a position is virtually dead, and high-flying theory has seen its elitism turn into lofty loneliness; to find the role of history and temporality has become perhaps theory's central concern, and no one any longer would think of writing a dissertation that was "pure" theory—that is, that did not ground its problem firmly in particular texts and specific historical moments and larger cultural issues that were in fact the focus more than the method used to probe them. My friend was right to notice a sharp change in interests and the habits of mind and work they would come to produce, and it is now almost a commonplace that the crucial issues to be discussed in texts are historical ones, even in brand-new texts. Some substantial part of the credit (or blame) for this shift goes to the movement usually called the "new historicism" and especially to the work of Stephen Greenblatt, who has a gift for focusing on important textual and hermeneutic issues in ways that make them seem historically compelling to large numbers of people. But ultimately the shift to a historical mode is larger than any single methodology or school, and it would be more accurate now to speak of new historicisms, for the kinds of historical investigations under way are legion—some radically new in method, some rather more traditional with new wrinkles; some Foucauldian, some Habermasian, a lot not. Subject matter is often new, involving texts and issues passed by in the long decades devoted to canonical and formalist narrowness, and all methodologies are highly contested because the lingering legacy of critical theory has made everyone self-conscious and argumentative about procedures and implications. What is important beyond labels is how fundamental and far-reaching the turn to historicism has been and how deep its roots seem to be. Most graduate students are, by their second or third year, deeply cognizant of and interested in historical issues, even if they are working in newer or contemporary literatures. And even those without passionate commitment "get it": they pursue ways of setting up dissertations so as to engage history in a meaningful way, not just (as they used to say rather patronizingly) "historicizing" the topic as if it were a patentable process, like martinizing, or a fashionable term, like downsizing, for an old and feared practice. The most notable result so far among graduate students is the stampede into American studies, with attention having shifted sharply to nineteenth-, eighteenth-, and even seventeenth- and sixteenth-century issues. As a result, the developing generation of Americanists is a whole new breed, far more ranging in knowledge, more talented, and more connected to other literatures and other disciplines than all but the best of their predecessors. On American texts and cultural issues, there is a genuine revolution.

The movement to historical issues in literary study does not seem to me ultimately surprising, and not just because I have always had strong historical interests and regard the revived interest in history with something like glee. (It is always nice to be able to feel trendy, especially when fashions catch up with you instead of vice versa, but there is deeper satisfaction, too, in thinking that powerful philosophical positions mostly suppressed during the long reign of the "new criticism" [or formalism as it is more properly called] are now being seriously explored). Too, it means a better chance, symbolized perhaps by the fact that the new historicism got its start in the Renaissance and especially in Shakespearean study, for the older literatures (that is, those periods before the Romanticism that altered perspectives continuously and that keeps presentism an eternal issue) to find again some crucial place in the minds and hearts of both graduate and undergraduate students who had tended to move, over the last several student generations, more and more to contemporary texts.

The move to historicism did not of course come out of nowhere. Marxism in its quixotic and stubborn way has always been, in all of its branches, in some sense historically committed, and some facets of structuralism and poststructuralism, especially when they were infused with or energized by Marxism, also showed occasional signs of historical curiosity. Too, historians themselves have transformed their craft and their profession over the past decade and a half, making their subject far more discussable, their work more available, and their methods more discoverable and self-consciously articulated. But the most important early indicators of "historicism on the rise" came in some of the directions of feminism, especially British and American feminism, where the importance placed on the rediscovery and resuscitation of older texts prompted archival work and led to important bibliographical and editorial projects. Recently, that kind of activity has increased and intensified, and many significant projects have led to the rehabilitation of writers as varied as Lady Mary Wroth, Aphra Behn, and Margaret Cavendish, Duchess of Newcastle. I suspect that everyone involved in university libraries knows how radically the teaching curriculum in some literary fields (most notably perhaps in seventeenth-, eighteenth-, and nineteenth-century studies) has changed in the past decade, but you may not all have pondered the historicist—as distinguished from the gender—implications of these changes and may not have noticed how scholarly projects and time commitments have shifted to reflect and further them.

The move to historicism in literary studies has a number of important ramifications in how faculty and students use their time and what kinds of materials they study in what ways—most of which influence how much and in what ways they use libraries—but let me mention only one here. You might have noticed that when I listed the disciplines of literary study, I mentioned literary history itself—the study of the making, relationship, and reception of texts. It is safe to say that ten years ago, no one would have mentioned literary history as something that anyone remotely tuned in to the times was doing. Now, suddenly, everyone is doing it, and quite beyond the superficial modishness of what intellectual hitchhikers are doing, basic revisionist projects are under way. Feminism of course fundamentally requires it, and so do (although many do not welcome it) most varieties of Marxism. Look at Margaret J. M. Ezell's *Writing Women's Literary History* for both a first-rate example of how it can be done and a judicious sense of what needs to be done.[1] Or think about the institutional projects under way: new or revised multivolume histories from Oxford, Cambridge, and Columbia; new major scholarly companions to genres, periods, and major figures (on old major figures such as Milton, as well as newly elevated ones); ambitious editions such as the Brown University–Oxford University Press women writers series (now truncated or abandoned, alas), the University of Kentucky Press editions of eighteenth-century women's novels, and the several projects undertaken by Pickering and Chatto; several series of new biographical dictionaries and relentless reprintings and repackagings of revisionist criticism. The recent proliferation of new or revised scholarly tools finding their place on old reference shelves—not even to begin to mention newly available and expanded electronic resources—suggests how much energy has shifted (largely driven by feminist concerns) into the production of projects in literary history.

Move to Cultural Studies

A second change involves cultural studies and the implications are far more complicated than I am going to make them sound, largely because cultural studies has such volatile political implications and the battle for control of the movement is still in progress. To simplify, cultural studies has two main thrusts: first, an interest in introducing a wider range of texts from a wider range of cultures than we usually study into the academic curriculum and to the working lives of literary scholars; and, second, a commitment to studying texts—all texts whether belletristic or otherwise—as cultural documents worthy of study both for themselves and for their roles and functions within their cultural economies.

It is only fair to say that the cultural studies imperative is, for some, far more a matter of political didacticism and ideological realignment than a question of intellectual directions (although both the political right and the impressionable media exaggerate this enormously) and that, therefore, some of the potential power of comparative culture is unnecessarily restricted to the alterity of contemporary *places* rather than fully explored in a historical way that conceives other *times* as a relevant kind of otherness that can clarify our own values and teach us about ourselves. But the intellectual potential of cultural studies, when logically pursued, both draws into the study of texts the considerations traditionally posed by disciplines such as anthropology, sociology, linguistics, economics, and political science, on the one hand and makes textual questions central to the investigation of cultural mores, habits, and values, on the other. Whether this makes English and other language and literature departments more central—or less so—to academic studies of cultural difference is debatable and likely to be contested for quite some time, and those of us whose business it is to read texts critically could still blow it, Big Time. But what is clear is that we are suddenly in the midst of an immense variety of questions none of us has been educated to investigate. Important work on these broadly cultural issues can only be done in an interdisciplinary way, and we are individually and collectively ill equipped by training to do this work. In our own "cultural" investigations, not to mention those we lead or provoke our students to do, we do not know our way around. We are going to be dependent—already are dependent in important ways—on those whose knowledge of the bibliographies, texts, and materials of other disciplines and other subject areas is larger, broader, and especially deeper than ours. I have come up against terms and issues over the past three or four years that I do not even know how to look up. The cries of help you hear from the faculty these days are aimed mostly at colleagues in other disciplines, but (inevitably) they will be redirected mostly to you.

My own awareness of how much I do not know has been enhanced by my research as much as by my teaching. A few years ago, for reasons too complicated to get into here and in any case not altogether clear to me, I began (with a former colleague from Emory) to work on a textbook that ultimately became W. W. Norton's *New Worlds of Literature*.[2] It included selections from the ethnic subcultures of many parts and regions of America; its focus was on the way different subcultures confronted the majority culture and how texts monitored, explored, and fostered the many results of those confrontations. It was the first text of its kind (now there are scores), and I have to say that I then had no idea what I was getting into, how many areas of the library new to me I would ultimately learn to explore. I got to know, among other things and people, a lot of librarians previously unknown to me. I found new kinds of research helpers; I found not only new kinds of help with making footnotes, but new kinds of help in finding footnotes that needed making. I am clearly not the only scholar-teacher to be led by new directions into kinds of work that are going to involve more consulting, negotiation, and dependency on others than I have ever known before. Footnoting canonical or newly canonical books such as

Moll Flanders, *Hard Times*, *Oroonoko*, or *Frankenstein* would seem to be a piece of cake after this, though (as someone involved in just such a revisionist editing project) I have found that even familiar texts and old informational questions now look different (and much more complex) because of multicultural explorations and their different focus on classic issues.

Distribution of Faculty Skills

The third area of change, involving the kinds of faculty English and related departments hire to "cover" the expanding areas we have imperialized, points even more to our limits and to areas where we are going to need professional research help to make up for education we have not had. If looking more deeply at historical texts such as *Moll Flanders* or teaching greater varieties of American texts that explore America beyond the old conventional categories takes us deep into whole continents of academic ignorance that our Eurocentric backgrounds have ill prepared us for, just wait until we thin our specializations out by trying to cover all the new "cultural" areas involving new traditions and new geographies we had not previously pretended we had access to. A quick and easy illustration: university English departments used to have five or six medievalists around, minimum; now they have two or three at most. We are still used to having four or five Renaissance specialists in a department the size of mine, and in most other "periods," a group of at least three or four. It is a luxury few other language departments have had, and they have learned to "cover" (it is only a metaphor) big areas with many fewer people: faculty members there teach several categories or have double or triple specialties, and are not always able to know all they would like to know to guide their students. As we in English add on Caribbeanists, specialists in Latino and various Asian literatures, postcolonialists in Anglophone literatures of India, Africa, Canada, and Australia, and specialists in non-English texts—all the while operating in a stable state or more likely downsized departmental economy—it does not take a mathematical whiz to notice that some concentrations of expertise are going to be diluted. We will not have as many people who know as much, and we are going to be turning to experts outside the faculty—as well as those in other disciplines—to help. Guess who my English colleagues will look to? More horizons of knowledge require more kinds of exploration, but we are globalizing in a time of diminishing resources. Already we are stretched too thin in our knowledge to do some of the things students have some right to expect of us; already we have virtually given up courses in editing and bibliography (and largely tossed them your way) because we are stretched in our offerings and lack the range of information and expertise to teach many skills thoroughly.

Our students now see more clearly than ever all the things they need to know, and there are too many of them, for them as well as us. They know that Shakespeare is not enough; that knowledge of Shakespeare's language and the social history of the theater and his cultural contexts and female contemporaries is not enough; that they need to know about Anglophone texts beyond England and America and disciplines beyond literary criticism, even beyond history and anthropology. More and more, we find ourselves using sections of the library we did not even know were there, asking questions we do not have even the foggiest notion how to phrase, and seeking information we could not translate even if we knew when we had found it. We will, I hope, seek out biologists and economists, and that will be good; for too long we have badmouthed, slighted, and even avoided experts in disciplines we do not understand, and we will no longer be able to afford that. But, too, as we find our way back to old texts, the texts of other disciplines, and the archives of others—not to mention our own archives that fifty years of literary directions have allowed us systematically to ignore—we are going to need more than the usual help with information resources. We will be lost even more than we are now; you will at least be our guides and often our teaching partners. I hope we become grateful enough.

In closing, let me describe briefly a project of mine that illustrates many of the demands placed on us and, in turn, shifted to you by the new directions of literary study. I am general editor, for Bedford Books, of a new series of classroom texts that will enable teachers to practice some important facets of the new historical and cultural directions in the classroom. In addition to providing a reliably edited and annotated text of novels such as *Evelina*, plays such as *She Stoops to Conquer*, and poems such as *The Rape of the Lock*, each volume contains a reception history tracing responses to the text from its first appearance to the present. More important, it will provide 150 to 200 pages of contemporary documents and excerpts from texts related to the central text. For example, in the *Moll Flanders* edition I am doing, there are maps of London, England, and Virginia; descriptions of Newgate Prison; spiritual biographies and criminal lives written about the same time; journals of other transported criminals; the text of the Transportation Act of 1718 and statistics on criminals transported to America from London as "colonists," not to mention chapbook versions of *Moll* and samples of abridgments and extensions produced by Defoe's rivals. I will not try to tell you about all the new things I learned about *Moll Flanders* from undertaking the project (about Defoe's propagandistic intentions on colonization and judicial reform, for example), and I will ask you only to imagine how much help I have got from people in research libraries around the world in putting the volume together. But consider for a moment what the implications for teachers and students may be in terms of projects they themselves undertake. Ultimately teachers could do these volumes themselves (with a little help from their friends) if they had the local library resources to do so, and they could have students do related projects on other texts. At the least, I expect, it will drive readers more often to rare book rooms and to many kinds of reference sources to check out different kinds of historicity and to compare the factual basis or uses of social information in texts studied as "literature." How much work that will make for you I will let you imagine, but I am pretty sure it will enliven some of the conversations you have with seeking students and seeking faculty. We are likely to be a more interesting bunch of teachers and scholars in this new kind of historicist climate, and I hope we will be more interesting to you as well as just more dependent.

Notes

1. Margaret J. M. Ezell, *Writing Women's Literary History* (Baltimore: Johns Hopkins Univ. Pr.: 1994).

2. Jerome Beaty and J. Paul Hunder, eds., *New Worlds of Literature: Writings from America's Many Cultures* (New York: W.W. Norton, 1989; 2d ed., 1994).

Chapter 12

A Typology of Literary Scholarship for Academic Librarians

Stephen E. Wiberley Jr.
University of Illinois at Chicago

Information technology is transforming all aspects of libraries, and if not yet transforming all aspects of literary scholarship, it is at least opening up the possibility for great change everywhere. Because information technology is central to what librarians do and because it changes so rapidly, librarians today spend much time attending to it. As a result, they have less time than in the past to study what users of libraries are doing. With less time to learn about users, they need intellectually parsimonious analyses of various user groups that will enable them to grasp, relatively quickly, the information needs of these users.

This chapter presents an analysis of literary studies that attempts to identify the basic types of work done by scholars in the field. This analysis derives principally from study of the sources scholars use and secondarily from assessment of the extent to which they consult librarians. It aims to be of value to both librarians who set policy and design services and librarians who help individual scholars. The analysis is parsimonious. It strives for power by risking oversimplification. It identifies and describes types of scholarship in terms of a few differentiating characteristics. In doing so, it ignores the complexity of what any one scholar actually does. It assumes that librarians who study it and similar analyses that support or correct it will extrapolate from these analyses to understand the needs of the departments and individuals they serve.

Literary Studies: A Field in the Humanities

An analysis of literary scholarship should be grounded in study of its products: humanistic publications. To have meaning to librarians, such an analysis should be theoretically based in library and information science. For librarians, the most basic question is, What sources of information does a person use? Indeed, it is differences in sources used that differentiates humanities disciplines such as literary studies from the social sciences. I define the humanities as those fields of scholarship that strive to reconstruct, describe, and interpret the activities and accomplishments of men and women by establishing and studying documents and artifacts created by those men and women. The social sciences also study the activities and accomplishments of men and women but use data social scientists themselves have developed through experiment, fieldwork, and surveys. The men and women whom social scientists study provide the data, but the social scientists greatly influence the data's content because they direct data collection and recording.

Crucial to the distinctiveness of literary scholarship or any other field in the humanities is the primary evidence or sources humanists use: documents and artifacts created by persons whose activities the scholar seeks to reconstruct, describe, and interpret. These documents and artifacts are called primary sources. Working from a definition of the humanities that stresses the role of primary sources and reflecting upon the kinds of work that literary scholars do, we can develop a typology of scholarship that roughly begins with types that use primary sources most intensively and exclusively and then considers the types that are more removed from them. The Modern Language

Association's *Introduction to Scholarship in Modern Languages and Literatures* and its predecessors help us identify the following types:

- descriptive bibliography;
- editing;
- historical studies;
- criticism;
- theory.[1]

In a given project or publication, a scholar may do more than one of these types, and such mixes can make it difficult to distinguish one type from another. And to verify that such types exist will take careful, bibliometric analyses of works that, nominally at least, fall into the different categories. But for the present discussion—an initial effort to develop an overall analysis of literary scholarship—these rough categories prove very useful.

Before beginning discussion of the different types of scholarship, it is worthwhile to review the course the analysis follows. This analysis combines induction and deduction. In a sense, I began deductively, using a definition of the humanities that William G. Jones and I offered in 1994.[2] But because this definition is based on years of reading humanistic scholarship and hours of interviewing humanists, it is, to a significant extent, derived inductively. The definition suggested an initial set of three types of humanistic scholarship: description, reconstruction, and interpretation. I then modified the types of scholarship given by this definition by comparing them to types of scholarship identified as important over the years by the Modern Language Association (MLA). This modified set of types in effect maps the literature of the humanities and enables me to identify specific works of scholarship (exemplars) that nominally, at least, fall into these types. I then study the sources that these exemplars cite. This bibliometric study leads to refining the definitions of some of the types to fit the questions posed by library and information science. Although many literary scholars probably would disagree with these definitions, the purpose of analysis is to answer questions important to librarians, not to conform to norms of literary scholarship. Thus, for example, even though literary scholars could contend from their perspective that it is possible to do historical studies without ever stepping into a special collections department, my analysis will argue that the use of rare materials is a distinctively important activity for one type of literary scholar and that this is what distinguishes historical studies, so defined, from criticism and theory.

Descriptive Bibliography

The humanistic activity most directly involved with sources is description. For literary sources description is called bibliography. Good bibliographies have a distinctive appearance. They have transcriptions of titles and description of physical characteristics and of significant content, all in a consistent format. The distinctive appearance of bibliographies is important. It reflects the fact that bibliographers have methods that, if not universally agreed upon, are held widely enough to allow uniformity that is unknown among other types of humanistic scholarship except scholarly editing. Agreement on methods has led to accepted rules for transcribing title pages, standards of notation for collation, and conventions in describing variant printings. A widely held methodological requirement is that a bibliographer study as many copies as possible of the works that are the subject of the bibliography in order to both differentiate variants and document the works' printing and publishing history.[3] This necessitates interaction between librarians and bibliographers.

Examination of a representative sample of descriptive bibliographies—the fourteen cited as exemplary in William Proctor Williams and Craig S. Abbott's *Introduction to Bibliographical and Textual Studies*—shows that bibliographers cannot be successful without libraries and librarians.[4] Bibliographers acknowledge this. For example, Edwin T. Bowden wrote in the preface to his bibliography of James Thurber: "My first thanks go to those libraries that have been particularly helpful, both in providing books and periodicals and in answering many detailed questions."[5] One gets a quantitative sense of the importance of libraries to the bibliographical enterprise by analyzing lists of location symbols that tell where the bibliographer found the copy described. For example, in the first and last volumes of the *Bibliography of American Literature*, libraries are 80 and 79 percent of the locations, respectively.[6] In bibliography, librarians and humanists collaborate. And for bibliographers of works that appeared as print on paper, collection of those printed documents is a central task of libraries. A universally shared digitized version or versions will not do; bibliographers must see the original.

At the same time, for works of the computer age, such as hypertext fiction, that are created for the video display terminal, not for paper, bibliographers will need the digitized — the original — sources. They will want to see the digital originals, exactly as they first appeared. This poses a great challenge for librarians and others involved in the preservation of digital sources. Jeff Rothenberg has summarized the basic technical requirements. Librarians will need to preserve not only the bit streams that are created today, but also the so-called bootstraps that enable them to decode these streams. They need to save the programs used to create digital documents as well as system software needed to run these programs. They also need to create emulators so future scholars will be able to run equivalents of past hardware.[7]

It is difficult to overemphasize the importance of libraries in the preservation of digital sources, and it is hard to exaggerate the complexity of the task. It also is worth noting that for most of the computer age the complexity of the task has been downplayed. Initially, the task of preserving digital information was seen as one of "refreshing" the data, copying them from an old medium to a new one. The very word *refreshing* is misleading because it calls up images of delightful reinvigoration, like opening up a window to bring a cool breeze into a stuffy room. Recently, however, librarians, if not others, have come to realize that the challenge of preserving digital information must be met by a more complicated and necessarily arduous process, one that solves all the problems outlined by Rothenberg. A landmark report by the Task Force on Digital Archiving of the Commission on Preservation and Access and the Research Libraries Group describes the process as *migration*, which it defines as "the periodic transfer of digital materials from one hardware/software configuration to another, or from one generation of computer technology to a subsequent generation."[8] Migration is a better word because it connotes the travail of moving from one place to another, of reestablishing life in a new location. Because of the rapidity and complexity of technological change and the certainty that it will never end, institutions, not individuals, whose lifetimes necessarily end, must take responsibility for the migration of digital sources. Libraries have the traditions and the expertise to do this for all types of sources.

Editing

Broad discussion of important topics in the humanities can occur only when sources that embody these topics are made widely available in reliable versions. Because key sources survive in either multiple forms or unique artifacts, it is necessary to make scholarly editions of them available. Today, scholarly editing is being transformed because of the computer. Of all literary scholars, editors are the most advanced in their interest in digital sources. This has developed because computer-based information systems allow editors to do things they have long wanted to do but been unable to do because of the limitations of print on paper sources. These capabilities include storage of images of variant versions of works so they can be quickly compared; the ability to have each component of a work's variants discretely encoded (that is, each word, line, sentence, etc., tagged) so it can be found and manipulated quickly; and, similarly, the ability to have all editorial materials and contextual sources discretely encoded so their components can be found and manipulated quickly.

Because the transformation of scholarly editing through digitization is just beginning, we can only speculate about how this type of scholarship will develop during the next century. Nevertheless, it seems probable that some key generalizations that apply to scholarly editing in the print world also will apply in the digital world. Printed scholarly editions have a distinctive format: the text of the edited work is central and is surrounded by an editorial apparatus. Similarly, the text of a digital edition will be central and will be displayed in a way that enables readers to link easily to its editorial apparatus.[9] Editors of printed scholarly editions intensively use originals of as many variants of the work being edited as they can. This brings editors to special collections where they interact with librarians. Examination of six exemplary printed critical editions shows that nearly all of the primary printed and manuscript sources they used were from libraries.[10] Similarly, current thinking about electronic editions and first efforts to produce them indicate that libraries will be crucial because they hold original manuscripts and published sources that will be the bases for digital editions.[11]

Besides providing the raw material that editors will work with, libraries are likely to be responsible for preserving the digital editions these editors create and for providing access to these editions through cataloging. Peter S. Graham has argued cogently that institutional commitments are essential to the long-term preservation of digital sources.[12] By their traditions and values and the expertise of their staffs, research libraries are ideally suited to take on such commitments. Furthermore, scholars assume that librarians "will increasingly take over the maintenance of electronic resources."[13]

Regarding access to digital sources, a crucial element is the development of standards for encoding, such as the Text Encoding Initiative (TEI). The TEI is a multilingual, international project that developed guidelines for the preparation and interchange of electronic texts for scholarly research. By design, TEI provides a structure for collaboration between librarians and humanists. Collaboration entails a division of labor in which literary scholars and their assistants mark up the digital file to reflect the source document's typographical layout, basic structure, and transcription. Scholars also tag thematic or stylistic elements. Library catalogers verify, correct, and expand the TEI header by standardizing author names, titles, and subject headings. They also may indicate the literary form of the text as well as related attributes such as the author's gender and nationality.[14] I would suggest that, as with bibliography and other aspects of scholarly editing, collaboration between librarians and scholars is possible because there is general agreement on method.

Historical Studies, Criticism, and Theory

One can tell at a glance that one has a descriptive bibliography or scholarly edition in hand. Descriptions of literary works dominate the bibliography, and the text of the literary work is central to the edition. In contrast, one cannot tell at a glance whether one has in hand historical, critical, or theoretical work. In format, all three are prose statements in which the words of the scholar predominate over those of literary works. This commonality of format reflects the absence of agreement among literary scholars upon method and the similarity of write-up among the three types. True, there is consensus enough in the discipline that these different types exist so that the MLA's *Introduction to Scholarship* has given significant attention to each. All five editions have had a chapter on literary history, four have had chapters on literary criticism (called in the latest edition literary interpretation), and the last two editions have had chapters on literary theory. But it is impossible to distinguish among historical works, criticism, and theory without at least reading them. Even reading may not be enough. Sometimes close analysis that measures against a standard may be necessary.

In the approach I am pursuing here, I look to the descriptions of these three types that literary scholars have given only to point in a general way to exemplars of scholarship to investigate. In the end, I will develop — because I think librarians must develop — definitions of each type that distinguish them in terms of the kinds of sources used, not the type's current or past status among literary scholars. These definitions may prove controversial because their aim is not necessarily to conform with literary scholarship but, rather, to provide librarians with a perspective on what literary scholars do.

To begin with, I divide the sources used by literary scholars into two categories, each of which has two subcategories. The two broad categories are familiar — primary and secondary. *Primary sources* are those created by the persons whose activities and accomplishments the literary scholar seeks to describe and interpret. In literary studies, these creators are called authors. Primary sources may be divided into original sources and later editions. Original sources are archives, manuscripts, and printed versions of a work in whose creation the author shares. Later editions are versions of original sources developed without the author's participation. For purposes of the present analysis, primary literary sources that have been classified in libraries (often older printed sources and usually archives and manuscripts have not been classified) fall into Library of Congress classes PA–PM, PQ–PZ.

FIGURE 1
Kinds of Sources for Literary Scholarship

I. Primary
    A. Original (when classified, PA–PM, PQ–PZ)
    B. Later Editions (PA–PM, PQ–PZ)
II. Secondary
    A. Literary (PA–PM, PQ–PZ)
    B. Nonliterary (A–N, P, much of PN, Q–Z)

Secondary sources are those written by persons other than the persons whose activities and accomplishments the humanist seeks to understand and interpret. These are usefully divided into two kinds: literary, those about works of literature, especially those that class in PA–PM, PQ–PZ, and those not about works of literature, including A–N and Q–Z and also P and much of PN. P and much of PN seem to belong more to theory than literature.[15] The different categories are summarized in figure 1.

The diversity of literary scholarship shows that these different kinds of sources can be used in virtually any combination. My research is too preliminary to discuss all of these combinations in detail, but I would like to focus on some of them and then begin to use the terms *historical, critical,* and *theoretical* in new ways, so that they begin to take on meanings useful for librarians.

Historical Studies

In relation to sources of information used, the historical scholar, as I am using the term, looks at original primary sources in much greater breadth and depth than the critic or theoretician. Although critics typically rely on standard editions they are studying and theoreticians principally use other theoretical works, historical scholars read a notable proportion of original sources, including manuscripts and first editions. Sometimes these first editions may be works of little-known authors, who, for whatever reason, have not merited scholarly editions. Historical scholars may be as interested in bindings, dust jackets, typefaces, and overall look of the edition as they are in what words they contain.

Because they are using original primary sources, some of them obscure, historical scholars, like descriptive bibliographers and editors, must use libraries. And like bibliographers and scholarly editors, literary historical scholars usually acknowledge the contributions of librarians. For example, after thanking those who funded her *Pastoral and Ideology: Virgil to Valéry*, Annabel Patterson said she was "particularly indebted to the curators of rare books and special collections at Cornell, at Princeton, at the British Library, at the Library of Congress where the Rosenwald Collection of illustrated *Virgils* is housed, at the Bibliothèque Nationale, and above all at the Folger Shakespeare Library, whose staff have been unfailingly and extraordinarily supportive."[16] Similarly, in *Writing Women in Jacobean England*, Barbara Kiefer Lewalski recognized that "many librarians and archivists . . . helped me locate and gain access to obscure materials, and facilitated this research at every stage."[17] Finally, in *Before Novels: The Cultural Contexts of Eighteenth-Century Fiction*, J. Paul Hunter thanked "many institutional libraries that have made their resources available and often provided aid and counsel" and whose collections and services were, he said, as important to his work as funding from Guggenheim, NEH, and the National Humanities Center.[18]

The acknowledgments quoted above and the sources cited in the books where those acknowledgments appear suggest that librarians in special collections work with literary historians more often and more significantly than do librarians who work with general collections. These acknowledgments and citations show that building collections, especially special collections, is crucial. They are the sine qua non for historical scholarship, as defined here. To cite just one example, Patterson told us how use of special collections changed her study of Virgil's *Eclogues*:

> This project began in an attempt to explain why it was that modern theorists of pastoral were often hostile to or contemptuous of the one era in which the genre could be said to be ubiquitous, namely, the Renaissance. Trying to answer that question took me back to Virgil . . . . But the inquiry itself opened my eyes to some remark-

able facts about Virgil's *Eclogues*. The size of the Virgil collections of the British Library, Princeton University Library, and the Library of Congress suggested that few texts can have been so frequently edited, annotated, translated, imitated, and illustrated in visual form. Moreover, the fame of the names involved indicated that here was a ready-made instrument for doing cultural history with a certain rigor, while at the same time raising the suspicion that there was more here than met the eye, that more had been invested in this text over time than our own cultural system anywhere admitted . . . . Beginning, therefore, as an exploration of Renaissance poetics, the project became impossible to complete without retracing the whole story of Virgilian interpretation, from its first major formulations in the early Middle Ages to developments that at least as I write can be spoken of as recent.[19]

My emphasis on special collections for historical scholarship is not to say that general collections are not important to these scholars. Whereas some humanists rely on their large personal libraries, all at some point or another use library general collections simply because the range of sources they cite is so vast that no individual could own them all.[20] General collections provide not only secondary, but also primary sources. But scholars, with few exceptions, use general collections without the help of librarians.[21] This is not to say that they use general collections as effectively as they would if they consulted librarians. Rather, it is simply an observation about usual behavior: when humanists who are used to working independently have an impersonal way (e.g., catalog, index, shelf location) to locate information, they seldom consult a librarian.

Currently, substantial efforts are under way to digitize sources in special collections and make them available over networks. Networked use of special collections is likely to lessen direct interaction between librarians and scholars because it will make them available through the impersonal mechanism of the computer. It seems fair to assume that this will occur increasingly because access to rare materials via the network is not only impersonal, but also less expensive than traveling to them. It also seems fair to assume that unless remote access to sources is accompanied by online assistance from curators, scholars will not use distant collections as effectively as ones they consult on-site. Finally, virtual reality ultimately cannot substitute for reality. Whenever disciplinary norms call for use of original sources, scholars will have to turn to special collections where the originals are preserved.

Criticism

Although I define historical scholarship as that based on original primary sources to such a degree that the scholar must utilize special collections, many literary scholars would disagree with this definition, possibly because they consider historical some scholarship not based on special collections material or because they see some studies I call historical to be what they call criticism. In assigning a differentiating characteristic to criticism, it is important to recognize that scholars can use a variety of sources when they criticize works of literature. Figure 2 outlines some of the variety. The one thing all the instances of criticism have in common is that they cite primary sources (PA–PM, PQ–PZ). Of course, it is a given that literary scholarship cites literary works. But in this analysis, I call criticism those prose works of literary scholarship that use literary works proportionally more than theory does, but without using original sources to the significant extent that historical scholarship does.

FIGURE 2

Use of Sources by Different Types of Literary Scholarship

Kind of Source	Type of Scholarship				
	Historical	Critical	Critical	Critical	Theoretical
Primary					
Original primary	x				
Later editions	x	x	x	x	x
Secondary					
Literary	x		x	x	x
Nonliterary	x			x	x*

*Use of nonliterary secondary sources greater in theory than in criticism.

One extreme form of criticism (extreme at least in terms of use of sources) is formalism. Formalism designates scholarship that focuses on the creative work itself with little (if any) regard for other sources. The emphasis is on the text, not its context. Probably the most famous movement in formalism was the New Criticism. Cleanth Brooks was perhaps its leading exponent. His critical works illustrate that critics usually do not need to consult librarians. These books do not acknowledge librarians, and although they constantly quote later editions of literature, they have few, if any, notes to other sources.[22]

New Criticism has long since passed from the scene, and scholarly norms for citations have changed since Brooks's time. Today, the norm of what I am calling criticism is to have many footnotes or endnotes and to cite, besides later editions, other criticism, literary theory, and, if the critic chooses, secondary sources from other fields. Thus, in figure 2, I have labeled as criticism three combinations of uses of sources: later editions of primary sources; later editions of primary sources and literary scholarship; and later editions of primary sources, literary scholarship, and nonliterary scholarship . All of these sources are ones whose dates of publication, authors, or publishers are such that one can fairly assume the scholar learned of them through tracing footnotes, from referrals from other scholars, or through everyday "keeping up" by scanning key journals and publishers' announcements.[23] In other words, the sources these scholars are using are so mainstream that there is very little need for them to consult librarians. Although critics (as defined here) have little need to consult librarians directly, such scholars will always rely on librarians to build local collections that support the main lines of their research; to provide interlibrary loan service that brings them materials about subjects tangential to those main lines; and to classify and catalog materials so that they have easy access to what they need and a shelf arrangement conducive to serendipitous discoveries.

An interesting question is whether critics will want to use digital sources. Anecdotal evidence is mounting as rapidly as computer printouts that people are unwilling to read documents on a video display terminal that are longer than two or three pages.[24] Given the propensity to read print-on-paper versions of longer documents, the relatively low cost of printed literary texts, and their ready availability in libraries, it may well be that critics will continue to read print-on-paper versions of primary sources. Librarians need to be ready for this possibility, even as they take increasing responsibility for digital collections.

Theory

Works of theory, Jonathan Culler has told us, succeed "in challenging and reorienting thinking in domains other than those to which they ostensibly belong because their analyses of language, mind, history, or culture offer novel and persuasive accounts of signification, make strange the familiar, and perhaps persuade readers to conceive of their own thinking and the institutions to which it relates in new ways."[25] Theory, in general, then, is unpredictable, destabilizing, and may deal with anything. Literary theory does of course relate to literature and literary theorists do cite works of literature (PA–PM; PQ–PZ). But an analysis of the sources cited by a handful of leading works of literary theory shows that they cite other works of literary theory (classed in P and much of PN in Library of Congress classification) and philosophy (B–BD and BH–BJ) much more heavily than do works that I am calling criticism. In other words, besides each other, literary theorists are likely to be as interested in Husserl as they are in Hardy, in J. L. Austin as they are in Jane Austen. Theorists almost never require first editions, archives, or manuscripts. Depending on their preferred medium, theorists will use digitized or print copies of the works they seek. Again, the length of the text needed should have a significant influence on whether the scholar reads a video display, a printout, or a printed copy.

Although theory has always been a part of literary scholarship, its importance to the field has become pronounced in the past three decades. (It did not have a chapter in the MLA *Introductions* until 1981.) The number of approaches in theory is great. The *Encyclopedia of Contemporary Literary Theory* has entries for forty-nine. The *Johns Hopkins Guide to Literary Theory and Criticism* has entries for twenty-seven of these forty-nine, as well as twenty-six others.[26] New theoretical positions develop regularly. Although there are a number of outstanding theorists, whose works must be collected by every library that supports a serious literary studies program, I have yet to find evidence that theory has a core literature. This challenges libraries to collect very broadly.

Because theory has such broad interpretative power, it can apply to fields outside literature. Arguably, literary studies has been the discipline more receptive to theory than any other. This has given it the foundation from which it can claim the right to interpret virtually any topic. Departments of English have been so aggressive in incorporating theory from other disciplines that, as M. H. Abrams has remarked, "if one wants to study Nietzsche, Marx, Freud, Derrida, or Foucault, one must apply not to departments of philosophy, psychology, or sociology, but to departments of English or comparative literature."[27] Consequently, librarians who develop collections in literature must keep their eyes on fields their predecessors did not have to follow. Also, they must stay abreast of new trends, particularly those that their local faculty find most important. Like critics, theorists usually cite works that are by well-known authors and are published by major presses. Thus, theorists are likely to find what they need in the library without consulting librarians. At the same time, because theory is so wide-ranging, no theorist could readily review all publications potentially relevant to his or her work. If the theorist is receptive to assistance, a librarian who understands the theorist's interests can send that scholar numerous useful recommendations of items to read. In either case, if librarians do not maintain a wide-ranging vigilance for trends in theory, their collections will not have the sources their theorists (and other) scholars need. This vigilance could include monitoring key publishers, cutting-edge journals, and leading departments.

Conclusion

Librarians face great challenges in providing effective services and maintaining efficient operations. Effective services must be tailored to meet individual needs, but efficient operations should be based in policies that fit general patterns of behavior. To provide effective service and maintain efficient operations, librarians need to know about the basic ways library users do their work. In the academic world, work is driven by scholarly traditions and disciplinary norms. Librarians gain mastery over these traditions and norms by investigating what academics have done, particularly by asking what sources of information scholars have used. By studying general guides to literary studies and selected exemplars of literary scholarship, this chapter has attempted to identify and describe basic types of scholarship (i.e., basic and distinctive patterns of use of sources in one humanistic discipline, literary studies). Even though others will undoubtedly challenge the typology presented here, this chapter provides a starting point for understanding humanistic scholarship. It has pointed to some of the most important things that librarians should do to support these different kinds of scholarship. This chapter's recommendations have largely been about policy and general practice, not about assistance to individuals. It is highly unlikely that any individual scholarly project will conform exactly to one of the types described here. These types, after all, although based on analysis of what sources of information scholars use, ultimately are derived from questions of librarians. It is equally unlikely that any individual project will not contain elements of the types described here. Given the latter probability, librarians can benefit from analyzing each scholar's needs in terms of the typology presented here. Given the former probability, they will need to adjust service to features of the scholar's work that do not conform to the types. In all cases, the mediator between the general and the specific, between sources of information and users, is the librarian.

The author is grateful to Anne C. Jordan-Baker, John M. Cullars, Joan B. Fiscella, William G. Jones, and William A. Wortman for commenting on earlier versions of this chapter.

Notes

1. "The Aims, Methods, and Materials of Research in the Modern Languages and Literatures," *PMLA* 67, no. 6 (1952): 3–37; *The Aims and Methods of Scholarship in Modern Languages and Literatures*, ed. James Thorpe (New York: MLA, 1963; 2d ed., 1970); *Introduction to Scholarship in Modern Languages and Literatures*, ed. Joseph Gibaldi (New York: MLA, 1981; 2d ed., 1992).

2. Stephen E. Wiberley Jr. and William G. Jones, "Humanists Revisited: A Longitudinal Look at the Adoption of Information Technology," *College and Research Libraries* 55 (1994): 503.

3. William Proctor Williams and Craig S. Abbott, *An Introduction to Bibliographical and Textual Studies*, 2d ed. (New York: MLA, 1989), 27–28.

4. Ibid., 101.

5. Edwin T. Bowden, *James Thurber: A Bibliography* (Columbus: Ohio State Univ. Pr., 1968), viii.

6. Jacob Blanck, comp., *Bibliography of American Literature*, vol. 1 (New Haven, Conn.: Yale Univ. Pr., 1955); Michael Winship, ed. and comp., *Bibliography of American Literature*, vol. 9 (New Haven, Conn.: Yale Univ. Pr., 1991).

7. Jeff Rothenberg, "Ensuring the Longevity of Digital Documents," *Scientific American* 272 (1995): 42–47.

8. Commission on Preservation and Access and Research Libraries Group, *Preserving Digital Information: Report of the Task Force on Archiving of Digital Information* (Washington, D.C.: Commission on Preservation and Access, 1996), 4–5.

9. William H. O'Donnell and Emily A. Thrush, "Designing a Hypertext Edition of a Modern Poem," in *The Literary Text in the Digital Age*, ed. Richard J. Finneran (Ann Arbor: Univ. of Michigan Pr., 1996), 193–212.

10. James Fenimore Cooper, *The Prairie: A Tale*, ed. James P. Elliott (Albany: State Univ. of New York Pr., 1985; Nathaniel Hawthorne, *The Scarlet Letter*, ed. William Charvat and Roy Harvey Pearce (Columbus: Ohio State Univ. Pr., 1962); W. D. Howells, *A Hazard of New Fortunes*, ed. David J. Nordloh et al. (Bloomington: Indiana Univ. Pr., 1976); Washington Irving, *Wolfert's Roost*, ed. Roberta Rosenberg (Boston: Twayne, 1979); Herman Melville, *Typee: A Peep at Polynesian Life*, ed. Harrison Hayford, Hershel Parker, and G. Thomas Tanselle (Evanston and Chicago: Northwestern Univ. Pr. and the Newberry Library, 1968); and Mark Twain, *Adventures of Huckleberry Finn*, ed. Walter Blair et al. (Berkeley: Univ. of California Pr., 1988).

11. Peter Shillingsburg, "Principles for Electronic Archives, Scholarly Editions, and Tutorials," in *The Literary Text in the Digital Age*, ed. Richard J. Finneran (Ann Arbor: Univ. of Michigan Pr., 1996), 23–35; Jerome McGann, "The Rossetti Archive and Image-Based Electronic Editing," in *Literary Text in the Digital Age*, ed. Richard J. Finneran (Ann Arbor: Univ. of Michigan Pr., 1996), 145–83; MLA, Committee on Scholarly Editions, "Guidelines for Electronic Scholarly Editions" (New York: MLA, 1997).

12. Peter S. Graham, "Requirements for the Digital Research Library," *College and Research Libraries* 56 (1995): 331–40.

13. Susan Hockey, "Creating and Using Electronic Editions," in *The Literary Text in the Digital Age*, ed. Richard J. Finneran (Ann Arbor: Univ. of Michigan Pr., 1996),13

14. Richard Giordano, "The Documentation of Electronic Texts Using Text Encoding Initiative Headers: An Introduction," *Library Resources and Technical Services* 38 (1994): 389–401; Edward Gaynor, "Cataloging Electronic Texts: The University of Virginia Library Experience," *Library Resources and Technical Services* 38 (1994): 403–13.

15. The Library of Congress's PN schedule includes several different segments

that are explicitly set aside for works of literary theory and other areas that are for works that deal with literature generally and can be applied to theoretical works. Most important is PN 45–57, which is for "Theory. Philosophy. Esthetics." There are also PN 1031–1049 for "Poetry. Theory, philosophy, relations, etc." and PN 3329–3352 for "Prose. Prose fiction. Philosophy, theory, etc." For general treatments of literature, there are call number areas such as PN 1010–1030 that are for works about poetry. This chapter's analysis of sources cited identifies as theory those classified below PN 440 and those areas of PN above 440 that are explicitly for works of theory or for general treatments of particular forms of literature. All other PNs, for example, PN 6010–6790 for "Collections of general literature," are counted with the sources of literature (i.e., PA–PH and PQ–PZ).

16. Annabel Patterson, *Pastoral and Ideology: Virgil to Valéry* (Berkeley: Univ. of California Pr., 1987), xiii.

17. Barbara Kiefer Lewalski, *Writing Women in Jacobean England* (Cambridge, Mass.: Harvard Univ. Pr., 1993), xi.

18. J. Paul Hunter, *Before Novels: The Cultural Contexts of Eighteenth-Century English Fiction* (New York: W. W. Norton, 1990), xxiii.

19. Patterson, *Pastoral and Ideology*, 8–9.

20. Mary Ellen Soper, "Characteristics and Use of Personal Collections," *Library Quarterly* 46 (1976): 397–415.

21. Stephen E. Wiberley Jr. and William G. Jones, "Patterns of Information Seeking in the Humanities,"*College and Research Libraries* 50 (1989): 638–45; Michaelyn Burnette, Christina M. Gillis, and Myrtis Cochran, "The Humanist and the Library: Promoting New Scholarship through Collaborative Interaction between Humanists and Librarians," *Reference Librarian*, no. 47 (1994): 181–91.

22. See, for example, Cleanth Brooks, *The Hidden God; Studies in Hemingway, Faulkner, Yeats, Eliot, and Warren* (New Haven, Conn.: Yale Univ. Pr., 1963); ———, *Historical Evidence and the Reading of Seventeenth-Century Poetry* (Columbia: Univ. of Missouri Pr., 1991); ———, *A Shaping Joy: Studies in the Writer's Craft* (London: Methuen, 1971).

23. See, for example, Terry Eagleton, *Myths of Power: A Marxist Study of the Brontes* (New York: Barnes and Noble, 1975); Naomi Schor, *Zola's Crowds* (Baltimore: Johns Hopkins Univ. Pr., 1978); Elaine Showalter, *Sister's Choice: Tradition and Change in American Women's Writing* (Oxford: Clarendon, 1991).

24. *Library of Congress Information Bulletin* 49 (26 Feb. 1990): 84; Marilyn Gell Mason, "The Yin and Yang of Knowing," *Daedalus* 125, no. 4 (1996): 165–67.

25. Jonathan Culler, "Literary Theory," in *Introduction to Scholarship in Modern Languages and Literature*, ed. Joseph Gibaldi, 2d ed. (New York: MLA, 1992), 203.

26. *Encyclopedia of Contemporary Literary Theory: Approaches, Scholars,*

Terms, ed. Irena R. Makaryk (Toronto: Univ. of Toronto Pr., 1993); *Johns Hopkins Guide to Literary Theory and Criticism*, ed. Michael Groden and Martin Kreiswirth (Baltimore: Johns Hopkins Univ. Pr., 1994).

27. M. H. Abrams, "The Transformation of English Studies: 1930–1995" *Daedalus* 126, no. 1 (1997): 124.

Chapter 13

Faculty Liaison: Librarians and Faculty as Colleagues

Marcia Pankake

University of Minnesota

Parts of this chapter touch on the content of other chapters in this book, because our liaison activities can deal with everything related to the library. If we regard librarianship—whether reference, collections development and management, cataloging, or technical and access services—as a process of communication, faculty liaison plays a pivotal role. Faculty liaison, both a means and an end, is a systematic way to communicate with, learn from, and serve important library patrons, to advance and publicize the library's agenda, and to ground the ideals and bureaucracy of the library in the real needs of its community. In faculty liaison you test your patience, articulate your ideals, demonstrate your technical competence, and display your practical skills. You also will gain much pleasure and gratification.

Faculty liaison can begin with graduate students because, of course, graduate students at your institution become faculty members at mine, and vice versa. Librarians who demonstrate to students—who model as well as tell them—that they command a body of sophisticated knowledge and technical skills prepare the faculty of the future to give library staff their confidence and respect.

Not all of us work at institutions with graduate programs, however, so faculty liaison for many of us begins with the faculty at hand. Most of us define *liaison* as a responsibility for, or a relationship with, faculty. A survey by the Association of Research Libraries reported that nearly 50 percent of respondents include responsibility for students in liaison work, but most of us focus first on faculty.[1] For some of us, work with faculty begins before they take their positions, when they interview on campus for jobs. I meet with all candidates (and sometimes with prospective graduate students) for the English department. Often librarians serve on search committees for faculty, but I prefer to stay off the committees. Each candidate is brought to the library, a bit puzzled sometimes, to meet with me. I have searched their CVs in advance, so I can say exactly how we can or cannot support their teaching and research. Young scholars and prospective faculty usually enjoy meeting librarians whose responsibilities relate to their research. While looking at the collections, they often discover materials they have sought. Even when our collections are weak in their particular interests, our services and general holdings compensate. I talk about the general level—regional relevant holdings, the general outlines of our collections relevant to their interests in, say, comparative Chinese and English drama—and at the detailed level of which journals we have and which ones we lack. Candidates respond with great interest to a comparison of holdings in their subjects, as, for example, saying that Minnesota's Irish literature collection is twice as big as Michigan's, equal in size to Indiana's, half as big as Wisconsin's, and one-tenth the size of Harvard's. We do not want people to arrive on campus and find unpleasant surprises in the library. If our holdings are weak, we discuss how I can direct purchasing to support their needs and how local and regional cooperation and interlibrary loan (ILL) will support their work.

This conversation often surprises, and usually pleases, the candidates. I learn much in talking with these new Ph.D.s about the sources of information they use in research. For them, this occasion often provides the first extended conversation with a librarian. I always refer to my national colleagues saying, "Do you know my colleague, Tim Shipe, your librarian at Iowa? We are acquainted through the American Library Association," thus insinuating that we are a national community of common interests as much as the American Society for Eighteenth Century Studies is.

This opportunity for a lengthy visit with job candidates allows me to inculcate some of my values into the new faculty members before they take up their jobs on campus. They learn that the department thinks the library is important and values their research. They learn I do not need them to suggest individual books to buy or to send me marked advertisements from the pages of *PMLA*. Instead, I want to know about their research, about works that are especially urgent for them individually, and about works that emanate from outside the organized English and American book trades. They learn how we work, how the budget constrains us, and what services we offer. And the department has learned that the visit to the library works as a recruitment device. Candidates return to the department enthusiastic about the library. Some candidates have exaggeratedly said they want to come to Minnesota, even without a job offer, simply to be able to use the library.

This positive effect is not due solely to my prowess. Often the hour has been a pleasant interlude in the candidate's day. Compared to a search for a library position, the interview for a job in English seems to have fewer activities. The candidate may meet a group of students, may give a lecture, will meet the department chair and the dean, and likely will dine with some faculty. The day is not that busy, so the library visit gives them something to do. More important, I do not judge the candidates. I do not affect whether they get the job offer, so they can relax with me. They are not competing with anyone when they are in the library.

As a result of this interviewing, the dean of faculty in the College of Liberal Arts asks me to speak with the group of new faculty who arrive on campus each fall. I cannot address their particular individual needs, of course, when they are coming to chemistry, journalism, history, and so on, but I manage to inform them about the library in a broader way. I can talk about general policies, the size of collections, our historical strengths, RLG and OCLC, and our bibliographic data-bases. And I can give them printed information and, most important, the names of their subject librarians.

Each year, several new people arrive temporarily on campus as visitors or sabbatical replacements. I write to these people in the summer to invite them to contact me for an introduction to the library or any particular help. I also call the newer assistant professors in the fall, if I have not had contact with them over the summer, to remind them of the library's interest in them and to encourage them.

Librarians who work in small institutions with little turnover in the teaching staff have limited opportunities in recruiting and welcoming new faculty. What other activities can librarians in all sizes of academic institutions pursue to serve faculty and build good relations with them? What models or paradigms will shape the services academic librarians offer to their faculty colleagues in the twenty-first century, especially given the social changes compelled by new technology?

Two sentences from novels that span the nineteenth century remind us that we are not the first to experience change and uncertainty. "It is a truth universally acknowledged, that a single man in possession of a good fortune, must be in want of a wife." Contrast this first sentence from *Pride and Prejudice* with this last sentence from *Heart of Darkness*: "The offing was barred by a black bank of clouds, and the tranquil waterway leading to the uttermost ends of the earth flowed sombre under an overcast sky—seemed to lead into the heart of an immense darkness."

Academic librarianship in our day recapitulates this movement from Jane Austen's static, civilized certitude to Joseph Conrad's modern uncertainty. When many of us began our careers, we began with the solidity of collections of good books, with the aesthetics of a stable ordered academic world. We saw a certain "housewifelyness" in librarianship: librarians kept books in order, and some faculty members perceived librarians as handmaids or servants. Now, at the end of the twentieth century, many librarians have faculty status and service has moved to expertise, but we perceive chaos in society, our institutions of higher education, and librarianship. Public support for higher education falters while private philanthropy increases. Conflicts within the academy over the literary canon, teaching methods, the purpose of literary study, and tenure embroil faculty and students alike. They ask, "What is literature?" "Is a billboard a text?" In the electronic environment, with the simultaneous consolidation of publishing firms and the growth of independent and desktop publishing, with the use of the Internet for both personal expression and organized communication of ideas, we ask, "What is a book?" "Are libraries and librarians necessary?" As our libraries reduce staff, pare acquisitions, invest in technology, and undertake new programs, we suffer the decline of society's investment—and even faith—in education. We experience a loss of staff, downsizing, restructuring. Much about our work, and even our values, seems intangible, shifting.

In the 1970s, some libraries adopted the model of the subject specialist, in which librarians paralleled members of the teaching faculty: librarians obtained equally advanced degrees and had experience teaching and doing research in the disciplines. They knew the work of their patrons firsthand. Librarians with teaching experience felt the practical effects that reserve room policies and deadlines had for teachers. When librarians had done research, they understood short deadlines, interlibrary loan, and other factors involved in expediently identifying, locating, and reading books—the practical impact libraries have on scholars. When librarians had published, they understood the toil and responsibilities involved in creating new publications as well as in their dissemination and use. With this knowledge, librarians could organize library collections and services better. Moreover, such intimate identification sometimes created instantly, and perhaps unjustifiably, a prejudice in the minds of some faculty in favor of the librarian. They regarded us as one of "themselves" rather than as one of "them."

Regardless of the educational background and functional responsibility and expertise of librarians, scholars and librarians can mutually respect their separate distinct expertise. Librarians provide scholars service without being servile. Even though scholars in literature work independently more than scholars in other disciplines, they understand separate complementary specialties. A linguist seeks help from a statistician, and neither feels inferior to the other.

Our professional literature contains many articles on the working relationships of faculty members and librarians. In the sphere of materials selection and collection management, Ung Chon Kim and Alfred Garvin Engstrom described methods of working with faculty.[2] Mark Sandler suggested the library train faculty in the tools and methods of selection.[3] Most recently, Robert Neville, James Williams III, and Caroline C. Hunt described diverse methods of faculty liaison relative to book ordering for computer science and English at the College of Charleston.[4] Catherine E. Pasterczyk has itemized liaison activities for librarians.[5] Some libraries have published guidelines for selectors. Librarians at Bobst Library (New York University) have assembled a concise list, reminding librarians that "there can be no single blueprint, schedule, or yardstick for success, given the diverse institutional, historical, political, and personal dynamics that different selectors are going to encounter in their own areas of activity."[6] RASD has guidelines for liaison work.[7] In serials literature, many articles have reported methods to consult faculty in serials cancellation programs. In teaching, of course, we have a large amount of literature on bibliographic instruction in general, some on working with faculty in instructional activities, and even some articles in our specialty, published in the *Literary Research Newsletter.*

Of great use to librarians in both collections work and reference are the publications by our colleagues who have analyzed the working methods and the sources of information used by humanists. Although fuller information appears elsewhere in this book, these valuable data merit reiteration, for they can shape our approach to faculty. One way to determine what scholars need is to ask them, which is what Stephen E. Wiberley Jr. has done. From interviews he observed that humanities scholars mostly work alone. They interpret documentary sources in a cultural context, and they work by reading. All read written primary sources. According to Wiberley and William G. Jones, "humanists spend most of their time alone, reading." They "rely partially or totally on library collections for their research." "They give little or no evidence of consulting librarians in general reference departments," but they do use librarians in archives, rare books, and special collections. How do they find what they read? Scholars rely, first, on references in publications they read; second, on communication directly from colleagues; third, on formal bibliography; and finally, on librarians. The formal bibliographic tool most often used is the serial bibliography published by their scholarly associations. They use the library catalog, whether in card form or online, "conveniently, independently, and unobtrusively" to find books and journals.[8]

Another way to examine what scholars need is to deduce it from their published work, and four citation studies in literature inform us. I do an injustice to these scholars by mentioning their findings so briefly, but I want to acknowledge our debt to them for their research. Richard Heinzkill showed us that scholars in literature rely more heavily on books than do scholars in other disciplines, but their use of serial literature is important and distinctive. Twenty percent of their citations were to serials; they cited a larger number and variety of journals than did scholars in other disciplines.[9]

Literary scholars use old books, more so than do scholars in other disciplines. Madeleine Stern found that 83 percent of their citations were to books and that scholars writing on writers from the more distant past, obviously, used books that were older than did scholars studying more modern writers. Milton scholars, for example, gave 44 percent of their citations to books published before 1900.[10]

John Cullars's study of scholars' published books found that 12.9 percent of scholars' citations were to manuscripts, and less than one percent to dissertations. John Budd identified a small core of thirty often-cited journals, a core, however, comprising only six percent of the 497 titles cited, but one of heavy use, reaping 38.6 percent of the total periodical citations.[11]

These studies bring us back to an Austenian universally acknowledged truth—the importance of collections. Most libraries with faculty liaison responsibilities associate them with collection development. Many libraries organize faculty liaison responsibilities by academic department, but in larger institutions, librarians may define liaison responsibilities, instead, by discipline. Obviously, American studies, women's studies, comparative literature, African-American studies, the law school, the college of education, and other departments may have faculty who work with literature. Our English department numbers only forty-five, but 109 faculty members' teaching and research needs depend on the collections in English and American literature. These faculty teach in eight departments in four colleges. Some departments will have a library committee; others may have one faculty member, sometimes the newest, sometimes the most senior, assigned responsibility for library liaison.

What practical things can one do when assuming new faculty liaison responsibilities? First, you must learn the work of either the departments you cover or the discipline as it is practiced at your school. Look at the faculty in the discipline or departments—their number, ranks, publishing records, and the courses they teach. Look at the departments—their administrators and support staff. Can you compare the relative proportion of money the college spends on a department to the money the library spends on it? Gather data on the students, both undergraduate and graduate—their numbers, their distribution in majors or special emphases. Identify readers who may work in other capacities at your school, as advisors or editors. Examine the funding supporting your readers—grants, gifts. Learn the history of your subject at your school by reading the archives and old annual reports and by talking to staff. What are the department's strengths and weaknesses, its regional or national stature, the awards won by students and staff, alumni? What directions do faculty plan to take in the near future? Does the department have a formal library committee? You can gather these data by reading locally published catalogs and meeting with departmental staff. Even having lunch and attending social events can lead to information and opportunities to promote the library.

In addition, you will want to understand how the discipline is practiced at your school by knowing what your faculty teach. Every year, look at the class schedule and course bulletins, paying special attention to new courses. Ask instructors for their syllabi, and visit the bookstore or check course Web sites to see what texts are required and recommended. As interdisciplinary work becomes more common, one must keep an eye out for teachers using literature in courses outside English departments and coordinate liaison activities with the librarians responsible for those departments.

Faculty research interests may diverge considerably from what they teach, and so we must speak individually with the faculty about their research needs. It is not sufficient to attempt to deduce their research needs from brief interactions at the reference desk. Probably each of us has gone to great lengths to help someone who seemed, from his questions, to be moving into a new direction, only later to learn he was getting information for his brother-in-law. Rather than attempt to deduce research needs from reference questions, one should take the time to meet with faculty about their research. After an initial interview with a faculty member, you must try to follow his or her publication records. Often departmental or college newsletters will report faculty members' conference papers. When I see their articles or books, or acknowledgments of their work in books related to their interests, I mention it. Sometimes we in the library are aware of their publications before their colleagues are.

In supporting faculty work, we also must support the work they direct their students to do. Graduate students' research interests can have greater impact on the library than those of the faculty because students often work on the newer frontiers of scholarship. Use teaching opportunities as occasions to let the graduate students know that you are willing to help them with their bibliographic research because you then learn what they are doing. Get a list of theses in progress from the department. Periodically look at the completed theses, to see what materials students have used and to observe the directions student research is taking. Your interlibrary loan unit may be willing to give you copies of filled ILL requests. Surveying these allows you to see what research materials readers are borrowing and to identify patterns of gaps in your collection.

The knowledge you obtain about your faculty and students allows you to select materials for the collection to meet immediate and near-future needs. My ideal has been to acquire most books in time for them to be cataloged in the library before the scholars know about them. Scholars know, of course, about those works immediately closest to their interests—the books closest to their research under way by colleagues and competitors. But for the wider circle of literature acquired by those of us fortunate enough to work in large libraries, our systematic coverage of professional, trade, and scholarly selection sources and our rapid acquisitions and cataloging methods will bring books into the library in advance of when readers want them. The sources a librarian uses to identify materials to purchase must differ from the sources of information that scholars employ to find materials to read.

The collection forms a natural bridge between librarians and faculty. We must use that bridge to explain our policies and our limits, unfortunately often in these days of diminished budgets. Librarians can do more than simply select materials, respond to faculty requests, or handle books selected by faculty. Every conversation with faculty members can inform them of our circumstances. An individual, for example, requesting a CD-ROM can lead to an exchange about license agreements. A meeting with a group, such as a library committee, can spread the word about costs and coverages of serial literature in the humanities. Few faculty members have thought about different patterns of scholarly communication and publication, or about the implications for the institution when the library has 95 percent of the serial literature of chemistry, but 56 percent of it in English. Moreover, every conversation can inform us of their expectations. Do our services meet their needs? You will hear about all aspects of the library, from the furniture to the hours, to the food and drink policy, to the printers. You must funnel the comments in the appropriate directions. Remember Wiberley's observation that people ask people they know, and so although your faculty liaison responsibility may begin with collections, it does not end there. Like the president's press secretary, the librarian with liaison responsibilities always represents the organization.

Rapid, thoughtful responses to faculty queries and requests build political support for the library among its most important constituents. Good professional service also can lead to the creation of gift funds for literature: gifts the faculty may make in memory of deceased colleagues; donations by family members for deceased students; or portions of special research grants scholars win. In some years these gifts, extra funds, grants, and various subsidies have increased my allocated funds by 25 percent.

Specialized reference services to specific disciplines, departments, or groups of faculty offer another avenue for liaison. Perhaps I generalized from my own experience as a student and teacher because I almost never consulted a reference librarian, but I also have drawn on publications by members of EALS. Scott Stebelman has argued that the specialized language of the humanities requires specialized knowledge of the discipline to exploit indexing tools to the fullest.[12] Michaelyn Burnette, Christina M. Gillis, and Myrtis Cochran have written about pairing librarians with humanities faculty to "foster individualized reference assistance" because the humanities scholar less often seeks help for a question with a specific answer than for a problem that needs a solution.[13]

We have many ways to deliver specialized reference so that patrons can use our resources independently. By creating guides to our holdings, we publicize and explain our collections and educate patrons. Some of these guides come about because people seek help or complain: "The library doesn't have any African literature." That assertion may be false, but people who do not know the names of writers of a specific country have trouble finding a place to start, especially when we use few or no subject headings for literature and the Dewey classification scheme lumps African with English literature. You examine your holdings and publish a guide, and soon the complainant is teaching African writers and postcolonial literature. When you publish the guide on your library's Web pages, patrons may consult it at any time from any place. Many of us issue regular annotated lists of new acquisitions or reference books or full-text files. One faculty member, a scholar of literature outside the English department, told me that receiving my quarterly lists made him feel like a member of a community. Another kind of liaison that overlaps with specialized reference occurs in large institutions when faculty members send us their research assistants. Sitting down with the research assistant, I plan the search strategy, I identify the sources, and I teach the assistant how to use them. Reading and writing remain the faculty member's bailiwick.

It is the rare faculty member who calls on me for what we might think of as regular reference assistance, the factual answer to a specific question. When they do, they ask me because, as Wiberley and

Jones said, "Assigning one specific librarian to a particular group of scholars might help to build interpersonal ties that will foster continued use of service."[14] When they do need regular reference help, it often occurs in rare circumstances, as for example, when planning a new course—Disabilities in Literature or Public Policy and Poetry—and they head into new territory. Occasionally, they seek bibliographic advice, again, to plan their excursions into new areas. Often they ask for specific, extra-library information about ISBN numbers, or copyright, or about publishing or archives. Providing specialized reference on demand requires tact as well as skill, for the librarian cannot allow him- or herself to be turned into the private librarian for aggressive individuals.

Given Wiberley and Jones's observations on scholars' use of reference services, we should warily regard as sufficient those reference services provided only at a reference desk. The solving of problems or the planning of extensive research strategies may need to be done in a quieter environment without the press of the next questioner standing by. Certainly reference is changed in the electronic environment. We all have many nonfaculty patrons whom we have never seen. They do not come to the library to put their hands on books. They communicate with us by voice- or e-mail, and using our computers, we direct them to remote, intangible sources of information.

Judy Reynolds discusses user education more fully in chapter 7 of this book, but I mention it here to reinforce it as an activity that faculty members value and one that directly links librarians to teaching faculty. Librarians in our disciplines offer a variety of instructional services, everything from full courses in bibliography and research methods to one-time lectures, with many variations between those two extremes. For example, Kenton B. Temple at Hodges Library (University of Tennessee) contacted eighteen faculty who offered courses with a research component in English and took to their classes a ten-minute presentation with a Web page that identified all library resources in one place.[15] This short introduction provided faculty and students with a name and face, and demonstrated the willingness of the librarian to help. A brief first session like this also can appeal to those faculty members who may jealously guard their classroom time. In English, we have the possibility of covering the range from the undergraduate composition student to the English undergraduate major and the graduate student. At Minnesota, we have even been flattered by faculty organizing conferences who ask us to present sessions in which we instruct scholars from other institutions in using the files, tools, and materials we own.

The content of our teaching, like that of all teachers, evolves over time, and also like other teachers, we have more content than classroom time. But we must demonstrate our belief in the value of librarianship as we teach practical skills. As we teach upper-level students, we use some of our specific knowledge to leaven the mass of skills. For example, in teaching how to use the *MLA International Bibliography*, we can say how many journals we subscribe to or what percentage of titles in the MLA the library holds, and then mention comparable figures for another institution. These data suggest there is more to learn and tell readers that libraries are not all alike and that individuals shape library collections and services. To suggest the intellectual power behind the practical details, we have a double duty because faculty members are present in the classroom when we teach students, so we have two audiences. We face the challenge of educating the teacher along with the students.

Students come to us when they prepare research papers, ranging from the undergraduate major paper to the honors thesis to the graduate student thesis. Linda George, English subject librarian at the University of Auckland library, sends a newsletter and flier to each new graduate student at the beginning of the year. Using a letter with a tear-off sheet and a return envelope, she announces her consultation service, her tailor-made research guides, and her several subject seminars on the research process, major tools, controlled vocabulary, and search strategy.[16] A few graduate students ask us to serve on their dissertation or exam committees. To advise dissertation students, of course, we must have appointments in the graduate faculty. Here we are well served by our own individual publication records.

Some librarians hold formal joint appointments with the academic departments they serve, but others choose not to do that. I do not want to support the view that an appointment in a teaching department confers more prestige than one in the library. I do not want to spend any time on running the department, on political or personnel or curricular decisions. I do not want to take sides in the inevitable internal departmental disagreements, because I want to be the librarian for all the faculty. As Huck Finn says, "It would a been a miserable business to have any unfriendliness on the raft; for what you want, above all things, on a raft, is for everybody to be satisfied, and feel right and kind towards the others."

Like Huck, we often move between two worlds as we direct consultation between the faculty and the library staff. This communication may be on matters as mundane as the shelving of books. If scholars of Dryden and Milton use many old books, certainly they will care about the preservation and storage of those books, and when the library moves these books into storage, scholars will get excited about it. To some library staff books are just so many feet of storage space, so many book trucks, but when patrons suddenly discover that their books no longer stand where they once stood, they justifiably become disturbed. Should we be surprised, considering that their primary work, according to Wiberley, is solitary reading from library collections?

Most of us contact or write to all faculty on single topics as we need to inform them, or seek their views on library matters. We can take advantage of three opportunities during any year for regular communication—the end or beginning of the fiscal year, the beginning of the school year, and the beginning of the calendar year. All of us benefit from electronic distribution lists. Some of us send newsletters to faculty. Scott Stebelman of George Washington University has offered his newsletters as models, first in paper and now in electronic form. Some of us send an annual report to the faculty. This report may announce impending changes, or expensive purchases, or may thank members of the department for their help during the year (giving them credit, and suggesting to others that they go and do likewise).

We should meet occasionally with the departmental officers, the chair, the director of graduate studies, and the director of undergraduate studies, each of whom has specific responsibilities. Smaller institutions may have less structure, but librarians should identify and use whatever structure exists. I always have the same agenda: What are your long range plans? These plans come to fruition in staff (faculty) and curricula, which directly influence our work. These conversations, repeated with different individuals over the years, can prove fruitful. I floated the idea with a couple of successive chairs that the department and I both would benefit if they were to use one of their graduate assistant positions for a computer assistant, who could extend my arm in the department. Although I have offered many sessions on our catalog and other computerized sources, I knew people needed more immediate help close at hand. Eventually the need became obvious, and finally the department gave a teaching assistant this responsibility, which lightened my burden. If we do not have time to do everything ourselves, we should scrounge around to find help.

Librarians get requests to write or talk about the collections when departments are evaluated for accreditation or when they propose new programs or degrees. These occasions give us an audience for our observations from collection evaluations. I told the chair of creative writing that we had 81 percent and 100 percent of the "best literary reviews," as identified in two articles. We had 68 percent of the relevant new periodicals in literary studies as identified in successive years of the Directory of Literary Biography (DLB); and I reported other measures of our holdings in contemporary drama and poetry. These communiqués give evidence of our expertise. Yet these collection evaluation activities stem from a view of an orderly and controllable world, a nineteenth-century world. How can we change them to apply to a world of access rather than assets, to a world of information in constant change? I do not know the answer, but I do know that we must ask the questions.

Frequent communication with faculty tends to lead to a collegial relationship, which leads to engaging with faculty in other work, such as preparing exhibits inside or outside the library, or work on grants, programs, conferences. We use our education in literature as we discuss interpretive SGML encoding of full-text files we create. Attending lectures, symposia, and conferences also is productive. When we do this, our colleagues in the office may wonder where we are, but meeting people on their own ground is important. Despite frequent e-mail, you must occasionally meet people face to face. A virtual community is a play on words, a fiction. We use the word *liaison*, with its senses of carrying over, binding, and intimacy, deliberately.

We have moved away from Jane Austen into Conrad's world. Access to information once was centralized in the library, but now it is decentralized by the Internet. Characteristics of the Internet undermine desires for control. We are adopting the new qualities and methods simultaneously with practicing the old. We pay for resources we do not have in the library, and we pay salaries of people who create temporary interfaces for these resources. I now no longer feel that I alone am responsible for preparing guides or teaching patrons. It would be folly to think that only librarians could construct Web pages. We do not regard Web pages as competition; we use these electronic sources rather than control them. Our information environment is much the richer for the initiatives from outside the library. This work reflects the weakening of old hierarchical structures. We do not command or control; instead, we confer, coordinate, and delegate.

We face greater social than technological changes. Our administrators are managing budget reductions and looking for new ways to transform the work environment and to economize on their staffs, to develop new systems, and to cooperate with other libraries. Five years ago we felt very pessimistic about our institutions, but the picture looks brighter now. As many local economies have improved, we are replacing the staff we lost. Systems people, distance education librarians, Web masters, these new staff do not fill the positions we lost, but they bring us talent for the new work our libraries do. We literature librarians must determine how we apply our subject skills in this changing environment. We must design the services our patrons will need and work with new staff to provide them.

Faculty liaison provides an avenue for us to learn from our patrons, but it also provides its own reward. Good relationships with people are both a means and an end. We may use new computerized methods to deliver new services with new materials when we negotiate special access to a remote database for one class, but the motive driving this activity has not changed. Our attitudes of service in librarianship and in the literary disciplines will help us to refine our specialization and to serve our patrons. Librarians who exercise intelligent discretion in building and managing collections can create collections, regardless of size, with distinctive characteristics that serve as independent centers of strength for the parent institution. Librarians who anticipate patrons' needs, who respond to local interests in their cataloging, subject, and authority work, who provide access to and deliver materials in innovative ways, who create new online reference, teaching, and research tools, who do research and publish—these librarians contribute directly to the credit, if not the glory, of their institutions. All is not dark and the book is not dead.

Notes

1. Gail F. Latta, comp., *Liaison Services in ARL Libraries*, SPEC Kit no. 189 (Washington, D. C.: Association of Research Libraries, Office of Management Services, 1992), i.

2. Ung Chon Kim, "Participation of Teaching Faculty in Library Book Selection," *Collection Management* 3 (1979): 333–52; Alfred Garvin Engstrom, "Methods of Fruitful Collaboration." *Journal of Academic Librarianship* 7 (1981): 150–51.

3. Mark Sandler, "Organizing Effective Faculty Participation in Collection Development," *Collection Management* 6 (1984): 63–73.

4. Robert Neville, James Williams III, and Caroline C. Hunt, "Faculty–Library Teamwork in Book Ordering," *College and Research Libraries* 59 (1998): 524–33.

5. Catherine E. Pasterczyk, "Checklist for the New Selector," *College and Research Libraries News* 49 (1988): 434–35.

6. Kent Underwood, *Faculty–Library Liaison: Goals and Guidelines for Selectors*, Bobst Library, New York University, 1990, 1.

7. "Guidelines for Liaison Work," *RQ* 32 (1992): 198–204.

8. Stephen E. Wiberley Jr. and William G. Jones, "Patterns of Information Seeking in the Humanities," *College and Research Libraries* 50 (1989): 638–45; Stephen E. Wiberley Jr., "Habits of Humanists: Scholarly Behavior and New Information Technologies," *Library Hi Tech* 9, no. 1 (1991): 17–21.

9. Richard Heinzkill, "Characteristics of References in Selected Scholarly English Literary Journals," *Library Quarterly* 50 (1980): 352–65.

10. Madeleine Stern, "Characteristics of the Literature of Literary Scholarship," *College and Research Libraries* 44 (1983): 199–209.

11. John M. Cullars, "Characteristics of the Monographic Literature of British and American Literary Studies," *College and Research Libraries* 46 (1985): 511–22; John Budd, "A Citation Study of American Literature: Implications for Collection Management," *Collection Management* 8 (1986): 49–62.

Literature in English

12. Scott Stebelman, "Vocabulary Control and the Humanities: A Case Study," *Reference Librarian*, no. 47 (1994): 61–78.

13. Michaelyn Burnette, Christina M. Gillis, and Myrtis Cochran, "The Humanist and the Library: Promoting New Scholarship through Collaborative Interaction between Humanists and Librarians," *Reference Librarian*, no. 47 (1994): 181–91.

14. Wiberley and Jones, "Patterns of Information Seeking in the Humanities," 644.

15. Kenton B. Temple, letters to author, 10 and 29 Oct. 1997.

16. Linda George, letter to author, 17 Oct. 1997.

Contributors

Michael Adams, Associate Professor at the City University of New York Graduate Center, is responsible for reference, library instruction, and the library's Web site. He holds a Ph.D. in English from the University of South Carolina and has contributed more than three hundred essays, reviews, and bibliographies to such publications as *Critique, Dictionary of Literary Biography, Magill's Literary Annual,* and *Masterplots II*. He was 1998–2000 editor of *Urban Library Journal*. E-mail: madams@gc.cuny.edu.

Shelley Arlen is Associate University Librarian at the University of Florida. A former Humanities Librarian, she is now responsible for collection management and library instruction in reference and in American and British history. Her book, *The Cambridge Ritualists: An Annotated Bibliography of Works by and about Jane Ellen Harrison, Gilbert Murray, Francis M. Cornford, and Arthur Bernard Cook*, was published in 1990 by Scarecrow Press. E-mail: shelarl@nervm.nerdc.ufl.edu.

Candace R. Benefiel is Senior Humanities Reference Librarian at Texas A&M University, with responsibility for humanities reference collection management, reference, library instruction, and liaison in the areas of world history and general humanities. She has published articles in *American Libraries, Journal of Academic Librarianship, College and Research Libraries, Reference Services Review,* and *Wilson Library Bulletin*. E-mail: candace@tamvm1.tamu.edu.

Betty H. Day is Coordinator for Electronic Resources and the MdUSA Program for the University System of Maryland. Previous to this position, she was the Humanities Bibliographer at the University of Maryland. She has served as chair of EALS and was bibliographic editor of *Literary Research: A Journal of Scholarly Method and Technique* (1987–1992). She received her MLS from the University of Maryland in 1979 and her Ph.D. in English from the same institution in 1992. E-mail: bd5@umail.umd.edu.

Richard Heinzkill is on the reference staff and is Selector for English and American literature, film, folklore, and theater at the University of Oregon. In addition to his book, *Film Criticism: An Index to Critics' Anthologies* (1975), he has published articles on both professional and literary topics in such journals as *Library Quarterly, Papers of the Bibliographical Society of America,* and *RQ,* and was a contributor to *English and American Literature: Sources and Strategies for Collection Development* (1987). E-mail: heinzkill@oregon.uoregon.edu.

J. Paul Hunter is the Barbara E. and Richard J. Franke Professor of Humanities at the University of Chicago. He has published extensively on 18th-century literature, most recently *Before Novels: The Cultural Contexts of Eighteenth-Century English Fiction* (1990), and prepared several successful anthologies. Currently he coedits the Bedford Cultural Editions series, which, he writes, "will enable teachers to use the latest historical approaches to textual analysis and cultural criticism."

Marcia Pankake, Professor and Bibliographer for English and American literature, French and Italian, manages collections and does faculty liaison, specialized reference, and bibliographic instruction at the University of Minnesota. She coedited *English and American Literature: Sources and Strategies for Collection Development* (1987) and *Selection of Library Materials in the Humanities, Social Sciences, and Sciences* (1985), for which she also coauthored the chapter on English. E-mail: m-pank@tc.umn.edu.

Susan L. Peters received her MLS from the University of Illinois in 1973 and her Ph.D. in literature from the University of Maryland, in College Park, in 1994. In 1992, she became Coordinator for Language and Literature at Emory University, where she also is responsible for selecting material in the areas of theater, film studies, and psycho-analysis. She is active in EALS. E-mail: libslp@unix.cc.emory.edu.

Judy Reynolds is Library Education and Assistant Program Head and Librarian at San Jose State University, with responsibility for library instruction, reference, collection management, and liaison for the English, foreign language, and linguistics and language development departments. She is currently a leader in a team teaching project to integrate information competence into the university curriculum. Her publications include "A Brave New World: User Studies in the Humanities Enter the Electronic Age" and "Master's Candidates' Research Skills." In addition, she edited the 1994 "Reference Service in the Humanities" issue of *Reference Librarian*. E-mail: judyr@sjsuvm1.sjsu.edu.

Timothy Shipe is Arts and Literature Bibliographer and Curator of the International Dada Archive at the University of Iowa Libraries. He received his Ph.D. in comparative literature from the University of Iowa. His publications include bibliographies and articles on the Dada movement in art and literature, the fiction of Max Frisch, and the cataloging of artists' books. A former chair of EALS, he also has chaired the Cataloging Advisory Committee of the Art Libraries Society of North America. E-mail: timothy-shipe@uiowa.edu.

Scott Stebelman has a Ph.D. in English from the University of Wisconsin and a MLS from the University of California, Berkeley. He is Group Leader for Education and Instruction and a subject specialist in English and American literature at George Washington University. His publications have appeared in a variety of library journals, on subjects ranging from collection development and user education to database evaluation. E-mail: scottlib@gwu.edu.

John L. Tofanelli, whose Ph.D. in English is from Stanford, is a Resource Services Librarian at Johns Hopkins University, with responsibility for collection management, reference, library instruction, and liaison for English, film and media studies, the Humanities Center, and the writing seminars. E-mail: johnt@milton.mse.jhu.edu.

Stephen E. Wiberley Jr. is Bibliographer for the Social Sciences and Professor at the University of Illinois at Chicago. He has authored several articles on the use of libraries and information in the humanities, including, "Humanists Revisited: A Longitudinal Look at the Adoption of Information Technology," *College & Research Libraries* (1994), with William G. Jones; and "Names in Space and Time: The Indexing Vocabulary of the Humanities," *Library Quarterly* (1988). E-mail: u30959@uicvm.uic.edu.

Perry Willett is the Bibliographer for English and American Literature, and Philosophy, and the Head of the Library Electronic Text Resource Service, at the Main Library of Indiana University, in Bloomington. His articles on electronic texts have appeared in *PACS Review* and *Library Hi-Tech*. In addition, he has chaired a task force of the Digital Library Federation charged with drafting a manual for best encoding practices using the Text Encoding Initiative guidelines. E-mail: pwillett@ucs.indiana.edu.

William A. Wortman is Humanities Librarian at Miami University (Oxford, Ohio) with responsibility for collection management, reference, library instruction, and liaison in the areas of English, theater, and foreign languages. The MLA published a second edition of his *Guide to Serial Bibliographies for Modern Literatures* in 1995, and the ALA published his *Collection Management: Background and Principles* in 1989. E-mail: wortmawa@muohio.edu.

Index